C0-CEP-575

UNEMPLOYMENT IN SOUTHERN EUROPE

COPING WITH THE CONSEQUENCES

Books of Related Interest

Immigrants and the Informal Economy in Southern Europe
Martin Baldwin-Edwards, Mediterranean Migration Observatory, Athens, and Joaquin Arango, Instituto Universitario Ortega y Gasset, Madrid (eds.)

The Politics of Immigration in Western Europe
Martin Baldwin-Edwards, Mediterranean Migration Observatory, Athens and Martin A Schain, Center for European Studies, New York (eds.)

Southern European Welfare States
Between Crisis and Reform
Martin Rhodes, European University Institute, Florence (ed.)

Crisis and Transition in Italian Politics
Martin Rhodes and Martin Bull, European University Institute, Florence (eds.)

Gender Inequalities in Southern Europe
Women, Work and Welfare in the 1990s
Maria Jose Gonzalez, Teresa Jurado, Manuela Naldini

Unemployment in Southern Europe

Coping with the Consequences

Editor

Nancy G. Bermeo

FRANK CASS
LONDON • PORTLAND, OR

First published in 2000 in Great Britain by
FRANK CASS PUBLISHERS
Newbury House, 900 Eastern Avenue, London IG2 7HH

and in the United States of America by
FRANK CASS PUBLISHERS
c/o ISBS
5804 N.E. Hassalo Street
Portland, OR 97213-3644

Website www.frankcass.com

British Library Cataloguing in Publication Data

Unemployment in southern Europe: coping with the consequences
1. Unemployment – Europe, Southern
I. Bermeo, Nancy Gina, 1951–
331.1'3794
ISBN 0 7146 4935 X (cloth)
ISBN 0 7146 4495 1 (paper)

Library of Congress Cataloging-in-Publication Data:

Bermeo, Nancy Gina, 1951–
Unemployment in Southern Europe : coping with the consequences / Nancy G. Bermeo.
p. cm.
Includes bibliographical references and index.
ISBN 0-7146-4935-X – ISBN 0-7146-4495-1 (pbk.)
1. Unemployment–Europe, Southern. 2. Labor market– Europe, Southern. 3. Full employment policies–Europe, Southern. I. Title.

HD5764.S66 B47 2000
331.13'794 – dc21 99-058701

This group of studies first appeared in a Special Issue on 'Unemployment in Southern Europe: Coping with the Consequences' of *South European Society & Politics*, 4/3 (Winter 1999) ISSN 1360-8746, published by Frank Cass.

Printed in Great Britain by
Antony Rowe Ltd., Chippenham, Wilts.

Contents

Introduction

This short collection of essays is a first attempt at assessing how the rising levels of unemployment have affected both political institutions and political behaviour in Southern Europe. Portugal, Spain and Greece provide most of the collection's empirical materials but France and other Western European states serve as important points of comparison.

Though much has been written about unemployment's causes and cures, systematic attention to its consequences is lacking. In an attempt to fill this void, these essays deal with the effects of unemployment on public policy, political parties, trade unions and individual opinions. Taken as a whole, they offer lessons about the multifaceted consequences of unemployment in general and highlight both the differences and the similarities among Southern European states specifically.

The volume begins with essays on how rising unemployment affects explicitly political institutions and their interactions. Katrina Burgesss offers the first of three essays on trade unions, looking at how high levels of unemployment affected Spain's two major labour federations and their interaction with the Spanish state. She delineates and explains three variations in interaction and shows how a final variation meant an end to a longstanding taboo on concessions for job security. Omar Encarnacion examines how the pressures of rising unemployment affected the nature of Spanish policy-making and argues that the process of social concertation that governed policy-making in the early years of Spanish democratization was a casualty of joblessness. Seraphim Sepheriades analyses how rising unemployment has affected trade unions in Greece. He argues that, contrary to the common wisdom, it has not lessened the likelihood of mobilization and confrontation but that it has made militant action less effective and forced labour into concession bargaining.

The essays by Miguel Glatzer and Rand Smith focus on the policies that have emerged from the changing interactions discussed above. Glatzer compares how a variety of governments in Portugal and Spain have coped with pressures to liberalize labor market policy. He concludes that failures and delays in liberalization are frequent and that success is rare and usually mixed. Put in the context of the other essays on trade unions, Glatzer's research highlights the importance of disaggregation and specificity in our discussions of trade union failure. Trade union and public pressure to prevent specific plant closures and layoffs seem not to be successful but pressures to prevent general nationwide changes in job protection policy seem more so.

Rand Smith's essay shows how unemployment undermined the cohesion of party-union coalitions in France and Spain and in so doing concurs with themes raised by Burgess, Ernarnacion and Sepheriades. In pointing to the different ways the left coalition tensions played themselves out in two different cases, he draws our attention to the importance of domestic institutional context.

The second set of essays in the collection deals with the effects of unemployment on individual political attitudes and behaviour. Here too, attention to the context in which unemployment occurs proves fruitful. Bacalhau and Bruneau use some of the first opinion polls conducted in Portugal to show that the unemployed have indeed seen the political world differently and more critically than other Portuguese. Amoretti's broad comparative study suggests that the differences we observe in Portugal and elsewhere might be based on class and education rather than unemployment per se.

The next two essays focus on the important question of how fears of unemployment affect attitudes towards immigrants. Margarida Marques shows that, despite relatively low levels of unemployment in Portugal, jobs are seen as a scarce resource and that specific types of immigrant labour are being targeted as responsible for rising joblessness. Martin Baldwin-Edwards and Constantina Safilou-Rothschild point out that immigrants are being blamed for rising unemployment in Greece despite what the authors find to be a complementary, rather than a competitive, role in the domestic labour market. In showing how resentment varies across immigrant groups, both of these essays show how scapegoating is socially constructed.

The essays by Manuel Villaverde Cabral and Neovi Karakatsanis address the intriguing question of why rising unemployment has had so few nationally salient consequences in Portugal and Greece respectively. Both authors argue that the answers derive from the social context in which unemployment occurs. Cabral attributes the Portuguese response to the low weight of wages in family incomes, regional differences in labour patterns and a longstanding tradition of pluri-employment. Karakatsanis also looks to traditional institutions in her explanation of Greek behavior. She explains how Greeks are coping with rising unemployment through political clientelism and personal familism but predicts that these mechanisms might weaken just as the causes of unemployment intensify.

The collection's conclusion joins the essays that focus on individuals to those that focus on institutions and asks why Southern Europeans have not reacted to rising unemployment in more politically destabilizing ways. The answer varies somewhat across states, with compensatory welfare policies playing a special role in Spain, but in Southern Europe as a whole the answers rest with familial networks and economic institutions that lie outside the formal economy.

How the unemployed will cope with joblessness and rising immigration in the future will depend on the crative use of the formal institutions discussed above. It will also depend on informal networks of actors who help shape public opinion. If this modest volume stimulates more research and communication within the network of scholars concerned with unemployment it will have served its purpose.

NANCY BERMEO
Princeton University

Acknowledgements
Three of these essays were originally written for a conference entitled 'Unemployment's Effects: Southern Europe in Comparative Perspective', held at Princeton University in the autumn of 1998. The editor gratefully acknowledges the Luso-American Development Foundation and the Spanish Ministry of Education for generously supporting the conference. Several Princeton University organizations contributed to the conference as well and also deserve thanks. These include the Southern European Research Group, the Center of International Studies, the Stanley J. Seeger Fund of the Program in Hellenic Studies, the Committee on European Studies and the Woodrow Wilson School. A final word of thanks is due to Ugo Amoretti and Megan Kennedy who contributed to the final product in a myriad of helpful ways.

Unemployment and Union Strategies in Spain

KATRINA BURGESS

The mid-1970s were heady days for Spanish trade unions. After being forced to operate in exile or at the margins of legality under the authoritarian regime of Francisco Franco, they burst onto the scene as important actors after Franco's death in 1975. According to one estimate, the combined membership in the General Workers' Union (UGT) and the Workers' Commissions (CCOO) grew by 60 per cent between 1977 and 1978 to reach a total of 1.6 million workers (Jordana 1996: 216). The unions themselves estimated a much larger increase, from 36,000 workers at the end of 1976 to nearly four million in 1978 (Van der Meer 1997: 41-2).[1] In addition, the unions demonstrated an impressive mobilizational capacity with strikes that caused an average annual loss of nearly 15 million workdays between 1976 and 1979 (Alonso 1991: 424).

This explosion in union activity took place, however, against the backdrop of a disturbing new trend in the economy. After more than a decade of steady growth, Spanish employment stabilized in 1975 and began a steep decline in 1977. This reversal sent Spain into an unemployment crisis from which it has yet to recover. Between 1977 and 1985, the number of jobless grew from 415,000 to nearly two million, translating into the highest rate of unemployment in western Europe (Jimeno and Toharia 1994: 1, 21). Not surprisingly, euphoria quickly soured into disillusionment for many workers, contributing to a precipitous decline in union membership. By 1981, combined membership in the UGT and the CCOO had declined to fewer than 800,000 workers, a 50 per cent loss in just three years (Jordana 1996: 216).

The UGT and the CCOO had no choice but to respond to Spain's unemployment crisis. They advocated similar remedies, including Keynesian demand management, an active industrial policy, protections against worker dismissal, a preference for permanent contracts, reduced working hours, and increased compensations for the unemployed. But

FIGURE 1
ANNUAL RATES OF UNEMPLOYMENT, 1977–97

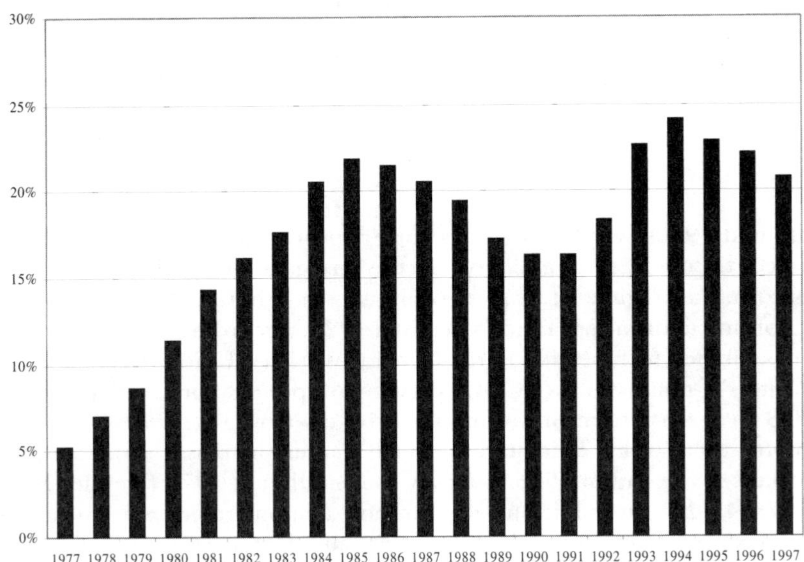

Sources: Anuario El País; MTSS (1993); MTAS (1996, 1997).

their strategies for achieving these goals passed through three distinct phases. During the first phase (1978-1986), the UGT and the CCOO competed fiercely, and the UGT participated unilaterally in social pacts that allowed for more flexible rules governing hiring and firing in return for support in its campaign to become Spain's hegemonic union. During the second phase (1986-1994), the UGT abandoned its conciliatory approach and joined the CCOO in resisting further flexibilization of the labour market. During the third phase (1994-1998), both unions became more willing to negotiate concessions with the government and employers, culminating in a bilateral pact that broke a long-standing taboo for the unions against compromising the job security of their core members.

I argue that these strategic shifts can be explained by three interrelated variables. The first variable is the institutional context in which the unions were operating. The most important features of this context were the construction and consolidation of a new system of labour relations, the electoral balance of power, and Spain's relationship to European integration. As these features changed, so did the incentives and options facing Spanish unions. The second variable is the 'insider-outsider' dilemma. The UGT and the CCOO faced a tension between protecting their core members and appealing to other collectivities that accounted for a growing share of the workforce. They altered their strategies partly to accommodate their search for a workable solution to this dilemma. The third variable is political learning. The unions based their strategic choices on expectations regarding the likely outcome of alternative strategies. When these exceptions proved unfounded, the unions 'learned' from the disjuncture between expectations and outcomes and adjusted their strategies accordingly.

This article is divided into four sections. In the first three sections, I discuss the origins, elements, and impact of each phase through which the UGT and the CCOO passed in their search for solutions to the unemployment crisis. With respect to the first two phases, I explain why the unions abandoned their existing strategies in favour of an alternative. In the fourth section, I synthesize my argument linking the unions' strategic choices to the institutional context, the insider-outsider dilemma, and political learning. I conclude with the observation that, while the unions' most recent strategies appear to be producing positive results, the entrenched nature of Spain's unemployment problem is likely to prompt further shifts in the strategic orientation of Spanish unions.

PHASE ONE: DIVIDED UNIONISM AND SOCIAL PACTS

Between 1978 and 1986, the UGT and the CCOO heatedly disagreed over the appropriate strategies for addressing Spain's escalating unemployment. Whereas the CCOO pushed for confrontation and mobilization, the UGT preferred concertation and exchange. To some degree, their contrasting styles reflected differing assessments of the intentions and capabilities of the government and employers. But they were also linked to each union's struggle to find a place in Spain's new system of industrial relations. Until the mid-1980s, this struggle took the form of intense competition that overwhelmed the points of agreement between the two unions regarding unemployment policies.

Legacy of Divided Unionism

To understand the competitive dynamic that shaped union policies during this period, we must examine the origins and evolution of the UGT and the CCOO prior to the outbreak of Spain's unemployment crisis. Although both unions existed before the transition to democracy, they have very different histories. Founded in 1888 and closely allied with the Spanish Socialist Party (PSOE), the UGT was one of Spain's most powerful unions until Franco took power in the late 1930s. Faced with severe repression, the UGT moved its headquarters to France and refused to collaborate in any way with the vertical unions established by Franco. Amazingly, the UGT survived its long exile and resurfaced inside Spain in the 1970s. But the union's nearly complete absence from workers' lives meant that it was 'little more than some historic initials, with a few thousand militants very concentrated in the Basque Country and Asturias' (Santos and Sánchez 1990: 255).[2] Even after membership levels soared in the late 1970s, the UGT had a long way to go before regaining the organizational and political stature it had enjoyed in the 1930s.

The UGT's recovery was further complicated by the existence of a new rival, the CCOO. In the late 1950s, Franco opened new spaces for worker organizations by allowing 'works committees' to engage in collective bargaining. A collection of *ad hoc* workers' commissions emerged to fill these spaces. With the active participation of the Spanish Communist Party (PCE), these commissions formed a national organization, the CCOO, and elected candidates to the works committees as a means of infiltrating the vertical unions. The regime initially tolerated the CCOO, which achieved major victories in the syndical elections of 1966. As labour mobilization increased, however, the regime reverted to repression, outlawing the CCOO in 1968, dismissing many workers from the works committees, and declaring states of emergency in 1969 and 1970.

Despite these setbacks, the CCOO dominated the labour movement when the political system began to liberalize in the 1970s. Unlike the UGT, which had steadfastly refused to participate in the works committees, the CCOO had established a firm foothold among Spanish workers.[3] The CCOO's relative strength became clear when the newly legalized unions presented candidates for election to factory councils in 1978.[4] The CCOO received 34.6 per cent of the vote, compared to only 21.6 per cent for the UGT (Führer 1996: 113). Moreover, the CCOO was the victor in 20 out of 22 sectors and 10 out of 15 regions, as well as dominating major firms in transport, automobiles, steel, and telecommunications (Pérez Díaz 1979: 17-19; Santos and Sánchez 1990: 255). Not surprisingly, this imbalance carried over to union membership.

According to a 1980 survey, the UGT accounted for only 31 per cent of unionized workers, compared to 46 per cent for the CCOO (UGT 1993: 15).

Together with developments in the political arena, the CCOO's resounding victory in the 1978 elections prompted both unions to reconsider their tactics. Previously, the UGT had advocated confrontation whereas the CCOO had favoured concertation. Their preferences were linked to the distribution of power in the party arena, which strongly favoured the PSOE over the PCE, particularly after the June 1977 elections. For the PCE, social pacts among the political parties became a means of remaining on equal footing with the PSOE despite the PCE's electoral weakness. The PSOE, on the other hand, sought to shift concertation away from the parties to the social partners (unions and employers). Although the PSOE signed the Moncloa Pacts in October 1977, it refused to consider another pact among the parties.[5]

The PSOE found support for this shift in unlikely quarters: the Spanish Confederation of Business Organizations (CEOE) and the conservative government of the Union of the Democratic Centre (UCD). The results of the 1978 factory council elections raised fears in conservative circles that the CCOO was becoming too powerful. Despite reservations about helping the PSOE, the CEOE and the UCD decided to side with the UGT against the CCOO (Díaz-Varela and Guindal 1990: 178-9). An essential part of this strategy was to negotiate pacts directly with the UGT.

This strategy helped convince the UGT to change its attitude toward social pacts. Particularly after its 1978 defeat, the UGT recognized that its comparative advantage lay in national agreements backed by the PSOE rather than in mobilization at the plant level, where it remained weak (Hawkesworth and Fina 1987: 74). Moreover, concertation became a way for the UGT to differentiate itself from the CCOO, which had begun to adopt more confrontational tactics. Hoping to ride the PSOE's coattails to a better showing in the 1980 factory council elections, the UGT started to cultivate an image of responsibility and pragmatism that contrasted with the CCOO's growing intransigence.

The altered terms of concertation had exactly the opposite effect on the CCOO. For the CCOO, pacts among the social partners held little appeal because they would grant disproportionate influence to its weaker rival. Moreover, these pacts reflected the pro-UGT bias of the UCD and the CEOE. In the 1979 Basic Interconfederal Accord (ABI) and the 1980 Interconfederal Framework Accord (AMI), the key issue on the table was the reconstruction of Spain's system of labour relations. The CCOO wanted to preserve the factory council model, which linked union power to the share of votes received in factory council elections. The UGT, on the other hand, preferred a system that linked union power to dues-paying membership by giving internal unions the right to bargain collectively and mobilize workers. This preference reflected not only the UGT's disadvantage relative to the CCOO in factory council elections, but also its long tradition as a membership-based union with a centralized authority structure.

Although entrenched practices and the CCOO's strength in the labour movement prevented a wholesale displacement of the factory council model, the UGT and the CEOE diluted the model in the ABI, which laid the foundations for the 1980 Worker's Statute. Against the virulent opposition of the CCOO, the Worker's Statute established two mechanisms of worker representation: the factory council and the union section. The factory council had the right to organize strikes and bargain collectively. Its delegates were elected by all workers in the workplace, regardless of whether or not they belonged to a union. If no union gained an absolute majority of seats, the factory council became the negotiating agent.

The union section, by contrast, consisted exclusively of union members who acted as 'the extended arm of unions in the enterprise' (Escobar 1993: 37). The union section's rights included disseminating information to workers and running candidates in factory council elections. If a union controlled an absolute majority of seats on the factory council, its union section became the negotiating agent. In workplaces with more than 250 workers, union sections were entitled to present closed electoral lists and to have at least one delegate on the factory council with a voice but no right to vote (Estatuto del Trabajador 1980: 75-6; Escobar 1993: 37).

This hybrid system of labour relations had two consequences that affected union responses to the crisis of unemployment. First, the system blurred the line between 'insiders' and 'outsiders' because the unions were answerable not just to their members but to all workers who voted in factory council elections. In the early 1990s, this latter group included around 50 per cent of all salaried workers, compared to a union affiliation rate of only between 10 and 15 per cent (Miguélez Lobo 1991: 220; Escobar 1993: 6). The line was further blurred by the *erga omnes* nature of collective agreements. Because all workers in the relevant domain (which could range from the workplace to the nation) bore the consequences of these agreements, the rate of coverage surpassed even the rate of participation in factory council elections (Prieto 1994: 376).

Second, the system created strong incentives for unions to compete rather than to co-operate, because their power rested so heavily on their performance in factory council elections. Within the workplace, this performance determined the distribution of seats on the factory council and, hence, the competencies of the union section. Beyond the workplace, the elections affected (a) the right to negotiate agreements at the provincial, regional, or national levels; (b) the legal capacity to convoke council elections in any workplace; (c) representation on the boards of public agencies; and (d) access to government subsidies.[6] Given these high stakes, the UGT and the CCOO sought to convince workers that they presented a unique and preferable alternative at the ballot box, particularly in the first decade after democratization when their identities were still in formation. As part of this strategy of differentiation, they advocated very different approaches to the unemployment crisis despite their basic agreement on optimal policies.

SOCIAL PACTS AND THE UNEMPLOYMENT CRISIS

The process and outcome of the negotiations surrounding the ABI and the Worker's Statute set the tone for union strategies into the mid-1980s. The UGT became determined to establish its hegemony in the labour movement, and social pacts promised to be an effective mechanism for achieving this goal. As a result, the UGT signed all five of the pacts negotiated between 1979 and 1984. The CCOO, on the other hand, concluded that it had little to gain from social pacts except in moments of political uncertainty. Thus, the only two national pacts signed by the CCOO came about, first, in the wake of an attempted military coup and, second, a few months after the PSOE established Spain's first leftist government since the 1930s.

These conflicting attitudes toward concertation quickly became entangled with the question of how the unions should respond to the unemployment crisis. Employers and government technocrats insisted that job creation required flexibilization of the labour market to reduce the costs of hiring and firing. They soon discovered that both unions considered dismissal procedures for permanent workers to be non-negotiable. Under Franco, permanent jobs had been protected by high dismissal costs in the form of redundancy payments and administrative procedures (Rhodes 1997: 107). The unions refused to entertain the idea of weakening these protections, some of which had been enhanced or formalized after Franco's death.[7] They also held firm against attempts to terminate the contracts of workers laid off in the process of industrial restructuring. After a bitter fight between the UGT and the PSOE government, the 1984 Law of Reconversion and Reindustrialization included an explicit guarantee that displaced workers would have their contracts suspended rather than terminated (Santos and Sánchez 1990: 345-50).

Advocates of flexibilization found a chink in the unions' armour, however, on the issue of fixed-term contracts. Although the government had begun allowing alternatives to indefinite contracts as early as 1976, these alternatives did not become a major item for social concertation until the 1980s. In June 1981, the UGT, the CCOO, the CEOE and the UCD government signed the National Employment Accord (ANE), popularly known as the 'pact of fear' (*pacto de miedo*) because it followed an attempted coup. A central concern among the pact's signatories was the country's rising unemployment rate. In exchange for significant financial and institutional benefits, the unions agreed to support non-traditional programmes for creating jobs, including apprenticeship contracts, temporary contracts, training contracts, part-time employment, and early retirement (Palacio Morena 1991: 13-15).

For the CCOO, this exchange was an aberration justified by the fragility of Spain's democracy. For the UGT, it conformed to a strategy of granting short-term concessions on flexibilization in return for the long-term benefits of concertation. This strategy seemed to be paying off. In 1980, the UGT nearly caught up with the CCOO in factory council elections, winning 29.3 per cent of the vote compared to 30.9 per cent for its rival. In addition, the UGT began to reverse the trend of CCOO domination across sectors and regions, winning in 11 out of 22 sectors and 9 out of 16 regions. Two years later, the UGT surpassed its rival, winning 36.7 per cent of the vote compared to 33.4 per cent for the CCOO. The UGT also prevailed in 13 out of 22 sectors and 14 out of 16 regions (Führer 1996: 113, 123-5).

The UGT's faith in concertation as a hegemony-building strategy received an additional boost when the PSOE won the 1982 elections in a landslide victory. The PSOE's leader, Felipe González, anticipated positive repercussions for the UGT: 'with a Socialist Party that has swept the political elections and is therefore initiating an epoch of government characterized by reforms and the modernization of the country, we are in real and objective conditions for the UGT to convert itself into the only

TABLE 1
RESULTS OF FACTORY COUNCIL ELECTIONS

Year	Number of Elected Delegates				%	
	UGT	CCOO	Other	Total	UGT	CCOO
1978	41,264	66,042	83,486	190,792	21.63	34.57
1980	48,194	50,817	65,581	164,592	29.27	30.86
1982	51,663	47,017	42,071	140,751	36.70	33.40
1986	66,411	56,065	39,908	162,384	40.92	34.54
1990	99,737	87,730	49,797	237,261	42.04	36.98
1995	70,746	77,040	55,975	203,761	34.70	37.80

Sources: Führer (1996: 113); UGT (1994: 71); EIRR (April 1996: 27)

union in Spain' (quoted in Díaz-Varela and Guindal 1990: 224). Likewise, the UGT concluded that the CCOO's failure to participate consistently in social pacts and the PSOE's decimation of the PCE meant that 'the UGT must prepare itself organizationally and strategically to be in our country not only the majority union, which it already is, but the union that unifies the vast majority of the labour movement' (UGT 1983: 205).

The UGT continued to harbour these expectations even after the PSOE abandoned its expansionary campaign platform (including a promise to create 800,000 jobs) in favour of tight monetary and fiscal policies. After a tumultuous year without a social pact, the UGT, the CCOO, and the CEOE met in July 1984 to renew negotiations. The CCOO quickly abandoned the table, however, when the CEOE pushed for removal of protections against the dismissal of permanent workers. In an attempt to salvage the pact, the Labour Minister sent a letter to the UGT secretary general, Nicolás Redondo, promising that the government would not modify the current labour legislation regarding lay-offs (Tuñon de Lara 1992: 498). Although the CCOO continued to boycott the negotiations, the UGT returned to the table and, in October 1984, signed the Economic and Social Accord (AES) with the CEOE and the government.

Like the ANE, the AES involved a trade-off that facilitated partial flexibilization of the labour market. But, this time, the terms of the trade-off were much less favourable to the unions. In particular, the AES supported a labour law reform that created 14 different kinds of employment contracts, most of which involved short-term work, exempted employers from paying full wages and benefits, and did not protect workers against dismissal (Palacio Morena 1991: 317-19). One analyst argues that the 1984 reform 'established the fixed-term contract in its multiple varieties as the ordinary form of contracting and made the indefinite contract the exception' (Falguera i Baró 1991: 282-3). In return for the UGT's support for this change, the government promised to extend unemployment insurance to 48 per cent of the eligible workforce by 1986.

The UGT agreed to these relatively unfavourable terms partly because 'there remained matters over which the UGT found it worth negotiating with the González administration' (Gillespie 1989: 430). The government resolved several of these matters in the UGT's favour over the next two years. The 1985 Organic Law of Union Liberty and the 1986 Accord on Union Participation in Public Enterprise reinforced the union sections by enabling them to operate more widely and with expanded rights on the shop-floor. The parliament also passed a Law on Union Patrimony in 1986 that created mechanisms for returning property confiscated from the unions by the Franco regime. These mechanisms clearly favoured the UGT, and the government delivered the bulk of the UGT's share just two weeks before the beginning of the factory council elections in October 1986 (Führer 1996: 187).

Ironically, the resolution of these issues contributed to the UGT's decision to shift from concertation to confrontation after 1986. This connection is clarified if we keep in mind Carlos Prieto's distinction between 'historic' exchange, which involves the construction of a system of industrial relations, and 'routine' exchange, which involves the daily administration of government (1994: 381-2). In the first decade after Franco's death, the UGT focused primarily on historic exchange, which encouraged a strategy of concertation. As long as the rules of the game had yet to be established, the UGT had strong incentives to make concessions on the management of routine exchange, including partial flexibilization of the labour market. The UGT was rewarded for its co-operation with a system of industrial relations that was quite favourable to the unions, particularly the UGT.

Once this system became law, however, the UGT had greater freedom to focus on routine exchange, which had been much less beneficial to the unions. Not surprisingly, one of the most contentious issues was unemployment. The unemployment rate reached 21.9 per cent in 1985, partly as a result of industrial restructuring and privatization. The 1984 Law on Reconversion estimated the loss of nearly 83,000 jobs, equivalent to 29.6 per cent of total employment in the 791 firms involved

FIGURE 2
UNEMPLOYMENT INSURANCE COVERAGE, 1978–97
(share of registered unemployed)

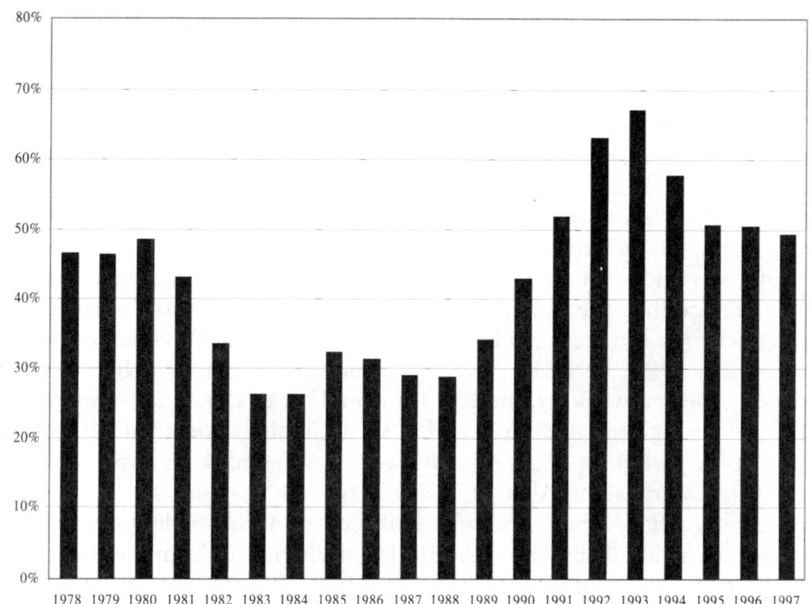

Sources: Anuario El País; MTAS (1998).

(**Fernández Marugan** 1992: 157). Two-thirds of the job losses took place in the steel, shipbuilding, and textile sectors, all of which had been traditional union strongholds. At the same time, rationalization and privatization in the state-owned sector led to the loss of 50,000 jobs between 1982 and 1986 (López-Claros 1988: 19-20).

Employment began to recover in 1986, but mostly through use of the less stable contracts allowed under the 1984 reform. Between 1985 and 1986, temporary contracts grew by 24 per cent, part-time contracts by 44 per cent, and apprenticeship and training contracts by 51 per cent (López-Claros 1988: 26-7). Although the 1984 reform extended factory council participation to any worker with at least one month of service, regardless of the type of contract, these workers were much more difficult to organize (*Claridad* 1984: 96-7). In the meantime, the government failed to live up to its promise to extend unemployment insurance to 48 per cent of the eligible workforce. Having fallen from 48.7 per cent in 1980 to 26.3 per cent in 1983, the rate of coverage increased to only 32 per cent by 1986 (Campos and Alvarez 1990: 199).

The UGT's concerns about the negative impact of these trends came to the fore during the 1986 factory council elections. Just as workers were going to the polls, the government and employers launched an offensive to flexibilize the labour market through deregulation and increased employer contributions to social security, which became known as 'the 27 liberalizing measures' (UGT 1989a: 321). Although the UGT won the elections with 40.9 per cent of the vote, compared to 34.5 per cent for the CCOO, the results debunked the UGT's expectation that the CCOO was on the verge of obscurity. Even worse, the aggregate figures 'hid the fact that the loss influence by UGT leaders was enormous in those factories and sectors where an organized labour movement existed' (Albarracín 1991: 418). In the 500 largest enterprises, which employed over one million workers, the CCOO won 43.2 of the seats compared to 31.6 per cent for the UGT. The CCOO also prevailed in public enterprises, with 46.4 per cent of the vote compared to 32.9 per cent for the UGT (Campos and Alvarez 1990: 74).

Despite official pronouncements of victory, UGT leaders interpreted the results as a call by the workers for a change in strategy. Redondo linked the UGT's disappointing showing to its co-operation with employers and the government:

> We are primarily responsible. But there are other factors that have taken away our votes: each time a minister speaks...we lose votes; each time the 27 liberalizing measures are mentioned, we lose votes; when [the leader of the CEOE] meets with the president, we lose votes...There is a problem of identification. Workers identify us with the actions of the government or with the actions of public managers. And nothing could be further from the truth (Quoted in *El País*, 18 December 1986).

Similarly, the UGT secretary general in the Metro argued that 'we have lost the elections because of a protest vote against the UGT...The undecided have voted for the CCOO not because they like this union but because they reject us' (quoted in *Cambio 16*, 5 January 1987).

The lessons learned from the results of the 1986 factory council elections prompted three related changes in UGT strategy. First, the confederation abandoned its commitment to global social pacts, preferring to negotiate narrow agreements on specific issues. Second, it refused to make further concessions on the flexibilization of the labour market. And, third, it abandoned its single-minded quest for hegemony in favour of unity of action with the CCOO. After tentative steps in this direction in 1987 and 1988, the UGT wholeheartedly adopted this shift in December 1988, when it organized a general strike with the CCOO against the labour policies of the PSOE government. The resounding success of the strike and its aftermath deepened the UGT's commitment to this approach into the mid-1990s.

PHASE TWO: UNITY OF ACTION AND HOLDING THE LINE

The UGT moved almost immediately after the 1986 factory council elections to reorient its strategy. In January 1987, Redondo wrote a letter to the CCOO's secretary general proposing unity of action in collective bargaining, a strategy that had not been considered since 1979 (*Cambio 16*, 5 January 1987). The following February, the UGT and the CCOO reached an accord that included a plan for collective bargaining and a demand for profound change in the government's economic policies (Campos and Alvarez 1990: 84). In the meantime, UGT leaders began to shift their negotiating strategy from global to specific agreements so as to maximize their flexibility in setting union policy (UGT 1987). Despite strong pressures from the government, the UGT refused to sign any agreement that ratified the PSOE's macroeconomic policies. In June 1988, Redondo explained that a global accord with the government was no longer possible, stating that 'it is necessary to pact concrete issues, but without committing ourselves to anything' (quoted in Díaz-Varela and Guindal 1990: 286).

The event that consolidated the UGT's strategy reorientation was yet another attempt by the government to flexibilize the labour market. Faced with an unemployment rate of 41.3 per cent among Spanish youth in 1987, the government proposed a Youth Employment Plan (PEJ) to provide employment for 800,000 youths over a three-year period by reducing employers' social security contributions and fixing wages at the statutory minimum (Rhodes 1997: 116). The UGT immediately expressed its 'radical opposition' to the plan, which it portrayed as a threat to job stability for young and old workers alike (UGT 1989a: 5). The CCOO was equally critical, proclaiming that the PEJ was 'the most blatantly conservative proposal regarding employment policy that had been made explicit in the last decade' (quoted in Campos and Alvarez

1990: 51). Both the UGT and the CCOO characterized the proposed contracts as 'garbage contracts' (*contratos de basura*) that 'hired the son to fire the father'.[8]

The UGT's Confederal Committee met in early November 1988 to denounce the government's proposal and to plan a series of mobilizations:

> The Confederal Committee of the UGT,...conscious that public denunciations have proven insufficient to modify the behaviour of the Administration and business, has resolved to invite the working men and women of our country to express their opposition to the social insensitivity that the government has manifested (UGT 1988: 2).

Among the UGT's demands were withdrawal of the PEJ and compliance with the AES, particularly the extension of unemployment insurance to 48 per cent of the registered unemployed. Later that month, the UGT and the CCOO issued a joint document reiterating the points in the Confederal Committee's resolutions (Campo and Alvarez 1990: 219-21). The centrepiece of the plan was a general strike to be organized jointly by the two unions for 14 December 1988.

The general strike was a resounding success. On 14 December, the vast majority of Spanish workers did not report to work.[9] In addition, hundreds of thousands of people took to the streets during the week of the strike to protest against the government. As only the fifth general strike in Spanish history, the mobilization emboldened the unions and dealt a serious blow to the government. In a joint manifesto issued on 15 December, the CCOO and the UGT declared that:

> The general strike of 14 December, carried out in a civic, orderly, and peaceful manner, has involved the most complete support for union claims and for demands for a more social orientation in the policies of the Government. The participation of millions of working men and women and many other social collectivities, with enthusiasm, in an unprecedented mobilization, has constituted a reaffirmation of democracy, as well as a consolidation of the unions...We want to indicate, finally, our conviction that the united action of the labour movement has been one of the key elements in the support received by the citizenry (quoted in Campos and Alvarez 1990: 236-7).

As these comments indicate, the strike's success validated for the unions the wisdom of holding the line against the government's flexibilization policies and of unity of action between the UGT and the CCOO.

This strategy received further validation over the next couple of years in the form of favourable policies and increased union membership. The government's only immediate concession was to withdraw the PEJ, but the policy environment became much more favourable to the unions after the general elections in October 1989. Although the PSOE won its third absolute majority in the parliament, it received 800,000 fewer votes than in 1986 and lost ground to the left-wing coalition, the United Left (IU) (Gillespie 1990: 59). This result, paired with the blow delivered to the PSOE's social democratic credentials by the 1988 general strike, heightened pressures within the party for more pro-worker policies. Meanwhile, the economy entered its fifth year of growth in 1990, which gave the government more room to make concessions to the unions.

The UGT and the CCOO followed the general strike with a major initiative called the Priority Union Proposal (PSP), which they launched just before the October 1989 elections. The PSP contained 20 demands organized into four areas: employment, social protection, income redistribution, and worker participation. The employment demands included union participation in the regulation of contracts, stricter limits on temporary employment, a reduction in work hours, and youth training and apprenticeship programmes based on the active participation of the unions and public agencies (UGT 1989b). Although most of these demands were long-standing, the PSP established a pattern of interaction that differed substantially from the social concertation of previous years: 'the negotiation took place over an extended period of time, with diverse interlocutors, with autonomous negotiations regarding each issue, and based in general concepts, leaving economic quantification until the end' (Calvo 1990: 68).

At first, the approach outlined in the PSP met with significant success, prompting a high-level UGT official to reflect that 'the strike of 14 December had its victory one year later.'[10] The unions achieved several important gains in 1990, including bargaining rights for public employees, improvements in pension benefits, and union participation in monitoring employment contracts (UGT 1994: 25). The accord on union regulation of contracts led to legislation requiring employers to divulge information regarding the initiation and termination of all contracts and creating tripartite commissions to monitor trends in the labour market. The explicit goal of the accord was to prevent fraud in the utilization of the 14 contract types allowed by the 1984 labour law reform (Campos and Alvarez 1990: 174-5). Beyond the negotiating table, the government finally met the unions' demand that at least 48 per cent of the registered jobless receive unemployment insurance. The rate of coverage grew from 29 per cent in 1988 to 52 per cent in 1991 and remained above 48 per cent through mid-1998 (see Figure 2).

The other area in which the new strategy seemed to reap significant benefits was union membership. After a precipitous decline in the early 1980s, the rate of union affiliation stabilized at around 11 per cent of the workforce between 1981 and 1986 (Jordana 1996: 215). This low rate was partly a function of the free-rider problem caused by Spain's hybrid system of union representation, which enabled workers to reap most of the benefits of being a union member without joining a union. The unions also faced three structural impediments to attracting members: high unemployment, labour market segmentation, and rapid growth in the service sector (Bilbao 1991: 252). Finally, some analysts and union leaders blamed the strategy of divided unionism and social pacts for worker disillusionment with the unions. Luis Enrique Alonso argues that social pacts delegitimized the unions by disempowering shopfloor leaders and

TABLE 2
UNION MEMBERSHIP
(thousands of workers)

Year	UGT	CCOO	Subtotal	Other	Total
1977	491.0	536.8	1,027.8	595.1	1,622.9
1978	729.5	910.5	1,640.0	817.1	2,457.1
1979	687.5	632.0	1,319.5	768.7	2,088.2
1980	357.0	483.0	840.0	340.8	1,180.8
1981	330.0	467.1	797.1	288.4	1,085.5
1982	378.1	453.1	831.2	255.9	1,087.1
1983	413.1	453.5	866.6	261.7	1,128.3
1984	381.3	429.6	810.9	267.2	1,078.1
1985	414.5	427.3	841.8	261.4	1,103.2
1986	442.2	398.4	840.6	269.9	1,110.5
1987	490.4	441.6	932.0	312.9	1,244.9
1988	531.1	486.4	1,017.5	355.8	1,373.3
1989	594.7	527.3	1,122.0	393.7	1,515.7
1990	655.2	610.1	1,265.3	431.7	1,697.0
1991	803.5	692.2	1,495.7	466.6	1,962.3
1992	874.1	761.8	1,635.9	488.8	2,124.7
1993	883.5	775.6	1,659.1	507.0	2,166.1
1994	820.8	787.4	1,608.2	518.6	2,126.8

Source: Jordana (1996: 216).

imposing salary caps without bringing discernible trade-offs (1991: 409).

This last interpretation gained credence after the unions shifted their strategy away from divided unionism and social pacts. Between 1986 and 1992, union affiliation increased by an average annual rate of 10 per cent, resulting in an overall increase of unionized workers from one to two million (Jordana 1996: 218). To some extent, these gains can be attributed to the rapid job creation that accompanied Spain's economic boom in the late 1980s. But most of the new workers between 1986 and 1992 were on fixed-term contracts and, hence, unlikely to join unions. Temporary jobs grew from 14 per cent of the total in 1984 to 35 per cent in 1994, compared to an EU average of only nine per cent (Miguélez 1995: 86; EIRR, January 1995: 15). Moreover, permanent contracts as a share of the total fell from 81.7 per cent in 1987 to 66.2 per cent in 1994, and fixed-term contracts with a duration of less than three years accounted for over 90 per cent of all new contracts between 1985 and 1995 (EIRR, November 1995: 28). In the meantime, high unemployment continued to shift many manual workers from big companies, where unions had a strong presence, to the largely non-unionized world of small companies, temporary jobs, self-employment, and welfare (Miguélez 1995: 85).

Given the persistence of these structural impediments to union affiliation, some credit must be given to the strategic reorientation of the unions. This reorientation, which was prompted by the same unemployment crisis that threatened the unions' membership, increased the incentives for workers to join unions. First, the success of the 1988 general strike relegitimized the unions as social actors and thereby provided 'identity incentives' for union membership. Second, the breakdown of centralized wage pacts gave sectoral and firm-level leaders more control over collective bargaining (Jordana 1996: 219). In a highly segmented labour market, this control allowed them to deliver increased benefits to permanent workers because competitive shocks to the firm could be absorbed by temporary workers (Rhodes 1997: 117). Finally, the unions sought to improve and expand the services they offered to their members. Some of these services derived from the PSP (such as the contract-monitoring agreement) while others consisted of union initiatives to provide their members with pensions, life insurance, housing, and legal assistance.

Flush with their new-found success, the UGT and the CCOO forged ahead with this strategy even when economic and political conditions began to turn against them. Beginning in 1991, economic recession and the impending formation of the European Monetary Union prompted the PSOE to adopt more restrictive policies. In June 1991, the government released a Social Pact of Progress, which had the same initials as the PSP but called for a global pact with the unions and emphasized inflation control and labour productivity. The UGT and the CCOO roundly rejected the pact and countered with their own proposal, the Union Initiative of Progress, in November 1991. They reiterated their commitment to issue-specific accords:

> The stage of global pacts has passed. Remedies do not exist that can bring solutions to complex problems in a short period of time nor that can ask of working men and women responsibilities that do not correspond to them. To achieve the objectives we seek, we believe in the necessity of a diversified process of negotiation of specific and concrete aspects (UGT 1991: 2).

Rather than responding favourably to the unions' demands this time, however, the PSOE relied on executive decrees and parliamentary alliances with conservative parties to adopt policies opposed by the unions.

Once again, Spain's unemployment crisis was at the heart of the battle between the government and the unions. Under growing pressure to rein in social spending, the government decreed cuts in unemployment benefits in 1992. The reform increased the minimum work period for benefit eligibility from six months to one year, lowered the average duration of benefits from 20 to 12 months, and delayed the initiation of benefits until after all severance payments had been exhausted (Rhodes 1997:109). Referring pejoratively to the reform as the '*decretazo*' (killer decree), the UGT and the CCOO organized another general strike in May 1992. The strike elicited widespread participation by the workforce, but it did not have the symbolic impact of the 1988 general strike. Nor did it persuade the government to soften its employment policies.

By 1993, the unemployment rate had once again reached epidemic proportions, growing from 16.3 per cent in 1991 to 22.7 per cent in 1993 (Anuario El País 1992; MTSS 1993). Unlike in the early 1980s, however, neither the government nor the unions were willing to make the necessary concessions to reach a negotiated solution to the crisis. The PSOE, which had lost its absolute majority in the June 1993 elections and was governing in coalition with a conservative party from Catalonia, stood firm on the need for further flexibilization of the labour market. In October 1993, Felipe González even went so far as to admit that:

> The great problem of the social pact is that the Government has nothing to give in exchange. We are asking for an incomes policy to improve competitiveness, for changes in traditional collective bargaining procedures and for a modification of the labour market that will make it more flexible...This requires a cultural change in union attitudes which makes it very difficult (quoted in EIRR, March 1994: 21).

Meanwhile, both the UGT and the CCOO continued to hold the line against any further liberalization of employment practices.

Unable to reach any agreement with the unions, the government unilaterally approved a decree-law on 'Urgent Measures to Promote Employment' in December 1993. The reform, which became law on 1 January 1994, flew in the face of the unions' demands. The reform had four central components. First, it liberalized restrictions on collective dismissals by raising the minimum number of workers considered to be 'collective' and expanding the valid reasons for engaging in such dismissals. Second, the reform effectively resurrected the PEJ by allowing employers to hire young workers on apprenticeship contracts at below the minimum wage and with reduced social security contributions. Third, the reform eliminated the government's monopoly on job placement by allowing for the operation of private placement and temporary work agencies. Finally, the reform imposed a tight deadline on termination of the labour ordinances that were left over from the Franco era but continued to regulate work conditions for 4.3 million workers (Rhodes 1997: 108-9; EIRR, March 1994: 22-3; EIRR, January 1995: 16-17).

The UGT and the CCOO reacted vehemently against these measures. Calling them a 'counter-reform of the labour market,' the UGT argued that the measures 'imply a radical and profound regression of the Labour Law, diminish the basic rights of workers and seriously affect the system of collective bargaining that was established – with broad social and political consensus – at the beginning of the transition' (UGT 1994: 29). To protest the reform, the UGT and the CCOO organized another general strike on 27 January 1994. Their strike demands focused on a revision of the reform that would guarantee job security, the purchasing power of pensioners and public employees, access to unemployment insurance coverage, and the individual and collective rights originally granted to workers under the Worker's Statute (UGT 1994: 324).

As in 1992, the general strike brought the economy to a standstill but did little to shift conditions in the unions' favour. The government essentially ignored the unions' demands and forged ahead with implementing the reform through amendments to the Worker's Statute. In the meantime, the unemployment rate remained above 20 per cent, and casualization of the labour market continued. After increasing slightly between 1990 and 1993, permanent contracts as a share of total employment began to decline in most regions of Spain (MTAS 1998). In addition, an estimated 250 private employment agencies concluded around half a million contracts in 1995, and half of all contracts signed in 1996 ran for less than one month (EIRR, November 1995: 30; EIRR, March 1997: 12). Perhaps most disturbing to the unions was a new trend in union affiliation. The rate of growth began to slow in 1992, and then, in 1994, the absolute number of union members declined for the first time since 1986. Although the CCOO continued to add to its rolls, the UGT's membership fell by 62,700 that year (see Table 2).

These disheartening results contributed to a re-evaluation by the unions of the strategy they had been pursuing since the mid-1980s. While remaining committed to unity of action, they began to soften their resistance to trade-offs on labour market policy. Once again, the initiative for this shift came primarily from the UGT. In 1994, Redondo handed leadership of the confederation over to Cándido Méndes, who was more willing to engage in dialogue with employers and the government. A serious shift in the unions' strategy did not occur, however, until both the UGT and the PSOE lost their majority status. In 1994-95, the UGT lost the factory council elections to the CCOO for the first time since 1980. This defeat, which was linked to an absolute decline in the number of factory council delegates in small firms, brought home the message that labour market segmentation threatened the organizational viability of the unions. The following year, the PSOE lost the general elections to the conservative Popular Party (PP), which threatened to reduce the unions' leverage even further.

PHASE THREE: JOINT RETURN TO THE NEGOTIATING TABLE

The unions' strategic reorientation in the mid-1990s was more gradual and less explicit than in the mid-1980s. Nonetheless, they began modifying their combative stance once they realized they would be unable to reverse the momentum toward flexibilization. Beginning in late 1994, the UGT and the CCOO negotiated several accords to ensure a role for organized labour in dictating the terms of the new environment. In October 1994, they signed their first national accord with the CEOE in ten years, agreeing to replace the expiring labour ordinances with collective bargaining (EIRR, December 1994: 25-6). The following year, they signed an unprecedented collective agreement with the new employers' association of temporary work agencies (GEESA) that set a minimum annual wage for temporary agency workers (EIRR, April 1995: 12). They negotiated another collective agreement with the GEESA in January 1997 that granted temporary workers the right to wages equivalent to those of permanent workers and pledged to create a monitoring commission (EIRR, March 1997: 12).

These agreements helped the unions extend their reach into under-represented collectivities, but they did little to address the segmentation of the labour market. By the mid-1990s, this segmentation was seriously threatening the organizational interests of the unions. Although they had been able to grow in the late 1980s and early 1990s despite the dramatic casualization of the workforce, the decline in membership growth after 1991 suggested that the shrinking size of their core constituency was finally catching up with them. There were also signs that the prevalence of fixed-term contracts was having a deleterious impact on the factory council system. As mentioned above, half of all employment contracts in 1996 ran for less than a month, which meant that these workers were not eligible to vote in factory council elections. Moreover, the use of fixed-term contracts was greatest in firms with fewer than 25 employees, which accounted for a growing share of the workforce.

The dangers of this last trend, particularly for the UGT, were brought home by the results of the 1994-95 factory council elections. The UGT lost the elections outright for the first time since 1980, winning only 34.7 per cent of the seats compared to 37.8 per cent for the CCOO (EIRR, April 1996: 26). While the CCOO performed slightly better than in 1990, the UGT's share plummeted by over seven points (see Table 1). Much of the UGT's loss can be explained by a sharp decline in the overall number of factory council seats. Eighty-one per cent of this decline (27,000 out of 33,500 seats) took place in firms with fewer than 50 employees, which had been the UGT's stronghold. Most likely, this outcome was linked to the sector's disproportionate share of fixed-term workers and the loss of over half a million jobs in firms with between six and 50 workers during this period. The end result, which hit the UGT particularly hard, was that Spanish workers had 33,500 fewer delegates to represent them on the shop-floor (EIRR, April 1996: 26).

The lessons learned from these disturbing trends in worker representation encouraged the unions to reconsider their options, which became even more limited after the PSOE lost to the Popular Party (PP) in the 1996 general elections. The PP's victory raised the spectre of a labour market reform that would reduce protection for permanent workers, which the unions had previously considered non-negotiable. At this point, however, the unions had few alternatives. They did not want to be left out of another major reform because they refused to compromise. Moreover, the costs of failing to negotiate concessions that might stop the haemorrhaging of the permanent workforce were becoming prohibitive. Thus, after long and difficult negotiations, they accepted some flexibilization of permanent contracts in the Interconfederal Accord for Employment Stability (AIEE), which they signed with the CEOE in April 1997.

The AIEE established a broad framework for labour market reform intended to boost job security and employment, streamline collective bargaining, and fill the regulatory vacuum left in some sectors by repeal of the labour ordinances (EIRR, May 1997: 24). Employers agreed to improve conditions for fixed-term and part-time workers in return for concessions by the unions on dismissal procedures for permanent workers. For the unions, the agreement reduced the types of employment contracts from 14 to five: (i) permanent, open-ended contracts; (ii) open-ended contracts for longer-term unemployed youth, first-timers, and those on fixed-term contracts; (iii) training contracts for youth; (iv) temporary contracts for a particular task or service; and (v) part-time contracts (EIRR, March 1997: 11). Workers on training contracts would receive wages at or above the national minimum wage and part-time workers would be granted the same social security benefits as their full-time colleagues. Moreover, the agreement mandated collective bargaining of training wages and the creation of a tripartite commission to monitor the temporary employment sector (EIRR, May 1997: 25-6).

In return for these changes, the unions agreed to a reduction in severance payments for the unlawful dismissal of permanent workers.[11] Although workers already employed on open-ended contracts would still be entitled to the old system of 45 days' pay per year of service, up to a ceiling of 42 months' pay, new open-ended contracts would carry a reduced payment of 33 days' pay per year of service, up to a ceiling of 24 months' pay (EIRR, May 1997: 24-5). This figure was higher than the 20 days' salary originally demanded by the employers (and supported by the conservative Catalan party), but it nonetheless represented a major concession by the unions. For the first time since the unemployment crisis began in the late 1970s, the unions agreed to renegotiate the protections for permanent workers that had been inherited from the Franco period and reaffirmed during the transition to democracy.

Not surprisingly, this concession caused some controversy within the unions, particularly the CCOO. While the UGT delegates approved the pact by 139 votes to one, only 78 per cent of the CCOO delegates endorsed the pact (EIRR, May 1997: 12). The moderates prevailed, however, because of fears that the unions were going down with the sinking ship of permanent employment under the old rules. As the UGT explained in the resolutions passed at its 37th Congress in March 1998, 'the Interconfederal Accord for Employment Stability aims to generate a culture of stability that clarifies the advantages of indefinite contracts and avoids the use of deregulation and a decrease in rights as instruments for improving the competitive position of firms' (UGT 1998: 49).

In May 1997, the government adopted decrees that formalized the AISS and offered government subsidies to employers who hired workers under the new permanent contracts.[12] These decrees had an immediate and positive effect. Government statistics showed that employers signed some 20,000 new open-ended contracts within the first month after the reform, with around 80 per cent being fixed-term contracts that became permanent and 30 per cent involving youths under 29 years of age (EIRR, July 1997: 11). In June 1997, open-ended contracts represented nearly 8.5 per cent of all new contracts, compared to 4.1 per cent in June 1996. Moreover, some companies began including commitments to permanent employment in their collective agreements (EIRR, August 1997: 12). In November 1998, the CCOO announced that the AIEE 'has promoted an increase in employment and has doubled the number of indefinite contracts' (CCOO 1998: 9).

The unions, meanwhile, continued their campaign to resolve the unemployment crisis in a way that preserved worker rights and union strength. As the UGT noted, 'we have to take into account that the Accord, and the legal modifications it implies, is only an instrument to permit us to improve the reality of contracting, requiring action through collective bargaining and the effective participation of worker representatives in the control of contracts to accomplish its objectives' (UGT 1998: 88). Similarly, the CCOO called for vigilance because 'the employers and the Administration continue abusing the use of temporary contracts' (1998: 9). Seeking to go beyond the AISS, the unions used a combination of negotiation and mobilization to push for a shorter work week, expanded protection for unemployed workers, and improved conditions for part-time workers. In November 1998, they signed an accord with the government that extended additional benefits to more than one million part-time workers. When the government refused to make concessions on the remaining issues on their agenda, they planned a series of mobilizations for December 1998 (CCOO 1998: 1-4).

UNDERSTANDING UNION RESPONSES TO UNEMPLOYMENT IN SPAIN

Despite 20 years of negotiation, conflict, and policy experimentation, Spain has not conquered the demon of high unemployment. On the contrary, the unemployment rate remains above 20 per cent of the economically active population. But beneath the persistence of the crisis are important changes in the structure and strategies of Spanish unions. The two unions that began as fierce rivals with an uncertain future during the transition to democracy in the late 1970s arrived at the end of the twentieth century with a new system of labour relations, greater organizational definition, increased autonomy from the political parties, and unity of action. Their journey has been profoundly shaped by the crisis of unemployment and the solutions proposed by the government and employers. As they have struggled to define themselves as social actors, the twists and turns of this crisis have repeatedly challenged their assessments of their interests and strategic options.

As shown in this article, the UGT and the CCOO passed through three strategic phases between 1978 and 1998. The first phase was characterized by divided unionism and the UGT's participation in social pacts that allowed for a dramatic rise in temporary employment. The second phase was a mirror image of the first, with the UGT and the CCOO opting for unity of action and joining together to hold the line against any further flexibilization of the labour market. Finally, the third phase combined certain aspects of the first and second phases (trade-offs on flexibilization and unity of action) while adding a new component: concessions on protections for permanent workers.

In the introduction, I presented three related variables for explaining the strategic choices made by the UGT and the CCOO: the institutional context, the insider-outsider dilemma, and political learning. Shifts in the institutional context prompted shifts in union strategy. For a decade after Franco's death, the unions were struggling to construct a new system of labour relations and to establish their respective positions within the labour movement. These institution-building concerns took first priority and, for the UGT, encouraged a strategy of concertation that required concessions on labour market flexibilization. Once the basic contours of this new system had been established, however, the context changed. Social concertation shifted from historic exchange to routine exchange, which centred on the unemployment crisis and was much less favourable to the unions. Combined with the UGT's realization that it was not going to establish undisputed hegemony over the CCOO, this shift prompted unity of action and resistance to further flexibilization of the labour market.

Initially, this new strategy received a boost from a booming economy and a governing party eager to re-establish its social democratic credentials. But the context changed again in 1992-93 when Spain entered another recession, the government faced the demands of joining the European Monetary Union, and the PSOE lost its absolute majority in the parliament and formed a coalition with the conservative Catalans. Unable to stem the resulting tide toward further flexibilization, the unions reconsidered their strategic options, which became even narrower after the PSOE lost to the PP in 1996. In recognition of their weakened position, they decided to return to the negotiating table in an attempt to obtain some benefits for workers and unions in exchange for concessions on labour market reform. Thus, they resigned themselves to a routine exchange that, while unfavourable, they deemed preferable to being left out in the cold altogether.

This shifting institutional context interacted with a second explanation for union strategies: the search for solutions to the 'insider-outsider' dilemma. From the beginning of the unemployment crisis, the unions struggled with a tension between protecting their core constituency, composed primarily of permanent workers in large public and private enterprises, and appealing to other collectivities that accounted for a growing share of the workforce. This tension was heightened by the ambiguities in Spain's hybrid system of worker representation, which forced the unions to operate in two overlapping but distinct arenas. Although permanent workers were more likely than other workers to vote in factory council elections, the greater inclusiveness of the factory council system (and its implications for union power) encouraged union leaders to be attentive to the interests of workers beyond their dues-paying membership.

Between 1978 and 1997, both the UGT and the CCOO refused to compromise on protection for permanent workers. They took a less consistent position, however, on conditions for workers outside the permanent workforce. At first, both unions agreed to more flexible rules on fixed-term contracts as a short-term mechanism to create jobs for less privileged workers while preserving the rights of permanent workers. The CCOO quickly abandoned this approach after signing the ANE in 1981, but the UGT continued to accept this trade-off into the mid-1980s. Rather than ameliorating the insider-outsider dilemma, however, this trade-off exacerbated it by creating a highly segmented labour market. Contrary to expectations, most workers hired under fixed-term contracts did not move into the permanent workforce (Fernández, Garrido, and Toharia 1991: 75). As a result, the labour market became increasingly divided into workers with job security, decent wages, and union representation, on the one hand, and workers with insecure (if any) jobs at low wages with weak ties to unions, on the other. Particularly alarming for the unions was the rapid growth of the latter group at the expense of the former.

The UGT finally rebelled against this trend, particularly after the government tried to adopt the PEJ in 1988. Taking its message to the streets in December 1988, the UGT joined the CCOO in rejecting any trade-off between guarantees for permanent workers and concessions on temporary employment. Instead, both unions held the line against easing protections for either group. Employers and the government portrayed this resistance as a narrow defence of insider interests, but the unions insisted that it was a solidaristic strategy aimed at defending the rights of all workers. Thus, when González asked, 'which is better, 800,000 temporary jobs or 400,000 permanent jobs?', the UGT replied that the dichotomy between quantity and quality was false and could be avoided by more enlightened policies (UGT 1989a: 322).

The unions received widespread support from young workers for their rejection of the PEJ, and they made a concerted effort to reach out to under-represented collectivities, particularly women, first-timers, and workers in the service sector. They also gained the right to monitor contracts and persuaded the government to extend insurance coverage to a greater share of the unemployed. But these attempts at solidarity were too little too late to stem the rising tide of temporary employment. After failing to prevent the government from undermining worker protections even further in 1992 and 1994, the unions began to reconsider the wisdom of their non-negotiable position on permanent contracts. With the negotiation of the AISS, they once again accepted trade-offs on the unemployment issue. This time, however, they exchanged concessions on permanent contracts for improved conditions for fixed-term and part-time workers. In particular, they sought to create the conditions for more temporary workers to make the transition to permanent employment.

The unions' reassessment of their options points to the third explanation for their strategic choices: political learning. Each episode of strategic reorientation was prompted by a perceived disjuncture between expectations and outcomes. The lessons learned from these disjunctures informed the unions' assessment of the implications of the institutional context and the insider-outsider dilemma for their interests and options.

Between 1978 and 1986, the UGT based its choices largely on the expectation that its participation in social pacts and the PSOE's implementation of Keynesian social democracy would put the CCOO out of business. By 1986, however, this expectation had been dashed. Not only was the CCOO still a powerful competitor, but the PSOE refused to abandon its market-oriented policies even after the economy began to recover. In addition, the UGT realized that it had underestimated the detrimental consequences of its concessions on temporary employment for the labour market. These revelations led the UGT to alter its strategy in favour of unity of action with the CCOO and greater combativeness toward the policies of the PSOE government.

The initial success of this strategy created a new set of expectations. Emboldened by the public response to the 1988 general strike, the government's adoption of more favourable policies, and the growth in union membership, the unions became convinced that they had sufficient bargaining power to block further flexibilization of the labour market and to win important victories without making any concessions. Once again, however, their expectations foundered on the sharp rocks of reality. In contrast to 1988, the general strikes of 1992 and 1994 had no discernible effect on government policy or union membership. In fact, the unions learned that their refusal to make concessions threatened to leave them completely marginalized. Thus, they adjusted their strategy for a second time to accommodate this unwelcome discovery.

Only time will tell whether the unions' latest strategy will produce the desired results. Thus far, their willingness to ease restrictions on the dismissal of permanent workers seems to be facilitating the growth of permanent contracts. As they argue, however, this outcome is necessary but not sufficient to resolve the larger problems of chronic unemployment and union weakness. As long as solutions to these problems remain elusive, the unions are likely to repeat the pattern of trial and error that has marked their response to the unemployment crisis since the late 1970s. Meanwhile, the crisis, by its very persistence, is likely to keep shaping the structure and strategies of the unions.

NOTES

1. These figures include sympathizers as well as dues-paying members and are highly suspect, since the unions lacked well-developed mechanisms for calculating membership at the time of the transition. They are politically significant, however, because they created the impression that the unions possessed sudden and intimidating strength in the late 1970s.
2. All translations by the author.
3. It should be noted, however, that despite the UGT's official boycott of the vertical unions, nearly 20 per cent of UGT leaders in the early 1980s had served in elected positions on the works committees, compared to around 33 per cent of CCOO leaders (Fishman 1984: 77).
4. In March 1977, one month before unions were legalized, the government issued a royal decree that replaced the works committees with factory councils. In addition to changing the name of these councils, the decree expanded their coverage to all firms with more than ten employees, reduced the role of the state in controlling the electoral system, and abolished the participation of employers (Escobar 1993: 3).
5. Not surprisingly, the UGT was much more critical of the Moncloa Pacts than the CCOO.
6. Spanish labour law reserved these privileges for unions that qualified as 'most representative' by receiving more than ten per cent of all delegates at the national level or more than 15 per cent of delegates at the regional level (Escobar 1993: 20). Until 1994, the last two privileges were distributed proportionally among the most representative unions on the basis of their electoral results.
7. The Worker's Statute lowered some of these barriers by (a) introducing an additional category for fair dismissals; (b) reducing indemnizations for unfair dismissals in firms with over 25 workers; and (c) offsetting dismissal costs in small firms through partial financing by a Guaranteed Salary Fund (Herrero 1991: 379). At the same time, however, the Worker's Statute imposed new restrictions on functional and geographical mobility and reduced wage flexibility and overtime (Rhodes 1997: 107).
8. Author interview with Mariano Guindal, economics editor at *La Vanguardia*, 22 June 1995, Madrid.
9. According to the CCOO, nearly eight million people, or 94.9 per cent of the economically active population, went on strike (Campos and Alvarez 1990: 105). The government later revised these estimates down to 75 per cent of the EAP.
10. Author interview with José María Zufiaur, Instituto Sindical de Estudios, UGT, 23 June 1995, Madrid.
11. Employers usually resorted to unlawful dismissals because 'lawful' dismissals were likely to involve a court proceeding that would end up costing more than the higher severance payments required for unlawful dismissals.
12. For example, the government would cover 40 to 60 per cent of the employer's social security costs for the first two years of the contract (EIRR, July 1997: 11).

REFERENCES

Albarracín, J. (1991): 'La política de los sindicatos y la dinámica del movimiento obrero' [Union policy and labour movement dynamics], in Miren Etxezarreta (ed.), *La re-estructuración del capitalismo en España, 1970-1990* [Capitalist Restructuring in Spain, 1970-1990], Barcelona: ICARIA, pp.401-25.

Alonso, L.E. (1991): 'Conflicto laboral y cambio social' [Labour conflict and social change], in Faustino Miguélez and Carlos Prieto (dirs.), *Las relaciones laborales en España* [Labour relations in Spain], Madrid: Siglo Veintiuno Editores, pp.403-26.

Alós-Moner, R. and A. Lope (1991): 'Los sindicatos en los centros de trabajo' [Unions in the workplace], in Faustino Miguélez and Carlos Prieto (dirs.), *Las relaciones laborales en España* [Labour relations in Spain], Madrid: Siglo Veintiuno Editores, pp.233-49.

Anuario El País [El País Yearbook], various years.

Bilbao, A. (1991): 'Trabajadores, gestión económica y crisis sindical' [Workers, economic management and union crisis], in Faustino Miguélez and Carlos Prieto (eds.), *Las relaciones laborales en España* [Labour relations in Spain], Madrid: Siglo Veintiuno Editores, pp.251-69.

Calvo, M. (1990): 'Análisis de los factores que han permitido acuerdos en la concertación' [Analysis of factors that have permitted concertation accords], *Claridad* 35/36, pp.63-9.

Cambio 16, various issues.

Campos, A. and J.M. Alvarez (1990): *Ayer, hoy y mañana del 14-D* [Before, during and after 14 December], Madrid: Comisiones Obreras.

CCOO (1998): 'Por el empleo y la solidaridad' [For employment and solidarity], Madrid: Comisiones Obreras.

Claridad (1984): 'Texto de la Ley Orgánica de Libertad Sindical. Reform del Estatuto de los Trabajadores' [Text of the Organic Law of Union Liberty. Reform of the Workers' Statute], Madrid: Unión General de Trabajadores.

Díaz-Varela, M. and M. Guindal (1990): *A la sombra del poder* [In the shadow of power], Barcelona: Tibidabo Ediciones.

EIRR [European Industrial Relations Review], various issues.

El País, various issues.

Escobar, M. (1993): 'Works or Union Councils? The Representative System in Medium and Large Sized Spanish Firms', Estudio/Working Paper 1994/43, Madrid: Instituto Juan March.

Estatuto del Trabajador [Worker's Statute] (1980), Madrid: Grafex, S.A.

Falguera i Baró, M.A. (1991): 'La legislación individual de trabajo' [Individual worker legislation], in Faustino Miguélez and Carlos Prieto (dirs.), *Las relaciones laborales en España* [Labour relations in Spain], Madrid: Siglo Veintiuno Editores, pp.271-87.

Fernández, F., L. Garrido, and L. Toharia (1991): 'Empleo y paro en España, 1976-1990' [Employment and unemployment in Spain, 1976-1990], in Faustino Miguélez and Carlos Prieto (dirs.), *Las relaciones laborales en España* [Labour relations in Spain], Madrid: Siglo Veintiuno Editores, pp.43-96.

Fernández Marugán, F.(1992): 'La década de los ochenta: impulso y reforma económica' [The decade of the eighties: economic momentum and reform], in Alfonso Guerra and José Felix Tezanos (eds), *La Década del Cambio: Diez Años de Gobierno Socialista, 1982-1992* [The Decade of Change: Ten Years of Socialist Government, 1982-1992], Madrid: Editorial Sistema, pp.135-94.

Fishman, R. (1984): 'El movimiento obrero en la transición' [The labour movement in the transition], *Revista Española de Investigaciones Sociológicas* [Spanish Journal of Sociological Research] 26, pp.61-112.

Foweraker, J. (1987): 'Corporatist Strategies and the Transition to Democracy in Spain', *Comparative Politics* 20/1, pp.57-72.

Führer, I.M. (1996): *Los sindicatos en España* [Unions in Spain], Madrid: CES.

Gillespie, R. (1989): *The Spanish Socialist Party*, Oxford: Clarendon Press.

Gillespie, R. (1990): 'The Break-up of the "Socialist Family": Party-Union Relations in Spain, 1982-1989', *West European Politics* 13/1, pp.47-62.

Hawkesworth, R. and L. Fina (1987): 'Trade unions and industrial relations in Spain: the response to the economic crisis', in William Brierly (ed.), *Trade Unions and the Economic Crisis of the 1980s*, Brookfield, VT: Gower, pp.64-83.

Herrero, J.L. (1991): 'Las relaciones de trabajo' [Labour relations], in Miren Etxezarrta (coord.), *La reestructuración del capitalismo en España* [The restructuring of capitalism in Spain], Barcelona: ICARIA, pp.81-97.

Jimeno, J. and L. Toharia (1994): *Unemployment and labour market flexibility: Spain*, Geneva: International Labour Office.

Jordana, J. (1996): 'Reconsidering union membership in Spain, 1977-1994: halting decline in a context of democratic consolidation', *Industrial Relations Journal* 27/3, pp.211-24.

López-Claros, A. (1988): *The Search for Efficiency in the Adjustment Process*, Washington, D.C.: International Monetary Fund.

Martínez Lucio, M. and P. Blyton (1995): 'Constructing the Post-Fordist State? The Politics of Labour Market Flexibility in Spain', *West European Politics* 18/2, pp.340-60.

Miguélez, F. (1995): 'Modernization of trade unions in Spain', *Transfer* 1, pp.80-97.

Miguélez Lobo, F. (1991): 'Las organizaciones sindicales' [Labour organizations], in Faustino Miguélez and Carlos Prieto (dirs.), *Las relaciones laborales en España* [Labour relations in Spain], Madrid: Siglo Veintiuno Editores, pp.213-31.

Moreno, N. (1994): 'Castigo a las centrales mayoritarias' [Punishment of the majority confederations], *El Siglo*, No. 151, pp.61-3.

MTAS (1996): *Anuario de Estadísticas Laborales y de Asuntos Sociales 1996* [Yearbook of Labour Statistics and Social Affairs 1996], Madrid: Ministerio de Trabajo y Asuntos Sociales.

MTAS (1997): *Anuario de Estadísticas Laborales y de Asuntos Sociales 1997* [Yearbook of Labour Statistics and Social Affairs 1997], Madrid: Ministerio de Trabajo y Asuntos Sociales.

MTAS (1998): *Boletín de Estadísticas Laborales* [Bulletin of Labour Statistics], November 1998, Madrid: Ministerio de Trabajo y Asuntos Sociales.

MTSS (1993): *Anuario de Estadísticas Laborales 1993* [Yearbook of Labour Statistics 1993], Madrid: Ministerio de Trabajo y Seguridad Social.

Navarro, M. (1990): *Política de reconversión: balance crítico* [Reconversion policy: critical review], Madrid: Eudema.

Palacio Morena, J.I. (1991): 'La política de empleo' [Employment policy], in Faustino Miguélez and Carlos Prieto (dirs.), *Las relaciones laborales en España* [Labour relations in Spain], Madrid: Siglo Veintiuno Editores, pp.307-29.

Pérez Díaz, V. (1979): 'Elecciones sindicales, afiliación y vida sindical local de los obreros españoles' [Union elections, affiliation and the local union life of Spanish workers], *Revista Española de Investigaciones Sociológicas* [Spanish Journal of Sociological Research] 6, pp.11-52.

Prieto, C. (1994): 'Sindicalismo' [Unionism], in Del Campo, Salustiano (ed.), *Tendencias Sociales en España (1960-1990)* [Social Trends in Spain (1960-1980)], Vol. II, Bilbao: Funcación BBV, pp.363-90.

Recio, A. (1991): 'La segmentación del mercado de trabajo en España' [Labour market segmentation in Spain], in Faustino Miguélez and Carlos Prieto (dirs.), *Las relaciones laborales en España* [Labour relations in Spain], Madrid: Siglo Veintiuno Editores, pp.97-115

Rhodes, M. (1997): 'Spain', in Hugh Compston (ed.), *The New Politics of Unemployment*, London: Routledge, pp.103-22.

Roca Jusmet, J. (1991): 'La concertación social' [Social concertation], in Faustino Miguélez and Carlos Prieto (dirs.), *Las relaciones laborales en España* [Labour relations in Spain], Madrid: Siglo Veintiuno Editores, pp.361-77.

Santos, R. and J.A. Sánchez (1990): *La conjura del Zar* [Conspiracy of the Czar], Madrid: Ediciones Tema de Hoy.

Tuñon de Lara, Manuel (1992): 'El movimiento laboral de 1981 y 1991' [The labour movement from 1981 to 1991], in Alfonso Guerra and José Felix Tezanos (eds), *La Década del Cambio: Diez Años de Gobierno Socialista, 1982-1992* [The Decade of Change: Ten Years of Socialist Government, 1982-1992], Madrid: Editorial Sistema, pp.487-520.

UGT (1983): *Gestión de la C.E.C. al XXXIII Congreso Confederal* [Report of the C.E.C to the XXXIII Confederal Congress], Madrid: Unión General de Trabajadores.

UGT (1987): 'La UGT reafirma su voluntad de concertación' [The UGT reaffirms its commitment to concertation], internal document.

UGT (1988): *Objetivos y criterios de actuación ante las movilizaciones generales* [Objectives and criteria of behaviour for the general mobilizations], Madrid: Unión General de Trabajadores.

UGT (1989a): *Gestión de la C.E.C. al XXXV Congreso Confederal* [Report of the C.E.C to the XXXV Confederal Congress], Madrid: Unión General de Trabajadores.

UGT (1989b): *Propuesta Sindical Prioritaria* [Priority Union Proposal], Información Sindical [Union Information], No. 75.

UGT (1990): *Resoluciones del XXXV Congreso Confederal* [Resolutions of the 37th Confederal Congress], Madrid: Unión General de Trabajadores.

UGT (1991): *Iniciativa Sindical de Progreso* [Union Initiative of Progress], Madrid: Unión General de Trabajadores.

UGT (1993): *Consideraciones sobre la afiliación sindical* [Considerations regarding union affiliation], Madrid: Unión General de Trabajadores.

UGT (1994): *Gestión de la C.E.C. al 36 Congreso Confederal* [Report of the C.E.C. to the 36th Confederal Congress], Madrid: Unión General de Trabajadores.

UGT (1998): *Resoluciones del 37 Congreso Confederal* [Resolutions of the 37th Confederal Congress], Madrid: Unión General de Trabajadores.

Van der Meer, M. (1997): 'Trade Union Development in Spain: Past Legacies and Current Trends', Working Paper, Nr. 18, Mannheim: Mannheim Centre for European Social Research.

A Casualty of Unemployment: The Breakdown of Social Concertation in Spain

OMAR G. ENCARNACIÓN

Of all the economic problems faced by the democratic regime inaugurated by Spain with the Constitution of 1978, none has proved to be more puzzling to scholars and more intractable to policy-makers than persistently high unemployment. As Spain approached the period of re-democratization that began with the death of General Francisco Franco in 1975, it enjoyed one of Europe's lowest rates of unemployment.[1] Between the years of 1965 and 1974, the unemployment rate stood at 1.5 per cent of the total population. However, by the mid-1980s, when Spain attained the highly elusive status of a consolidated democracy, the nation had developed the most extreme condition of high unemployment among OECD countries. During the critical years of democratic transition and consolidation (1977-86), the average annual unemployment rate stood at 12 per cent. It then climbed to 18.4 per cent between 1986 and 1990. The crisis may have reached its peak in 1994 when the unemployment rate soared to 24 per cent, or 3.7 million of the active population. This dramatic upheaval in the nation's employment picture has led some observers to suggest that with the transition from dictatorship to democracy, Spaniards swapped job security for political freedoms (Balfour 1989: 248).

As might be expected, the spectacular rise in unemployment in Spain in the post-Franco era has generated a vast literature in which a variety of domestic and international factors are vigorously debated as the

This research is culled from dissertation fieldwork conducted in Spain between the years of 1994 and 1997. For a summary of this work see: Encarnación (1997). The author gratefully acknowledges the financial support provided by grants and fellowships from the Council of European Studies, the Fullbright Program, and the Program for Cooperation between United States' Universities and the Spanish Ministry of Culture. A 1997–98 Ford Foundation/National Research Council Post-doctoral Fellowship permitted the author to return to Spain in the Spring of 1998 to update the research.

underlying roots of this crisis (Toharia 1988; Martínez Lucio and Blyton 1995; Maravall and Fraile 1997; Martin 1997; Rhodes 1997). Chief among them is the domestic repercussions of the international energy crisis of the mid-1970s. Rising oil prices occasioned the collapse of many firms and the return of thousands of Spanish migrant workers from northern European countries whose economies were similarly affected by escalating energy costs. More recently, the pressures of economic globalization and integration have further exacerbated the nation's unemployment picture. Spain's entry into the European Community in the mid-1980s came at the cost of a painful program of industrial restructuring and modernization that entailed the destruction of hundreds of thousands of jobs in key sectors of the economy such as steel, automobile, textiles and shipbuilding.

Another contributing factor in inducing high unemployment in Spain concerns shifting attitudes among state technocrats about the role of the state in the economy. Under Franco, the state was committed to full employment. This reflected the paternalism of the old regime as well as a survival strategy. Full employment was meant to minimize mass opposition to the dictatorship and to compensate the workers for the lack of authentic labour representation within the regime. The democratically elected governments of the post-transition period, by contrast, have increasingly operated under the assumption that the market rather than the state bears responsibility for employment conditions. Paradoxically, such beliefs gained currency under a socialist government. During the long rule of the *Partido Socialista Obrero Español* (PSOE), 1982-96, the employment protections instituted by the state under the Franco period were vastly weakened while the discretionary ability of employers to fire and hire workers was significantly expanded.

While explanations for Spanish unemployment abound, considerably less attention has been paid to the effects of vast unemployment in Spain on national institutions, social relations, political processes, and the like. In this regard, the case of Spain mirrors the broad trend in the comparative study of the politics of unemployment that privileges the examination of its causes over its consequences. Seeking to steer the study of the politics of unemployment towards its effects, this essay uses the Spanish experience to explore the question of what are the consequences of persistently high unemployment upon the realm of governance in general and the policy-making arena in particular.

The central contention of the essay is that unemployment in Spain contributed significantly to the end of societal consensus on economic policy. This development is illustrated in the breakdown of social concertation (hereafter 'concertation') born with the return of democracy in 1977 with the all-important Moncloa accords.[2] The policy of concertation is one of the most innovative and unexpected developments in Spain's political economy of democratization, given the country's reputation as a setting for elite conflict, class confrontation, and combative labour politics. It provided the mechanisms that allowed the government, employers and trade unions to orchestrate a highly successful process of democratic transition and consolidation. But by 1986, the social and economic pacts that stand at the heart of concertation – most notably agreement in regards to wages – were no longer possible. The breakdown of concertation ushered in a period of intense conflict in labour relations captured in the general strike of 1988, Spain's first since 1934.

Critical to the demise of concertation, I argue, was the manner in which the unemployment crisis created an inhospitable political climate for the collective pursuit of economic goals among the state, labour and capital. Reflecting the complexity of the process of concertation itself, this argument is developed in three steps. Each line of contention is geared toward illustrating how the unemployment crisis affected a different concertation actor. Firstly, I demonstrate how the crisis of unemployment induced economic prescriptions that undercut the government's need for cross-class consensus in policy-making. Secondly, I suggest how the unemployment crisis raised the risks for participation in policy-making for the labour movement. Thirdly, I illustrate how conditions of high unemployment worked against concertation by eroding proclivities for co-operation among the employers.

The subsequent discussion is organized as follows. Part one provides an overview of the literature on the consequences of high unemployment for governance and the policy-making arena and examines the extent to which the insights provided by this literature are applicable to the case of Spain. Part two summarizes the rise and fall of the process of concertation in Spain and highlights its relevance to policy-making in the post-Franco era and particularly with regard to unemployment. Part three demonstrates the independent and pivotal role that the crisis of unemployment played in creating a political context that prevented the continuation and deepening of the policy of concertation. Emphasis is placed on the first administration of the socialist party (1982–86), under whose tutelage the last of the great social pacts between the government, employers and unions expired. I conclude the essay with some thoughts on the implications of the argument defended in this essay to the comparative study of the effects of unemployment on politics.

UNEMPLOYMENT'S EFFECTS ON GOVERNANCE AND POLICY: SPAIN IN COMPARATIVE PERSPECTIVE

What is the impact of high unemployment on governments and their capacity to rule? The available literature on the subject provides few surprises. By and large, conditions of vast unemployment are thought to be highly conducive to governmental vulnerability in both the electoral and policy-making spheres. Unsurprisingly, the most commonly cited consequence of vast unemployment is punishment at the polls for ruling parties. Cross-national research by John Goldthorpe (1987) and Douglas Hibbs (1987), suggests that, despite the efforts of elected officials to portray unemployment as a problem that is beyond the control of their policy-making abilities, politicians are routinely punished at the ballot box under conditions of high unemployment. A more recent and extensive study by Adam Przeworski and José A. Cheibub reaches a similar conclusion (see Maravall and Fraile 1997: 29). Their analysis of the impact of economic conditions on the survival of Presidents and Prime Ministers for 222 regimes between 1950 and 1990 concludes 'that unemployment was the only outcome that appears to affect the political survival of heads of governments in parliamentary democracies' (Maravall and Fraile 1997: 29).

Curiously, considering the magnitude of unemployment in Spain and the fact that this crisis unravelled in the context of a newly-institutionalized democracy, politics in the post-transition period show remarkably few of the consequences of high unemployment noted above. This point is best articulated by José M. Maravall. He writes (1997: 95) that in Spain 'high unemployment had only limited political consequences. Not only did it not weaken support for democracy, but neither did it prove politically catastrophic for the government.' The first sign of the seemingly inconsequential political impact of unemployment in Spain is the fact that since the transition to democracy in 1977, the country has experienced only two transfers in government. This first happened in 1982 when the socialist PSOE defeated the centre-right UCD, and then in 1996 when the PSOE was defeated by the conservative PP. More remarkable is the electoral resilience demonstrated by the PSOE, the party that governed Spain during the worst years of the unemployment crisis. As I will note shortly, the PSOE survived and thrived as millions of Spaniards were unable to find suitable employment. This development points to one of the most puzzling aspects of the politics of unemployment in Spain. As suggested by Maravall and Fraile (1997: 2), the Spanish electorate appears to have 'exonerated' political leaders for their inability to solve or at least significantly alleviate the unemployment situation.

Indeed, judging from the experience of the PSOE, it appears that high unemployment has been of relatively little consequence to the ability of elected governments to hang on to political power at election time. Under the leadership of Felipe González, the PSOE repeatedly won national elections between 1982 and 1996 and retained an absolute majority in parliament until 1993. And even when the socialist party lost vast numbers of votes, the party continued to hold onto its parliamentary majority. This was the case of the 1986 elections, when the unemployment rate had already passed the 20 per cent mark. The PSOE lost three million votes in 1986 but still managed to retain an absolute majority of seats in parliament. More revealing is the fact that while in power and even during its defeat in 1996, the PSOE retained significant support from those whom we might think were most likely to defect from the party: the unemployed. During its long rule the PSOE did experience a decrease of support among this group. According to data provided by Maravall and Fraile (1997: 30), during the 1982 elections the PSOE won 55 per cent of the unemployed vote and by 1993 this support had declined to 35 per cent. But they stress that support for the PSOE by the unemployed was always higher than that for the opposition. For example, during the 1996 elections, the winning party (the PP) received 30 per cent of the unemployed vote versus 38 per cent for the PSOE.

Also noteworthy is the fact that although the unemployment crisis hampered the deregulation of the labour market, it did not diminish the capacity of the PSOE to implement a broad programme of economic restructuring that included the pursuit of policies that actually exacerbated unemployment conditions. In the comparative literature on economic reform among newly-democratized countries, the PSOE is often held up as a model of success, mostly because on the tenacity with which the party embraced privatization of state enterprises, liberalization of the financial sector, and other components of economic neo-liberalism (López-Claros 1988; de la Dehesa 1993; Bermeo 1994). And notwithstanding strong opposition from labour, these policies do not appear to have engendered negative impressions of the government.

Public opinion polls suggest that throughout the PSOE's tenure in government, the party received largely positive appraisals from the general public, despite persistently high unemployment (Mancha 1993: 165-71). This goes a long way towards explaining why the public continued to prefer the PSOE's guardianship of the economy over that of its alternatives from either the right or the left.[3] And, as observed by Maravall (1997: 160), when this changed finally in the mid-1990s 'it was the result of political rather than economic circumstances.'

Beneath the picture of regime stability, electoral resilience, and policy success depicted above rests considerable political turmoil and social unrest. The unemployment crisis that erupted in Spain during the 1980s had important reverberations upon both the governing party (the PSOE) and society at large. Assessing them, however, requires looking beyond the nation's electoral politics. An area of concern to this study is cross-class consensus in policy-making, one of the hallmarks of the post-Francoist political economy and one of the critical factors in understanding Spain's successful transition to democracy. The demise of concertation debilitated the PSOE by occasioning the severance of ties between the government and labour, a factor that over time contributed to the PSOE's electoral weakness, and threw industrial and labour relations into a highly confrontational mode. Before illustrating the links that can be made between the unemployment crisis and the demise of concertation, a recapitulation of Spain's concertation experience is in order.

THE RISE AND FALL OF CONCERTATION IN SPAIN

On 27 October 1977, Adolfo Suárez, Spain's first democratically elected ruler in nearly 40 years, concluded the negotiations that led to the signing of the Moncloa accords. This momentous event, the cornerstone of Spain's democratization, provided the political foundations for the development of the process of concertation in the post-Franco era.[4] The Moncloa accord expressed the wish of the government and the nation's most important political forces to confront and solve the economic and political problems that converged around the transition to democracy in 1977 in a climate of responsible co-operation with the aim of contributing to the consolidation of democracy. Driving this intent among the architects of Spain's new democracy was the intense desire to put to rest a long history of elite fragmentation, ideological extremism, and class conflict. They shared the view that these conditions had contributed significantly to the collapse of the Second Republic and the coming of a bloody civil war in the 1930s.

The Moncloa accords committed political parties from a broad ideological spectrum including centrists, social democrats, communists, conservatives, and regional-nationalists to a program of economic stabilization whose immediate goal was the moderation of wages as a way to curb runaway inflation. To that end, the most important component of the Moncloa accords was the implementation of a wage band that dictated that salary increases could not exceed 20-22 per cent in anticipation of an inflation rate of 20 per cent. This practice of fixing wages based on predicted inflation contrasted with the previous practice of decentralized collective bargaining where past inflation plus productivity was the norm. Other features of the pacts included close control of state expenditures, restoring the nation's fiscal balance, and reforming an antiquated and inefficient tax system.

The economic compromises contained in the Moncloa accords had immediate, positive results, especially in the area of inflation control. The annual rate of inflation fell from almost 25 per cent in 1977 to 14 per cent by 1982 and the rate of wage inflation was reduced from 30 to 15 per cent (Bermeo with García Durán 1994: 94). This meant that in Spain, in striking contrast to many other post-authoritarian democracies, hyper-inflation would be successfully avoided. More impressive, however, were the political accomplishments of the Moncloa accords in the area of democratic consolidation. The spirit of co-operation embedded in the Moncloa accords neutralized the political arena in a manner that made it possible for the political class and the general public to agree on the parameters of the country's new Constitution (Fuentes Quintana 1980: 155).

The process of societal co-operation in policy engendered by the Moncloa accords differed significantly from that encapsulated in this landmark pact. First and foremost, there were notable changes in the configuration of the bargaining cartel. While the making of Moncloa depended upon political parties as the principal bargaining agents, subsequent pacts negotiated between 1978-86 were forged either in the form of tripartite agreements between the government and peak representatives from employers' associations and trade unions or as bilateral accords between the employers and the unions. The principal protagonists in the process of social concertation (other than the government) have been the nation's leading labour federations, the Communist-oriented *Comisiones Obreras* (CCOO) and the Socialist-oriented *Unión General de Trabajadores* (UGT), and the *Confederación Española de Organizaciones Empresariales* (CEOE), Spain's most important business association.

A second notable development concerns the scope of the concertation bargaining process. The economic and political compromises contained in subsequent pacts have been considerably more limited than those stipulated by Moncloa. Generally speaking, these compromises have been restricted to wage policy and other matters related to labour and industrial relations. That noted, it is important to stress that there is no prototype of a social concertation pact in Spain. Instead, each accord has responded to a particular situation in the nation's political economy. The 1979 *Acuerdo Básico Inter-confederal* (ABI) (Inter-confederal Basic Accord) and the 1980-81 *Acuerdo Marco Inter-confederal* (AMI) (Inter-confederal Framework Accord), signed by the CEOE and the UGT, sought to stabilize and reform industrial and labour relations following the dismantling of the Franco regime's vertical syndicates. These agreements regulated pay guidelines, working hours, and productivity. They also served as the basis for the drafting of Spain's Workers' Charter, a sort of bill of rights of Spanish workers. It recognizes the right to strike, the legitimacy of trade union representation at the company level, and the autonomous role of employers' organizations and trade unions in regulating the process of collective bargaining.

The 1982 *Acuerdo Nacional del Empleo* (ANE) (National Employment Accord) represents the peak of the concertation process in Spain, a characterization that reflects the fact this is the first accord to be signed by all the relevant actors from government, business, and labour (UCD, CEOE, UGT and CCOO, respectively). This pact is also notable for the highly charged political context that surrounded its formulation. The ANE is known as 'The Pact of Fear' because it was negotiated on the heels of the military coup of February 1981 triggered by the return of political autonomy to regional governments in Catalonia and the Basque country. The military uprising served as a waking call to the political class that democracy was still threatened by the nation's authoritarian past. Along with dictating new wage provisions for 1981-82, the principal goal of the ANE was to confront the growing unemployment problem. Accordingly, the centrepiece of the pact was a government promise to take whatever actions necessary to maintain intact the salaried population. That meant creating 350,000 jobs in the public sector and guaranteeing an expanded role for the trade unions in a variety of governmental bodies including the INSS (social security), INEM (employment), and INSALUD (health).

The 1983 *Acuerdo Interconfederal* (AI) (Interconfederal Accord), signed by the CCOO, UGT and the CEOE, accompanied the socialist victory of 1982 and the first transfer of political power within the new democracy. The 1985-86 *Acuerdo Económico y Social* (AES) (Social and Economic Accord), signed by the UGT, the CEOE and the PSOE, is the last of the great accords. Together with wage stipulations, the AES suggested the directions in economic policy that the PSOE would adopt to alleviate the unemployment crisis. The AES generally sought to inject more flexibility into the labour market by increasing options for temporary employment, reducing restrictions on part-time and seasonal employ-ment, and lowering minimum wage standards for workers under 18.

The absence of social pacts in the Spanish economy since 1986 suggests that the country has entered a period of concertation breakdown in which confrontation has replaced co-operation as the dominant feature into industrial and labour relations. This was dramatically illustrated on 14 December 1988, when the leadership of the UGT and CCOO jointly convened Spain's first general strike in the democratic period. By most accounts, the general strike succeeded in paralyzing the nation. Union leaders estimate that over 85 per cent of salaried workers participated in the strike by choosing not to go to work. However, the best indication of the success of the general strike was provided by Felipe González, who recognized it as a 'political success for the unions' (Gillespie 1990: 59).

Multiple factors account for the breakdown of the concertation process in Spain. Perhaps the most obvious one is that after 1986 compromises on behalf of democracy (which was the *raison d'être* of the majority of the pacts) were no longer deemed necessary by either the government or the social partners. By the time the last accord expired in 1986, democratic institutions were no longer perceived to be at risk and the collective memory and ghosts of the Civil War and the Franco dictatorship had generally receded into history. To be sure, some of the 'demons' that haunted the democratization process in Spain (political violence and regional nationalism and separatism, in particular) have settled into seemingly permanent fixtures of political life. But these factors are no longer regarded as direct threats to the stability of democratic institutions. Paradoxically, a nationwide sense that the transition from dictatorship to democracy was irreversible was created by the failed military take-over of 1981. In short, it is important to acknowledge that, to a significant extent, concertation died a victim of its own success.

A second explanation for the demise of concertation in Spain concerns its institutional weakness. While the early literature on the rise of concertation in Spain mistakenly analogized this process to the neo-corporatist experiences of northern European countries (Pérez-Díaz 1987), revisionist assessments have interpreted the concertation experience as a temporary, state-led strategy of regime change lacking the institutional foundations that characterized democratic corporatism (Martínez-Lucio and Blyton 1995: 357; Bermeo 1994: 609; Encarnación 1997). By the time the last pact expired, it was clear that while the social actors had spent much political capital to secure social pacts, few resources had been used to develop institutions specifically designed to facilitate routine intra-group negotiation. A tripartite chamber, such as Austria's Parity Commission or the Netherlands' Social and Economic Council, envisioned in the 1978 Constitution, never materialized during the period of pact-making. The absence of a formal bargaining framework had important consequences on the capacity of concertation to ensure its own continuity. Above all, it prevented the deepening of societal trust and interdependence and hindered the expansion of the bargaining scope beyond the issue of wage policy.

Shifts in proclivities toward co-operation across the social actors provide a third explanation for the demise of concertation in Spain. The unemployment crisis stimulated such a shift. As suggested next, vast unemployment had a profound impact upon all the social partners, but chiefly upon the government which since the inception of democracy had played the central role in the management and maintenance of the process of concertation since its inception in 1977.

THE GOVERNMENT AND THE POLITICAL ECONOMY OF UNEMPLOYMENT

Among the more notable paradoxes in the development of concertation in post-Franco Spain is that it floundered under the rule of a social democratic party with a century-old tradition of close ties to organized labour. Such governments are traditionally viewed as highly conducive to concertation (Lange 1986; Schmitter 1991). As remarked by Schmitter (1991: 69), the European experience suggests that 'there is a close connection between social democracy and the persistence of social concertation.' The key assumption made by scholars in linking labour-based parties to concertation is that, because of their ties to organized labour and their commitment to socialist ideologies, these parties find it easier and more palatable than conservative or centrist governments to incorporate participation of the unions in the making and implementation of economic policy. These were certainly the expectations that greeted the advent of a socialist government in Spain in 1982.

Indeed, it was the hope of labour leaders and the left in general that a socialist administration would serve to deepen union participation in policy-making well beyond the level reached during the first five years of democracy under a centre-right government. In striking contrast to these expectations, however, the PSOE distanced itself from both the labour movement and the concertation process. Instead, it adopted a policy-making style that stood in direct opposition to the notion of concertation by seeking to preserve state autonomy in the design and implementation of economic policy. Critical to understanding this development is the manner in which the economic recession that accompanied the transition to democracy, and that crystallized in a dramatic rise in the ranks of the unemployed by the mid-1980s, conditioned the nature of the policies that the PSOE felt were necessary for the country to overcome its economic problems.

During the elections of 1982 the PSOE campaigned on a platform that called for *El Cambio* (the change), an egalitarian reform of society affecting income distribution, education, health, social security and housing policy (Maravall 1985: 158). But upon entering government, PSOE leaders changed their minds and instead of *El Cambio*, they implemented a radically new approach to managing the economy. This emphasized privatization of state assets, liberalization of the financial sector, reduction of budget deficits, industrial re-conversion, and flexibilization of the labour market.[5] In defending the abandonment of *El Cambio*, PSOE leaders argued that the depth of the economic crisis, as illustrated most dramatically by the rise in unemployment, demanded new economic solutions (Maravall 1991: 26). High among the PSOE's policy priorities was ridding the economy of the labour market rigidities inherited from the Franco dictatorship, which the previous government, preoccupied with the democratic transition and unwilling to confront a resurgent labour movement, had retained largely intact. As explained shortly, the incoming PSOE administration perceived the paternalistic labour laws of the Franco era as a central cause behind the unemployment crisis as well as an obstacle for the creation of new jobs in the new democratic regime. In turn, the emphasis that the PSOE placed upon economic reform in general and labour flexibilization in particular undercut governmental support for class compromises in policy-making.

The implementation of the PSOE's programme of economic reform required a fundamental re-orientation of the manner in which social accords had been negotiated in the past. Under the UCD, the first party to control the state in the post-Franco era (1977-82), the wheels of concertation had been greased by expansionist policies. Most of the pacts negotiated during this period contained significant increases in the 'social wage.' This was especially the case of the Moncloa accords. Although this foundation pact incorporated the UCD's principal package of structural reform and economic stabilization, it also stipulated increases in state spending on education, housing, unemployment coverage, subsidies for the development of trade unionism, and other welfare benefits. These expenditures mirrored the Keynesian orientations of the technocracy inherited from the late Franco period and their commitment to the development of the welfare state in Spain (Encarnación 1997: 397; Gunther 1996: 50). They also had a pragmatic side since they reflected the UCD's recognition that obtaining co-operation from the labour movement with an opposition, centre-right party was contingent upon the delivery of tangible compensation to the unions in exchange for the wage sacrifices being requested from the workers (Bermeo with García Durán 1994: 102).

Under the PSOE, however, concertation was subjected to the demands of fiscal austerity and structural reform. As suggested previously, a key component of the reform process was de-regulation of the labour market which many within the PSOE and outside the government (most notably the business community) felt was necessary to enhance the competitiveness of the economy, to prepare it for integration into the European Community, and to overcome the unemployment crisis. For important segments within the PSOE, the haemorrhaging of jobs that began in the late 1970s could be traced to the steady raising of wages that preceded the advent of democracy. During this period real wages grew faster than productivity, paternalistic Francoist legislation had created important rigidities in the labour market, and low investment resulted in a serious lack of productive capital (Bresser Pereira, Maravall and Przeworski 1993: 107). Stemming from these conditions was the perception that central to the creation of jobs was de-regulation of the labour market, targeted at reducing the costs involved in the hiring and firing of workers.

The understanding of the unemployment crisis in Spain outlined above was promoted most strongly by the 'neo-liberal' wing of the PSOE which by 1982 had gained full control of the Ministries of the Economy and Industry. The individuals in charge of these institutions, Miguel Boyer and Carlos Solchaga, respectively, were the principal architects of the restructuring of the economy that marked the tenure of the PSOE in government and that sought to allow market forces and mechanisms to play a greater role in the management of the nation's economic affairs. The new economic mantra of the PSOE was best expressed by Solchaga in 1985. He noted that 'no one in the PSOE today thinks that the state by itself can or should design an industrial profile which will bring us out of the economic crisis. This we can only do with (more) recourse to the market and its general laws' (Bermeo 1990: 149).

The PSOE's adoption of neo-liberalism, particularly with regard to employment laws and regulations, did not augur well for the continuation of cross-co-operation in the context of concertation. Worsening economic conditions only served to strengthened the government's resolve to push through market-oriented economic reforms, and this in turn translated into a retreat of the state from the bargaining table. As explained by Martínez Lucio and Blyton (1995: 356), 'concertation had no place' in an economic environment in which the early expansionary thrust of government economic policy began to be replaced by a variant of Thatcherite economic and monetary discipline, especially in the context of rising unemployment. On the one hand, the drive for fiscal austerity enhanced the rationale of the view of many technocrats allied to Boyer and Solchaga that regarded concertation as an 'expensive, inefficient and unnecessary' means to make economic policy (Maravall 1991: 59). These views were made public in an infamous leaked memorandum in which Boyer and Solchaga stated that 'no concertation was cheaper than concertation' (Martínez Lucio and Blyton 1995: 356).

On the other hand, there was the sense that real reform, especially with regard to the labour market, could not be attained as long as the government's hands were tied to a process of negotiation with the unions. Indeed, there was the perception within the PSOE that 're-structuring of the role of the state in the labour market was not compatible with any systematic union role within the state' (Martínez Lucio and Blyton 1995: 356). Accordingly, during the years of 1983 and 1984, the government skilfully avoided an agreement with the unions because it 'wanted to push through its harshest readjustment measures and saw concertation as an impediment to what needed to be done' (Gillespie 1990: 51). These efforts materialized, first, with the 1984 Law of Reconversion and Re-industrialization, a legislation that targeted 11 sectors for re-structuring, entailing the elimination of over 80,000 jobs, and second, with the first real efforts aimed at liberalizing the labour market. The latter came with the 1984 reform of the Workers' Charter that allowed for the introduction of temporary contracts into the economy. This development, as will be shown shortly, dramatically changed the nature of employment in Spain.

Despite a palpable decline in its commitment to negotiation and compromise in policy-making, the PSOE continued to seek pacts with the unions after the expiration of the AES in 1986. For Prime Minister Felipe González, obtaining explicit collaboration with the unions was paramount to the maintenance of the PSOE's identity as a social democratic and labour-based institution (author's interviews with PSOE leaders, Madrid, 1994). This explains the government's efforts to reactivate the process of concertation after the hostilities generated by the strike of 1988 dissipated. In the late 1980s, the government offered to negotiate the national budget with the unions in advance of its presentation to parliament. In 1991, it established an economic and social council to facilitate policy co-operation with both employers and unions. None of these efforts produced the return to a negotiated approach to policy-making, largely because the government demanded that future pacts did not disrupt the pace and scope of the economic reform process (author's interviews with labour leaders, Madrid, 1994). In doing so, the government significantly raised the cost of co-operation in policy-making for the labour movement. As suggested in the next section, already weakened by persistently high unemployment and declining membership, Spanish unions could not afford to support a government whose policies were cutting through the very heart of the working class that had brought it to power.

LABOUR, UNEMPLOYMENT AND THE RISING COSTS OF PARTICIPATION IN POLICY-MAKING

Spanish labour eagerly welcomed the PSOE administration. Indeed, the pact of 1982 (the AI) is regarded by labour leaders as a honeymoon gift from the unions to the newly elected government (author's interview with José María Zufiaur, Madrid, 1984). This was one of the few pacts signed by both the CCOO and the UGT, and as such, it raised high hopes for the strengthening of the concertation process under the new socialist government. By 1984, however, when the earliest intentions of the PSOE to pursue neo-liberal policies began to surface, labour support for pacts began to wane significantly.

The first labour defection from the negotiating table was that of the CCOO, which, despite its reputation as the most confrontational of the major unions, had played a central role in the policy of concertation.[6] It is worth recalling that it was the CCOO, rather than the more moderate UGT, which first committed labour to the practice of bargaining wages with capital and the state. The CCOO leadership enthusiastically endorsed the Moncloa accords, qualifying them as 'substantially advantageous to the workers' and made possible by 'pressure from the masses' (Zufiaur 1985: 213). By contrast, the UGT questioned the morality of labour's participation in a political pact orchestrated by former Francoist officials and eventually chose not to endorse it (Zufiaur 1985: 213). The CCOO also embraced the ANE and the AI. Marcelino Camacho, General Secretary of the CCOO, described the former accord as 'the first stone in our country for the building of a new policy of solidarity which would make it possible to face up to the unemployment crisis' (de la Villa and Sagardoy Bengoechea 1986: 387). The CCOO, however, fiercely opposed the AES as too costly to the working class.

The unemployment crisis and its repercussions on the working class, especially job insecurity, rest at the heart of the decision by the CCOO not to support the ANE, an important development in the breakdown of the concertation process. In the view of the CCOO leadership, the ANE 'did not create sufficient employment, would increase unemployment by opening the possibility for the collective firing of employees in enterprises of fewer than 25 employees; reduced wages and attacked on social security; in short, the agreement is designed to meet the needs of both the employers and the government and their desire to legitimate their economic policies' (CCOO 1987: 25). After 1986, the CCOO decisively turned its back on concertation and concentrated its efforts on militant actions aimed at capitalizing upon the grievances of the workers against the government and the sense of social insecurity engendered by the PSOE's economic programme. The organization contended that the government had no right to expect co-operation from labour in an environment dominated by the loss of job security and increasing unemployment (author's interviews with CCOO leaders, Madrid, 1994).

The refusal of the CCOO to support the AES left the UGT, the historic labour branch of the PSOE, the sole union participant in the concertation process. In agreeing to sign the AES and other bilateral pacts with the government, the UGT reluctantly settled into a relationship with the PSOE based on concessions in the areas of job security and industrial re-structuring in exchange for compensatory programmes and the expansion of union's and workers' rights. Although the UGT succeeded in avoiding the dreaded *despido libre* (unrestricted firing), by signing the AES, the organization effectively gave the government the green light to begin dismantling the regime of social protection erected under the Franco era that had made employment in Spain a virtual lifetime guarantee. This was, perhaps, the workers' only truly cherished legacy of Franco's repressive rule. Compensating for such sacrifices was a 'comparatively' advantageous scheme of early retirement or eventual re-deployment that covered some 70,000 workers (Gillespie 1990: 51). The UGT also was successful in securing legislation, such as the 1985 Organic Law of Union Liberty (LOLS), that authorized union presence at the workplace and the right of public workers to strike. The UGT was also favoured by the government over the CCOO in the return of the *patrimonio histórico*, the union property confiscated by Franco after the civil war. These assets, which also included the fees collected from the workers during the dictatorship and whose value in 1985 was estimated to be around 2 billion dollars, were vital to labour's rehabilitation in the new democracy (McElrath 1989: 105).

After the AES expired, the UGT, as the CCOO had done in previous years, arrived at the realization that the costs of co-operation with the PSOE were outweighing its benefits. And as in the case of the CCOO, factors intimately linked to the unemployment crisis led to that conclusion. For a start, the government did not always deliver on the promises which had become the basis for the UGT's justification for continued co-operation with the government. A notable example is the PSOE's failure to expand unemployment coverage to workers displaced by industrial re-structuring to 43 per cent by 1985 and 48 per cent by 1986, as agreed in the AES. The 48 per cent target would not be reached until 1989 (Alvaro Espina 1990: 456). The UGT's abandonment of concertation was also encouraged by the fact that although by the late 1980s the Spanish economy was generating new jobs, the unemployment crisis as a whole remained unabated, and in some respects it had actually worsened. The continuing crisis of unemployment, as I will explain shortly, gave rise to real fears among UGT officials of a backlash from the workers against the union's continuing reliance on co-operation in its interaction with the government.

Between the years of 1982 and 1987, the number of unemployed increased from 2.2 million to 3 million, a situation that pointedly suggested to UGT leaders that co-operation with the government was proving useless in bringing about change in the nation's employment landscape. After 1986, the unemployment picture changed as the socialist programme of economic liberalization began to yield some impressive results including the creation of 1.7 million jobs between 1986 and 1991 (Richards and García de la Polavieja, 1997: 17). These gains, however, did little to compensate for the haemorrhaging of jobs that took place between 1982-86. Although by 1990 the unemployment rate had dropped to 16 per cent (the lowest it had been in nearly a decade) it was about the same as when the PSOE came to power in 1982. More significant was the deterioration in the quality of employment created in Spain after the liberalization of the labour market in 1984. Since the mid-1980s, over 90 per cent of all employment contracts signed each year are temporary (Martínez Lucio and Blyton 1995: 351). As a result, today Spain not only has the highest unemployment rate among OECD countries but also the highest level of temporary work (33.59 per cent of the salaried population) (Richards and García Polavieja 1997: 16).

For UGT leaders, pursuit of the policy of negotiation and co-operation with the government in the context of persistently high unemployment, deteriorating employment conditions and a widespread fear about job security, posed numerous risks. First and foremost, the continued association of the UGT with the PSOE began to jeopardize the union's standing as the nation's leading workers' federation. This prospect materialized dramatically during the national union elections of 1986, which determine representation of the unions in collective bargaining. Although the UGT won the elections, it was badly defeated by the CCOO in some of the largest public companies. The first lesson that the UGT leaders drew from the 1986 elections was that its opposition had successfully capitalized on the growing dissatisfaction of the workers with the PSOE. A second and related lesson was that the UGT 'had become too closely associated with government policies that demanded sacrifices from the labour movement' (Gillespie 1990: 58). As remarked by Nicolás Redondo, the head of the UGT, the elections demonstrated that 'the workers have come to identify us with the actions of the government' (*Anuario El País* 18/12/86).

Continuing affiliation and co-operation with the PSOE in the context of high unemployment also threatened to exacerbate the depletion of union membership. In particular, labour leaders were fearful that participation in future pacts would send the workers the message that union leaders were unwilling to confront the government in an effort to protect their jobs. Such fears are well understood considering the magnitude of the decline in trade union membership experienced by Spain in the democratic period. While the collective membership rate in

Spanish trade unions exceeded 50 per cent during the euphoric years following the legalization of free unions in 1977, by the mid-1980s it had dropped to below 20 per cent (Pérez-Díaz 1987: 234). In the mid 1990s, it stands at 9.3 per cent, the lowest in western Europe (Schmitter 1995: 294). The decline in union membership is faithfully mirrored in the sharp decline in membership experienced by the UGT, which went from a high of 1,000,000 in 1978 to 663,000 by 1985 (McElrath 1989: 104). A central explanation in the decline of the unions was, of course, the unemployment crisis, since both some its causes (the energy crisis of the late 1970s) as well as its prescriptions (industrial re-conversion and liberalization of the labour market) hit particularly hard the areas of the economy where union membership was strongest.[7]

A battle over solutions to the unemployment crisis eventually led the UGT to end its official affiliation with the PSOE, a partnership forged in the late nineteenth century and sustained throughout the repressive years of the Franco dictatorship. This divorce within the socialist family effectively ended nearly ten years of consensus-driven policy-making in democratic Spain. The straw that broke the camel's back was a government plan designed to create 800,000 temporary jobs under a youth employment proposal which the government was forced to withdraw due to complaints from the unions that it increased the workers' vulnerability vis-à-vis the employers and reduced job security. The youth employment scheme also generated calls from disenchanted union leaders for adoption of strategies of confrontation against the socialist administration (Saracíbar 1988). It also provoked the UGT into seeking closer ties with its rival organization (the CCOO) as it sought to orchestrate a broad strategy of opposition to the PSOE. Such efforts culminated with the 1988 general strike, an event notable for its intense anti-government nature. In the aftermath of the strike, the UGT joined the CCOO in calling for a *giro-social*, a fundamental re-orientation of the government's economic programme that demanded the extension of social protection, a new focus on wealth re-distribution and job creation, and abandonment of the liberal approach to economic policy-making implemented to date. These actions were coupled with intense strike activity that made Spain one of the most contentious industrial settings in western Europe during the 1980s.

UNEMPLOYMENT AND THE EROSION OF SUPPORT FOR CONCERTATION AMONG EMPLOYERS

By the time the AES expired in 1986, employers' reliance on social pacts as a means to control wages had diminished significantly, a development intimately linked to the unemployment crisis and its repercussions on the labour movement. This trend, however, was hardly evident in the employers' official assessment of the break-up in the relations between the PSOE and the UGT and, by extension, the end of concertation. The employers' response to these events was one of great regret and, unsurprisingly, given the rise in industrial conflict that accompanied the demise of concertation, the employers pointedly blamed the unions for the breakdown of the system of social pacts which had guided economic policy since 1977. Commenting on the failure to reach a pact in 1987, the president of CEOE, José María Cuevas (1989), noted that the unions have gone from a model of relations with employers based on 'negotiation and dialogue to a model based on permanent confrontation, strikes, and mobilization.' In his view, the unions, the UGT in particular, bears 'direct responsibility for breaking the social compromise and for driving the nation into a phase of 'ruptured concertation.'

There is much irony in the employers' response to the events leading to the end of concertation since the business community never fully embraced the process of concertation. Indeed, among major social actors, employers exhibited the most ambivalence about entering into pacts and, despite the facts that the social pacts facilitated the consolidation of democratic institutions within a capitalist framework, left property rights virtually intact, and moderated workers' salaries. Employers happily complied with the wage stipulations of the social accords but they remained ambivalent, and at times outright hostile, to the notion of sharing policy decision-making with the unions. For instance, the CEOE declared the Moncloa accords 'illegitimate' (CEOE 1977), and soon after their implementation, employers began to defect from the UCD in droves, occasioning a crisis within the party that culminated in its electoral defeat and total collapse in the 1982 elections.[8] The bilateral pacts that the CEOE negotiated with the UGT between 1980-81, and that led to the creation of the Workers' Charter, were subsequently criticized by the organization as a 'loss of a unique opportunity for reform' since these pacts preserved the rigidities of the labour market inherited from the dictatorship (Iglesias: 1990: 151). The CEOE, however, reserved its harshest criticism for the ANE, the last pact negotiated under the UCD. Its vice-president, Arturo Gil (interview with the author, Madrid, 1994), criticized this pact for its 'heavily compromised political nature and its generous incentives to the unions.'

A number of reasons closely linked to the evolution of concertation and the employers' role in that process explain the employers' lukewarm embrace of concertation. UCD officials, and especially Adolfo Suárez, purposefully avoided contacts with the business community during the negotiations of the Moncloa accord as a way to entice both the Communist and Socialist parties to the bargaining table. Consequently, it is widely acknowledged that the employers did not play a role in the design of the Moncloa pacts (Bermeo with García Durán, 1994: 105). Indeed, by their own admission, employers learned of the details of the pacts just prior to their presentation in parliament (author's interviews with CEOE leaders, Madrid, 1994). Employers were also threatened by the prospect that a comparatively better-organized labour movement could use the pacts as a means to enhance their political standing in the new democracy.[9] Such fears were undoubtedly encouraged by the euphoria created by the legalization of trade unions in 1977 which gave Spain, albeit for a very short time, an impressive level of unionization. Just as worrisome to the employers was that, at the inception of democracy, the majority of the workers were choosing to join the Communist-controlled federation (CCOO).

By the mid-1980s, employers' ambivalence toward concertation had turned into real lack of interest in seeking accommodation and compromise with the unions. After the expiration of the AES, employers were expressing the view that 'social pacts as an institution should not be extended indefinitely' and that the institutionalization of bargaining in the form of a social and economic council 'would only serve symbolic rather than real purposes' (Pérez-Díaz 1985:18). Critical to the emergence of these sentiments was growing awareness among the employers that concertation was neither desired nor needed in the management of the economy. This realization was influenced by both political and economic events. The collective sense that Spanish democracy had attained consolidation significantly devalued concertation among employers by projecting the impression that all-out confrontation was no longer a threat to democratic stability. This message was compellingly demonstrated by the labour movement with the general strike of 1988. In the economic realm, concertation also lost its rationality among employers, a development largely influenced by the crisis of high unemployment.

The crisis of unemployment significantly eroded employers' interest in concertation in both direct and indirect ways. First and foremost, the unemployment crisis contributed to the decline in support for concertation among employers by simply acting as a more effective moderator of wages and labour militancy than social pacts. This development manifested itself in a variety of ways, but most notably in the decrease in appeal of national centralization of wages among employers. By the mid-1980s, the CEOE began to favour either the full-fledged decentralization of the wage setting process or wage agreements negotiated by the employers with individual unions rather than through a 'peak' or national union. These alternatives allowed employers a significantly more favourable negotiating environment than concertation. For a start, they allowed employers to prevent the rise of the compensatory schemes that had traditionally accompanied the negotiation of national wage accords and thus increase the 'marketization' of policy-making. The move away from national wage agreements also permitted Spanish employers to better exploit the anxiety, fears and insecurities of the workers about their own employment situation in the midst of rising and vast unemployment.[10]

The unemployment crisis further diminished the rationality of concertation among employers by curtailing the organizational capacities of the unions. High unemployment, as noted previously, had an enormous impact upon union density as reflected in the dramatic loss of membership that Spanish unions sustained in the early 1980s. In turn, the growing institutional weakness of the labour movement occasioned a fundamental re-thinking among employers about the value of concertation. On the one hand, the union's own organizational difficulties meant that the employers had less incentive to contain labour demands through negotiation and concessions and to grant them a voice in the management of labour and industrial relations. As suggested by Martínez Lucio and Blyton (1985: 356), in the face of labour's weakness, employers were disinclined 'to pay the price of wage moderation in terms of improved social provision and possibly expansionist economic policy.' On the other hand, by the mid-1980s, when union membership levels may have dropped into single digits, employers were seriously and legitimately questioning whether the unions had the capacity to deliver upon their wage commitments (author's interviews with CEOE leaders, Madrid, 1994).

CONCLUSION

This essay has used the breakdown of concertation in Spain since the mid-1980s to illustrate the consequences of high unemployment upon governance and policy-making. In particular, the essay has been concerned with explaining how persistently high unemployment eroded the foundations for societal co-operation in policy-making across and within the social actors most centrally concerned with the process of concertation. The unemployment crisis that exploded and consolidated in Spain in the early 1980s first affected concertation by forcing the government to curtail the economic incentives and social protection that had previously facilitated the making of social accords especially in the area of wages. This development, in turn, exposed the labour movement to the vagaries of the market thus raising the costs of its participation in the policy arena. Finally, the unemployment crisis diminished the interest of employers in concertation by acting as a more effective moderator of wages than social pacts and by weakening labour's bargaining position vis-à-vis both capital and the state.

As is customary in almost any scholarly endeavour possessing 'comparative' ambitions, the tendency in the conclusion is to locate the broad meaning of the empirical findings and the theoretical implications of what has been argued. In this case, these tasks must be approached with considerable trepidation given, first, the limitations imposed on comparative political analysis by a single case study, and second, the peculiarities of the case itself. That noted, Spain is hardly alone among western European nations in having experienced the convergence of rising unemployment and a decline in the propensity of social actors to rely upon concertative arrangements in national policy-making. In the last two decades, Sweden and Germany, two cases traditionally associated with harmonious, consensus-driven policy-making especially in regard to wage policy, have experienced unprecedented high unemployment and significant instability and decline in the realm of concertation. Unsurprisingly, a recurring theme in recent writings on industrial and labour relations and interest representation in advanced industrial economies is the decline of concertation, neo-corporatism and the like (Streeck 1984; Streeck and Schmitter 1991).

It is beyond the scope of this essay to investigate the full extent to which the theoretical contentions developed for this study are applicable to other cases. But it is interesting to note that this study's central assertion – that unemployment is a central explanation for the demise of concertation – resonates well beyond the confines of the Spanish case, thus suggesting a high degree of generalizability for our arguments. Moreover, the very precise manner in which unemployment eroded the foundations for concertation in Spain can be found in the experience of other countries. The component of the model most often found in other explanations of the demise of concertation is that which concerns the state's withdrawal from direct bargaining with both capital and labour.

As in Spain, the state's retreat from concertation is largely explained as a reflection of efforts by government elites to secure a significant degree of autonomy to implement the policies of economic adjustment demanded by international competition, globalization, and economic integration (Streeck and Schmitter 1991: 146-7). Such policies are not believed to be successful if the government has to compromise with capital and especially the labour movement. As in the case of Spain, the era of economic adjustment and reform in most countries has included attempts at de-regulating the labour market as a means to promote employment. And, as in Spain, such an approach to unemployment policy has placed enormous strains on the relations between the government and the labour movement even in cases in which these relations are sustained by long-standing historical affiliations. France under socialist government is a shining example. In this case, effective progression towards social concertation has been hindered by the government's attacks on welfare provisions and the unions' fears of close association with the government in the context of rising unemployment.

Finally, we find in the experience of other European countries an important role for capital and its response to the unemployment problem in the demise of concertation. A number of recent studies of concertation's demise in a variety of European settings make a forceful case for placing the employers' at the centre of the breakdown of concertation (Streeck, 1984; Gobeyn 1993). In the view of one author (Gobeyn 1993: 93), the demise of corporatist concertation in western European economies can be attributed largely to growing capitalist opposition to maintaining corporatist forms of relations with organized labour and the state. It is further noted that 'for industrialists, the highest possible levels of capital accumulation are currently realizable through less centralized processes of industrial relations and economic policy-making; thus corporatism's provision of official economic policy-making and administrative roles to labour is now being viewed by capital as more of a hindrance to rather than as a facilitator of such accumulation.'

More directly related to our analysis is the fact that in the broader

European context, as in the case of Spain, high unemployment is seen as a leading cause behind the employers' rejection of decades-old traditions of centralized wage bargaining. It is reported that in countries such as Germany, where employers had once embraced concertation for its capacity to moderate wages and labour conflict, such arrangements are currently perceived as 'constraining their adaptive responses to market contingencies' (Streeck 1984: 294). These anti-concertation stances derive in great measure from the employers' awareness of the growing weakness of labour being occasioned by high unemployment. It is observed that

> with the arrival of recent expansions in unemployment levels, particularly in those industrial sectors where trade unionism is most extensive, there exists less of a need to give organized labour a 'voice' in the making of public policy, for the docile, disciplined labour environment that the granting of this 'privileged' policy making position generated can now be realized through market forces, as substantial supplies of reserve labour are at present in place in many west European societies to act as external restrains in the emergence of labour militancy and high wage demands (Gobeyn 1993: 92).

In sum, this essay suggests that the political consequences of high unemployment are indeed far reaching and go well beyond the toppling of governments and political leaders. Concertation has long been a staple of European public policy. Indeed, this mode of policy-making has traditionally stood at the very heart of the democratic cross-class consensus which has been pivotal to Europe's economic prosperity and political stability in the post-war era. It has also made post-Franco Spain a paradigmatic example of cross-class co-operation and democratic consolidation and a model to still-fragile democracies in eastern and central Europe and Latin America. Its demise raises, at best, the prospect of increased class conflict and strains on the social fabric of European societies, and at worst, diminished democracy. These outcomes suggest the manner in which the arrival and entrenchment of high rates of structural unemployment is transforming the very nature of European governance.

NOTES

1. Unemployment statistics in Spain are notoriously unreliable. The data presented in this study are gathered from various reports from the Instituto Nacional del Empleo (INE), the European Community, and the Secretaría de Estado y Comercio.
2. Following common usage of the term, in this study social concertation refers to a mode of policy-making based on the co-operative pursuit of common objectives by the government, employers and trade unions. More specifically, social concertation is linked to the establishment of 'social pacts' aimed at regulating a variety of economic issues including wages, inflation and industrial and labour relations. For theoretical conceptualizations of social concertation see Lange (1986).
3. The fact that the voters did not blame the PSOE for the unemployment crisis does not explain why the voters continued to support the party in the first place. Maravall and Fraile (1997: 37) observe that the negative consequences of the unemployment crisis under the PSOE were mitigated by the influence of ideology, income levels, and evaluations of the general economic conditions and of social policies. Other reasons include the weakness of alternatives to the PSOE from either the left or the right. This meant that voters angry with the policies of the PSOE had limited opportunities to punish the party at the polls. Moreover, despite a high unemployment rate, the PSOE ruled over a booming economy. As many as two million new jobs were created during the economic expansion of the late 1980s, forcing a drop in the unemployment rate from 21 per cent in 1986 to 15 per cent by 1990 (Jimeno and Toharia 1994: 20).
4. A full examination of the politics and policies of social concertation in post-Franco Spain is beyond the scope of this paper. Fortunately, the subject of concertation in Spain has generated a substantial and diverse literature, a reflection of its importance to post-transition politics. For transcripts of the Moncloa pacts and other agreements of the concertation process during the consolidation of Spanish democracy see: de la Villa (1985) and CCOO (1987). For an analysis of the political factors aiding in the rise of concertation in the aftermath of the Franco regime see: Encarnación (1997). For an analysis of the relevance of the politics of concertation to the consolidation of Spanish democracy see: Foweraker (1986), Pérez-Diaz (1990), and Encarnación (1997). For assessments of the economic legacies of concertation see: Fuentes Quintana (1980), Pérez-Díaz (1987), de la Villa and Sargadoy Bengoechea (1987) and Bermeo (1994). For theoretical and conceptual discussions of the political architecture of concertation, especially in light of the more ambitious concept of corporatism, see: Giner and Sevilla (1986); Martínez-Alier and Roca (1987); Bermeo (1994) and Encarnación (forthcoming).
5. Between 1982 and 1986, the PSOE sold or dissolved more than 30 public enterprises (Bermeo 1990: 140). Many of these enterprises belonged to the National Institute of Industry (INI), whose employment roster fell from 219,000 in 1982 to 169,000 by 1986 (López-Claro 1980: 20).
6. Between 1977-82, the CCOO was particularly supportive of tripartite accords that incorporated participation of the state. However, it rejected bilateral accords between the unions and the employers. The explanation for this behaviour resides primarily in the relationship of the CCOO with the Spanish Communist Party (PCE). After the electoral collapse of the PCE in the 1977 elections, the CCOO became the party's principal instrument for participation in national politics. Among the objectives the PCE pursued via the CCOO and the concertation process was a more moderate political orientation. In this context, political pacts carried more weight than social pacts with the employers.
7. High unemployment is only one factor behind Spain's low level of workers' unionization. Other factors include the largely blue-collar membership of the UGT and the CCOO, the recent shift toward a service economy, the huge size of the informal

economy, and the low participation of women in union affairs. The percentage of male workplace leadership within the CCOO is 92.3 per cent and 98.8 per cent for the UGT. An additional factor is the often-noted aversion of Spaniards to join associations of any kind.

8. Support for the UCD among employers dropped precipitously from 44 per cent in the general elections of 1979 to 8 per cent in 1982. Simultaneous with the decrease of business support for the UCD was a dramatic increase in support for AP, a right-wing party closely associated with the old authoritarian regime. Support for AP among employers increased from 25 per cent in 1979 to 46.5 per cent by 1982. See: Pérez-Díaz (1985: 26-7).
9. Spanish capital, unlike labour, had no history of formal organization prior to the democratic transition. The CEOE, organized in 1977, was Spain's first employers organization to be formed with the explicit intent of defending the interests of Spanish employers. It was created partly in response to the perception by the business community that the UCD was ignoring the concerns of the employers, a message conveyed by the manner in which the Moncloa accords were negotiated. On the formation of the CEOE and the role of business in the consolidation of Spanish democracy see: Martínez (1993).
10. This point brings to light the issue of the psychological impact of unemployment upon the workers, a subject thoughtfully explored by Frances Fox Piven and Richard Cloward (1981). They have observed: 'that because insecurity makes workers vulnerable, it also saps their strength. When people fear for their subsistence, they accept onerous and dangerous working conditions. They accept discipline, follow orders, and submit to humiliation. An insecure labor force is thus a more productive labor force and a cheaper one' (p. 13).

REFERENCES

Anuario El País (various issues).

Balfour, Sebastian (1989): *Dictatorship, Workers and the City: Labour in Greater Barcelona*, Oxford: Clarendon.

Bermeo, Nancy (1990): 'The Politics of Public Enterprise in Portugal, Spain and Greece', in Ezra Suleiman and John Waterbury (eds), *The Political Economy of Public Sector Reform and Privatization*, Boulder, CO: Westview.

Bermeo, Nancy (1994): 'Sacrifice, Sequence and Success in Dual Transitions: Lessons from Spain', *The Journal of Politics* 56/3, pp.601-27.

Bermeo, Nancy with José García Durán (1994): 'Spain: Dual Transition by Two Parties', in Stephan Haggard and Steven Webb (eds), *Voting for Reform*, New York: Oxford University Press.

Comisiones Obreras (1989): *De los pactos de la Moncloa al ASE*, Madrid: C.S. de Comisiones Obreras.

Confederación Española de Organizaciones Empresariales (1977): Statement on the Moncloa Accords, Madrid.

Cuevas, José María (1989): Speech to the CEOE General Assembly, Madrid: CEOE.

Encarnación, Omar G. (1997): 'Social Concertation in Democratic and Market Transitions: Comparative Lessons from Spain', *Comparative Political Studies* 30/4, pp.387-419.

Encarnación, Omar G. (Forthcoming): 'Federalism and the Paradox of Corporatism: Illustrations from Spain', *West European Politics*.

Espina, Alvaro (1991): *Empleo, Democracia y Relaciones Industriales en España*, Madrid: Ministerio de Trabajo y Seguridad Social.

Foweraker, Joe (1987): 'Corporatist Strategies and the Transition to Democracy', *Comparative Politics* 20/1, pp.57-72.

Fuentes Quintana, Enrique (1980): 'Economía y política en la transición democrática española: fundamentos y enseñanza de una experiencia', *Pensamiento Ibero-Americano* 1/1, pp.43-159.

Gillespie, Richard (1990): 'The Break-up of the Socialist Family: Party-Union Relations in Spain, 1982-89', *West European Politics* 13, pp.47-62.

Giner, Salvador and Enrique Sevilla (1984): 'Spain: Form Corporatism to Corporatism', in Allan Williams (ed.), *Southern European Transformed*, London: Harper and Row.

Gobeyn, Mark James (1993): *Corporatist Decline in Advanced Capitalism*, Westport, CT: Greenwood Press.

Goldthorpe, John (1987): 'Problems of Political Economy after the Post-War Period', in Charles Maier (ed.), *Changing the Boundaries of the Political*, Cambridge: Cambridge University Press.

Gunther, Richard (1996): 'From Dictatorship to Democracy: Policy-Making in Spain', Manuscript, The Ohio State University.

Hibbs, Douglas A. (1987): *The Political Economy of Industrial Democracies*, Cambridge, Mass: Harvard University Press.

Iglesias, Rodrigo (1990): 'La concertación social desde la perspectiva de las organizaciones empresariales', in Angel Zaragoza (ed.), *Pactos sociales, sindicatos y patronal en España*, Madrid: Siglo Veintiuno.

Jimeno, Juan and Luis Toharia (1994): *Unemployment and Labor Market Flexibility: Spain*, Geneva: International Labour Office.

La Dehesa, Guillermo de (1983): 'Spain', in John Williamson (ed.), *The Political Economy of Reform*, Washington DC: Institute for International Economics.

La Villa, Luis Enrique de (1985): *Los grandes pactos collectivos a partir de la transición*, Madrid: Ministerio de Trabajo y Seguridad Social.

La Villa, Luis Enrique de and Juan Antonio Sagardoy Bengoechea (1987): 'Social Concertation in Spain', *Labour and Society* 12, pp.386-407.

Lange, Peter (1987): The Institutionalization of Concertation, *Working Paper*, Duke University Program in International Political Economy.

López-Claros, Augusto (1988): *The Search for Efficiency in the Adjustment Process*, Washington, DC: International Monetary Fund.

McElrath, Roger (1989): 'Trade Unions and the Industrial Relations Climate in Spain', Industrial Relations Unit, The Wharton School, University of Pennsylvania, Philadelphia, PA.

Mancha, Tomás (1993): *Economía y Votos en España*, Madrid: Instituto de Estudios Económicos.

Maravall, José María (1985): 'The Socialist Alternative: The Politics and Electorate of the PSOE', in Howard R. Penniman and Eusebio Mujal-León (eds), *Spain at the Polls: A Study of the National Elections*, Durham: Duke University Press.

Maravall, José María (1991): 'The Politics of Economic Reform: The Southern European Experience, *Working Paper* no. 2, Program on East-South Transformations, University of Chicago.

Maravall, José María (1997): *Regimes, Politics and Markets: Democratization and Economic Change in Southern and Eastern Europe*, New York: Oxford University Press.

Maravall, José María and Marta Fraile (1997): 'The Politics of Unemployment: The Spanish Experience in Comparative Perspective', Paper presented at the conference 'Unemployment's Effects: The Southern European Experience in Comparative Perspective', Princeton University, 14-16 November.

Martin, Rhodes (1997): 'Spain', in Hugh Compston (ed.), *The New Politics of Unemployment*. New York: Routledge.

Martínez Lucio, Miguel and Paul Blyton (1995): 'Constructing the Post-Fordist State? The Politics of Labour Market Reform in Spain', *West European Politics*, 18/2, pp.340-60.

Martínez-Alier, J. and Jordi Roca (1987): 'Spain: From Corporatist Ideology to Corporatist Reality', *Journal of International Political Economy* 177/56-97.

Pérez-Díaz, Victor (1985): 'Los empresarios y la clase política', *Papeles de la Economía Española* 25: 2-35.

Pérez-Díaz, Victor (1987): *El retorno de la sociedad civil* [The Return of the Civil Society], Madrid: Instituto de Estudios Económicos.

Piven, Frances Fox and Richard Cloward (1981): *The New Class War*, New York: Pantheon Books.

Richards, Andrew and Javier García de Polavieja (1997): 'Trade Unions, Unemployment and Working Class Fragmentation in Spain', Paper presented at the conference 'Unemployment's Effects: the Southern European Experience in Comparative Perspective, Princeton University, 14-15 November, 1997.

Saracibar, José Antonio (1988): 'Las razones que se quieren ocultar', in Santos Julia (ed.), *La desavenencia*, Madrid: Ediciones El País.

Schmitter, Philippe (1989): 'Corporatism is Dead! Long Live Corporatism!', *Government and Opposition* 24/54-73.

Schmitter, Philippe (1991): 'La Concertación Social en Perspective Comparada', in Alvaro Espina (ed.), *Concertación Social, Neocorporatismo y Democracia*, Madrid: Ministerio de Trabajo y Seguridad Social.

Schmitter, Philippe (1995): 'Organized Interests and Democratic Consolidation in Southern Europe', in Richard Gunther, P. Nikiforos Diamandouros and Hans-Jürgen Puhle (eds), *The Politics of Democratic Consolidation: Southern Europe in Comparative Perspective*, Baltimore: The University of Johns Hopkins Press.

Streeck, Wolfgang (1984): 'Neo-Corporatist Industrial Relations and the Economic Crisis in West Germany', in John Goldthorpe (ed.), *Order and Conflict in Contemporary Corporatism*, Oxford: Clarendon Press.

Streeck, Wolfgang and Philippe Schmitter (1991): 'From National Corportism to International Pluralism', *Politics and Society*/19, pp.133-63.

Toharia, Luis (1988): 'Partial Fordism: Spain between Political Transition and Economic Crisis' in Robert Boyer (ed.), *The Search for Labor Market Flexibility: The European Economies in Transition*, New York: Clarendon Oxford University Press.

Zufiaur, José María (1985): 'El sindicalismo español durante la trancisión y la crisis', *Papeles de la Economía Española* 22: 202:34.

Unemployment, Informalization and Trade Union Decline in Greece: Questioning Analytical and Prescriptive Orthodoxies

SERAPHIM SEFERIADES

Like most other European nations, Greece is troubled by high and growing unemployment. In 1996 10.34 per cent of the economically active were unemployed, up from only 4.04 per cent in 1981 and 7.65 per cent in 1991. Along with Spain and, to a lesser extent Italy, Greece is now cited as a high unemployment country in the literature (see, e.g., Symes 1995). Of the total number of unemployed, the high rates of unemployment among youth (29.8 per cent in 1995) and long-term unemployment (52.4 per cent in 1995) have been particularly worrisome. In both these aspects, Greece ranks above the EU average, though still slightly below the other three southern European countries. However, whereas youth and long-term unemployment have been declining in Italy, Spain, and Portugal, in Greece they have been rising (Eurostat 1996: 163).

The way most scholars and policy makers have interpreted growing unemployment has centred on short- and medium-term developments in the labour market. The factors most usually cited include the contraction of employment in the agricultural sector, the increased participation of women in the labour force, and the restrictive monetary and exchange-rate policies adopted to meet the criteria for participation in the EMU (see, e.g., Petrinioti 1998; Demekas and Contolemis 1996). Since very little can be done about any of these factors, however, the argument which increasingly tends to dominate synthetic and prescriptive analyses is that unemployment is caused by structural rigidities in the labour

---

This paper was prepared during the author's stay at the European University Institute as a Jean Monnet Fellow. He wishes to thank Professors Stefano Bartolini and Martin Rhodes for their valuable comments.

market. According to the most recent European Commission report on the Greek labour market, '[t]he existing employment protection legislation contributes to the protection of certain jobs but restricts flexibility, raises costs and reduces employment opportunities available to those who are out of work' (European Commission 1997: 38, ix; see also OECD 1996a). Sometimes one has to read between the lines of mainstream argumentation, but the generally neo-classical orientation, venerated not only in Athens but in most European capitals, is quite clear: dismantle employment protection, and there will be jobs. The first part of this article proposes to briefly examine the merits of this contention. By briefly analyzing features of the Greek labour market (especially the large, and eminently flexible, 'informal sector'), I will suggest that, contrary to the predominating orthodoxy, the experience of Greece casts doubt on the view that labour-market flexibility can serve as a cure to unemployment.

The issues raised in this skimpy first part of the article are, of course, extremely complex and variegated. Naturally, no definitive propositions regarding the causes of Greek unemployment can be offered. The modest goal is, rather, to prompt and assist the open-ended reflection needed to gain a better understanding of the precise nature of the problem at hand. This, in turn, can serve as valuable background for the second, and major, part of the article examining the effect of unemployment on trade unions.

Here, too, there is an orthodox view (both journalistic and scholarly) with which to grapple. It can be summarized in just two words: union retreat. A recent issue of the influential weekly *Οικονμικός Ταχνορόμος* painted the following gloomy canvas, replete with normative statements:

> The decline of the trade union movement both in Greece and internationally is beyond question. The relevant data on the number of unionized workers are overwhelming. What is even more remarkable is that the general influence of unions is dwindling. In other periods the movement could topple governments and enforce the introduction of legislation. Nowadays it is fighting not to lose its voice....Soon the trade-union movement will amount to nothing unless it changes orientation....The answers the trade-union movement gives to contemporary problems are outdated and, in practice, lead to its own decimation. Restructuring will continue no matter what, and trade unionism is unable to stop it....Until today, the movement has not succeeded in coming up

> with new ideas, neither internationally nor in Greece. If this continues, the trade-union movement will be forced to write on its own tombstone: 'I died because I lacked imagination' (FC 23 July 1998, my translation).[1]

The gruesome imagery of the last admonition notwithstanding, the prescription underpinning the analysis is, once again, unmistakable: either accede to policies of wage restraint and labour-market flexibility and thrive, or resist and perish. My goal in what follows will be to scrutinize both the analysis and its underlying policy prescription. Relying on a conceptual distinction between the institutional-organizational features of labour movements (principally trade union density) and their protest outlook (principally their propensity to strike), I will argue that, contrary to a widespread assumption, the low/declining membership of the Greek trade union movement has not entailed a reduced propensity to strike. This, in turn, casts new light on the usual objectivist, environmental renderings of the problem of declining membership as a direct function of high unemployment. Are factors associated with capitalist restructuring and rising unemployment all we need to know to interpret shrinking union membership? What is the role of union tactics and politics (unions as strategic actors)? Finally, is the strategic dilemma facing unions 'acquiesce and thrive *or* resist and perish', or is it, perhaps, the other way around?

I. FLEXIBILITY AND UNEMPLOYMENT

Nowadays the point seems to have been sufficiently hammered home that the issue of labour market flexibility is much more complicated than we once thought. Bewildering variation in labour-market structures and policies, as well as in scholarly analytical approaches interpreting these policies make conclusive theorization exceedingly risky and cumbersome (Bamber and Lansbury 1998; Hyman and Ferner 1994; Baglioni and Crouch 1990; Boyer 1988;). For practical purposes, however, it is possible to distinguish among three kinds of flexibility: *numerical flexibility*, which denotes employer capacity to hire and fire employees in response to developments in the business cycle; *wage-level flexibility*, referring to a capacity to freely determine wages; and *working-time flexibility*, which gives employers the freedom to extend or shorten the workday (see Moody 1997b: 95-6; Dedousopoulos *et al.* 1997, 1988; Rhodes 1997: 2).

Often conflating the various aspects of the issue, the question has been recently posed in Greece: Is the labour market flexible or rigid? The answer, of course, can only be relative, partial, and inconclusive – flexible/rigid compared to which model? Even so, it is possible to start providing an answer where it is simplest, i.e. at the level of wages. Though the proponents of further wage-level flexibility are correct in pointing out that the current system, determining minimum wages at the national level, could be reformed to allow lower, sub-minimum wages at the local level (presumably reflecting variations in the supply of and demand for skills), the fact of universally low wages remains.[2] It follows that further wage-level flexibility is unlikely to contribute to any significant job creation. As one analyst put it, if high, inflexible wages were a factor in Greek limited competitiveness and unemployment, then Greece ought to have solved these problems long ago (Kouzis 1997: 119).

The issues surrounding the other two, workplace kinds of flexibility are considerably thornier. Though Greece has an exceedingly weak welfare state (Spyropoulos 1998; Stathopoulos 1996; Kritsantonis 1992), elaborate labour-market legislation regulating employment and working time (most of it introduced in the 1980s) remains in place. Law 1387/1983 sets limits for the maximum number of employees who can be dismissed (2-3 per cent per month), while other pieces of legislation regulate overtime, weekly rest periods, holidays, night work, and firing compensations.[3] This, in turn, has caused many to argue that removing the protective legislation interfering with employer freedom to hire and fire would contribute to job creation. Plant-level flexibility has been advanced as a panacea for curing unemployment. Is it?

Reflecting on the notion of workplace flexibility a decade ago, Robert Boyer stressed that it is, from its very definition, associated with productivity. Higher flexibility is aimed at stimulating overall productivity. Assuming that the contemporary unemployment problem facing Greece and other European countries stems from the inability of their labour markets to absorb technological change and adapt to increased international competition because of Fordist rigidities, flexibility ought to be associated with an increased capacity to modernize which, in turn, would have a positive long-term job-creating influence. The association, however, is not causal.

> In the short-term it is the rate of investment, the growth of the market, and the skill of the work-force that condition the rate at which technical change is incorporated into the economic system. In the long term, it is only the emergence of a coherent

technological system that will enable cumulative growth of productivity to be achieved (Boyer 1988: 230).

To the extent that investment remains timid, the market sluggish, and the labour force unskilled, no such technologically advanced system is likely to emerge. In that case, flexibility usually becomes but a euphemism for downgrading most of the rights of wage earners (Gilbert et al. 1992; Pollert 1991; Rubery 1989; Hyman 1988). Indeed, the danger looms large that approaching the 'need for higher flexibility' as part of a larger plan for reducing short-term costs of production may well end up being an obstacle to long-term changes in socio-productive organization, which alone offers the best chance for sustainable job creation (Shaikh 1996).

Boyer's argument is a good starting point for assessing the Greek experience, especially as it helps account for developments in that sector of the economy which is flexible *in extremis*, the informal sector. Pondering over issues associated with the nature of this sector requires a short detour.

As elsewhere in Mediterranean Europe, 'invisible' informal activities, absorbing low-paid labour, and avoiding the reach of the state with regard both to the enforcement of labour legislation (safety, insurance, length of the workday, etc.) and the observation of collective bargaining agreements are extremely widespread in Greece, accounting for anything between 18 and 30 per cent of the GNP (Hadjimichalis and Vaiou 1990; Lolos 1989, 1991; Pavlopoulos 1987). Informal activities usually have been considered as factors contributing to 'unemployment relief' (see, e.g., Leontidou 1993: 62-6). Considering the enormous flexibility associated with them, however, they can, equally well serve as a laboratory for testing the promise of flexibility. Are informal activities *cum* flexible production associated with technological innovation and employment creation?

Informal work takes many forms (Skolka 1985). Hadjimichalis and Vaiou (1990) have suggested the following fourfold categorization: *criminal activities*; *profitably exploiting inadequacies of the formal regulatory system* (mainly denoting tax evasion); *reproduction of traditional forms of production* (involving activities such as petty-trade, illegal construction, tourism in summer, harvest of fruits and vegetables in summer and spring, T-shirt production in autumn and winter); and those generated by *specific restructuring strategies* of individual firms in agriculture, industry, retail, and services. Among all four, it is the last one that has been hailed as a model for overcoming Fordist rigidities, onto the road of 'flexible specialization'. Relying on apparent success stories such as, most notably, Third Italy, the argument has been put forward that the internal, plant-level flexibility associated with this form of production will lead inevitably to technological upgrading on the basis of computers and other multi-purpose machinery and the emergence of 'economies of scope'. Relying on batch-production techniques, these will be able to penetrate market niches with just-in-time production, thereby increasing their productive utilization and creating the prerequisites for further investment and productivity-increasing technological innovation. This, in turn, will lead to considerable job creation (see, e.g., Sabel and Zeitlin 1997; Sabel 1989; Wickens 1987; Sabel and Zeitlin 1985; Piore and Sabel 1984).

The 'flexible vision', Boyer's objections, and the Greek experience can now be fruitfully joined. Recent research on the evolution and intricacies of the Greek informal sector indicates that, contrary to the expectations of the flexibility theorists, plant-level flexibility has led neither to productivity-increasing technological upgrading nor to sustainable job creation. Pelagidis (1997: 158-70, 216-17), who researched textile production in the Thessaloniki area, discovered that, despite the general dynamism and adaptability characterizing the sector in the late 1980s, the use of new technologies was conspicuously absent and that most comparative advantage was derived from low-paid work, especially piecework and outwork. Similarly, Lyberaki (1988), who researched flexible small-medium enterprises, discovered that

> Their flexibility and responsiveness [were] not geared towards differentiation and product development but rather towards auxiliary activities....Flexibility and responsiveness [appeared] to exhaust their beneficial potential in a defensive/survival strategy; they [did] not appear capable of generating expansion and growth (Lyberaki 1988: 328).

Even more tellingly, Moschonas and Droucopoulos (1993: 116, 118) discovered that in the period 1963-90 the productivity gap between large (rigid) and small (flexible) establishments in Greece widened by no less than 23 per cent. (Naturally, the gap also widened in terms of wages. Whereas in 1963 the annual remuneration per employee in flexible establishments was 75.9 per cent of its counterpart in large establishments, by 1990 it had fallen to 67.1 per cent.)

In their extensive research, encompassing flexible informal activities both in agriculture and manufacturing in northern Greece, Hadjimichalis and Vaiou (1997) reached largely similar conclusions. Once again, flexibility was found to be primarily 'defensive', increasingly failing to generate economies of scale and relying almost exclusively on low production and management costs. In the early 1990s, far from offering a way out of the employment crisis characterizing the official economy, informal activities were found to be in the midst of a severe crisis of their own. Especially after 1993, a large number of them were forced to close down (according to the researchers' estimates, 30-40 per cent of the textile units that had been founded between 1981 and 1988) and lay off their workers. To schematize a rather complex state of affairs, plant-level flexibility led not to flexible specialization, but to a growing *crisis of informalization*; not to sustained employment creation, but to a frustrating increase in the (informal/invisible) jobless rate.

In the summer of 1998 the Greek government introduced new legislation in the direction of more working-time flexibility.[4] Under the new law, employers are able to vary the length of the working week and the distribution of the hours worked during the year.[5] As stated in the law's preamble, the government expects the restructuring/flexibilization of the labour market to 'contribute decisively to the preservation of existing jobs and the formation of new ones, as well as to improvement in the overall competitiveness of the Greek economy' (Elliniki Dimokratia 1998: 23). By highlighting the problematic nature of the association between flexibility, technological innovation, and productivity growth, and illustrating with a brief reference to the experience of the Greek informal sector, however, I have suggested why some of these high hopes, viewing flexibility as a panacea, may be misguided.[6] The extent to which further flexibility will carry the day, however, depends largely on the stance of the labour movement.

II. LOW UNION DENSITY, PROTEST, AND PROSPECTS FOR TRADE UNIONISM

The prophets of trade union doom in Greece rely on some hard data. In the 1990s unions have come under increasing strain, membership has been declining and, as the quote from the *Οικονμικός Ταχνορόμος* cited at the beginning of this paper suggests, union discourse has been losing much of its erstwhile appeal. Indeed, largely due to unemployment, 'power and initiative appear to have drifted from trade unions' (OECD 1991: 97). But does this mean, as some have suggested, that unions are in the process of dissolving? What is precisely the nature of the retreat? What causes it and how can it be reversed? Is it simply rising unemployment? Moreover, how does this retreat relate to the unions' capacity to mobilize? Answering these questions and specifying the exact nature of the retreat is extremely important, not the least because crucial policy prescriptions flow from the analysis that will be made.

Greek authors and commentators who evoke the 'resurgence of labour quiescence' theme (Shalev 1992) to describe long-term trends in the evolution of the labour movement and the effects of unemployment usually conflate two levels of analysis: union membership and density on the one hand, and union mobilizing potential on the other (see, e.g., Toutziarakis 1997).[7] But in Greece (and other countries of Mediterranean Europe), the correlation between density and mobilizing capacity implicit in the blending is spurious. Even if unemployment tends to drive down trade union membership, it does not also erode labour's capacity for job actions of all sorts.

Historically, the repressive labour environment, characterized by limited political-legal space, persistent state repression, and low living standards, effectively precluded the institutionalization of the labour movement. As a result, membership has been low and unstable, and overall organization precarious. This situation of limited institutionalization continued also after World War II, during the 'guided democracy' of the 1950s and 1960s and after the restoration of parliamentarism in the mid-1970s (I will return to these issues below). After some considerable gains in the period 1977-82, when union density grew from 35.8 per cent to 36.7 per cent, the traditionally low pattern set in again. Among 24 OECD countries Greece ranked nineteenth in 1988 (OECD 1991: 101) and continued to experience a decline in the 1990s, when union density fell from 34.1 per cent in 1990 (OECD 1994: 184) to 27 per cent in 1995 (Koukoules 1998: 104).

Low and declining union density, however, did not lead to a low propensity to strike. On the contrary, recent quantification of labour disputes revealed that Greece is the country which, if anything, defies the pan-European 'labour acquiescence' trend. In a recent study covering the 15 member states of the European Union, plus the three members of the European Free Trade Area (Iceland, Norway, and Switzerland), Greece, apparently unaffected by rising unemployment, ranked first in terms of most of the measures suggested, a slight variation of Shorter and Tilly's

TABLE 1
STRIKE PROPENSITY IN GREECE AND OTHER EUROPEAN COUNTRIES

	1980-85 GR/rank	EU	1985-90 GR/rank	EU	1990-93 GR/rank	EU	1970-93 GR/rank	EU
SR	0.30/1	0.12	0.49/1	0.07	0.68/1	0.05	0.40/1	0.10
RDNW	0.74/1	0.31	4.06/1	0.19	4.41/1	0.14	2.52/1	0.3
MR	0.76/7	1.30	2.33/3	1.25	4.06/2	1.40	1.35/3	1.18
SDR	2.46/12	2.50	8.18/2	2.60	6.46/3	2.61	6.20/6	2.91
RIPS*	+2.56/3		+7.19/1		+7.89/1		+6.10/1	
SIPS*	–0.99/10		+2.76/1		+2.80/1		+1.14/3	
GIPS*	+1.57/4		+9.95/1		+10.69/1		7.24/1	

*Figures for the RIPS, SIPS, and GIPS are recalculated so that the average for all countries equals zero. Propensity to strike increases where the sign is positive, and falls where the sign is negative.
Source: Adapted from Aligisakis (1997); ILO (1990-95).

(1974) conceptual scheme (Aligisakis 1997). These involve the *Strike Rate* (number of strikers by number of wage earners – SR); the *Rate of Days not Worked* (the ratio of days not worked because of strike action by the number of wage earners – RDNW); the *Mobilization Rate* (number of strikers by number of strikes – MR); and the *Striker Determination Rate* (days not worked by number of strikers – SDR). The first two measures comprise the *Relative Index of Propensity to Strike* (RIPS) and the third and fourth the *Structural Index of Propensity to Strike* (SIPS). Added together, they form the *General Index of Propensity to Strike* (GIPS). The data are summarized in Table 1.

Whereas in the early 1980s Greece ranked low in terms of the mobilization and striker determination rates (respectively, Shorter and Tilly's 'size' and 'duration'), in the mid-late 1980s and the 1990s this was reversed. For the last decade or so, strikes in Greece have been characterized by high frequency, long duration, and large average size. It also merits attention that, in terms of its General Index of Propensity to Strike for the period 1970-93 (7.244), Greece ranks far above second-ranked Italy (4.813), the country usually cited as the hotbed of industrial unrest (Edwards and Hyman 1994).

This remarkably high propensity to strike subsided after 1993, but the trend is by no means unambiguous. Although the number of strikes, strikers, and hours lost declined abruptly between 1993 and 1995, 1996 (a year when there was an upsurge in unemployment) was marked by increases in all three criteria. This was especially so in terms of the hours lost because of strikes. Compared to 1995, the hours lost in 1996 increased by 70 per cent (Koukoules 1998: 111). Though it remains to be seen whether this new upsurge in labour militancy will continue, it is nonetheless evident that to speak of 'labour acquiescence' in Greece is, to say the least, premature.

Moreover, regardless of short-term developments, the prediction that strikes will somehow wither away in the future seems inconceivable on historical grounds. As Franzosi (1995: 347-8) argued, since strikes are ultimately caused by conflict over the distribution of scarce resources, long-term prosperity is an absolute prerequisite of a society free of conflict and such a state of affairs nobody dares to predict. Instead, in 'each European country sudden eruptions of new conflict have appeared at several moments in history and there is no reason why they may not recur in the future' (Leisink et al. 1996: 14).

Challenging as it may be, adequate explanation of – and possible theory building on the basis of – Greek strike patterns lies beyond the scope of this paper. (Any future effort, however, must be based on Franzosi's (1995) superb blending of economic, organizational, institutional, and political explanatory factors.) But the extreme nature of the divergence between unionization and mobilization rates in the context of rising unemployment, flying in the face of the usual assumptions in the political economy literature, Franzosi's findings (who discovered that 'union organizational strength and strike activity [go]...hand in hand' – p. 345), as well as resource mobilization theory (see, e.g., McAdam, McCarthy and Zald 1996), certainly calls for an explanation. This too, however, is exceedingly complex to be fully pursued in the context of a short paper. All I can aspire to do here is suggest what I think may be prerequisites for an adequate explanation. For that we must turn to history.

In particular, I want to suggest that the Greek labour movement's contemporary crisis of low union density *without* a simultaneous crisis of mobilizing capacity (and despite rising unemployment) cannot be adequately explained unless we take into account the historically learned patterns of labour activation. These we may provisionally dub 'historically cumulative labour strategies' (see Lipsig-Mumme 1989; see also Crouch 1993). This notion bears important parallels with Charles Tilly's (1978) notion of 'collective action repertoires', and refers to the ways in which labour movements learn to turn their resources into collective action. Profoundly interactive and relational (Tilly's subsequent studies of 'contentious repertoires' stress that the concept refers to pairs of politically constituted actors, one of whom is the state

– see, e.g., Tilly 1998), these ways depend a great deal on the legacy of what Valenzuela (1992) termed the 'mode of a labour movement's political insertion' into the socio-political system (see also, Collier and Collier 1991; Seferiades 1998a). Below I will attempt to sketch what I think are the crucial features of the Greek case.

III

> The workers' movement in Greece never knew a period of genuine legality. The things which a lot of people of diverse social backgrounds experienced in the course of the last military dictatorship [of 1967-74] were to [the interwar] workers...a permanent condition under all the regimes, republican, monarchist, or military. Arbitrary arrests, house searches without a warrant night and day, beatings, torture, humiliation, detention, exiles. And when the workers, badly beaten and bleeding would bring a charge to court, or publicize their predicament in the press, the clichéd reaction was: 'typical communist lies' (Stinas 1985: 145, my translation).

Because of late industrialization, a labour movement emerged relatively late in Greece, only in the last quarter of the nineteenth century. The economic behaviour of the Greek elites, largely an outcome of the country's semi-peripheral articulation into the world system and the structure of economic opportunities that this articulation entailed, created an environment conducive to the exclusion of the new collective actor. Excessive elite reliance on trade, with a concomitant hesitance to invest in industry, and a strong penchant for financial speculation and economic adventurism, produced a fluid labour market and made projects for the strategic incorporation of the labour movement appear both relatively expensive and useless (see Hadjiiossif 1993: 447; Liakos 1993: 174-6).

This does not mean, of course, that no political will for such an incorporation existed. Especially during the first period of Venizelist rule in the early/mid-1910s, exceptionally progressive labour legislation was introduced, only to be stalled by acerbic employer resistance (Mavrogordatos 1983). During the interwar period, repression returned to centre stage. It has been tellingly argued that, unlike the situation in western Europe, where the evolution of state-labour relations could be described by the scheme 'prohibition → tolerance → recognition,' in

Greece the evolution has been distressingly Sisyphian: 'prohibition → tolerance → prohibition' (Liakos 1993: 163).

The extremely narrow political-legal space allotted to the labour movement, the constant intervention of the state in the internal life of trade unions, and the coercive presence of the police and army in virtually all forms of labour protest precluded the ideological incorporation of the labour movement and produced an intensely conflictual political culture. As a result a vicious circle was set in motion: the more coercive the state became, the more coercion was needed (Seferiades 1998b).

These structural features had two important consequences. First, the labour movement was characterized by the strong role that politics and party organisations played in its operation. Unlike the situation in western Europe, such organisations had a longer history than trade unions and, as a result, trade-union discourse developed not as a forerunner but as a sub-species of political discourse. Even more crucially, by precluding genuine union autonomy, the constrictive political environment made it appear that having a well-defined political goal was a prerequisite for undertaking meaningful trade union action. Playing by the rules of the game was largely untenable, so the game had to be changed.

Second, as mentioned earlier, the labour movement was characterized by intense segmentation and an almost permanent organizational fluidity. Although trade unions and the outer trappings of a generally robust trade union life existed, they had only limited functional content, concealing a constantly low union density, membership instability, and a broad array of organizational irrationalities (such as the inability to hold regular conferences, collect union dues, etc.). This had contradictory consequences regarding the political sociology of trade union leaders. Whereas it was relatively easy for them to rise to the leadership (especially when they were linked to the state), the bureaucratic structures they were erecting were exceedingly weak, unable to control the movement and, much less, ensure its incorporation into channels of vertical communication with the state. This, in turn, precluded the institutionalization of the movement, giving it an informal, intermittently convulsive dynamic, which, though explicable, was usually unforeseen.

Itself a reflection of limited institutionalization, this convulsive dynamic tended to spread to society at large though informal communication networks, not through the industrial shop floor. It is not surprising, then, that its relationship with unemployment was neither direct nor predictable – contextual and political considerations were always of paramount significance.

Unions had a low membership, but, whenever they called militant action, the response was likely to be significant. An important instance of this convulsive dynamic characterizing the labour movement was the way that small confrontations would snowball to engulf entire regions, quite irrespective of local unemployment rates. Dynamic as they may have been, however, these confrontations would not bring about much in the way of solid organizational gains for the official trade union movement. Though a constant source of anxiety for the state, labour militancy was organizationally intractable.

A related feature was that general popular demands (sometimes with a distinctly pre-industrial character) were prominent in trade-union discourse and the opposite, a situation in which trade-union practices tended to influence innocuous popular activities (such as, most notably, around popular housing). This informal mode of communication between unions and their potential membership rendered labour's mobilizing capacity largely immune to unemployment's adverse effects, and became particularly evident during the years of the German occupation in the 1940s, when the labour movement played a decisive role in the national resistance movement. The eruption of a wave of political strikes in 1942-43 (when more than 100 strikes broke out) and the emergence of new participatory institutions despite the coercive presence of the German occupation forces, essentially abolished the old state and created hopes for the development of rational organizational structures. These, however, were viciously crushed in the 1946-49 civil war.

As trade unions were denied all autonomy by the repressive state in the 1950s and 1960s, the problem of trade union under-representation increased. At a time when genuine labour activists were persecuted, a

> caste of leaders developed who were ironically known as *ergatopateres* (workers' fathers). Sustained by patronage relations with the government, they also confected a spurious legitimacy by convening rigged conferences, de-registering troublesome branches, and similar stratagems. Since their income was received from the government rather than from members' [dues], they were under no real pressure to act effectively as workers' representatives (Kritsantonis 1992: 613-14).

This period further crystallized the Greek labour movement's contentious repertoire. If union autonomy was severely compromized by the actions of a repressive state, then the response would have to be similarly political, albeit organizationally erratic and intractable. The eruption of labour militancy that marked the mid-1960s took place at a time of low unemployment. Judging by the labour movement's history and the fact that this militancy developed largely outside union organizational channels, however, it is very unlikely that labour activism would have been deterred if unemployment were higher. It is also telling that the militancy of the 1960s was spearheaded by political, not narrowly economic, developments (Seferiades 1998c). The major goals pursued were also political, involving the liberalization of the post civil-war regime and an end to royal interference into the workings of the political system. As in the past, politics was understood not as the culmination of economic demands, but as a prerequisite for their meaningful articulation. This being the case, it is not surprising that membership in the trade unions was relegated to secondary status and union density remained low as usual, below the 20 per cent mark.

After 1974 there was considerable liberalization and efforts were made for the institutionalization of the labour movement. Union autonomy remained compromised, however, and union affairs open to government intervention, despite the formal guarantees of Article 12 of the 1975 Constitution (Zambarloukou 1996; de Roo and Jagtenberg 1994; IRS 1991: 25; Mavrogordatos 1988). As a result, the Greek workers' traditionally low propensity to organize along with their strong penchant for plebiscitarian political action remained, this time in the context of progressively rising unemployment. This helps explain both the outbreak of intermittent strike waves in the background of continually low union density and the enormous political factionalism that beset the trade union movement in the late 1970s and 1980s. It also lies at the core of contemporary union dilemmas.

IV

If, as seen, low union density and general organizational feebleness does not reflect a reduced willingness and/or capacity to act (Offe and Wiesenthal 1985), it does however, limit this action's effectiveness. As Visser (1992: 23-4) argued, high union membership may not be a prerequisite of labour militancy, but it is necessary if this militancy is to become a truly 'strategic resource', capable of being used in a conscious and purposeful manner. Both in the recent and the more distant past, the Greek labour movement waged titanic battles, but most of them ended in defeat. Despite the momentous eruption of May 1936, the movement was unable to stop the imposition of the Metaxas dictatorship in the interwar period. And though the 1964-66 strike wave has tellingly been described as the prelude to the pan-European 1968 (Vernardakis and Mavris 1991), the labour movement was subsequently so numbed that scholars have naturally concluded that the Colonels' dictatorship had little need to repress it further (see, e.g., Bermeo 1995). The strike waves of the late 1970s and 1980s were successful in gaining economic concessions and opening up labour's political-legal space in the short term, but were unable either to end state intervention in internal trade union affairs or, as seen above, effectively address the problems of low wages and informal labour markets.

In the 1990s the defeat involves what Lipsig-Mumme (1989: 230) called 'qualitative decline', a lessened ability to influence the political, social, and economic agenda. This, in turn, is manifested in a variety of ways, including a large number of strikes lost, the inability to influence legislation, and the increasing distancing of PASOK, the ruling socialist party, from union influence. Moreover, unions may be losing their ability to influence the 'general public' and create a favourable ideological climate. Data on this issue are difficult to come by, but according to survey 1.3b of Eurobarometer 48 (Commission Européenne 1997: B.5), more Greeks 'tend not to trust' trade unions (49 per cent) than those who do (45 per cent). (On the other hand, the percentage of positive attitudes is considerably higher than the EU15 average of 38 per cent.)

The irony of the matter is that all this is happening at a time when, at long last, the movement has been granted the status of an official 'social partner', especially after the introduction of Law 1876/1990 establishing free collective bargaining at the peak level, and laying the grounds for what Crouch (1994: 210) aptly called 'a very loose neo-corporatism'. Although, as seen, unemployment has been rising, nowadays the General Confederation of Labour (GSEE) enjoys not only the freedom its quasi-clandestine predecessors lacked, but has its own research institute (INE/GSEE), the opportunity to assess and evaluate contemporary trends in the labour market, and the chance to reflect on international experience.

Developments in the spring of 1998 represent a meaningful condensation of contemporary labour movement dilemmas. Reacting to policies of welfare-state retrenchment and privatization, teachers and bank employees came out on strike and confronted the police on several occasions. Though they were able to demonstrate to the privatizing state and the elites that the route to labour-market flexibilization is going to be long and thorny, their strikes, unable to spearhead a larger movement, met with defeat. What is worse, unionists estimate that in their wake, union membership seems to have further declined (Balaouras 1998).

This being so, it would appear that the biggest challenge facing the labour movement at the end of the 1990s was to overcome its historical organizational feebleness precluding the strategic and purposeful deployment of worker militancy. What are the prospects?

V

In light of the continually high strike propensity of the labour movement, it is clear that any search for solutions to the present crisis must avoid the pitfalls of environmental determinism, and approach unions as organizing agencies, or strategic actors (Leisink et al. 1996). After all, recent research in political economy has amply demonstrated that environmental factors such as unemployment are, by themselves, extremely unstable and weak predictors of union decline (see, e.g., Visser 1994; Lange and Scruggs 1997a, 1997b; Richards and Polavieja 1997). Unions in Greece are not facing a crisis because capitalist restructuring and high unemployment have made workers too afraid or too segmented to fight. The strike data we examined indicate that workers are anything but tamed. Neither are unions the victims of the much discussed 'free rider' problem suggested by rational choice theorists – as a rule, militant strikes are far more costly to the individual than deciding to join a union. It is, rather, because unions have failed to convey to their potential membership why it is important to belong to a union in a manner sufficiently strong to overcome the labour movement's historically embedded plebiscitarian contentious repertoire and its landmark low propensity to organize. That is, to convince workers that union 'goals matter to them, that their own participation makes a difference, that others will join, and that together they stand a chance of success' (Klandermans cited in Visser 1994: 85).

The way the union leadership has been trying to address this problem over the last few years has been characterized by an effort to cherish the unions' recently earned 'social partnership' status, albeit at the expense of their traditional social-movement outlook. The GSEE has prepared elaborate proposals for purposes of conducting 'social dialogue' (see GSEE/ADEDY 1997), which, though well documented and critical of neo-classical policies, are based on the assumption that the solution to

Greece's economic and social problems lies in co-operation and consensus-building. Employers and the state must be made to understand why low wages and further informalization of the labour market offer no solution to the problem of unemployment, it is argued, but this can be achieved merely through competent argumentation. Concurrently, the movement's traditional politicization is silently abandoned in the name of an increasingly technical discourse (*vide* GSEE's otherwise excellent proposals about the promise of the 35-hour week – INE/GSEE 1996) and the goal of 'union autonomy'. Although party factionalism inside GSEE bodies continues, unions increasingly abstain from offering informed commentary on political issues. In short, the union leadership has sought to address the problem of low membership by attempting to curb the labour movement's historical confrontationism and politicization. It is reasoned that this will create the conditions for the organizational rationalization of unions, and will allow them to play an important role in Greece's advancing social and political 'modernization', the rhetorical buzzword of the late 1990s (see, e.g., Protopappas 1997, 1998).

This stance has earned the GSEE a good name with employers and European Commission analysts,[8] but has done nothing to arrest declining density, or lead the quasi-wildcat strikes which broke out to success. As elsewhere in Europe, worker 'collective willingness to act' has been light-heartedly squandered and this has contributed to a net decline in 'union power' (Offe and Wiesenthal 1985; Hyman 1994: 128). In the summer of 1998, GSEE officials could not conceal their profound disappointment with the evolution and prospects of the 'social dialogue' (Linardos-Rylmon 1998). George F. Koukoules (1997: 70) described the situation as follows:

> The present crisis...embroils the trade union movement into the following contradiction: on the one hand, because of the several favourable institutional reforms that have been put in place in recent years, it is a privileged interlocutor in negotiations with employers and the state. On the other hand, neither the employers nor the state show any willingness to grant any concessions to the unions but, on the contrary, keep asking unions to concede more and more (my translation).

Koukoules concludes tellingly that 'unless the union movement finds ways to overcome this contradiction, it will suffer its most decisive defeat'.

The problem, of course, is not particularly Greek. In the hard economic times of the 1980s and 1990s, governments and employers the world over can be expected to sustain the regimes of consensual industrial relations established in the post-war era '*only* to the extent that unions underwrite policies of retrenchment and restraint' (Hyman 1994: 115, emphasis in the original) – even in cases where the state does not seek the liquidation of the welfare state, but merely its replacement with what Rhodes (1997) aptly called 'competitive corporatism'. All the same, union leaderships have tended to cling to the paradise lost of societal corporatism, even when struggles break out. Kim Moody (1997a: 54) gave a fine description of the process:

> A fight is called for and sometimes waged by these...leaders. Typically, it is waged in the name of the old stable relationship. For the top leaders there is no contradiction. There is, however, an underlying contradiction between the new demands of capital and the unions' old line of defence. Stability is gone, but the paradise lost of stability and normal bargaining continues to inform the actions of the leaders even when they are confrontational. Their actions sometimes push forward even though their eyes are focused clearly on the past. That this contradiction is likely to limit the effectiveness of the unions is obvious...

What is particular (and ironic) about the Greek case is that the societal-corporatist 'past' Moody is talking about has never existed. And, evidently, it is not likely to come about in the 1990s.

On the other hand, concession bargaining, increasingly seen as 'conceding defeat without attempting to wage a fight' (Balaouras 1998), has eroded union credibility. If, historically, workers were unwilling to join unions because of state repression, in the 1990s they are sceptical because of continually limited union effectiveness (compounded, of course, by low density and rising unemployment). In an environment of continual concession bargaining the 'free rider' dilemma is reversed. If no benefits are to be won by collective bargaining, the theoretically challenging task ceases to be explaining why the outsiders refuse to join a union, but why the insiders have not yet left.

VI

It is appropriate, therefore, to conclude by offering some tentative thoughts on how the problem may be overcome. I propose to do so along the six complementary dimensions for conducting research on union strategy in the era of rising unemployment and declining union membership recently suggested by Leisink et al (1996). The authors believe that, though not exhaustive, these dimensions are essential for unions to examine if they want to overcome contemporary crisis and organizational dilemmas. They involve the following: *mission of unions*, *solidarity*, *items on the bargaining agenda*, *relations with the state*, *relations with the employers*, and *internationalism*. Though some of the remarks below read like a manifesto, they are to be seen also as summary of a future research agenda.

(1) Union mission: Economic stringency and rising unemployment put in doubt the post-war mode of union representation relying on sustained GNP growth and relatively tight labour markets (Hyman 1994: 114). If this is the case for countries of the European core, it is much more true for countries such as Greece, where a long heritage of political repression and 'an unusually autocratic set of employers never made free collective bargaining an option' for trade unions (Kritsantonis 1992: 619). Clinging to notions of 'social partnership' (new in Greece, but, for practical purposes, also hopelessly outdated) at a time of rising unemployment can only lead to concession bargaining and, through that, to further erosion of union credibility and strength. Greek unions cannot overcome their problem of low density unless they actively re-politicize their discourse, transcending the immediate implications of work relations at the enterprise level and exposing social forces behind economic phenomena, which lie at the core of the problem of rising unemployment. This is especially true in the era of globalization. As Hyman (1988: 59) put it, 'the *what* and the *why* as well as the *how* of production decisions [are] of key relevance'. In the 1990s and beyond, 'the labour movement's old demand that production should be determined by social need rather than profit assumes new meaning'. In keeping with the historical traditions of the Greek labour movement, Greek unions must seek a contentious, encompassing, social-movement kind of unionism. According to Moody (1997b: 4-5), this means a movement that will be deeply democratic, militant in collective bargaining, political in acting independently of the retreating forces of social democracy, and universal in terms of the scope of the demands that it puts forward.

(2) Solidarity: Both in Greece and internationally authors have long suggested that union decline in the context of rising unemployment is causally linked with a crisis in traditional working-class values (see, e.g., Koukoules 1997; Visser 1994). What most of these analyses fail to point

out, however, is that solidarity is, and has always been, constructed – no golden era of organic labour unity has ever existed (Moody 1997b: chapter 7; Hyman 1992; 1994: 117-19). It follows that declining solidarity is not so much a cause of declining union density, as it is an effect. As in the past, unions can and must address the problem. In Greece special emphasis must be placed on five categories of workers. Those employed in the informal sector, women, youth, immigrants (see Baldwin-Edwards 1998; Petrinioti 1993), and, of course, the unemployed. Thoughts on their particular demands and how they can be articulated with those of the rest of the union movement already exist (see Hadjimichalis and Vaiou 1997: 218-19; Sianou 1997: 164; Katsoridas 1998: 85-8, 1994: 36-8), but need to be developed further, not so much by scholars as by union leaders.

(3) New items on the bargaining agenda: The most direct way unions can enhance solidarity is by reconsidering and substantially innovating the bargaining agenda in ways that will have a positive effect on the working class as a whole, especially the unemployed. This, of course, means taking to heart the interests of unorganized workers, especially those belonging to the five categories mentioned above. Unions must frame and pursue the interests of their own membership in ways which do not 'exclude and oppose those of other constituencies' (Hyman 1994: 120). Employment creation can and must be immediately put on the bargaining agenda. The problem is particularly thorny in Greece, however, because of the unequal density of public and private sector unions (the famous 'insider-outsider' issue), a problem compounded by the rising numbers of the unemployed. Scholars have long noted that this situation has tended to bias the bargaining agenda in favour of the public sector (Fakiolas 1985), tying unions to a core and ageing workforce and making them unable to defend the interests of the rest (either because they are not unionized or because they work in the black market). Many have also argued that, for the sake of protecting the interests of private sector workers and the unemployed, public sector workers ought to moderate their demands (see, e.g., Manos 1998). However, the conclusion does not flow from the premise. By compromising their typically militant stance[9] public sector unions will not help private sector unions solve their low-density problem. One can hardly expect a smashed backbone to help a meagre body gain weight. On the contrary, international experience and social movements theory (see, e.g., Tarrow 1998: chapter 9) suggest that by extending their demands and flexing their mobilizing muscle, so-called

elite union organizations (such as the public sector workers in Greece) have lowered otherwise high costs of participation and collective action and opened precious new space to previously unorganized workers and other strata, thereby improving their aggregate density (Moody 1997b: 278-79; Lipsig-Mumme 1989). Unless unions undertake extensive campaigns to address the issues in a comprehensive manner along the lines suggested above, however, a contentious mobilizing strategy might be misunderstood, threatening to turn once sympathetic people against unions. These campaigns must stress that new items are being put on the bargaining agenda and hammer home that the old maxim, 'an injury to one is an injury to all', still holds.

(4) Relations with employers: Leisink et al. (1996: 23) have argued that nowadays it is pointless to try charting beforehand a good-for-all industrial relations' practice, *either* co-operative *or* conflictive. Instead, unions must 'master the whole repertoire of union-employer relationships and be able to choose whichever model seems appropriate' (see also **Olney** 1996). This is probably true, but what *will* be appropriate depends to a large extent on the nature of the demands unions put forward. For instance, considering economic crisis and unemployment to be quasi-natural phenomena and ossifying the notion of a positive business climate can only lead to concession bargaining. In times of economic strain, versions of 'business unionism' and 'productivity coalitions' essentially mean an end to unionism. In the 1990s and beyond, genuine flexibility in union industrial relations practice presupposes clearly demarcated lines and an aggressive programme of requisitions. 'Institutional commitments to labour peace, the avoidance of non-economic issues, and reduction of strike militancy…[have all been found to] do workers a...disservice' (Cohn 1993: 226). Even in cases where advanced demands put forward cannot be won, unions can gain a great deal by approaching the issues in a politically provocative manner, exposing specific social interests behind given proposals (taking special care to demonstrate how specific business practices fail to alleviate unemployment), and campaigning to show why the existing balance of social forces prevents a better outcome. Especially during the time of negotiations for a National General Collective Agreement, these can be transformed into highly successful union recruitment campaigns.

(5) Relations with the state: If, as has been pointed out above, societal corporatism is gone, there is no point in daydreaming about it. The

sooner union leaders realise this, the better. As 'oppositions that never become governments, unions must fight from the outside' (Moody 1997b: 285). Of course, this does not mean that unions must stop talking to the state. But unions, more than scholars, must, once again, come to grips with the fact that, particularly in the 1990s, the state's role has been to guarantee 'control of the major means of production, distribution, communication, and exchange by private, inherently undemocratic banks and corporations' (Panitch 1996: 108). It follows that negotiations can no longer exhaust themselves in the effort to solidifying an imaginary social partnership with 'socialist monetarism'. Instead, unions must seek to clarify to the workers the nature of the issues involved, including the state's and the unions' respective positions, and use the publicity associated with peak-level negotiations as a fulcrum for establishing a relationship both with other social movements and with workers' movements in other countries. As with many other items on this agenda, however, here too the problem is one of agency. As Moody (1997a: 54) argued, the step from a merely symbolic to an ideological or even institutional 'social partnership' between the labour bureaucracy and capital's bureaucracy and the state is not always a big one. In Greece, the current Under-secretary of Labour, Evangelos Protoppapas (particular agile in promoting the 'accede or die' ideology), was GSEE's last president. Will future labour leaders be prepared to forfeit their potential political careers? No answer can be given, of course, but the outcome will depend to a large extent on whether or not unions combine their drive to grow in numbers with one for greater internal democracy and leadership accountability. Contrary to earlier assessments (Streek 1988), we now know that the two can be compatible (see Moody 1997: 275-7; Hyman 1994: 124-5).

(6) Internationalism: Much in the logic of concession bargaining rests on the notion of national competitiveness. The argument runs something like the following: Workers must accept further wage cuts and the dismantling of labour legislation, because otherwise the national economy will lose whatever competitive edge it possesses. The questionable technical merits of this argument notwithstanding, its common-sense prowess is, nevertheless, depressingly evident. It can be addressed only if one takes into account that it its being monotonously repeated the world over. This requires the international co-operation of union forces, internationalism. Though scholars are just beginning to discuss the issue, noting the enormous opportunities and difficulties

involved (e.g., Moody 1997a and b; Goetschy 1996; Hyman 1996), it seems warranted to suggest that an international orientation can in the short-term recast the terms of the national debates and help unions grow.

SUMMARY

The first part of this paper briefly examined the merits of neo-classical arguments regarding the causes of the recent upsurge in Greek unemployment. I showed that at least the Greek experience casts doubt on the view that labour-market flexibilization can serve as a sustainable cure to unemployment. The focus in the second, and major, part of the paper has been on unions. Unlike the situation in most European countries, rising unemployment has not affected the mobilizing capacity of the Greek labour movement. More than a century after its emergence, however, this movement has yet to overcome its historically embedded low union density. This may not prevent the outbreak of militant strikes, but hampers their effectiveness. In recent years union leaders have attempted to address this problem by progressively abandoning the movement's traditional politicization, and by trying to check its penchant for confrontational action, in favour of a co-operative industrial relations model. In the context of economic crisis and rising unemployment, however, this has led to concession bargaining which, instead of improving, further worsened the problem of declining union credibility and density. I have suggested that, contrary to orthodox prescriptions, the way forward for unions is not to undo militant traditions, but to enrich, deepen, and enhance them.

NOTES

1. Trade union death is a favourite theme of serious European journalism. *The Economist* of 1 July 1995, for instance, suggested that unions have just one choice: 'adapt or die'. In a similar vein, the European Commission Report cited above argues: 'In recent years the labour unions have been facing a crisis of confidence among workers and have experienced losses in their member support and in their strength. Their partisan character and their use for political...purposes have disappointed their membership and have reduced their vigour' (European Commission 1997: 54).
2. Although it is true that real wages in Greece grew between 1980 and 1985, the picture changed dramatically after 1985. Whereas in the period 1985-90 and 1990-94 employee compensation in the OECD countries increased by 9.56 per cent and 3.94 per cent respectively, in Greece it declined by 8.60 per cent and 11.29 per cent. All the same, unemployment continued to increase, especially after 1990 (1990-96 unemployment rise: 3.3 percentage points), when real compensation decline was even

more pronounced than between 1985-90. I have analyzed this point in more detail in S. Seferiades 1999.

3. Other relevant legislation includes law 1892/1990 regulating part-time work. For a recent synopsis in English, see European Commission 1997: 60-6. The perennial inability (or unwillingness) of the Greek state to enforce labour legislation, however, is a factor stressed by many analysts (see, e.g., Georgakopoulou 1995).
4. This legal trend is international. The UNCTAD recently estimated that, of the 373 national legislative changes governing foreign investment between 1991 and 1994, only five were not in the direction of greater flexibility (cited in Moody 1997: 43).
5. Employers will be able to extend the workday up to ten hours for a period of up to six months. Few failed to notice, however, that, anti-unemployment rhetoric aside, the law's major short-term effect will be reduction in job creation. Moreover, the new law causes workers who in the past were employed for extra hours during peak seasons to lose their overtime pay.
6. See, also, Georgakopoulou (1995, 1996). For a similar conclusion about Europe as a whole, see Martin (1998: 36-8). Martin stresses the British experience, where increasing flexibility led not to employment creation, but to the loss of jobs. See also Nolan (1994), who, examining Europe and the United States, shows both that unregulated markets do not necessarily correlate with low unemployment and that the increased flexibility in employment has been brought about at the expense of technological dynamism. Authors such as Knudsen (1995), on the other hand, suggested that a likely condition of technological innovation is employee participation.
7. Of course, this tendency to extrapolate statements about trade union strength or weakness on the basis exclusively of union density is not particularly Greek. For instance, most of the recent comparative scholarship on the impact of globalization on trade union strength relies on figures of trade union density. For a succinct review of the main themes, see Lange and Scruggs (1997a). On the other hand, there is a large literature stressing that there is no automatic link between high unionization and militancy. For a review, see Visser (1992). The literature examining the factors explaining strike incidence is literally voluminous. For succinct reviews, see Franzosi (1995) and Edwards and Hyman (1994). One common theme that needs to be borne in mind for what follows, however, is that although economic conditions (unemployment, inflation, etc.) are not to be discarded, their effects on strike rates have been found to be limited and extremely unequal.
8. Take, for instance, the following appraisal by the European Commission: 'On the whole, labour unions seem to have become more mature and responsible and this has been reflected in their behaviour in recent years' (European Commission 1997: 54).
9. Precise data are lacking, but it is widely known that, as elsewhere in Europe, public sector workers have been the lead group of most strikes (Kritsantonis 1992: 625-2).

REFERENCES

Aligisakis, M. (1997): 'Labour Disputes in Western Europe: Typology and Tendencies', *International Labour Review* 136/1, pp. 73-94.

Alogoskoufis, G. (1990): 'Ανταγωνιστικότητα, Προσαρμογή Μισθών και Μακροοικονομική Πολιτική στην Ελλάδα', [Competitiveness, Wage Adaptation and Macroeconomic Policy in Greece] Working Paper, Αθήνα: ΚΕΠΕ.

Ashton, D. N. (1986): *Unemployment under Capitalism. The Sociology of British and American Labour Markets*, Sussex: Harvester Press.

Baglioni, G. and C. Crouch (eds.) (1990): *European Industrial relations. The Challenge of Flexibility*, London/Newbury Park/New Dehli: Sage.

Balaouras, M. (1998): Interview (July).

Baldwin-Edwards, M. (1998): 'Κρατικές Πολιτικές για τη Μετανάστευση: Συγκριτική Ανάλυση στον Ευρωπαϊκό Νότο', [State Policies for Migration: Comparative Analysis of the European South] in X. Petrinioti and G. F. Koukoules (eds.): *Επετηρίδα Εργασίας 1998*, [Labour Almanac 1988] Αθήνα: Πανεπιστημιακές Εκδόσεις Παντείου, pp. 191-98.

Bamber, G. J and R. D. Lansbury (eds.) (1997): *International and comparative Employment Relations: a Study of Industrialised Market Economies*, London: Sage.

Bermeo, N. (1995): 'Classification and consolidation: some lessons from the Greek dictatorship', *Political Science Quarterly* 110/3, pp. 435-52.

Boyer, R. (1988): 'Defensive or Offensive Flexibility', in R. Boyer (ed.): *The Search for Labour Market Flexibility. The European Economies in Transition*, Oxford: Clarendon Press, pp. 222-51.

Cohn, S. (1993): When Strikes Make Sense – And Why. Lessons form the Third Republic French Coal Miners, New York/London: Plenum Press.

Collier, D. and R. B. Collier (1991): *Shaping the Political Arena. Critical Junctures in the Labor Movement, and Regime Dynamics in Latin America*, Princeton: Princeton University Press.

Commission Européenne (1997): Eurobaromètre. L'opinion Publique dans l'union Européenne, 48/Automne.

Crouch, C. (1993): *Industrial Relations and European State Traditions*, Oxford: Clarendon Press.

Crouch, C. (1994): 'Beyond Corporatism: the Impact of Company Strategy', in R. Hyman and A. Ferner (eds.): *New Frontiers in European Industrial Relations*, Oxford/Cambridge, Mass: Blackwell, pp. 196-222.

Dedousopoulos, A., K. Foteinopoulou *et al.* (1997): *Κοινωνικές Προϋποθέσεις της Απασχόλησης και της Ανεργίας*, [Social Prerequisites of Employment and Unemployment] Αθήνα: Πάντειο Πανεπιστήμιο και Υπουργείο Ανάπτυξης.

Dedousopoulos, A. (1998): 'Ακαμψίες, Ευελιξίες, και Απορύθμιση στην Ελληνική Αγορά Εργασίας', [Rigidities, Flexibilities , and De-regulation in the Greek Labour Market] in X. Petrinioti and G. F. Koukoules (eds.): *Επετηρίδα Εργασίας 1998*, [Labour Almanac 1988] Αθήνα: Πανεπιστημιακές Εκδόσεις Παντείου, pp. 151-59.

Demekas, D. G., Z. G. Kontolemis (1996), 'Unemployment in Greece: A Survey of the Issues', IMF Working Paper (WP/96/91).

de Roo, A. and R. Jagtenberg (1994): *Settling Labour Disputes in Europe*, Duventer/Boston: Kluwer.

Edwards, P. K. and R. Hyman (1994): 'Strikes and Industrial Conflict: Peace in Europe?' in R. Hyman and A. Ferner (eds.): *New Frontiers in European Industrial Relations*, Oxford/Cambridge, Mass: Blackwell, pp. 250-80.

Elliniki Dimikratia (1998): *Εισηγητική Έκθεση στο Σχέδιο Νόμου «Ρύθμιση Εργασιακών Σχέσεων και Άλλες Διατάξεις»*, [Preamble to the Law 'Regulation of Labour Relations and Other Provisions'] Αθήνα.

Eurostat (1996): *Community Labour Force Survey (Employment in Europe)*, Bruxelles/Luxembourg: Statistical Office of the European Communities.

European Commission (1994): *European Economy*, Bruxelles/Luxembourg: Statistical Office of the European Communities.

European Commission (1997): *Labour Market Studies, Greece*, Brussels/Luxembourg: Office for Official Publications of the European Communities.

Fakiolas, R. (1985): 'The Greek Trade Unions: Past Experience, Present Problems and Future Outlook', in G. Spyropoulos (ed.): *Trade Unions Today and Tomorrow*, Maastricht: Presses Interuniversitaires Européennes, pp. 123-38.

Franzosi, R. (1995): *The Puzzle of Strikes. Class and State Strategies in Postwar Italy*, New York: Cambridge University Press.

Georgakopoulou, V. (1995): *Αγορά Εργασίας και Σύγχρονες Εργασιακές Σχέσεις*, [Labour

Market and Modern Industrial Relations] Αθήνα: INE/OTOE.

Georgakopoulou, V. (1996): *Ευελιξίες της Επιχείρησης και της Εργασίας*, [Company and Labour Flexibilities] Αθήνα: INE

Gilbert, N., Ñ. Burrows, Á. Pollert (eds.) (1992): *Fordism and Flexibility: Divisions and Change*, London: Macmillan.

Goetschy, J. (1996): 'The European Trade Union Confederation (ETUC) and the Construction of European Unionism', in P. Leisink, J. Van Leemput, J. Vilrokx (eds.): *The Challenge to Trade Unions in Europe. Innovation or Adaptation*, Cheltenham/Brookfield: Edward Elgar, pp. 253-65.

GSEE/ADEDY (1997): *Οι Προτάσεις του Κοινωνικού Διαλόγου*, [Proposals for the Social Dialogue] *Tetradia tou INE* 10-11/April-September.

Hadjiiossif, C. (1993): *Η Γηραιά Σελήνη. Η Βιομηχανία στην Ελληνική Οικονομία*, [The Old Moon. Industry in the Greek Economy] Αθήνα: Θεμέλιο.

Hadjimichalis, C. and D. Vaiou (1990): 'Whose Flexibility? The Politics of Informalisation in Southern Europe', *Capital and Class* 42, pp. 79-107.

Hadjimichalis, C. and D. Vaiou (1997): *Με τη Ραπτομηχανή στην Κουζίνα και τους Πολωνούς στους Αγρούς. Πόλεις, Περιφέρειες και Άτυπη Εργασία*, [With the Sewing Machine in the Kitchen and the Polish Workers in the Farms. Cities, Regions and Informal Work] Αθήνα: Εξάντας.

Hyman, R. and A. Ferner (eds.) (1994): *New Frontiers in European Industrial Relations*, Oxford/Cambridge, Mass: Blackwell.

Hyman, R. (1988): 'Flexible Specialisation: Miracle or Myth?' in R. Hyman and W. Streeck (eds.): *New Technology and Industrial Relations*, Oxford: Basil Blackwell.

Hyman, R. (1992): 'Trade Unions and the Disaggregation of the Working Class', in M. Regini (ed.): *The Future of Labour Movements*, London: Sage, pp. 150-68.

Hyman, R. (1994): 'Changing Trade Union Identities and Strategies', in R. Hyman and A. Ferner (eds.): *New Frontiers in European Industrial Relations*, Oxford/Cambridge, Mass: Blackwell, pp. 108-39.

Hyman, R. (1996): 'Changing Trade Union Identities in Europe', in P. Leisink, J. Van Leemput, J. Vilrokx (eds.): *The Challenge to Trade Unions in Europe. Innovation or Adaptation*, Cheltenham/Brookfield: Edward Elgar, pp. 53-73.

ILO (1995-97): *Yearbook of Labour Statistics*, Geneva: International Labour Organization.

Ioakimoglou, E. (1993) *Κόστος Εργασίας, Ανταγωνιστικότητα, και Συσσώρευση Κεφαλαίου στην Ελλάδα (1960-1992)*, [Labour Cost, Competitiveness, and Capital Accumulation in Greece (1960-1992)] Αθήνα: INE.

Ioakimoglou. E. (1997): 'Η Οικονομική Πολιτική, η Ανταγωνιστικότητα και η Ανεργία', [Economic Policy, Competitiveness and Unemployment] in GSEE/ADEDY: *Οι Προτάσεις του Κοινωνικού Διαλόγου*, [Proposals for the Social Dialogue] *Tetradia tou INE* 10-11/April-September, pp. 61-94.

Ioakimoglou, E. (1998): 'Οι 35 Ώρες και η Πολιτική Ηγεμονία ', [The 35 hour week and Political Hegemony] in M. Hletsos, D. Katsoridas *et al.*: *Ανεργία. Μύθοι και Πραγματικότητα*, [Unemployment. Myths and Reality] Αθήνα: Εναλλακτικές Εκδόσεις, pp. 113-35.

Ioakimoglou, E. and J. Milios (1993): 'Capital Accumulation and Over-Accumulation Crisis: The Case of Greece (1960-1989)', *Journal of Radical Political Economics* 25/2, pp. 81-107.

INE/GSEE (1996): *Η Μείωση του Χρόνου Εργασίας. Προκαταρτική Μελέτη*, [The Shortening of Working Time. Preliminary Study] *Tetradia tou INE* 5/January-February-March.

IRS (1991): *Collective Bargaining, Trade Unions and Employers' Organisations in Europe. A Guide to 15 European Countries*, London: European Industrial Relations Review.

Katsoridas, D. (1994): 'Φασόν: Ζωή και Δουλειά με το Κομμάτι', [Outworking: Life and Work by the Piece] *Theseis* 48, pp. 25-38.

Katsoridas, D. (1998): 'Αιτίες και Συνέπειες της Ανεργίας και η Ανάγκη Δημιουργίας Κινήματος Ανέργων', [Causes and Effects of Unemployment and the Need for the Creation of a Movement of the Unemployed] in M. Hletsos, D. Katsoridas *et al.*: *Ανεργία. Μύθοι και Πραγματικότητα*, [Unemployment. Myths and Reality] Αθήνα: Εναλλακτικές Εκδόσεις, pp. 31-92.

Knudsen, H. (1995): *Employee Participation in Europe*, London/Thousand Oaks/New Dehli: Sage.

Koukoules, G. F. (1997): 'Αναδρομή σ' ένα Αμφιλεγόμενο Παρελθόν', [Review of a Contested Past] in K. Kassimati (ed.): *Το Ελληνικό Συνδικαλιστικό Κίνημα στο Τέλος του 20ου Αιώνα*, [The Greek Trade Union Movement at the End of the 20th Century] Αθήνα: Gutenberg, pp. 25-74.

Koukoules, G. F. (1998): 'Συλλογικές Εργασιακές Σχέσεις', [Collective Industrial Relations] in X. Petrinioti and G. F. Koukoules (eds.): *Επετηρίδα Εργασίας 1998*, [Labour Almanac 1988] Αθήνα: Πανεπιστημιακές Εκδόσεις Παντείου, pp. 101-15.

Kouzis, Y. (1997): 'Για το παρόν και το μέλλον των εργασιακών σχέσεων', [On the Present and Future of labour Relations] in GSEE/ADEDY: *Οι Προτάσεις του Κοινωνικού Διαλόγου*, [Proposals for the Social Dialogue] *Tetradia tou INE* 10-11/April-September, pp. 113-26.

Kritsantonis, N. (1992): 'Greece: From State Authoritarianism to Modernization', in A. Ferner and R. Hyman (eds.): *Industrial Relations in the New Europe*, Oxford: Blackwell.

Lange, P. and L. Scruggs (1997a): 'Where Have All the Members Gone? Union Density in the Era of Globalization', Paper Presented at the 1997 Annual Meeting of the American Political Science Association, Washington, D.C., August 28-31.

Lange, P. and L. Scruggs (1997b): 'Unemployment and Density: A Research Memo', Paper Presented at the Conference on 'Unemployment and its Effects: The Southern European Experience in Comparative Perspective', Princeton University, November 14-15.

Leisink, P., J. Van Leemput, J. Vilrokx (1996): 'Introduction,' in P. Leisink, J. Van Leemput, J. Vilrokx (eds.): *The Challenges to Trade Unions in Europe. Innovation or Adaptation*, Cheltenham/Brookfield: Edward Elgar, pp. 1-27.

Leontidou, L. (1993): 'Informal Strategies of Unemployment Relief in Greek Cities: the Relevance of Family, Locality and Housing', *European Planning Studies* 1/1, pp. 43-68.

Liakos, A. (1993): *Εργασία και Πολιτική στη Ελλάδα του Μεσοπολέμου. Το Διεθνές Γραφείο Εργασίας και η Ανάδυση των Κοινωνικών Θεσμών*, [Labour and Politics in Interwar Greece. The International Labour Office and the Energence of Social Institutions] Αθήνα: EMNE.

Linardos-Rylmon, P. (1998): Interview (August).

Lipsig-Mumme, C. (1989): 'Canadian and American Unions Respond to Economic Crisis', *The Journal of Industrial Relations* June, pp. 229-56.

Lolos, S. (1989): 'Ανεπίσημη Οικονομία: Κριτικές Επισημάνσεις Ποσοτικές Προσεγγίσεις', [Informal Economy: Critical Remarks and Quantitative Approaches] *Synchrona Themata* 38, pp. 34-9.

Lolos, S. (1991): 'Εννοιολογική Ταξινόμηση της Ανεπίσημης Οικονομίας', [A Conceptual Classification of the Informal Economy] *Synchrona Themata* 45, pp. 40-6.

Lyberaki, A. (1988): *Small Firms and Flexible Specialisation in Greek Industry*, Ph.D. Thesis, University of Sussex.

Manos, S. (1998): 'Ποιο το Μέλλον του Συνδικαλιστικού Κινήματος;' [What Future for the Trade Union Movement?] *Οικονμικός Ταχνορόμος* 23 July, p. 43.

Martin, R. (1998): 'Regional Dimensions of Europe's Unemployment Crisis', in P. Lawless, R. Martin, S. Hardy (eds.): *Unemployment and Social Exclusion. Landscapes of Labour Inequality*, London/Philadelphia: Jessica Kingsley Publishers.

Mavrogordatos, G. Th. (1983): *Stillborn Republic. Social Coalitions and Party Strategies in Interwar Greece 1922-1936*, Berkeley: University of California Press.

Mavrogordatos, G. Th. (1988): *Μεταξύ Πιτυοκάμπτη και Προκρούστη. Οι Επαγγελματικές Οργανώσεις στη Σημερινή Ελλάδα*, [Between Pityokamptes and Prokroustes. Professional Organizations in Contemporary Greece] Αθήνα: Οδυσσέας.

McAdam, D., J. D: McCarthy, M. Zald (eds.) (1996): *Comparative Perspectives on Social Movements: Political Opportunities, Mobilizing Structures, and Cultural Framings*, Cambridge: Cambridge University Press.

Moody, K. (1997a): 'Towards an International Social-Movement Unionism', *New Left Review* 225/September-October, pp. 52-72.

Moody, K. (1997b): *Workers in a Lean World. Unions in the International Economy*, London/New York: Verso.

Moschonas, A. and V. Droucopoulos (1993): 'Small and Medium-Scale Industry in Greece: Oasis of Dynamism or Symptom of Malaise?' *Review of Radical Political Economics* 25/2, pp. 108-31.

Nolan, P. (1995): 'Labour Market Institutions, Industrial Restructuring and Unemployment in Europe', in J. Michie, J. G. Smith (eds.): *Unemployment in Europe*, London/San Diego/New York/Boston/Tokyo/Toronto: Academic Press, Harcourt Brace & Co. Publishers.

OECD (1989): *Economic Outlook*, Paris: Organisation for Economic Co-operation and Development.

OECD (1991): *Employment Outlook*, Paris: Organisation for Economic Co-operation and Development.

OECD (1994): *Employment Outlook*, Paris: Organisation for Economic Co-operation and Development.

OECD (1996a): *Economic Surveys, Greece*, Paris: Organisation for Economic Co-operation and Development.

OECD (1996b): *OECD Economics at a Glance. Structural Indicators*, Paris: Organisation for Economic Co-operation and Development.

OECD (1997): *Historical Statistics, 1960-1995*, Paris: Organisation for Economic Co-operation and Development.

Offe, C. and H. Wiesenthal (1985): 'Two Logics of Collective Action', in C. Offe and J. Keane (eds.): *Disorganized Capitalism*, Cambridge, Mass.: The MIT Press.

Oikonomou, G. (1991): *Για Μια Εισοδηματική Πολιτική Σταθεροποιήσεως και Ενισχύσεως της Παραγωγής και της Απασχολήσεως*, [For an Incomes Policy Conducive to Stabilization, Production Enhancement and Employment] Αθήνα: ΙΟΒΕ.

Onley, S. L. (1996): *Unions in a Changing World. Problems and Prospects in Selected Industrialized Countries*, Geneva: International Labour Office.

Panitch L. (1996): 'Rethinking the Role of the State', in J. Mittelman (ed.): *Globalization: Critical Reflections*, Boulder/London: Lynne Rienner Publishers, pp. 83-113.

Pavlopoulos, P. (1986): *Εισοδηματικά Μερίδια*, [Income Shares] Αθήνα: ΙΟΒΕ.

Pavlopoulos, P. (1987): *Η Παραοικονομία στην Ελλάδα. Μια Πρώτη Ποσοτική Οριοθέτηση*, [The Shadow Economy in Greece. A Preliminary Quantitative Delimitation] Αθήνα: ΙΟΒΕ.

Pelagidis, T. (1997): *Η Διεθνοποίηση της Ελληνικής Οικονομίας: Ευελιξία και Αναδιάρθρωση*, [The Internationalization of the Greek Economy: Flexibility and Restructuring] Αθήνα: Εξάντας.

Petrinioti, X. (1993): *Η Μετανάστευση προς την Ελλάδα. Μια Πρώτη Καταγραφή, Ταξινόμηση και Ανάλυση*, [Immigration into Greece. A Preliminary Charting, Classification and Analysis] Αθήνα: Οδυσσέας.

Petrinioti, X. (1998): 'Η Ανεργία,' [Unemployment] in X. Petrinioti, G. F. Koukoules (eds.): *Επετηρίδα Εργασίας* 1998, [Labour Almanac 1998] Αθήνα: Πανεπιστημιακές Εκδόσεις Παντείου, pp. 55-76.

Piore, M. J. and C. F. Sabel (1984): *The Second Industrial Divide*, New York: Basic Books.

Pollert, A. (ed.) (1991): *Farewell to Flexibility*, Oxford: Basil Blackwell.

Protopappas, E. (1997): 'Η Συμβολή του Εργατικού Κινήματος στην Ανάπτυξη της Οικονομίας', [The Contribution of the Labour Movement to Economic Development] in K. Kassimati (ed.): *Το Ελληνικό Συνδικαλιστικό Κίνημα στο Τέλος του 20ου Αιώνα*, [The Greek Trade Union Movement at the End of the 20th Century] Athens: Gutenberg, pp. 85-101.

Protopappas, E. (1998): 'Η κρίση στα Συνδικάτα', [Crisis in the Trade Unions], *Οlκονμικός Ταχνορόμος* 23 July, pp. 41-2.

Rhodes, M. (1997): 'Globalisation, Labour Markets and Welfare States: A Future of "Competititve Corporatism?"' in M. Rhodes and Y. Mény, *The Future of European Welfare: A New Social Contract?* London: Macmillan, pp. 178-203.

Richards, A. and J. G. Polavieja (1997): 'Trade Unions, Unemployment, and Working Class Fragmentation in Spain', Paper Presented at the Conference on 'Unemployment and its Effects: The Southern European Experience in Comparative Perspective', Princeton University, November 14-15.

Rubery, J. (1989): 'Labour Market Flexibility in Britain', in F. Green (ed.), *The Restructuring of the UK Economy*, Hemel Hempstead: Harvester Wheatsheaf.

Sabel, C. (1989): 'Flexible Specialisation and the Re-emergence of Regional Economies', in P. Hirst and J. Zeitlin (eds.), *Reversing Industrial Decline?* New York: Berg.

Sabel, C. F. and J. Zeitlin (1985): 'Historical Alternatives to Mass Production', *Past and Present* 108/August, pp. 133-76.

Sabel, C. F. and J. Zeitlin (eds.) (1997): *World of Possibilities: Fexibility and Mass Production in Western Industrialization*, New York: Cambridge University Press.

Seferiades, S. (1999): 'Low Union Density Amidst a Conflictive Contentious Repertoire: Flexible Labour Markets, Unemployment and Trade-Union Decline in Greece', IUE Working Paper.

Seferiades, S. (1998a): *Working-Class Movements (1780s-1930s). A European Macro-Historical Analytical Framework and a Greek Case Study*, Ph.D. Thesis, Columbia University.

Seferiades, S. (1998b): 'Institutionalized Coercion and Informal Protest: An Interactive Approach to State-Labor Relations in Interwar Greece', Paper presented at the 1998 Annual Meeting of the American Political Science Association, September 3-6.

Seferiades S. (1998c): 'Διεκδικητικό Κίνημα και Πολιτική: Ο Ελληνικός Συνδικαλισμός πριν τη Δικτατορία (1962-1967)', [Protest Movement and Politics: Greek Trade Unionism before the Dictatorship (1962-1967)] *Hellenic Political Science Review* 12/November.

Shaikh, A. (1996): 'Free Trade, Unemployment, and Economic Policy', in J. Eatwell (ed.): *Global Unemployment. Loss of Jobs in the 90s*, Armonk, NY/London: M. E. Sharpe, pp. 59-78.

Shalev, M. (1992) 'The Resurgence of Labour Quiescence', in M. Regini (ed.): *The Future of Labour Movements*, London: Sage, pp. 102-32.

Shorter, E. and C. Tilly (1974): *Strikes in France, 1830-1968*, Cambridge: Cambridge University Press.

Sianou, F. (1997): 'Η Θέση των Γυναικών στο Συνδικαλιστικό Κίνημα', [The Role of Women in the Trade Union Movement] in K. Kassimati (ed.): *Το Ελληνικό Συνδικαλιστικό Κίνημα στο Τέλος του 20ου Αιώνα*, [The Greek Trade Union Movement at the End of the 20th Century] Αθήνα: Gutenberg, pp. 155-66.

Skolka, J. (1985): 'The Parallel Economy in Austria' in W. Gaertnet and A. Wenig (eds.): *The Economics of the Shadow Economy*, Heidelberg/New York/Tokyo: Springer-Verlag, pp. 80-104.

Spyropoulos. G. (1998): *Εργασιακές Σχέσεις. Εξελίξεις στην Ελλάδα, την Ευρώπη και τον Διεθνή Χώρο*, [Industrial Relations. Developments in Greece, Europe, and Internationally] Αθήνα: Εκδόσεις Αντ. Σάκκουλα.

Stathopoulos, P. (1996): 'Greece: What Future for the Welfare State?' in Vic George and P. Taylor-Goody (eds.): *European Welfare Policy. Squaring the Welfare Circle*, London:

Macmillan, pp. 136-55.
Stinas, A. (1985): *Αναμνήσεις*, [Recollections] Αθήνα: Υψιλον.
Streek, W. (1988): Editorial Introduction. *Economic and Industrial Democracy*, 9/3, pp. 307-17.
Symes, V. (1995): *Unemployment in Europe. Problems and Policies*, London/New York: Routledge.
Tarrow, S. (1994): *Power in Movement. Social Movements, Collective Action and Politics*, Cambridge/New York/Melbourne: Cambridge University Press.
Tarrow, S. (1998): *Power in Movement. Social Movements and Contentious Politics*, Cambridge/New York/Melbourne: Cambridge University Press.
Tilly, C. (1978): *From Mobilization to Revolution*, New York: McGraw-Hill Publishing Company.
Tilly, C. (1998): 'Stories of Social Construction', Lecture for the Fiftieth Anniversary Celebration of the Institute for Social Research, University of Michigan Ann Arbor, 4 December 1997, Revised 6 October 1998.
Toutziarakis, Y. (1997): 'Κρίση των Συνδικάτων: Οργανώσεις Καθολικής Αλληλεγγύης ή Λειτουργικό Εξάρτημα της Κοινωνίας των 2/3;' [Trade Union Crisis: Organizations of General Solidarity or a Functional Appendage to the Two-thirds society?' in K. Kassimati (ed.): *Το Ελληνικό Συνδικαλιστικό Κίνημα στο Τέλος του 20ου Αιώνα*, [The Greek Trade Union Movement at the End of the 20th Century] Αθήνα: Gutenberg, pp. 217-59.
Valenzuela, S. J. (1992): 'Labour Movements and Political Systems: Some Variations', in M. Regini (ed.): *The Future of Labour Movements*, London/New Dehli: Sage, pp. 53-101.
Vernardakis, C. and Y. Mavris (1991): *Κόμματα και Κοινωνικές Συμμαχίες στην Προδικτατορική Ελλάδα οι Προϋποθέσεις της Μεταπολίτευσης* [Parties and Social Coalitions in Pre-Dictatorship Greece. The Social Preconditions of the Return to Democracy] Αθήνα: Εξάντας.
Visser, J. (1992): 'The Strength of Union Movements in Advanced Capital[ist] Democracies: Social and Organizational Variations', in M. Regini (ed.): *The Future of Labour Movements*, London/New Dehli: Sage, pp. 17-52.
Wickens, P. (1987): *The Road to Nissan*, London: Macmillan.
Zambarloulou, S. (1996): 'Συνδικαλιστικό Κίνημα και Κρατικός Παρεμβατισμός στη Μεταπολιτευτική Ελλάδα: Μια Συγκριτική Προσέγγιση', [Trade Union Movement and State Interventionism in Greece in the Period after the Restoration of Democracy: a Comparative Approach] in C. Lyrintzis, E. Nikolakopoulos, D. Sotiropoulos (eds.): *Κοινωνία και Πολιτική: Όψεις της Γ' Ελληνικής Δημοκρατίας*, [Society and Politics: Facets of the Third Greek Republic] Αθήνα: Θεμέλιο, pp. 91-118.

Rigidity and Flexibility: Patterns of Labour Market Policy Change in Portugal and Spain, 1981–96

MIGUEL GLATZER

The Portuguese and Spanish labour markets have recently become the object of great interest among economists. Indeed, in a widely cited article, Blanchard and Jimeno argue that high unemployment in Spain and low unemployment in Portugal 'may be the biggest empirical challenge facing theories of structural unemployment' (Blanchard and Jimeno 1995: 212-18). The puzzle over the two countries' drastically different unemployment rates emerges because labour market policy in Spain and Portugal is regularly classified as not only highly similar, but also as amongst the most rigid in the OECD. Explaining how rigid and rather similar labour market policies have produced these different unemployment outcomes has been the underlying question animating most economists' investigations of the Iberian labour markets (Bank of Portugal 1997).

This essay asks a somewhat different set of questions. It is concerned primarily not with labour market policy's effects, but with labour market policy change. Its aims are two-fold. First, it attempts to develop a model that can usefully aggregate and describe labour market policy change possible across multiple sub-areas. Second, it presents results for Portugal and Spain for the period from 1981 to 1996.

The paper focuses on the following sets of questions: Are the reforms characterized by programmatic coherence or do they often include contradictory elements, reflecting the exigencies of political bargaining? Do reforms emerge singly or in large policy packages where side-payments can be carefully crafted? Do the reforms change direction over time, or is there sustained movement towards a rather stable goal? Does unemployment make particular reforms more difficult?

Removing labour market rigidities is a notoriously difficult enterprise. Indeed, recent work on the contemporary political economy of unemployment has focused on the political barriers which strongly reduce the probability of certain policy prescriptions from being adopted. Europe's high unemployment problem has elicited many calls for change, ranging from standard prescriptions of labour market deregulation, to alternative calls for work-sharing, working-hour reductions, improved active labour market policy, and increased public investment made possible through changes in current macroeconomics policy.[1]

Despite a general perception that European labour market policy has remained immobile and stagnant in the face of rising and persistently high unemployment, there has indeed been change.[2] From the perspective of those who advocate liberalized and deregulated labour markets, however, the change clearly has not been nearly enough. From such a perspective, the change has often been in precisely the least desirable direction, i.e. towards greater rigidity. Gilles Saint-Paul provides clear examples. Despite very significant productivity differentials between East and West Germany, the post-reunification government encouraged a process of wage convergence which substantially increased eastern Germany's unemployment rate. Despite a high rate of unemployment, the French presidential campaign of 1995 included a proposed rise of the (already high) French minimum wage (Saint-Paul 1996).

Reforms which move in the direction of liberalizing the labour market (or reducing social protection) are notoriously difficult. Reform attempts can result in failure (where the reform is withdrawn or substantially watered down, as in the 1994 French attempt to lower the minimum wage for young workers, or subsequent attempts to raise the retirement age for privileged groups of workers), government collapse (Italy and pensions reform 1997), or electoral failure (Sweden 1994).

THE NEED FOR A MODEL

Given the complexity of labour market policy change (described below), a model that usefully aggregates the wide variety of change possible can provide a guide to the kinds of change that are most likely to be implemented, or most likely to be resisted.

Policy-makers face a large array of options when changing labour market policy. In any given year, a policy-maker could change any one or more of several policy areas, including but not limited to the minimum wage, restrictions on firing, restrictions on hiring, social security taxation, unemployment compensation, union power, collective bargaining, restrictions on functional and regional mobility (internal flexibility), and strikes.

For each of these sub-areas of labour market policy, the policy maker again has multiple options. Consider the case of unemployment compensation. The minimum contributory period to qualify for unemployment benefit could be extended or diminished. The benefit period could be lengthened or diminished. The benefit amount could be increased or reduced. Workers excluded from the scheme could be made eligible. Unemployment assistance provided when benefits have been exhausted could similarly be increased or reduced. A further set of decisions concerns the provision of special benefits to particular groups of workers (e.g. those near retirement), or to particular regions (those suffering from high unemployment for example), or to particular industries (e.g. dying smokestack industries).

Even a relatively simple case such as the minimum wage offers many options. In addition to being increased or decreased, the minimum wage is often itself subdivided to provide different minimum wages for different groups (agriculture, industry, services, domestic services, craft). These differences can be increased, reduced or eliminated. In addition, the minimum wage is often applied differently to young workers (e.g. 15 year-olds receiving 50 per cent of the minimum wage, 16 and 17-year olds receiving 75 per cent of the minimum wage, reflecting notions of apprenticeship, skill development and the family wage). These differences can in turn be deepened or reduced. By coding the direction of each change, the framework allows one to take a wide-angle shot of the forest, instead of a narrowly focused picture of the trees.

CODING LABOUR MARKET POLICY CHANGE: THE MODIFIED SAINT-PAUL MODEL

This paper develops a modified version of Saint-Paul's elegant model, which codes labour market policy and relates it to underlying economic and political conditions (Saint-Paul 1996).[3] The Saint-Paul model classifies changes in firing costs according to a four-part scheme. The basic classification concerns whether a policy increases or decreases firing costs. An increase in firing costs is classified as a move towards greater labour market rigidity; a decrease as a move towards greater flexibility. Because partial reforms that affect only a sub-group of workers rather than the whole workforce are politically easier to implement, Saint-Paul's coding scheme also provides information on whether the move towards greater rigidity or flexibility occurs across the board (affecting the whole workforce), or whether it affects only part of the workforce (two-tier reforms, resulting in dual labour markets).

This paper modifies the Saint-Paul model in the following ways. First, the classification scheme has been extended to focus not only on firing costs, but also on the minimum wage, hiring restrictions, unemployment benefits and social security taxes levied on employment. This allows one to investigate whether certain areas of labour market policy are more frequently the target of reform than others. In addition, such a scheme allows one to investigate the presence of policy packages, whereby reforms in one area are linked with reforms in other areas. Under the right conditions, such policy packages might facilitate reform.

Reflecting a concern with dual labour markets, the original Saint-Paul model focuses on major examples of labour market reform but draws a critical distinction between reforms that affect the whole of the workforce and those that affect only part of it. By contrast, the scheme presented here includes smaller-order changes in labour market policy. Developing the classification scheme this way allows one to investigate whether reform occurs incrementally or in 'big bangs.' Third, the scheme presented here includes failed attempts at policy reform and distinguishes these from successful reforms.[4]

The potential contributions of this model in mapping patterns of labour market policy change are considerable. First, a classification scheme that focuses on rigidity and flexibility employs what is arguably the reigning model in economics for understanding labour market policy. Restrictions on firing, constraints on various types of employment contracts, the level of the minimum wage, and social security charges levied on employment are among the most important instruments in labour market policy, and can be comparatively evaluated using the common framework of rigidity and flexibility.

Furthermore, this is a model that has direct relevance to the Portuguese and Spanish cases. Analyses of the Portuguese and Spanish labour markets frequently focus on distorting rigidities in these markets and the perverse effects these have generated. Examples include concerns about the negative effects of rigid dismissals legislation on foreign investment (Portugal), the creation of dual labour markets of protected and unprotected workers with the serious equity issues involved in the maldistribution of job security and access to social security thereby generated (both countries), to high unemployment (Spain). In addition, the rigidity/flexibility schema is one adopted by local actors, often explicitly but certainly implicitly.[5]

Nonetheless, there are costs associated with the proposed scheme. There are a number of important labour market policy instruments that are not easily classified using the rigidity/flexibility dimension. Active labour market policy, for example, is not readily classifiable as rigid or flexible. Similarly, public employment programmes fall outside of the classification scheme. Furthermore, in the interests of clarity, the scheme makes a binary distinction between small- and large-scale change. Inevitably, the cost is some loss in detail.

Nonetheless, the model does highlight differences in the direction of labour market policy change over time and across subfields. The model also highlights the existence of policy change moving in contradictory directions at the same time, which may constitute evidence of policy packages and political bargains.

Applying the Model to Spain and Portugal, 1981 to 1996

The period 1981 to 1996 was selected for analysis because it maximizes variation in three important respects. First, the difference in unemployment rates between Spain and Portugal becomes manifest and permanent during this period. Spain's unemployment rate throughout this period is significantly higher than Portugal's. From 1983 onwards, Spain's unemployment rates always exceeded that of Portugal by over 10 percentage points.

Second, both Spain and Portugal experienced changes in the direction of unemployment during this period. Spanish unemployment rose from 11.5 per cent in 1980 to 21.5 per cent in 1985, and has hovered between 16 and 22 per cent since then. By contrast, unemployment in Portugal only rose from 6.9 per cent in 1980 to a peak of 9.9 per cent in 1986, and then descended to hover between 4.4 per cent and 8.7 per cent.

Third, government preferences regarding labour market policy had changed substantially by 1981. In the preceding period, particularly in Portugal and to a lesser extent in Spain, governments wanted to increase labour market rigidities (as defined in this paper), not reduce them. Democracy meant increasing workers' rights in multiple areas (Bermeo 1986; Morrison 1981; Fishman 1990).[6] Thus the transition from dictatorship to democracy brought substantial changes in both countries in the legal and de facto treatment of unions, collective bargaining, and strikes. Portugal's minimum wage dates from the revolutionary period, although studies of the desirability of a minimum wage had been carried out in the waning years of the dictatorship. Although restrictions on firing had been substantial during the dictatorship, they became severe during the revolutionary period. Similarly, the policy goal in social policy was to increase coverage and increase social spending, not reduce it.

However, in both countries, the expansion of worker rights through legislation or de facto tolerance becomes increasingly problematic, and this becomes highly visible in government policy and proposals by 1981. In Portugal, for example, dire balance of payments problems led to IMF agreements which call explicitly for labour market liberalization. Economic problems in Portugal led to a strange phenomenon of wage arrears, whereby bankrupt or insolvent firms are unable to pay their workers. The lack of jobs, however, leads these workers to continue labouring at the firms, creating social and political problems whose solutions are quite different from previously contemplated labour market policy.

In Spain, the problem is of a different nature. Instead of inflation, falling wages, and wage arrears, the principal Spanish problem is one of high unemployment, leading to important insider-outsider dynamics. De-industrialization of Spain's heavy industry creates unemployed older workers. Young job-seekers also find it hard to get a job. The exploding unemployment problem in turn causes repeated budgetary crises in the unemployment benefit system, as well as political struggles over taxes on employment. Employers in particular place special emphasis on reducing social security contributions, which they view as escalating wage costs and as one of the causes of high unemployment in the first place.

Thus, in both countries, economic difficulties had placed serious obstacles in the path of consistent movement towards greater labour market rigidity. Although worker protection and increased social expenditure were the long-term goal of most governments in both countries, a range of economic problems made those options increasingly costly.[7]

As a result, these governments faced hard choices, exacerbated by the low growth rates of the early 1980s. The second half of the 1980s brought high growth rates, and this provided more room to manoeuvre. However, governments that had attempted labour market reform in the early 1980s and failed, or had seen other governments fail, saw in the high growth rates of the 1980s a window of opportunity to attempt necessary reform.

Using the modified Saint-Paul model described above, the following tables and findings code and analyze the success and failure of labour market policy reform initiatives in Portugal and Spain.

THE TABLES

The two tables present coded labour market policy data for the years 1981 to 1996 for the sub-fields of the minimum wage, firing restrictions, hiring regulations, social security taxation levied on employment and unemployment benefits. Data are culled from the European Industrial Relations Review. Changes in legislation, failed reforms and government policy proposals are summarized in the Appendices.

L indicates a change in policy towards labour market liberalization.
R represents a change towards labour market rigidity.
FL and **FR** indicate failed liberalization and failed rigidity.

Before analyzing the charts, two caveats should be mentioned about the use of the terms 'rigidity' and 'liberalization.' First, the use of the term 'liberalization' conforms to its use in the economics literature, where labour market liberalization involves the lifting of rules that attempt to protect workers by taming the market. As used here, the term is thus very different in meaning from its use in the social policy literature, where liberalization often implies increases in programme generosity. Second, although these terms have become value-laden in political debate, they are used here solely for their analytical coherence. Indeed, this paper makes no claim about the ideal degree of liberalization or rigidity in the Portuguese and Spanish labour markets.

TABLE 1
LABOUR MARKET POLICY CHANGE – SPAIN

1981:
Implemented:
— UB more generous **(R)**
— Part-time and temporary contracts eased **(L)**
— At the same time, workers on part-time contracts are given improved entitlement to social security **(R)**
— National Employment Pact signed (ANE) signed

1982:
Implemented:
— UB more generous **(R)**
— Collective agreements' extension to non-signatory parties extended **(R)**
— Min. wage increased 11.9 per cent (1980 inflation 15.6 per cent) **(L)**
— Hiring temporary workers eased **(L)**
— New Job Creation/Training Package reduces soc. sec. contributions paid by employers when they hire young workers who participate in vocational training programmes **(L)**

— Decree aimed at speeding court procedures better to assist workers with unfair dismissal complaints **(R)**

Failed:

— Soc. Sec. reform that would have reduced employer contributions and cut the number of benefits available **(L)**

Elections:

— UCD disintegrates; 28 October election
— Labour Market Policy Platforms:
— PCE (Communists):
  — retirement age reduced to age 60 from current 65
  — four-year plan to create 400,000 jobs
  — improve unemployment benefits

PSOE:
  — substantial reform of existing labour legislation covering strikes, union rights, collective bargaining and employee participation in large firms

Centre and right (UCD and CDS)
  — greater aid to small firms
  — further liberalization of temporary and part-time contracts

PSOE wins. Plans to
  — create 400,000 jobs by 1986
  — lower the retirement age
  — increase the school-leaving age
  — reform the labour exchange

1983:

Implemented:

— Min. wage increased 13.08 per cent (inflation in 1982 was 14.4 per cent) **(L)**
— Temporary work law restricted (stricter limits on numbers of workers by firm size who may be on temporary contracts) **(R)**
— Temporary work law eased by removing prohibition on the use of temporary contracts in firms where workers have been dismissed in the last 12 months **(L)**
— Reduction in employers' arrears in soc. sec. contributions **(L)**
— UB: unemployed liable to be called for work **(L)**
— UB: coverage and entitlement period extended **(R)**
— Weekly working hours reduced from 41 to 40; annual holiday entitlement increased from 3 weeks to 4 **(R)**

Proposed in New Central Agreement: *Acuerdo Interconfederal* (AI)
— Ban on systematic overtime **(R)**
— Controls over multiple employment, registration with social security **(R)**
— Possibility of early retirement at 64 with full pension when the firm will fill the subsequent vacancy with workers on the unemployment register

1984:

Implemented:
— Social security charges reduced for employers and employees **(L)**
— Employment subsidies and reduction in social security for firms hiring older unemployed workers **(L)**
— UB system made more generous: benefit extended from 18 months to 2 years **(R)**
— Workers Statute reformed, easing restrictions on atypical contracts **(L)**

Proposed in Social and Economic Accord: ***Acuerdo Economico y Social*** **(AES)**
— Social security contributions reduced by 0.3 per cent **(L)**
— Creation of special aid fund for unemployment and commitment to hire 200,000 in public sector **(R)**
— Employment legislation to be gradually harmonized with European standards
— No agreement on modifying dismissals legislation

1985:
Implemented:
— Min. wage rises 6.99 per cent (inflation in 1984 was 11.3 per cent) **(L)**
— Multiple employment prohibited in public sector
— Social Security reform
— Minimum contributory period extended from 10 to 15 years **(L)**
— Eligibility rules and benefit levels for disability pensions tightened **(L)**
— Training and employment promotion involves reduced social security contributions and employment subsidies for unemployed workers **(L)**
Failed:
— Single comprehensive overhaul of the social security system abandoned

Context:
Unemployment rises to 22.07 per cent.

All opposition parties and trade unions opposed the social security reform bill. The bill leads to strong strains between the UGT and the PSOE. To try to mend relations with the UGT, the government promises not to amend current legislation on collective redundancies, but this leads to complaints from the CEOE (employers' association) that this violates the terms of the Economic and Social Agreement (AES).

CCOO (Communist-leaning trade union confederation) wants job creation through public investments, reduction in working time to 39 hours, reduction in overtime, reduction in the retirement age to 64, the conversion into permanent contracts of existing temporary contracts, and a pay rise of 8.75 per cent.

1986:
Implemented:
— Min. wage rises 8 per cent (inflation in 1985 was 8.8 per cent) **(L)**
— UB: plans to increase coverage ratio **(R)**
— UB: plans to increase the number of unemployed receiving training on 75 per cent of the national minimum wage **(R)**
— UB: sanctions on unemployed who refuse offers of training **(L)**

Other:
Employers call for reducing labour market rigidities and social security taxation on employment.

PSOE wins second absolute majority in 22 June election.

1987:
Implemented:
— UB benefit period extended for 18 months beyond the present 3 years **(R)**
— Recipients must be prepared to be geographically mobile and to move anywhere in Spain as opposed to only within a 25 km. radius **(L)**

Failed:

— Solution to the three-year limit on temporary contracts authorized under the 1984 reforms. These contracts are now expiring. Employers want them renewed, but legally the job is supposed to become permanent or disappear.

Other:

Law regulating strikes (and restricting current practice) drafted.

1988:

Implemented:

— Reduced social security contributions when employers create jobs in development zones where unemployment is high, as part of the Ley de Incentivos Regionales **(L)**
— Min. wage rises 4.5 per cent (inflation was 5.2 per cent) **(L)**
— Subsidies and reduced social security contributions for firms hiring young first-time job seekers on fixed short-term employment contracts **(L)**
— UB extended to cover more long-term unemployed over the age of 45 who have run out of benefit **(R)**

Other:

Bitter fight ensues over the minimum wage increase, with unions appealing to the ILO, but unemployment remains above 20 per cent.

Unions criticize the social dumping of the employment promotion schemes; employers argue that an overall decrease in social security contributions would be preferable.

1989:

Implemented:

— Modified youth employment program **(L)** for subsidies; **(R)** for benefits, but again heavily criticized by unions
— More generous unemployment benefits, under pressure from unions **(R)**

Failed:

— Youth employment program shelved, following strike by unions against social dumping.

Proposed:

— Incentives for employers to conclude permanent employment contracts with categories of disadvantaged workers (young unemployed, temporary workers, and mothers returning to the labour market).

Other:

Relations between the government and the unions remain tense. Unions demand recovery of a 2 per cent loss in purchasing power suffered by pensioners and public employees, an increase in the coverage rate of the UB system, the raising of pension rates to bring them in line with the minimum wage, and the recognition of full collective bargaining rights of public employees.

1990:

Implemented:

— Government-union agreement on contract-monitoring will allow better monitoring of the 14 variants of employment contract on the Spanish labour market to reduce abuse **(R)**
— Decree-Law on Labour Procedures increases the penalties to employers of unfair dismissal by increasing the compensation due workers unfairly dismissed **(R)**

1991:
Implemented:
Min. wage increased 6.5 per cent (inflation in 1990 was 6.7 per cent) **(R)**

Parliament authorizes government to amend labour laws to
- — Provide greater flexibility in the use of employment contracts **(L)**
- — Increase vocational training
- — Eliminate the Labour Ordinances **(L)**
- — Oblige unemployed persons to accept job offers and take part in training programmes **(L)**

Proposed:
- — Pact on competitiveness that would involve wage restraint. But unions remain adamant that problems of competitiveness cannot be resolved by either lower wages or greater labour market flexibility. Instead, a solution would be dependent upon reduced interest rates, lower appreciation of the peseta, improvements in vocational training and public investment
- — Strike legislation that would penalize strikes in essential services **(R)**

1992:
Implemented:
- — Cutback in unemployment benefit to reduce the INEM deficit and provide individuals with greater incentive to seek work **(L)**
- — Removal of the *Ordenanzas* that limit functional and regional mobility **(L)**
- — Improvement in vocational training
- — Strike legislation that limits strikes in essential services **(L)**

Failed:
- — Transfer of management of the unemployment insurance system to the social partners to control fraud, and to allow the social partners to decide whether a deficit should be covered by an increase in contributions or a reduction in benefit

Other:
UGT reacts furiously to the labour market reforms, calling for two general strikes. The UGT leader, Nicolas Redondo, describes the reforms as 'the most serious onslaught against workers in the entire period of democracy.'

The unions attribute much of the alarming rise in workplace accidents to the increase in fixed-term contracts and the informal economy, where training is low.

1993:
Implemented:
Employment package (inspired by proximity of the election)
- — Increase in labour-intensive public spending on infrastructure
- — Fixed-term contracts due to expire in 1993 extended for one more year **(L)**
- — Subsidies awarded for each fixed-term contract converted into an open-ended contract

After the election:
- — Minimum UB reduced to 75 per cent of the minimum wage from 100 per cent **(L)**
- — To qualify for UB, unemployed individuals may draw an income (from rent or interest, for example) no greater than 75 per cent of the national minimum wage **(L)**
- — Social security contributions levied on UB, but at a lower rate than for employed workers **(L)**
- — Unemployment insurance contributions to rise by 0.5 per cent **(R)**

Failed:
— Workers who receive redundancy payments would be ineligible for unemployment benefit for some time **(L)**
— Full social security contributions would be levied on UB **(L)**

Proposed:
Labour reform package that would
— Reduce the number of different types of fixed-term contracts **(R)**
— Promote wider-use of open-ended employment contracts **(L)**
— Ease restrictions on functional flexibility and regional mobility **(L)**
— Ease the process of termination of contract **(L)**

Social Pact proposal would:
— Substitute labour ordinances with collective agreements
— Increase the flexibility of working time arrangements **(L)**
— Provide incentives for part-time working **(L)**
— Restrict use of fixed-term contracts **(R)**

Other:
PSOE wins fourth consecutive term in general election of 6 June.

1994:
Implemented:
Decree-Law on Urgent Measures to Promote Employment.
— Pay for practical work contracts can fall to 60 per cent to 70 per cent below fully collectively agreed rates **(L)**
— Social security costs for apprenticeship contracts lowered by excluding apprentices from coverage for non-work-related sickness and from the right to draw unemployment benefit **(L)**

Amendments to the Workers' Statute.
— Collective redundancies made easier by increasing the objective grounds for collective dismissal, raising the number of employees involved for redundancy to be considered collective, speeding the authorization process **(L)**
— Functional and geographical mobility made easier **(L)**
— Opt-out from collective bargaining agreements loosened **(L)**

Labour ordinances to be replaced by collective agreements. **(L)**

Statutory supplements to the minimum wage for overtime, night work and arduous work eliminated. **(L)**

Other:
General strike of 27 January obtained only limited participation.

1996:
Other:
General elections of March 3 result in the victory of the PP under Aznar.

TABLE 2
LABOUR MARKET POLICY CHANGE – PORTUGAL

1981:
Failed:
— Labour law reform prompted by pressure from the IMF to encourage foreign investment
— Reforms would relax the stringent dismissals law and discourage short-term contracts **(L)** + **(R)**

1982:
Failed:
— Labour law reform redrafted. Would allow for the suspension of employment contracts 'in times of proven work recession' subject to prior approval of the workers and authorization from the Labour Ministry **(L)**
— Labour law reform postponed by the revision of the constitution

1983:
Implemented:
— Lay-off law approved in parliament. **(L)**

Proposed:
— Dismissals law passes general approval step in parliament **(L)**
— Limits on overtime **(R)**
— Improved training and apprenticeship programmes

Other:
Political crisis following Pinto Balsemao's surprise resignation in December 1982. Elections called for 25 April. Austerity measures. Escudo devalued. Unemployment rises from 7.5 per cent in late 1982 to 10.5 per cent. Companies unable to pay workers, both in public and private sector.

1984:
Failed:
— Liberalization of labour laws. Strikes and redundancies are among the most controversial issues **(L)**

Other:
Inflation continues to grow, reaching 31.1 per cent. Workers experience plummeting purchasing power. Labour affairs dominated by the problem of pay arrears. Inability of government to act leads to massive protests by opposition parties, entire union movement and Catholic Church.

1985:
Implemented:
— Min. Wage raised 23 per cent (but 1984 inflation was over 30 per cent) **(L)**
— New UB system introduced: UB (*subsidio de desemprego*) + UA (*subsidio social de desemprego*) **(R)**
— System of wage guarantees developed to ensure that workers' receive their last four months' wages in case of employers' insolvency or bankruptcy **(R)**

Failed:
Comprehensive labour law reform package (pacote laboural) covering

— Strikes and lock-outs **(L)**
— Temporary work **(L)**
— Fixed term contracts **(L)**
— Dismissals **(L)**

Other:
Controversy over the labour reform package exacerbates tension in the PS-PSD coalition, and is a factor in the PSD withdrawing from the coalition in June. Parliament dissolved 12 July; early elections called for 5 October. PSD wins with 29.8 per cent of the vote, up 2.6 per cent. PS falls from 36.8 per cent to 20.8 per cent, its worst ever result. PRD, a new party, wins 18.0 per cent.

ILO rules that the Portuguese government has failed to enforce four ILO conventions covering the payment of wages in arrears, holiday pay, the provision of information on labour conditions and adequate labour inspections.

1986:
Implemented:
— Decree on wage arrears, allowing workers to choose either the termination of their entitlement or suspension of the contract (suspension also provides them with unemployment benefit, but for a reduced period) **(R)**
— Rise in min. wage of 17.2 per cent, but inflation in 1985 was 19.3 per cent **(L)**
— Decree on wage arrears, suspending tax payments and eviction notices when individual concerned is not in regular receipt of his wage

Failed:
— Easing of dismissals and short-term contracts law **(FL)**

1987:
Implemented:
— Min. Wage rises 12 per cent (inflation in 1986 was 11.7 per cent) **(R)**
— Min. Wage applies to workers 18 and 20, who previously received only 75 per cent of the rate **(R)**
— Min. Wage rates will be lowered for craft sector and small companies, for whom it causes problems **(L)**
— UB extended to cover young workers who have completed school or training and have been looking for a job for over a year **(R)**
— Relocation subsidies for unemployed who move to areas of relatively full employment or skills shortages, e.g. transportation and rent subsidiess. Rent subsidies are paid by the employer who deducts the amount from the company's tax bill **(L)**
— Sick pay scheme eligibility tightened **(R)**
— Further UB for young people passed in parliament under the minority PSD government but likely to be revoked by the government, now that it has an absolute majority **(R)**

Failed:
— Deregulation of working hours, increasing statutory working day to above eight hours, and allowing women to work night shifts in industrial plants **(FL)**
— Decree deregulating working conditions vetoed by President

Other:
Wage arrears problem recedes.

3 April: PSD Government falls on censure motion, but wins absolute majority in subsequent elections.

Planned changes in labour laws include trade union rights, collective bargaining, holidays and absences, working time and – above all – individual dismissals.

1988:

Implemented:

— Min. wage rises 7.9 per cent (inflation in 1987 was 9.4 per cent) **(L)**

— Narrower bill liberalizing dismissals **(L)**

— Increase in fines for child labour **(R)**

Failed:

— Important bill liberalizing dismissals by widening the definition of just cause. The bill passed in parliament, under the absolute majority of the PSD, but was found procedurally and materially unconstitutional by the Constitutional Court **(FL)**

Other:

Dismissals bill causes large demonstrations, and the first general strike jointly called by the two rival trade union confederations.

1989:

Implemented:

— Minimum wage up 10.3 per cent (inflation the past year was 9.5 per cent) **(R)**

— Weekly working hours reduced from 48 to 45. **(R)**

— Liberalizing labour law reforms (*pacote laboural*) approved **(L)**

  — widens the concept of just dismissal to include the circumstances of the firm

  — places limits on automatic re-engagement of employees found to be unjustly dismissed

  — restricts the power of judicial appraisal for assessment of blame

  — for collective redundancies, abolishes the requirement of administrative authorization from the Ministry of Labour

— The law also seeks to discourage short-term contracts **(R)**

  — they can be renewed only twice – total duration of the contract cannot exceed three years

  — the contract becomes permanent if the three year period is exceeded.

— 2nd revision of the constitution

  — the period of employment required to qualify for social security, redundancy pay and retirement pensions is extended **(L)**

Other:

CGTP and UGT issue joint nine-point demand for higher wages, reduced taxes, higher pensions, improvements in social security, reduced working hours, better vocational training and more action against child labour.

1990:

Proposed:

Economic and Social Agreement (*Acordo Economico Social*)

— Five year social contract proposed by the government would allow certain workers to retire early, reduce working time, increase the min. working age from 14 to 16, reduce taxes on employment, increase the minimum wage at a rate faster than average wage increases, improve training and make redundancies due to technological progress easier

1991:

Implemented:

— Rise and harmonization of the minimum wage. The min. wage in agriculture has been raised to equalize it with the min. wage for industry and services. The min. wage for domestic services remains lower **(R)**

Parliament authorizes the government to amend the law on dismissals to include the worker's unsuitability for the job as grounds for dismissal. **(L)**

1992:
Implemented:
— Central pay agreement to obtain wage moderation would increase the minimum wage in real terms
— Parliament approves legislation allowing the government to ease restrictions on temporary lay-offs and short-time working **(L)**
— More restrictive strike law modifies prior notice and compulsory minimum services **(L)**

Failed:
— Strike law that would curtail sympathy strikes, prohibit certain forms of industrial action and require a secret ballot before initiation of a strike **(L)**

Proposed:
— Reduction in the employment protection of civil servants which would permit transfers, early retirement and redundancy to allow rationalization of public administration. The bill is found unconstitutional by the Constitutional Court **(L)**

1993:
Implemented:
— Decrees regulating child labour performed between the ages of 14 and 16. Children this age can only perform light work, stipulated in the decrees, and only if they have completed their compulsory schooling **(R)**
— Substantial increase in active labour market policy

1995:
Implemented:
— Social security charges for new hires covering young people who have never had a job, are in vocational training programmes, or have been registered with job centres for more than a year, are exempted for a period of three years **(L)**

Other:
Socialist Party wins 1 October legislative elections with 43.7 per cent of the vote.

1996:
Implemented:
Social Pact (Acordo de Concertacao Social)
— Gradual reduction of working time from 44 to 40 hours per week **(R)**
— Greater flexibility in other aspects of working time **(L)**
— Unemployment benefit increased for unemployed people over 45 **(R)**
— Employee social security contributions reduced **(L)**

Universal statutory right to the 13th month bonus (equal to one month's pay), which had previously been limited to collective agreements. **(R)**

Use of temporary contracts tightened. **(R)**

Other:
Jorge Sampaio elected President in 14 January election.

FINDINGS

The tables demonstrate significant variation in labour market policy reform during this period. Labour market reform varies in direction, by year, in content, and in the extent to which reform proposals are linked together in policy packages.

Over the period from 1981 to 1996, and using the European Industrial Relations Review as a data source, Spain experienced 45 instances of labour market policy change in the areas of the minimum wage, firing laws, hiring regulations, taxation on employment, and unemployment benefit. In Portugal over the same period the number is 26.

In addition to these successful examples of policy change, there were three cases of failed attempts at policy reform in Spain, two in unemployment benefit and one in employment taxation. By contrast, there were ten cases of failed reform in Portugal. There are multiple paths towards failure. The government proposal may fail to win approval in parliament, or, in the Portuguese case, the President may doubt its constitutionality and refer the reform to the Constitutional Court. In addition, the government may find the costs of implementing the measure to be too high, either due to resistance from unions or from employers. Employers can threaten non-cooperation in tri-partite negotiations. In addition to non-cooperation in negotiations and in efforts to secure wage restraint, unions can also threaten popular protest and strike action.

All but one of the 13 failed policy reforms involved attempts at labour market liberalization, indicating clearly the political difficulties governments face in removing worker protection. The extent that anticipated opposition to certain reforms led governments to avoid or delay attempts at policy reform is not counted as failure by the tables. Viewed in this larger sense, the continued existence of important labour market rigidities in these countries attests to the difficulty in achieving comprehensive labour market reform. Despite agendas which included comprehensive reform, the long-lasting governments of the PSOE and PSD achieved reforms which although significant, remain partial.

The most important failure of the reform programmes of both governments was the failure to reduce dismissals costs. In Portugal many attempts were made to reduce firing costs, but most of these failed. As the reforms ultimately required change in the constitution, the barriers to reform were high. In Spain, reducing firing costs for permanent employees was viewed as particularly difficult to accomplish. The result in both countries has been liberalization of the employment contract through the easing of regulations on hiring temporary workers. By so doing, governments can lower employers' risks, provide employment opportunities to those without work, but still maintain the protections enjoyed by workers with permanent contracts. The proliferation of temporary contracts nonetheless promotes the rise of inequitable labour market segmentation, in which some workers enjoy comprehensive protections while others do not. The division of the labour market by temporary and permanent work contracts significantly affects the distribution of job security, the accrual of pension time, and access to unemployment benefits.

The charts indicate that in most of the sub-areas of labour market policy analyzed, reforms change direction at least once, and often many more times. In Spain, for example, all of the categories of labour market policy experience both liberalizing and rigidifying reforms. In Portugal the only two exceptions to this rule are taxation on employment and changes in dismissals policy, both of which experience only liberalizing reforms. The change in direction of the reforms is clearly visible in the minimum wage. Despite a downward trend in the value of the minimum wage, there are years where the minimum wage is either revalued or consolidated upward through the elimination of lower-tier minimum wages for agricultural workers or young workers. Changes in the direction of reform are also salient in unemployment benefits, which are extended and then tightened from year to year.

It is also quite common for policy reform within a sub-area to exhibit change in contradictory directions within the same year, often as part of the same reform. An example of this is the 1987 reform of unemployment benefits in Spain. The unemployment benefit period was extended for 18 months beyond the existing three years (coded as greater rigidity), but recipients were required to be geographically mobile and to accept jobs anywhere in Spain (coded as a move towards liberalization). Recipients had previously only been required to accept job offers within a 25 km. radius of their home. This kind of policy change, where a move towards liberalization is balanced by a move towards greater rigidity, is more common in Spain than in Portugal. There are ten examples of this kind of contradictory movement in Spain. Six of these examples occur in the area of unemployment benefit, three in the area of hiring policy, and one in employment taxation. By contrast, in Portugal there is only one example of change in contradictory directions within the same area, and this occurs in the minimum wage domain.

The charts support the notion that the effect of high unemployment is curvilinear. The initial policy reaction is to compensate the unemployed by increasing unemployment benefits. After a certain point, however, the costs of unemployment benefit start to cause budgetary problems. Combined with pressure from employers to lower the taxation of employment, the budgetary problems lead to pressures to limit unemployment benefits. As the volume of expenditure mounts, and as unemployment remains high, policy experts recommend shifts in labour market expenditure from passive transfers to more active policies involving training and human capital investment. During the period of rising unemployment, Spanish reform of the unemployment benefit system expanded coverage and increased the generosity of benefits, making the system more rigid. From 1990 on, however, the trend shifts dramatically. Since 1990, changes in unemployment benefit rules tilt strongly towards liberalization.

The charts also indicate that in both countries the minimum wage is the easiest of the domains to liberalize. The likely explanation for this is two-fold. First, minimum wages policy is generally set unilaterally by the government, and thus does not require parliamentary approval where it can either be blocked or become the focus of substantial media attention. Second, low minimum wages affect only a small proportion of the workforce and thus command considerably less interest to the workforce as a whole than do changes in the unemployment benefit system, dismissals policy, hiring, or employment taxation.

CONCLUSION

This paper has charted labour market policy reforms in Portugal and Spain. It has contextualized particular types of reforms, assessed the coherence of reform trends, and monitored movement toward and away from the goal of liberalization. As labour market policy consists of many domains, each of which consists of bundles of rules, reform can take many forms. Charting labour market policy reform aggregates the many changes in different areas to a level where these changes can be compared to one another across domains and across time. The coding scheme used here is a tool that can be used to classify reforms, and identify patterns and puzzles. Like all tools, the coding scheme has a limited purpose. Although it can be used to identify patterns, generate hypotheses and pose puzzles, it does not offer explanations for the patterns.

Rigidity and liberalization were used as the classifying principle not only because of their importance in the economics literature but also because the removal of many rigidities was among the main goals on the labour market reform agendas of governments in both Spain and Portugal during this period. Although it constitutes a core element in the solution to high unemployment proposed by the OECD, labour market deregulation remains a highly contested policy option for many, who rightly see it as undermining many of the worker protections that help constitute the European model of society. Full labour market liberalization is indeed incompatible with the European model, and some forms of rigidity not only protect workers' rights but also enhance economic efficiency.

Analytically distinct from the desirability of labour market liberalization is the question of whether it is achievable politically. The comparative evidence indicates that it remains a perilous political enterprise. Unlike the Juppe and Balladur governments in France, the governments of Felipe Gonzalez did not fall over labour market and social security reform. Nonetheless, as the charts demonstrate, the process of labour market reform was a halting and partial one. Although major changes such as the liberalization of temporary contracts were achieved, many of the reforms appear to have traded liberalization in one area for rigidity in another. In Portugal, where policy reform towards liberalization was less frequently packaged with increases in rigidity, the rate of failed attempts at liberalization was higher. Charting labour market policy reform usefully aggregates the multiple changes in policy, but also demonstrates the difficulties in achieving labour market liberalization in a European context.

NOTES

1. For recent reviews of policy options see OECD 1995; Compston 1997; and Michie 1997.
2. For a review, see OECD 1997.
3. The classification scheme is found in Saint-Paul 1996, Tables 4 and 5, pp. 284 and 285.
4. Saint-Paul recognizes the value of so doing in a later part of the same article, and indeed compares a successful Spanish reform to a failed French reform: see Saint-Paul, p.297.
5. Interviews with Socialist party leaders and Labour Ministry officials in Portugal revealed that the decision not to employ the terms 'liberalization' and 'flexibilization' was strategic. Several core elements of the proposed labour reforms were privately acknowledged to be rigidity-reducing in their goals.
6. For an excellent detailed discussion of Portuguese labour market policy in this period see Rodrigues 1988.
7. Social spending continued to rise throughout the 1980s. The argument here is not that economic difficulties prevented the rise in social spending. Rather, the argument is that

economic difficulties (ranging from inflation, balance of payments problems, and falling real wages to unemployment) posed particular challenges to the growth of the welfare state and to the increase in workers' rights. For accounts of the search for economic efficiency and social fairness and the political sustainability of economic reform in this period see Maravall 1993; Bermeo 1994 and Barreto 1996.

REFERENCES

Bank of Portugal conference 'The Portuguese Labour Market in International Perspective', Lisbon, 18-19 July 1997.

Barreto, A. (ed.) (1996): ***A Situacao Social em Portugal: 1960-1995***, Lisbon: Instituto das Ciencias Sociais da Universidade de Lisboa.

Bermeo, N. (1986): *The Revolution within the Revolution: Workers' Control in Rural Portugal*, Princeton: Princeton University Press.

Bermeo, N. (1994): 'Sacrifice, Sequence and Strength in Successful Dual Transitions: Lessons from Spain', *Journal of Politics* 56/3, pp.601-27.

Blanchard, O. and J., Jimeno (1995): 'Structural Unemployment: Spain versus Portugal', *American Economic Review* 85/2, pp.212-18.

Compston, H. (ed.) (1997): *The New Politics of Unemployment*, New York: Routledge.

European Industrial Relations Review

Fishman, R. (1990): *Working-class Organization and the Return to Democracy in Spain*, Ithaca: Cornell University Press.

Maravall, J. (1993): 'Politics and Policy: Economic Reforms in Southern Europe', in L. Pereira, J. Maravall and A. Przeworski, *Economic Reforms in New Democracies: A Social-Democratic Approach*, Cambridge, UK: Cambridge University Press.

Michie, J. (ed.) (1997): *Employment and Economic Performance: Jobs, Markets and Growth*, Oxford: Oxford University Press.

Morrison, R. (1981): *Portugal: Revolutionary Change in an Open Economy*, Boston: Auburn House.

OECD (1995): *The OECD Jobs Study*. Paris: OECD.

OECD (1997): *Implementing the OECD Jobs Strategy: Lessons from Member Countries' Experience*. Paris: OECD.

Rodrigues, M.J. (1988): ***O Sistema de Emprego em Portugal: Crise e Mutacoes***, Lisbon: Publicacoes Dom Quixote.

Saint-Paul, G. (1996): 'Exploring the Political Economy of Labour Market Institutions', *Economic Policy* 23, pp.263-300.

Unemployment and the Left Coalition in France and Spain

W. RAND SMITH

High and persistent unemployment, one can claim without exaggeration, has been the central economic policy issue throughout western Europe during the past two decades. After averaging 2.4 per cent annually between 1960 and 1973, unemployment in European Union nations more than tripled, to an annual average of 8.5 per cent, between 1974 and 1995. Since 1990 unemployment has continued to rise, to over 11 per cent, despite an economic upturn since 1994. Rising joblessness, predictably, has carried political implications. For governments of all partisan tendencies, the twin concerns of combating unemployment and coping with its consequences have influenced all aspects of public economic management, including fiscal, monetary, labour, social welfare, regional, and industrial policies. Governments everywhere have sought, assiduously and at times desperately, to generate new jobs while providing sufficient social protection to the unemployed to prevent electoral defection or mass protest.

The impact of unemployment on economic policy has been especially strong in nations governed by left (socialist or social-democratic) parties. Not only do left parties draw much of their electoral support from those groups that are most vulnerable to job loss, especially unskilled service and industrial workers, but these parties have typically made full employment a central plank in their electoral platforms (Scharpf 1991: 15). In starkest terms, the unemployment crisis has sharpened the classic social-democratic dilemma: the trade-off between capitalist efficiency and social solidarity.

Doctrinally committed to defending working-class interests – and in some cases even pledged to break with capitalism and launch a transition to socialism – left governments also face market pressures that contradict

---

Some of the material in this article is derived from the author's book, *The Left's Dirty Job: The Politics of Industrial Restructuring in France and Spain* (Pittsburgh: University of Pittsburgh Press and Toronto: University of Toronto Press, 1998).

such aims. When jobs are threatened, one would naturally expect these governments to use such measures as subsidies, protectionist trade policies, and ownership changes such as worker-owned co-operatives or even nationalization, in order to save those jobs. For both structural and political reasons, however, left governments also confront pressures to privilege market efficiency. Whatever their ideological goals, left governments depend on private capital to generate investment, growth, employment, and tax revenues, and thus must promote capitalist interests in order to ensure their own political survival. Such promotion may mean permitting firms to restructure their operations in line with market pressures, a process that typically eliminates large numbers of jobs. Moreover, for electoral reasons left governments must appeal to non-workers as well as workers, but in so doing they tend to dilute their ideological commitment to the working class (Przeworski 1985).

Rising unemployment has not only sharpened policy quandaries for left governments, it has also created tensions within the coalitional elements that support those governments, including left parties and affiliated organizations such as labour unions. Perhaps nowhere has the impact of unemployment been more profound than on the internal politics of left coalitions, which typically encompass a range of organizations bearing distinct, often disparate, visions of the unemployment 'crisis'. Left governments must not only negotiate the policy dilemmas of unemployment, they must also manage the political tensions arising within their own coalitions. A full assessment of unemployment's impact on left governments must, therefore, take account of both the policy dilemmas and political dynamics that such governments face.

The following discussion compares how recent Socialist governments in France and Spain addressed these issues. These are two promising cases for analysis because of the longevity and political dominance of Socialist parties since the early 1980s.[1] In both nations, Socialist leaders had both the time and the opportunity to enact measures to deal with the unemployment crisis, and an examination of their experiences can shed light on the policy and political implications of unemployment for left governments. This analysis raises two interrelated questions: How have French and Spanish Socialist governments defined and responded to the challenge of unemployment? What impact, in turn, has the unemployment issue had on the left governing coalitions themselves?

The central argument to be developed is that despite contrasting initial approaches to unemployment, the governments of François

Mitterrand and Felipe González eventually adopted economic approaches emphasizing business profitability and investment over the reduction of unemployment. At the same time, these governments, in line with governments throughout western Europe, enacted measures to cushion the shock for unemployed and displaced workers, mainly through early retirement and other income-maintenance programmes. The primacy given to fostering private investment and profits proved controversial, however. In both countries, the unemployment issue undermined the cohesion of the left political coalition, as government economic policies created divisions within the Socialist parties themselves, between the Socialists and other left parties, and between the Socialist parties and their allies in the labour movement.

While the unemployment issue created divisions within the left in both countries, the pattern of those divisions differed, creating contrasting political dynamics and economic outcomes. In France, the chief conflicts occurred within the Socialist Party (PS) and between the PS and its ally, the French Communist Party (PCF). Conflicts over unemployment between the government and organized labour, while occasionally bitter and explosive, did not generally preoccupy government leaders, and tended to decline over time. In Spain, by contrast, Socialist political leaders faced relatively little discord over unemployment within their own party, and they did not have to contend with significant opposition from the other main left party, the Spanish Communist Party (PCE). Rather, Socialist leaders met growing opposition toward their employment and other economic policies from organized labour, which became increasingly united and mobilized.

The following section sets the context by tracing the rise in unemployment in France and Spain during the past two decades. Then we analyze Socialists' attempts to cope with growing unemployment in the 1980s and early 1990s. The third section compares the impact of rising unemployment on the respective left coalitions themselves, and the conclusion considers the larger implications of intracoalitional conflict for these governments' management of the public economy.

UNEMPLOYMENT: THE PROBLEM

France and Spain shared the fate of other European nations in suffering deteriorating labour market conditions, notably rising unemployment rates, following the first oil shock in 1973. Moreover, since the late 1970s, unemployment in both nations has remained stubbornly high by historical standards. Within this broad similarity, however, the two nations have followed contrasting labour-market trajectories. From similar levels of unemployment in the mid-1970s, France and Spain diverged by the late 1970s, as Spain's new democratic leaders gradually exposed the national economy to external competition. One result was a rapid, dramatic jump in unemployment that gave Spain the highest unemployment rate in western Europe. Since that time, Spain's rate has remained roughly twice that of France (and of the EU generally), averaging nearly 20 per cent per year since the early 1980s.

Spain's poor unemployment record has accompanied, paradoxically, an impressive burst of job creation. Between 1975 and 1985, a period of democratic transition and economic adjustment, the Spanish economy lost nearly 2 million jobs, as the unemployment rate leaped from 3.6 to 21.1 per cent. But approximately as many jobs were created in the subsequent boom years of 1985-90, at a rate three times the OECD-Europe average. Although unemployment dropped during this period – from 21 to 16 per cent – it remained high by European standards for two reasons. The first was a vast expansion of the labour force, due to a baby boom that took place in the 1960s and early 1970s and to the entry of a much higher percentage of females into the labour force (Espina 1991: 365-7). Second, most of the new jobs created were temporary (fixed-term contract) or part-time, and thus their impact on the overall unemployment rate was slight. Indeed, Spain's labour market remains singular throughout western Europe in its reliance on temporary workers. For example, between 1987 and 1997, the percentage of workers on fixed-term contracts has climbed steadily from 16 to over 33 per cent, compared with about 15 per cent for the European Union as a whole (OECD 1994: 104; OECD 1998: 24).

Economists conventionally attribute much of Spain's poor job performance to the rigidity of its wage-formation system.[2] Wage rigidity, which causes wages to respond slowly if at all to changes in employment levels, makes it difficult for employers to adjust to recession by reducing wages. To keep wage bills under control during downturns, employers often resort to layoffs. But employers face legal and administrative obstacles in seeking to lay off workers individually or in small numbers because of Spain's strong tradition of job protection – a lingering legacy of Francoism. More typically, employers often postpone labour adjustment until the point of financial crisis, and then undertake large-scale layoffs (OECD 1994: 73).

This wage rigidity has tended to maintain and even reinforce a highly segmented labour market. One segment is a core of about 8 million workers who are generally older, permanent and secure in status, and relatively well-paid. Another segment is a periphery of about 2 million underemployed (part-time or temporary) workers, while a third component is the 3.5 million unemployed, who are disproportionately young and female. Spain's labour market remains distinctive throughout the OECD by combining a high average duration of employment for those with jobs, along with a high proportion of long-term unemployed among those without jobs. Spain also has the EU's highest youth unemployment rate: 34.4 per cent among the 16-24 year old category (López-Claros 1992: 22; Cornilleau 1994: 48).

France's employment record, as mentioned, has been considerably better than Spain's. Since the early 1980s, France has performed close to the EU average. Along with other EU nations, however, France has experienced a deterioration in job creation since 1990. After descending below 9 per cent in that year, unemployment climbed back into double-digits in 1992 and has since remained at around 12 per cent. Moreover, France's labour market evidences some of the same traits as Spain's, albeit in less extreme fashion, notably segmentation between secure and precarious workers and a high level of youth unemployment (OECD 1994: 67; Maruani and Reynaud 1993: 27-47).

UNEMPLOYMENT: SOLUTIONS SOUGHT

Upon gaining power in the early 1980s, Socialist governments under Mitterrand and González were well aware of the political risk of rising unemployment. Both governments owed much of their electoral success to the policy failures of their predecessors, especially in responding to the global recession following the second oil shock of 1979. With unemployment climbing rapidly to post-war highs, voters in France and Spain soundly rejected incumbents Giscard and Calvo-Sotelo and their conservative allies. Although the elections of 1981 and 1982 prescribed no clear policy 'mandate,' they did convey voters' sentiment that the new governments should play an active economic role, notably to reduce unemployment (López-Pintor 1985: 308-11; McDonough, Barnes, and López Pina 1998: 67-71).

French and Spanish Socialist leaders began with very different visions of how they would do so. For Mitterrand and his followers, attacking unemployment directly was a core goal of their governing programme. Applying equal doses of Colbertism and Keynesianism, French Socialists sought to preserve existing jobs and generate new ones by 'reconquering the domestic market' through increased public spending and nationalizations. A reflation (*relance*) of the economy would stimulate consumer spending, which would then fuel new investment and job creation. This virtuous cycle would be reinforced by a vast wave of nationalizations of key industrial firms and of the banking sector that would enable the government to restructure and recapitalize these firms. In the process, these firms would increase investment and create new jobs.

The González team began with no illusions that such a voluntarist approach would succeed. Spanish Socialists in 1982 were little inclined to experiment with *dirigismo*, an attitude that stemmed from several factors, including the fragility of the country's new democracy, the vulnerability of its economy, and González's own growing moderation as he consolidated control over the Spanish Socialist Party (PSOE). (The fact that the PSOE came to power 18 months after the Mitterrand government also played a role. Since by then the latter had begun retreating from its reflation strategy, PSOE leaders were well aware of the risks of such an approach.)

With Spain's entry into the European Community (EC) slated for 1986, less than four years hence, the González government faced strong pressures to encourage market-driven modernization. The new leaders had to prepare businesses to compete in Europe, which meant reforming an outmoded small-scale agricultural sector, an ill-adapted financial system hobbled by undercapitalized banks and securities markets, and an inefficient system of state-run firms. Whereas the French Socialists stressed growth and job creation while worrying little about inflation, their Spanish counterparts sought to restore a favourable investment climate by drastically cutting inflation and providing incentives for domestic and foreign investors. Only by first fostering such a climate, Spanish Socialists believed, could they cope effectively with rising unemployment.

Subsequent experience served to dissolve these divergent policy approaches, as the French Socialists were ultimately forced to abandon their *relance* in favour of a new strategy much more aligned with that of the PSOE government. Although a government spending increase (+27 per cent between 1981 and 1982) and direct public-sector job creation did provide the French economy with a short-lived stimulus, the *relance* proved unsustainable. Within a year, it became clear that reflation was aggravating inflation, failing to revive investment, and, most seriously, boosting imports and worsening the trade deficit. By early 1983, less than two years after taking power, the Mitterrand government decided to reverse course definitively. The new strategy, euphemistically labelled '*rigueur*,' sought to limit spending and restrict household consumption, while seeking to increase business profits through lowered taxes and low-interest loans. The driving force behind *rigueur* was Mitterrand's March 1983 decision to tie France's economic fate irreversibly to 'Europe.' Exchange-rate policy was tightly linked to the European Union's Exchange Rate Mechanism (ERM), and a central goal of macroeconomic policy became the maintenance of a strong franc vis-à-vis other ERM currencies. Under this strategy the French economy's international competitiveness would increase by lowering inflation (and not by devaluing the currency), a process that required restrictive monetary policy and the reduction of budget deficits and business taxes.

This new approach, put in place between 1983 and 1985 under prime ministers, Pierre Mauroy and Laurent Fabius and finance minister, Jacques Delors, henceforth became accepted orthodoxy among Socialist leaders, providing the framework for economic policy generally, and employment policy specifically, throughout the late 1980s and early 1990s. Although the government did enact various measures to stimulate job creation – for example, a youth jobs program (*les Travaux d'Utilité Publique*) and a 'reconversion leave' to support laid-off workers undergoing new job training – it also gave private businesses and even public firms a green light to lay off workers in order to boost profits. Labour-market policy came to centre on encouraging work force flexibility by enabling employers to more easily hire and fire temporary workers (Howell 1992: 186-205). Accompanying this employer-friendly approach was an effort to socialize the costs of unemployment by providing laid-off workers with various forms of income support, chiefly early retirement (Holcman 1997: 46-61).

Throughout the second five-year period of Socialist legislative dominance (1988-1993), successive prime ministers Rocard, Cresson, and Bérégovoy maintained the strong franc strategy. Although emphasizing monetary stringency, these leaders sought to counteract the strategy's depressive effects on employment by a series of modest employment-stimulus plans and retraining schemes. This approach produced little effect on unemployment, however, which climbed sharply during the recession of the early 1990s. On the other hand, this strategy did contribute to eliminating the inflation gap with Germany, boosting profit margins, and shifting income shares from households to firms (Blanchard and Muet 1993: 27-31; Smith 1998: 87-8).

Effectively out of power between 1993 and 1997 (although Mitterrand remained as an increasingly ill and lame-duck president until 1995), the Socialists regained a working parliamentary majority in the 1997 elections, when voters repudiated the economic policies of Chirac's hand-picked prime minister, Alain Juppé. Under the new Socialist prime minister, Lionel Jospin, the government returned to a more activist approach to unemployment reminiscent of the early Mitterrand government. Taking direct aim at the problem, labour minister Martine Aubry pushed through plans to create 350,000 public-sector jobs for young people. The most controversial reform was a bill designed to stimulate job creation by reducing the legal working week from 39 to 35 hours without loss of pay. (The measure would take effect in 2000 and apply to firms with more than 20 employees.) With work hours shortened, Socialist leaders argued, employers would have an incentive to hire more workers. Opposed vociferously by the employers' association, the government eventually diluted the bill by merely setting a limit (35 hours) above which overtime would be paid and eliminating any requirements regarding pay, while offering employers financial incentives to hire new workers. The bill was finally approved by parliament in May 1998, and its long-term effects will not be known for several years (*Liaisons Sociales* 1998).

Unlike the French Socialists, González and the Spanish Socialists stuck consistently to their initial policy path, although their four parliamentary terms were marked by specific emphases. During the first term, 1982-86, the PSOE government focused primarily on reducing inflation through tightening monetary policy, reducing the fiscal deficit, and moderating wages (including sponsorship of several wage-limiting 'social pacts' between business and labour). The government also sought to improve the competitive position of both public and private firms through an early devaluation of the peseta, a programme of 'reconversion and reindustrialization' in 15 targeted sectors, and efforts to improve the efficiency and financial condition of the national industrial holding agency, the Instituto Nacional de Industria (INI). Rising unemployment was not entirely ignored, but the emphasis was on labour flexibility, including the use of part-time and fixed-term contracts. For example, a 1986 law permitted firms to hire workers on provisional six-months contracts for up to three years (OECD 1986: 60-2).

The PSOE government's second term, 1986-89, reaped the rewards of the first term, as rapid investment and growth followed from the improved business conditions. Especially strong was foreign direct investment, which leaped 43 per cent from 1985 to 1986 (López-Claros 1992: 28), and Spain enjoyed the highest growth rate within the EC. Yet, as we shall see, this term was also the PSOE government's most contentious, as organized labour grew increasingly dissatisfied with the government's efforts vis-à-vis unemployment and social equality.

The González government's final two terms (1989-93, 1993-96) were marked by dwindling popularity and growing political fragility due to scandals and to the loss of an absolute parliamentary majority in the 1993 elections. Caught between public demands for more social spending and EC mandates for monetary stringency, the government followed a contradictory strategy. On the one hand, it enacted a permissive fiscal policy that increased government spending generally and social spending specifically while tolerating a rapidly growing budget deficit. Between 1989 and 1993, for example, government spending as a percentage of GDP rose from 40.9 to 47.6, while the overall public deficit as a percentage of GDP increased from 2.8 to 7.5 per cent (OECD 1994a: A30, A32). On the other hand, Spain's new membership in the Exchange Rate Mechanism meant that the government had to maintain the peseta's value vis-à-vis other EC currencies, which implied a tight monetary approach. This policy of applying the monetary brakes while pressing on the fiscal accelerator proved unsustainable, and the peseta came under speculative attack in late 1992 and early 1993, resulting in three devaluations totalling 19 per cent (*Financial Times*, 14 May 1993). Other than providing generous income support for the unemployed, the government took no new initiatives in labour-market policy.

Although beginning with contrasting visions of how to resolve the unemployment crisis, French and Spanish Socialist leaders converged by the mid-1980s in a broadly similar economic approach, one I have labelled a market-adapting strategy (Smith 1998). That strategy sought to promote a gradual adjustment of the economy to international and domestic market forces so as to avoid sudden and massive losses of jobs and incomes. Encouraging firms to modernize and to re-allocate labour according to market-efficient criteria, both governments used income-support and other measures to cushion the shocks of labour displacement. On balance, this approach was generally in line with the labour-market strategies of governments throughout western Europe regardless of their partisan composition.

UNEMPLOYMENT: IMPACT ON THE LEFT COALITION

In both France and Spain, the political implications of unemployment extended deeply into the left coalitions themselves, as the question of how to respond to growing unemployment became a focus for contending visions of a 'socialist' economic strategy. In both nations, discord over unemployment polarized the left's main groups and undermined its unity. This discord took place at all levels: within the Socialist parties themselves, between Socialists and their chief ally-adversary on the left, the Communists, and between the Socialist party and the principal labour organizations.

The pattern of internal dispute varied in the two cases, however. In France, conflict over unemployment took place mainly within the PS and between the PS and their initial allies, the Communist Party (PCF). Disputes between the government and the unions, by contrast, while often vociferous, were relatively less disruptive. In Spain, conflict over unemployment was relatively slight within the PSOE and between the Socialists and Communists, but acrimonious between the PSOE government and the labour movement. The following discussion develops this contrasting pattern by comparing the impact of unemployment on each of these elements of the left coalition: the Socialist Party, other party allies, and organized labour. As we shall see, many of these variations were strongly influenced by differences in the leadership strategies and development trajectories of the two coalitions.

Socialist Party

The issue of employment policy bitterly divided the French Socialist party, especially during the Mitterrand government's first three years. By contrast, the PSOE experienced relatively little internal discord over employment questions. The explanation for this difference can be found in the respective parties' development as they struggled for power during the 1970s.

In Spain, Felipe González rose to political prominence by taking over the PSOE from within. Coming of political age during Franco's final decade, González emerged in the late 1960s as the leader of a group of young '*renovadores*' who contested not only Franco's rule but also that of the PSOE's ageing leadership, most of whom were living in exile. Through grassroots organizing and successful challenges to the leadership at party congresses, González and his supporters eventually captured control of the PSOE in 1974 (Gillespie 1989: 264-88; Maravall 1985:

169-72). For the next two years, which included Franco's death and the first steps toward a democratic transition, the PSOE under González pushed an increasingly radical line, culminating in a December 1976 congress that, for the first time in the party's history, officially embraced Marxism and espoused a governing programme based on workers' self-management, widespread nationalizations, and other reforms.

As the democratic transition continued during the next three years, the PSOE's influence and political popularity grew rapidly. Accompanying this growth was a dual tendency within the PSOE: a strengthening of González's personal power within the party along with a progressive moderation of the party's ideology (Share 1985). This tendency did not go uncontested, however, as an emerging 'critical sector' accused González of deserting the party's commitment to radical change, rejecting an alliance with the PCE and other leftists, and centralizing party power. But in a fierce internal struggle between May and September 1979, González defeated the dissidents, moved the party away from Marxism, and extended his hold over party organization (Nash 1983).

When the PSOE won the 1982 elections, González was the uncontested leader of a party that was firmly committed to a moderate economic programme. Spanish Socialist leaders were virtually unanimous in believing that economic policy had to promote modernization in a context of growing European co-operation. An explicit strategy to create new jobs or defend existing ones was not a priority. As the exception proving the rule, the PSOE's 1982 campaign promised to create 800,000 jobs, but that commitment was quietly dropped once the elections were over. Having had its 'Bad Godesberg' prior to coming to power,[3] the PSOE did not undergo an internal crisis of identity as unemployment and workers' protests mounted during the early 1980s. The unemployment issue, therefore, had little impact on the party itself.

Such was not the case in France, where, as mentioned, a fierce debate took place within the PS over basic economic policy, including the government's approach to unemployment. As in Spain, the impact of unemployment on the French Socialist Party can be best understood by tracing the party's trajectory as it rose to power. The key point is that the PS, far from becoming centralized and virtually monolithic like the PSOE, developed as an unsteady coalition of factions (*courants*) united around a charismatic leader, Mitterrand. During the decade 1971-81, four such factions jockeyed for influence, each one seeking to promote its own leaders and viewpoints within the party structure: the leftist

CERES, the Rocardians (followers of Michel Rocard, Mitterrand's arch rival), the 'social democrats' organized around old-line Socialists, Pierre Mauroy and Gaston Defferre, and Mitterrand's own faction (Bergounioux and Grunberg 1992).

Mitterrand may have been the undisputed leader (at least until a 1979 challenge by Rocard), but his power depended on the support of other factions. The Socialists' programme, therefore, tended to reflect the shifting balance of forces among these factions. Although there were major continuities in party positions over time, the PS's ideology was not a package of fixed positions, but the product of internal factional conflicts (Ross and Jensen 1981). Far from hurting the PS's electoral prospects, however, this factionalism probably helped it by forcing the party to appease the various factions and therefore to appeal to a wide range of voters and interests.

The elections of 1981, of course, did nothing to erase the PS's factionalism, and thus the new government was publicly united but internally divided. The failed *relance* of 1981-82 brought those divisions to the surface and created a veritable identity crisis for the party as government leaders sought to cope with a faltering economy. Unemployment was a principal focus of the policy debate, for by early 1983 Socialist leaders had to decide whether the government would pursue its reformist strategy, with its emphasis on reconquering the domestic market and creating jobs, or abandon its reformism in favour of a more orthodox approach stressing austerity and monetary discipline. Proponents of the former strategy, including the CERES and several prominent government ministers, argued that France should maintain its commitment to social reforms, even if it required leaving the European Monetary System and adopting protectionist measures. Opponents of this strategy, including prime minister Mauroy, finance minister Jacques Delors, and Rocard (now planning minister), countered that domestic inflation had to be brought into line with France's main EC partners, and therefore that considerably more austerity (and, inevitably, more unemployment) was necessary (Favier and Martin-Roland 1990).

In the protracted government crisis of March 1983, Mitterrand finally sided with the latter group. Although that decision did not quell all discord within the PS, and it certainly did not eliminate factionalism, it did ratify a definitive new policy path. Henceforth, the protectionist CERES approach, with its stress on national economic autonomy, was not a serious policy option. The 1983 U-turn represented the Socialists' acceptance that France's economic future would be tied irrevocably to that of its European partners.

Whereas the Spanish Socialists confronted the economic and employment problems of the 1980s with a united front based on moderate pragmatism, their French counterparts engaged in a divisive internal struggle. Although the ultimate outcome was generally the same in that both governments eventually embraced market-adapting economic approaches by the mid-1980s, the two cases sharply contrast in the way in which that outcome was achieved. The Spanish Socialist government 'never doubted the need to sacrifice national sovereignty in the area of macroeconomic management' (Boix 1998: 110), which rendered the unemployment issue mainly a question of how to maintain the incomes of laid-off workers. French Socialists, by contrast, did doubt this need, and that doubt gave rise to a fractious intragovernmental debate in which unemployment was a chief focus of contention.

Socialists and Communists

Unemployment also created tensions between the Socialists and the other main left party, the Communists, but the pattern varied between the two countries. This conflict was much more severe in France and had direct consequences for Socialist governance, whereas in Spain the Socialist-Communist dispute, while present, was more muted and had little bearing on how the Socialists governed.

An explanation for this difference can be found in the alliance strategies of the two Socialist parties. During the 1970s, French and Spanish Socialists took divergent approaches to the question of co-operation vs. rivalry with Communists. Mitterrand based his electoral strategy on an explicit alliance with the Communist Party, believing that co-operation would profit the Socialists and help bring them to power. González, on the other hand, rejected co-operation with other parties, notably the Communists (PCE), and sought instead to rally the rest of the left to his own party's banner. These contrasting alliance strategies would largely define how the unemployment issue would affect relations between Socialists and Communists in each country.

Mitterrand wagered in the early 1970s that an electoral partnership with the Communists would work systematically to his and the Socialists' advantage by allowing him to pose as the *candidat unique* of the alliance and by drawing votes away from the PCF. Such an alliance was formally struck in 1972 with the signing of the Common Programme of the Left, and it soon became clear that Mitterrand had bet correctly. In late 1977, the Communists, by then disillusioned with the alliance, cancelled their adherence to the Common Programme, and co-operation broke down. In the run-up to the 1981 elections, however, Mitterrand maintained the fiction of unity with the Communists, and once elected, appointed four Communists to minor ministerial posts. Thus the PCF was officially part of the new left government, albeit cast in a secondary role.

As the *relance* turned to *rigueur* in 1982-83, however, the PCF became an increasingly vocal critic of government policy. With the 1983 'Delors plan' imposing new taxes and limiting public spending, the PCF found itself caught in a contradiction, holding four ministerial posts yet rejecting rigeuer and blaming the crisis on a capitalist conspiracy. By the spring of 1984 this conflict had become untenable, for both the PCF and the Socialists, as massive layoffs in coal, steel, and other heavy industries brought the Communists to the verge of an open break with the government. The final divorce came in July 1984 with the appointment of a new prime minister, Mitterrand protégé Laurent Fabius, who portrayed himself as a champion of both industrial modernization and social justice. For the Communists, however, Fabius's appointment signalled the government's determination to pursue austerity at the expense of workers, and the PCF chose this moment to resign from the government. The Communists' withdrawal met with little resistance, however, because the PCF's electoral decline, capped by its dismal 11 per cent showing in the 1984 elections (versus 16 per cent in the 1981 legislative elections), made it expendable as a coalition partner (Ross and Jenson 1985). For the remainder of Mitterrand's tenure as President, the Communists remained a hostile but increasingly marginal presence, gaining, for example, just 27 of 577 seats in the 1988 elections.

Unlike Mitterrand, González rejected the prospect of a formal alliance with the Communists, a reluctance that stemmed from a history of mutual recriminations between the parties during the Second Republic, the Civil War, and even the Cold War. This antipathy remained strong even as the balance of power between the two parties reversed during the 1970s, and the PSOE surged well ahead of the Communists in members and voters. Following the first legislative elections in 1977, in which the PSOE far outpolled the PCE, 28.9 to 9.2 per cent, González and other top leaders saw even less reason for an alliance that they believed would likely benefit only the Communists. There was little ideological basis for this split, however, since both parties sought to convey a moderate and responsible image. Rather, their division owed more to electoral competition, since both parties occupied the same electoral space and were competing for many of the same voters (Maravall 1985: 161-72). In any case, the issue of a PCE alliance became increasingly moot during the early 1980s as the PCE became embroiled in internal conflict and finally broke apart; its descent to less than four per cent in the 1982 elections consigned it thereafter to the political margins.

The issue of unemployment (and economic policy issues in general) did not cause great conflict between Socialist and Communist leaders for the simple reason that the two parties operated largely independently. The Communists were finally able to improve their electoral fortunes in the late 1980s by constituting the leading element in a new formation, the United Left, that became a vocal critic of Socialist economic policies. But the key factor was Socialist electoral dominance. Until 1993, the PSOE enjoyed a clear parliamentary majority, and even during its final term (1993-96) the Socialists were able to cobble together a working majority without the Communists.

Socialists and the Unions

Differences over employment policy created tensions between Socialists and their labour allies in both countries, but those tensions were considerably greater in Spain than in France. In Spain, the main union confederations, the Socialist-affiliated General Workers Union (UGT) and the Communist-influenced Workers Commissions (CCOO), became increasingly disenchanted with PSOE economic policy, especially its '*fatalismo*' regarding unemployment, and were able to mobilize a significant proportion of the working class in opposition. Co-operating closely over several years, the two unions culminated their efforts in a massive general strike in late 1988. In France, however, the two principal confederations, the Communist-aligned General Confederation of Labour (CGT) and the Socialist-leaning French Democratic Confederation of Labour (CFDT), also opposed the government's employment policies, albeit for different reasons (see below), but proved generally ineffective in mobilizing against those policies. Contributing to labour's relative weakness was the inability of the two main confederations to resolve their differences and form a united labour front. On balance, the unemployment problem created more overt conflict between the government and labour in Spain than in France.

This outcome is surprising in that the PSOE, compared with the PS, maintained much closer relations with the union movement, in particular with the UGT. PSOE leaders had founded the UGT in 1888, and the two organizations overlapped considerably in membership. Indeed, Socialist

Party members were required by party statutes to join the UGT, and the PSOE enjoyed strong electoral support among UGT members. Moreover, even though the PSOE and the other main confederation, the CCOO, did not maintain a formal relationship, more CCOO members voted for the PSOE than for their own confederation's fraternal ally, the PCE (Pérez-Díaz 1980).

By contrast, the PS had tenuous ties to organized labour. Despite the PS's vow that 'the first task of a left government will be to organize the effective power of workers in the firm' (quoted in Cayrol 1978: 296), the party failed to develop solid organizational links to the working class. The largest of the union confederations, the CGT, had long been under the control of the Communist Party, and thus the PS's relationship with the CGT, always mediated by the PCF, varied according to shifts in PS-PCF relations. The confederation which contained the most PS members and was ideologically the most sympathetic was the second largest, the CFDT, but after 1979 the CFDT had decided to 'recentre' its strategy on workplace bargaining, thus rejecting any party alliance. Finally, the third major confederation, the Workers Force (FO) closely guarded its political independence, refusing privileged ties with any political party.

The breakdown in relations between the PSOE and the labour movement did not occur immediately. In fact, during the first three years (1982-85), the UGT generally supported the government's austerity and other economic measures. A case in point was industrial restructuring. To stimulate modernization, the Socialists enacted a 'reconversion and reindustrialization' plan that targeted several key sectors and required sizeable reductions in their work forces. In two core industries, for example, steel and shipbuilding, the plan aimed to eliminate over half the work force, a total of nearly 50,000 jobs. (In return, displaced workers would be offered various income-support and retraining measures.) In the elaborate sectoral-level *concertación* process to define these plans, the UGT played an active role, negotiating with employers and state officials and signing agreements on labour issues for all of the affected sectors. The UGT thus initially backed the government's reconversion efforts, recognizing, in the words of its leader, Nicolas Redondo, that 'sometimes unions have to negotiate sacrifices and not benefits' (*El País*, 17 October 1983).

The CCOO rejected such an approach, opposing the government's plans from the start. With regard to industrial restructuring, for example, a CCOO leader labelled the government's plan a 'deindustrialization plan' that manifested a 'real obsession...with reducing employment' (*El*

País, 23 June 1983). The CCOO faulted not only the plan's goals but also its procedures, and refused to participate in the sectoral negotiations. Government officials found the CCOO intransigent; according to one ministry of industry official involved in the plan, 'the *Comisiones* didn't want to be part of the dialogue and so they turned to confrontation in the streets' (author interview, 27 June 1994). Choosing an oppositional stance, the CCOO played its single card: mobilization of worker discontent in the targeted regions. Throughout 1983, 1984, and 1985 the confederation spearheaded countless strikes and demonstrations in the industrial regions such as the Basque Country, Asturias, and Galicia that would suffer heavy job losses.

This pattern of UGT support and CCOO opposition changed in 1985, however, as the two confederations joined in a campaign of protest against government economic policy. Since the CCOO's basic opposition did not shift, one must account for the UGT's change in attitude. Part of that change stemmed from competitive pressures within the union movement and from growing personal animosity between González and the UGT leader, Nicolas Redondo. In the worker-delegate elections in 1986, for example, the UGT lost ground to the CCOO in several key sectors and firms, especially in the public sector, and, according to a top CCOO official, these losses convinced UGT leaders that support of the government's austerity policies had become a handicap (author interview, 27 October 1993). Moreover, an increasingly bitter rivalry between UGT leader Redondo and González poisoned relations between the UGT and the government. Whereas Redondo had been one of González's earliest backers and had remained a confidant during the first two years of government, the union leader by 1985 was claiming that González had failed to compensate the UGT for its initial support. According to a UGT metalworkers' leader during this period, 'the conflict between the UGT and the government became, purely and simply, a personal fight between Redondo and González' (author interview, 23 July 1994).

Although inter-union competition and personal rivalries contributed to the break, the main factor was growing economic policy differences between the government and the UGT, especially vis-à-vis unemployment. The UGT's initial opposition in 1985 focused on the government's attempt to reform the pension system by increasing employees' contributions while reducing the number of beneficiaries and the amounts they could receive (López-Claros 1992: 27). On this issue, the UGT publicly opposed the reform but refused to join the CCOO in calling for a general strike. During the following three years, however, the two unions increasingly joined together to fight against the government's 'regressive' policies. Chief among the government's failures, according to the unions, was its poor employment record. The unions charged that far from stimulating the creation of secure, well-paying jobs, the government's flexibility reforms had mainly fostered various types of part-time or temporary work. The unions' disenchantment with labour-market policy climaxed in 1988 over the government's three-year plan to create 800,000 jobs for young people by subsidizing employers to offer short-term, minimum-wage contracts.

This discontent culminated on 14 December 1998 in a forceful display of working-class protest: a 24-hour general strike that attracted about 80 per cent of the work force and paralyzed the country. According to the head of the United Left, 'On December 14 the unions brought to a head all the bad feelings in Spanish society – about the huge earnings of a rich few, about a majority still struggling for a living, about profits not trickling down' (quoted in *Financial Times*, 24 February 1989). The strike apparently got the government's attention, for thereafter Socialist leaders tried to appease the unions. In 1990, pensions and unemployment coverage were increased, and the government passed a law allowing unions to monitor temporary contracts. Attempting to re-open the pact-making process, the government also sought to enlist the unions in a 'competitiveness' agreement that would link wage increases to productivity. The government was constrained, however, in its ability to grant significant concessions to labour because its commitments within the EC placed a premium on fighting inflation. Indeed, by mid-1992 the government was attempting to cut unemployment subsidies, which prompted the unions to call a second (and less successful) general strike. A third general strike followed in late 1993, when the government sought to facilitate the layoff process for employers. Thus the early 1990s saw little change in the tense stand-off between the government and the unions.

Whereas government-union conflict built over time in Spain, it tended to decline in France. During the *relance* of the first year, the main unions granted the government leeway to carry out a strategy that the government promised would create jobs and bring down unemployment. But as the government turned to austerity, union opposition predictably increased, reaching a peak during the years 1983-85. For the CGT, the break came as the government sponsored or approved a wave of restructuring in such industries as steel, automobiles, shipbuilding, and coal. Following their Communist allies who, as we have seen, left the government in July 1984, the CGT became a harsh critic of the government's new economic strategy. CGT leader Henri Krasucki, for example, denounced the layoffs as 'humanly and socially intolerable.' He added, 'We don't accept the alibi of modernization. Many of these job cuts don't result from technological changes, but from industrial surrender, from reduction of production capacity – for example, in coal, steel, shipbuilding, and textiles. The number one problem is not to reduce capacity, but to increase it' (*Le Monde*, 17 January 1984).

The other major labour confederation, the CFDT, also criticized the government, although more for the latter's methods than for the content of its policies. Although its leader, Edmond Maire, had been an early advocate for rigeuer, the CFDT accused the government of merely pretending to consult rather than taking the union's positions seriously. According to the head of the CFDT's Economic Sector:

> We weren't recognized as an actor. The government didn't comprehend the respective proper roles of unions and the government. The government felt itself to have a double legitimacy. On the one hand, it said, 'We were elected by universal suffrage, and now we hold political power.' At the same time, it said, 'We are the party of the working class, thus we know what is good for the people' (author interview, 24 April 1987).

Yet even when their opposition to the government's employment policy was at its zenith, the unions had difficulty mobilizing workers and exerting effective influence. A case in point was the steel industry, where a 1984 restructuring plan sought to eliminate 40,000 jobs. When the plan was announced in late March, public reaction, as expected, was hostile in those regions such as Lorraine that were targeted for closures and cutbacks, yet protests remained scattered. At the national level, union reaction was divided and largely ineffectual. The CGT opposed the cuts but could mobilize only limited demonstrations, while all other unions at least tolerated the decision. The CFDT, favouring the industry's modernization, considered the cuts inevitable but urged retraining and new regional investment to ease the plight of dislocated workers. Among other national union groups, one (the General Confederation of Managers, or CGC) accepted the plan, whereas two others (Workers Force and the French Confederation of Christian Workers, or CFTC) opposed the plan but refused to organize protests against it. On balance, union-inspired protest, while intense, remained fragmented and localized, insufficient to force the government to rescind or substantially modify its plan.

After 1984, however, worker mobilization against unemployment declined. Even a modest strike burst in 1988 demonstrated not a rebirth of union influence but its debility, as many strikes, especially in such public-sector firms as EDF (electricity), SNCF (railroads), Air France, and PTT (post office and telephone) were led by *coordinations*, or informal, independent rank-and-file leadership groups. Throughout the late 1980s and into the 1990s, France had one of the lowest strike rates in western Europe.

Several factors contributed to the failure of the French labour movement to mobilize effective protests against the rise in unemployment. One was a long-term decline in membership and organizational capacity beginning in the late 1970s. By one estimate, overall membership density declined by more than half, from 30 to 14 per cent, between 1975 and 1991 (Labbé 1994: 148). Another factor, ironically, was the impact of the government's own labour reforms, notably the Auroux laws, which encouraged a decentralization of negotiations concerning wages and working conditions from national, regional, and federational arenas to the firm level. On balance, this trend tended to give employers greater discretion than before in determining wages, working hours, and working conditions, while increasingly weakening union leverage (Howell 1992).

Probably the most important factor that sapped the unions' ability to contest the government's employment policies was the failure of the CGT and CFDT to forge any kind of co-operative relationship. After working together under a formal agreement from 1966 to 1979, the two unions split bitterly, and thereafter remained locked in cold war, making concerted action virtually impossible. This split stemmed from both political and programmatic differences. Whereas the CGT remained closely tied to the Communist Party, and tended to subordinate its action to the PCF's political goals, the CFDT vigorously defended its political independence and concentrated on workplace issues. Moreover, the CFDT took a more conciliatory line regarding employment issues, arguing that job cuts were sometimes necessary, but that they should be negotiated with management in exchange for retraining programmes and job placement agencies that the unions themselves could help administer. The CGT, on the other hand, rejected such views, holding that the employment crisis was largely a capitalist plot to boost profits. Given these profound differences in perspective, the two unions appeared to struggle as much against each other as against the government or employers.

CONCLUSION

This analysis has argued that in response to growing unemployment in the 1980s, Socialist governments under Mitterrand and González ultimately adopted generally similar economic strategies. Both governments sought to establish favourable conditions for capitalist investment, encourage the modernization of industrial firms, and create more jobs only as a long-term goal. Temporary unemployment was viewed as a regrettable but unavoidable by-product of this process, and both governments gave the green light to firms to proceed with layoffs. The governments' principal labour-market role then became the crafting of measures to ensure the 'orderly exit' of those workers affected, with the primary mechanism being a form of attrition whereby older workers would be 'retired' early and not replaced. Some public expenditures were devoted to active labour-market policies such as regional reindustrialization, worker retraining and 'reinsertion,' and the like, but most measures were passive ones providing forms of income support. On balance, these programmes were not notably different from those adopted by other western European governments of varying partisan composition (Houseman 1991).

This comparison also indicates that the paths by which these governments arrived at these strategies differed strikingly: the PSOE government pursued this approach consistently from the outset, whereas the PS government underwent a wrenching reversal in 1982-83. Given these contrasting trajectories, it is not surprising that the internal dynamics of their respective coalitions would also differ. The core of this paper has sought to analyze those dynamics with respect to a central economic problem, unemployment. To state the contrast in capsule form: in France, intra-coalitional conflict vis-à-vis unemployment tended to be concentrated within the PS and between the PS and PCF, not between the government and organized labour, whereas in Spain, disputes occurred chiefly between the PSOE government and organized labour, not within the PSOE or between the PSOE and the Communists.

One final question needs to be addressed: What difference did these contrasting patterns of conflict make? The answer is nuanced. On the one hand, the Spanish union's greater mobilization did make some difference in terms of the conditions of labour adjustment in many industries. There is evidence, for example, that in Spain adjustment (i.e., layoffs) was delayed and income-support and other measures were increased because of union pressure. In such industries as steel and automobiles, Spanish unions mounted widely-supported protest campaigns that wrested concessions from the government. Union influence in France was considerably weaker, due mainly to the problems of organization and mobilization discussed previously (Smith 1998: 154-209).

On the other hand, what is striking in both cases is that, in the final analysis, these contrasting patterns are not associated with substantially different policy outcomes. Stated otherwise, in both France and Spain, conflict within their respective coalitions over unemployment (and economic policy generally) did not prevent Mitterrand and González from pursuing a market-adapting approach that succeeded in reducing inflation, deregulating financial institutions, and shifting income to firms, but manifestly failed to reduce unemployment and in fact increased it. Such an outcome suggests the importance of two countervailing factors: international pressures and the progressive insulation of Socialist leaders from coalitional influences. There is no denying that international economic constraints, notably each nation's obligations within the EU's Exchange Rate Mechanism, severely limited the Socialists' policy options. The PSOE government willingly accepted those constraints from the outset, and French Socialists did so, perhaps grudgingly but dutifully, in March 1983. In so doing, the prospects for any autonomous national solution to the employment crisis became virtually impossible.

But just as crucial is the extent to which Socialist leaders succeeded in using their governmental positions to progressively separate themselves from their own political base, especially from organized labour. In both France and Spain, the unemployment issue highlights the veritable gulf that developed between left political leadership and the union movement. To some extent, that gulf was inevitable, given the natural tension between broader economic constraints and labour's interest in defending employment. Yet the creation of this gulf was also the result of a political choice, a decision by Socialist leaders to restructure their own governing coalitions so as to marginalize organized labour's voice. In this tendency French and Spanish leaders were not alone; similar trends characterize left party-union relations in nations as disparate as Sweden and Britain (Pontusson 1992; Wickham-Jones 1995). These experiences suggest that a major casualty of Europe's unemployment crisis may be the dissolution of the fraternal party-labour relationship that has sustained European social democracy for the past century.

NOTES

1. In France, François Mitterrand was elected president in 1981, re-elected in 1988, and served until May 1995. During the first 12 years of his presidency (through the 1993 legislative elections, which the right won decisively), his *Parti Socialiste* (PS) controlled the parliament in all but two years (1986-88). Although Gaullist leader Jacques Chirac won the 1995 presidential election, his conservative coalition lost its parliamentary majority to the Socialists in the May 1997 elections. Since then, Chirac has had to 'co-habit' with Socialist prime minister, Lionel Jospin. In Spain, Felipe González and his Socialist party (PSOE) won four consecutive elections (1982, 1986, 1989, 1993), albeit with steadily declining margins. In March 1996 elections, the PSOE was defeated by the conservative Popular Party, after nearly 14 years in office.
2. Wage rigidity is linked to several aspects of the country's labour relations system, including the inertia of a centralized bargaining and wage-setting system, the maintenance of high pay levels within public enterprises (given traditions of strong unionism and public bailouts), the wide use of indexation (upwards of 90 per cent of workers are covered by agreements containing indexation clauses), and the rapid escalation of non-wage labour costs (OECD 1994: 68-83).
3. Social democrats often point to the landmark 1959 Bad Godesberg conference of the German Social Democratic Party as the turning point in that party's post-war history. At the conference the SPD disavowed Marxism and class struggle while embracing a market-based economy.

REFERENCES

Bergounioux, A. and G. Grunberg (1992): *Le long remords du pouvoir: le parti socialiste français,* Paris: Fayard.

Blanchard, O. and P.A. Muet (1993): 'Competitiveness Through Disinflation: An Assessment of the French Macroeconomic Strategy', *Economic Policy* 16, pp.12-56.

Boix, C. (1998): *Political Parties, Growth and Equality: Conservative and Social Democratic Economic Strategies in the World Economy*, Cambridge: Cambridge University Press.

Cayrol, R. (1978): 'Le Parti Socialiste à l'entreprise', *Revue Française de Science Politique* 28/2, pp.296-312.

Cornilleau, G. (1994): 'Données de base sur le chômage en Europe', in P.A. Muet, *Le Chômage persistant en Europe*, Paris: Presses de la FNSP.

Espina, A. (1991): *Empleo, democracia, y relaciones industriales en España*, Madrid: Ministerio de Trabajo y Seguridad Social.

Favier, P. and M. Martin-Roland (1990): *Le décennie Mitterrand: Tome 1, Les ruptures*, Paris: Seuil.

Gillespie, R. (1989): *The Spanish Socialist Party: A History of Factionalism*, Oxford: Clarendon Press.

Holcman, R. (1997): *Le chômage: Mécanismes économiques, conséquences sociales et humaines*, Paris: La Documentation Française.

Houseman, S.N. (1991): *Industrial Restructuring with Job Security: The Case of European Steel*, Cambridge, MA: Harvard University Press.

Howell, C. (1992): *Regulating Labor: The State and Industrial Relations Reform in Postwar France*, Princeton, NJ: Princeton University Press.

Labbé, D. (1994): 'Trade Unionism in France Since the Second World War', *West European Politics* 17/1, pp.146-68.

Liaisons Sociales (1998): '35 heures: Loi d'orientation et d'incitation relative à la réduction du temps du travail', 7864 (May 25), pp.1-15.

López-Claros, A. (1992): *The Search for Efficiency in the Adjustment Process: Spain in the 1980s*, Washington, D.C.: International Monetary Fund.

López-Pintor, R. (1985): 'The October 1982 General Election and the Evolution of the Spanish Party System', in H.R. Penniman and E. Mujal-León (eds), *Spain at the Polls, 1977, 1979, and 1982*, Durham, NC: Duke University Press, pp.293-313.

McDonough, P., S.H. Barnes and A. López Pina (1998): *The Cultural Dynamics of Democratization in Spain*, Ithaca, NY: Cornell University Press.

Maravall, J.M. (1985): *La política de la transición*, Madrid: Taurus, 2nd edn.

Maruani, M. and E. Reynaud (1993): *Sociologie de l'emploi*, Paris: Editions la Découverte.

Nash, E. (1983): 'The Spanish Socialist Party Since Franco: From Clandestinity to Government, 1976-1982', in D.S. Bell (ed.), *Democratic Politics in Spain: Spanish Politics After Franco*, London: Frances Pinter, pp.29-62.

OECD [Organisation for Economic Co-operation and Development] (1986): *Economic Surveys: Spain*, Paris: OECD.

OECD (1992): *Economic Surveys: France*, Paris: OECD.

OECD (1994): *Economic Surveys: Spain*, Paris: OECD.

OECD (1994a): *Economic Outlook*, 56 (December), Paris: OECD.

OECD (1998): *Economic Surveys: Spain*, Paris: OECD.

Pérez-Díaz, V.M. (1980): *Clase obrera, partidos, y sindicatos*, Madrid: Fundación del INI.

Pontusson, J. (1992): *The Limits of Social Democracy: Investment Politics in Sweden*, Ithaca, NY: Cornell University Press.

Przeworski, A. (1985): *Capitalism and Social Democracy*, Cambridge: Cambridge University Press.

Ross, G. and J. Jenson (1981): 'Strategy and Contradiction in the Victory of French Socialism', in R. Miliband and J. Saville (eds), *The Socialist Register 1981*, London: Merlin, pp.71-103.

Ross, G. and J. Jenson (1985): 'Pluralism and the Decline of Left Hegemony: The French Left in Power', *Politics & Society* 14/2, pp.147-183.

Santesmases, A. G. (1985): 'Evolución ideológica del socialismo en la España actual', *Sistema* 68-69, pp.61-78.

Scharpf, F. (1991): *Crisis and Choice in European Social Democracy*, Ithaca: Cornell University Press.

Share, D. (1985): 'Two Transitions: Democratisation and the Evolution of the Spanish Socialist Left', *West European Politics* 8/1, pp.82-103.

Smith, W.R. (1998): *The Left's Dirty Job: The Politics of Industrial Restructuring in France and Spain*, Pittsburgh: University of Pittsburgh Press and Toronto: University of Toronto Press.

Wickham-Jones, M. (1995): 'Anticipating Social Democracy, Preempting Expectations: Economic Policy-Making in the British Labor Party, 1987-1992', *Politics & Society* 23/4, pp.465-94.

Political Crises and Unemployment: Popular Perceptions in Post-Revolution Portugal

MARIO BACALHAU and THOMAS BRUNEAU

This article reviews data from three nation-wide surveys conducted in Portugal between 1978 and 1993 on public perceptions about unemployment and responses to 'crisis' situations. The responses show that unemployment looms large in a commonly held definition of 'crisis', and that the attitude of the unemployed sets them apart from those with jobs. By focusing on the term 'crisis', it is hoped that the chapter will convey a broad sense of how the Portuguese population has evolved in their understanding of economic, political and social problems.

Indeed, the surveys were undertaken by both authors in order to 'gauge' the political opinions and behaviour of the Portuguese population from the period of transition from authoritarian rule to the consolidation of democracy. The data are drawn from three public opinion surveys covering the whole of continental Portugal, but excluding the two island archipelagos of the Azores and Madeira. The first survey was conducted in 1978 during the less than year long second constitutional government, an awkward coalition between the social democratic Socialist Party (*Partido Socialista*, PS) and conservative and Catholic Social Democratic Center Party (CDS). The second survey was conducted in 1984 during the ninth constitutional government, constituted by the so-called Central Bloc (*Bloco Central*) government of the PS and liberal oriented Social Democratic Party (*Partido Social Democratico*, PSD) that lasted for two years. The third and final survey was conducted in 1993 during the twelfth constitutional government, the second majority government of the PSD, which, like the previous PSD government, lasted a full term of four years.[1] In contrast with the period immediately before and after it, however, this was a time of recession with a negative Gross Domestic Product (GDP) of about 1.2 per cent, even if politically stable.

It is necessary to place the research in a broader context of transition to democracy and democratic consolidation. Two things are especially important: first Portugal underwent a revolution, which culminated in the consolidation of its democracy. Second, the country has one of the lowest unemployment rates in the European Union (EU). In the second quarter of 1997, it stood at 6.6 per cent , compared with the EU average of 10.7 per cent.[2]

The coup of 25 April 1974 came about because of the unwillingness of the junior officers assembled in the Armed Forces Movement (*Movimento das Forcas Armadas*, MFA) to continue fighting to preserve the Portuguese colonies in Africa. The coup and the political events it unleashed led to a rapid process of de-colonization and to a revolution within Portugal. Up until then, there had been virtually no opportunities for democratic participation in political life for 50 years, as the structures and processes for political participation were lacking. In less than two years, Portugal lost a 500 year old colonial empire, witnessed major transformations in all sectors of its economy and society, and experienced great political turbulence. The Armed Forces, which split into several factions, and the Portuguese Communist Party (*Partido Comunista Portugues*, PCP) played central roles in these turbulent times. It was only gradually, and in the face of great resistance that the more democratic political parties emerged and began to struggle for power. The economy was severely affected by de-colonization, revolution and political strife, as well as by the return of about 600,000 refugees from Africa, at a time when Portugal had a total population of less than 9 million.[3]

The political situation gradually stabilized as a result of a combination of events involving domestic and international actors. In 1976, a new constitution defined the parameters of the political system, which contained a number of undemocratic features. In 1982, a constitutional revision led to the elimination of the military-dominated Revolutionary Council (Concelho da Revoluçao, CR), such that Portugal became what can be considered a consolidated democracy.

Economic stabilization was initiated with the aid of two IMF programs (1977-78 and 1983-84 respectively) and stability finally began to take root in 1986, with Portugal's accession to the European Economic Community (EEC), which paved the way for major transfers of resources and foreign investment.[4] In 1989, another constitutional revision led to the abolition of 'socializing' provisions that had governed the economy. By 1991, when the second PSD government was in power, the political and economic systems were fairly stable. The first two surveys were conducted in this context, prior to accession to the EEC, while the third was undertaken during the recession in 1993.

It should be remembered that Portugal was the poorest and most underdeveloped country in western Europe at the time of the revolution. There was no 'scientific organization of labour', the unions had little capacity to negotiate salaries, work conditions and labour relations. Consumption levels were low due to low wages, and wage income was often supplemented by agricultural cultivation for self-consumption, small trade, handicraft making, as well as remittances from emigrants. Welfare was incipient and education levels low, as were opportunities for training for productivity and specialization. There were great obstacles to geographic and professional mobility. The industrial and agricultural sectors were unequally developed, leading to de-capitalization and impoverishment in the latter. Internal competition was restricted by the so-called 'industrial conditioning' mechanisms. The colonies supplied raw materials and engaged in low-technology level production, while an increasing association between domestic monopolies and foreign capital allowed for technological improvement and entry into new markets.[5]

It was only in the 1960s that very modest reforms were initiated to permit collective agreements on wages and to expand parts of the social welfare system. After the revolution in 1974, extensive changes and improvements were introduced regarding union rights, collective bargaining, minimum wages and social security, among other reforms, many of which were included in the 1976 constitution. Among them were the imposition of limits on individual and collective hiring and firing, the establishment of minimum and maximum wages, paid vacations, and the payment of a 14th monthly wage. It also expanded other benefits such as unemployment and retirement payments, a shorter working week and increased access to public and private education.

As Portugal prepared for and finally acceded to the EEC in 1986, major changes were made to the organization of productive sectors and all aspects of employment. The EEC provided fairly specific guidelines as well as financial and other support to facilitate the transformation of what was a poor underdeveloped country into one that could compete within what later became the European Union (EU). The emphasis on the interests of business or labour shifted, however, depending on the government in power. In 1996, for example, the incoming PS government stressed 'social obligations' regarding labour and the unemployed, focusing on professional development and the utilization of regional resources for the creation of jobs and firms. Funds from the EU played a central role in supporting this emphasis.

UNEMPLOYMENT

Before 1974 the concept of unemployment had little meaning. Indeed, studies undertaken before that year did not even mention the term, with the unemployed being included in a wider group of 'non-active' individuals such as those on pensions and retired. This can be explained by the reduced number of people receiving wages in what was a semi-industrial economy and by the absorption of surplus labour in the 1950s and 1960s by emigration and the military draft. Unemployment exploded after 1974, as a result of the revolution coinciding with the oil shock, the massive return of refugees from Africa, and the loss of the colonies and the more developed countries as a destination for surplus labour.

Unemployment increased rapidly from 1.3 per cent of the active population (about 3,620,000 people) in the first half of 1974 to 3.5 per cent in the first half of 1975. It increased again to 6.1 per cent in the first half of 1976, 7.1 per cent in 1977, 7.9 per cent in 1978, 8.3 per cent in 1979, 7.6 per cent in 1980, 8.8 per cent in 1981, and 7.6 per cent in 1985. In the first half of 1995 unemployment stood at 7.3 per cent, remained the same in 1996, and declined in 1997 to 6.6 per cent. The importance of these admittedly relatively low figures increased greatly for the public, given limited state support for the unemployed. Surveys and anecdotal evidence show that despite the various efforts to create jobs, and alternative sources of income sought by people in small agricultural activities and the 'grey' market, unemployment has remained a major concern for the population.

It should be noted that the public expects the state to play a central role in the resolution of the unemployment problem. The role the state has to play ranges from macroeconomic policy to determining legal and organizational issues. This is in large part due to the fact that unions and employers' organizations have an unstable and weak social and economic basis and must therefore rely on the action of either political parties or the state. Because of the central role ascribed to the state, the ideology and political action of political parties place a great deal of emphasis on the problem of employment and unemployment. Indeed, the data shows that the public's definition of 'crisis' is closely linked to the issue of unemployment and that the jobless tend to have opinions that distinguish them from the employed.

Perceptions of 'Crisis'

The response to the question of whether there is a 'crisis' in Portuguese society has been pretty constant over time. Table 1 shows how all those over 18 years of age responded to the question of whether they thought Portuguese society faced a 'crisis'.

TABLE 1
IS THERE A CRISIS?

	1978	1984	1993
Yes	63.2	93.2	80.1
No	5.3	1.3	9.3
Do not know	27.5	5.0	9.5
No response	3.9	0.6	1.1
Base (thousands)	6091	6481	7948

Source: Bacalhau (1978), Bruneau and Macleod (1986), and Bacalhau (1994).

Table 2 shows how, regardless of their employment status, a majority of people in all groups felt there is was crisis in 1993.

TABLE 2
IS THERE A CRISIS? (BY OCCUPATION)

	Self-employed	Salaried	Unemployed	Retired	Student	Housewives
Yes	81.3	83.2	83.6	74.4	86.8	76.3
No	8.4	8.1	8.2	12.0	9.7	9.0
DNK	8.7	7.6	6.8	12.0	3.5	13.6
NR	1.6	0.7	1.4	1.7	0.0	1.1
Base	310	680	73	484	144	279

Source: **Bacalhau (1978)**, Bruneau and Macleod (1986), and Bacalhau (1994).

Table 3 shows how more people that placed themselves on the left than those who placed themselves on the right of the political spectrum thought that there was a crisis facing Portuguese society in 1993.

Table 4 shows how responses appear to be linked to whether respondents voted for the party in power or not. In 1978 and 1993 those who reported voting for the PCP thought there was a crisis in both periods, while voters for other parties adopted different responses in 1978 and 1993. In 1978 those who reported voting for the PS were less inclined to think there was a crisis. The same is true in 1993 for PSD and CDS voters.

Table 5 shows that respondents considered unemployment, including lack of employment opportunities, to be the most serious 'crisis' in 1978

TABLE 3
IS THERE A CRISIS? (BY POLITICAL AFFILIATION)

	Extreme Right	Right	Centre Right	Centre Left	Left	Extreme Left
Yes*	2.0	16.2	23.0	22.8	17.0	0.6
No*	2.0	30.2	26.4	13.4	6.5	0.0
DNK	2.2	15.0	18.9	16.4	9.4	0.1
NR	0.0	24.0	16.9	4.4	11.2	0.0
Total	2.0	18.0	22.9	21.3	15.2	0.6

· Yes: 1+2+3 = 41.2 % - 4+5+6= 40.4% and No: 1+2+3 = 58.4 % - 4+5+6= 19.9%

Source: Bacalhau (1978), Bruneau and Macleod (1986), and Bacalhau (1994).

TABLE 4
IS THERE A CRISIS? (BY PARTY AFFILIATION/YEAR)

	PCP		PS		PSD		CDS		None	
Year	1978	1993	1978	1993	1978	1993	1978	1993	1978	1993
Yes	78.6	92.7	65.2	8.3	70.7	75.4	66.8	86.3	71.8	82.0
No	5.0	2.7	11.1	5.1	11.8	15.1	1.0	4.9	7.0	7.8
DNK	10.8	3.6	22.1	6.3	14.8	8.5	30.8	8.3	19.4	10.2
NR	5.6	1.0	1.6	0.4	2.7	0.9	2.1	0.5	1.8	0
Base (1000)	480	251	936	2232	450	1549	532	179	769	259

Source: Bacalhau (1978), Bruneau and Macleod (1986), and Bacalhau (1994).

TABLE 5
WHAT IS THE MOST SERIOUS PROBLEM?

	1978	1984	1993
Unemployment	29.5	33.8	56.9
Other*	68.1	59.4	36.4
DNK/NR	2.4	6.8	6.7

Source: Bacalhau (1978), Bruneau and Macleod (1986), and Bacalhau (1994).

(29.5 per cent) and 1993 (56.9 per cent), and the second most important problem in 1984 (33.8 per cent). In 1993, unemployment was overwhelmingly the most important issue; it was cited approximately five times more frequently than the next most important problem, inflation.

In 1978, the other most cited problems were the economic situation (29 per cent), lack of money (4 per cent), increase in the cost of living (26 per cent), social disorder (3 per cent), disagreement among the parties (3 per cent), lack of food (3 per cent) and the external debt (3 per cent). In 1984 they were inflation/lack of food (49 per cent), the delayed payment of wages (3 per cent), the external debt (7 per cent), the decrease in productivity (6 per cent) and housing (4 per cent). Finally, in 1993 the main problems were inflation (12 per cent), low wages (4 per cent), housing (1 per cent), the failure of businesses (3 per cent), low agricultural growth (3 per cent), education (1 per cent), lack of food and impoverishment (3 per cent) and decreasing standard of living (5 per cent).

Table 6 shows what the public thought was the most serious problem according to their employment status in 1993. Respondents were asked to indicate to what extent they agreed that unemployment or other issues where the main problems affecting Portuguese society.

TABLE 6
WHAT ARE THE MAIN PROBLEMS? (BY OCCUPATION)

	Self-employed	Salaried	Unemployed	Retired	Student	Housewives
Unemployment	58.3	62.1	68.9	46.7	51.8	55.9
Other	35.3	32.0	26.2	45.2	44.8	34.7
DNK/NR	6.4	5.9	4.9	8.1	4.0	9.4
Base	310	680	73	484	144	279

Source: Bacalhau (1978), Bruneau and Macleod (1986), and Bacalhau (1994).

Table 7 shows the link between views on which party was best prepared to govern the country and an emphasis on unemployment as the key problem facing Portuguese society. In 1993, for example, those that considered the PCP most able to govern considered unemployment the most important problem. Those favouring government by other parties did not place as much emphasis on unemployment. Respondents were asked to say which was the most important problem facing Portuguese society, according to political party sympathies.

Reasons for the Crisis

Table 8 shows what respondents thought was the cause of the country's main problems. Most felt that 'bad government' and the 'world economic crisis' were the main causes. Indeed, the importance attributed to these causes grew between 1984 and 1993. It is notable that respondents gave such a broad range of reasons for current problems, including the nationalization of businesses in the revolutionary period, strikes,

TABLE 7
WHAT ARE THE MAIN PROBLEMS? (BY PARTY AFFILATION/YEAR)

	PCP		PS		PSD		CDS		None	
Year	1984	1993	1984	1993	1984	1993	1984	1993	1984	1993
Unemployment	15.9	62.6	27.5	58.7	31.1	59.1	32.5	54.2	29.9	62.6
Other	82.7	36.6	64.8	35.3	61.2	34.5	63.9	39.6	64.7	29.6
DNK/NR	1.4	0.8	4.7	6.0	7.7	6.4	3.6	6.2	5.4	7.8
Base	561	271	1570	2529	755	2054	346	207	854	410

Source: Bacalhau (1978), Bruneau and Macleod (1986), and Bacalhau (1994).

TABLE 8
WHAT ARE THE CAUSES OF PROBLEMS?

	1984	1993
Government	20.4	27.8
World economic crisis	20.2	31.5
Managerial class	4.0	5.4
Accession to the EEC		4.4
Parties	7.9	1.0
AR		2.5
President	0.1	0.9
The Revolution of 1974	4.1	1.4
Nationalization	8.0	3.2
Privatization		1.1
Unions		1.6
Professional associations		1.1
Capitalist class		0.7
Strikes	9.1	1.6
Other	2.1	0.8
NR	24.1	15.0

Source: Bacalhau (1978), Bruneau and Macleod (1986), and Bacalhau (1994).

ineffective parties in 1983 (a period of party and political instability), and finally accession to the EEC and poor government in 1993.

Table 9 shows that there was a very strong link between respondents' views on the main causes of current problems and their employment status in 1993. The unemployed blamed the government most of all, far above any other cause.

Table 10 shows to whom respondents attributed responsibility for the problems facing Portuguese society according to political party

TABLE 9
WHAT ARE THE CAUSES OF PROBLEMS? (BY OCCUPATION)

	Self-employed	Salaried	Unemployed	Retired	Student	Housewives
Government	24.2	31.7	37.7	24.2	20.8	27.7
World economic crisis	33.3	31.3	24.6	33.3	48.8	24.4
Capitalist class	5.6	6.3	9.8	3.9	6.4	4.2
Accession to EEC	6.3	5.3	4.9	1.7	6.4	8.8
Other	19.5	12.5	14.8	14.7	13.6	13.3
DNK/NR	11.1	12.9	8.2	22.2	4.0	21.6

Source: Bacalhau (1978), Bruneau and Macleod (1986), and Bacalhau (1994).

sympathies or affiliation. Between 1984 and 1993, with the exception of PSD and, to a lesser extent, CDS, voters blamed the government, specifically the PSD government of Prime Minister Cavaco Silva. The data shows that the causes of social problems vary widely according to political party affiliation, as do views about which problems are the most important.

Responsibility for Resolving Problems

Table 11 shows what respondents thought was the solution for resolving the problems facing Portuguese society. Respondents began to point to the government as the agent to solve problems only after its stabilization. Until 1987, neither the government nor the political parties were stable. In this context, respondents pointed to a wide range of actors or actions in 1984 and many (32.7 per cent) either did not know how to respond or declined to do so. Thus, the emphasis on governmental solutions after 1984 represents a major shift in attitudes.

Table 12 shows that the unemployed, much like all other groups in 1993, point to the government (60.7 per cent) to resolve social problems. The relatively high percentage of references to the presidency can be explained by its being considered the power of last resort. The EU also figures large, revealing an awareness of international factors and the expectation that integration could solve economic problems.

Table 13 reveals that in 1993, respondents differed over who they consider responsible for resolving social problems according to party-preferences. Those favouring parties in opposition to the PSD, in power at the time, pointed to the government more frequently. Thus, 68.6 per cent of PS supporters held that it was up to the government to resolve social problems, in contrast with 57.4 per cent of PSD supporters.

TABLE 10
WHAT ARE THE CAUSES OF PROBLEMS? (BY PARTY AFFILATION/YEAR)

	PCP		PS		PSD		CDS		None	
Year	1984	1993	1984	1993	1984	1993	1984	1993	1984	1993
Government*	50.1		17.4		20.5		17.1		18.6	
C. Silva	66.0		41.8		6.8		18.6		26.1	
World economic crisis	11.2	4.9	28.7	26.9	23.4	37.5	11.9	37.8	20.2	20.6
Managerial class	10.4	9.9	5.4	6.1	0.7	5.3	1.5	2.2	2.1	5.0
Accession to EEC	0.0	3.9	0.0	3.5	0.0	5.1	0.0	7.3	0.0	5.8
1976 Constitution	3.2	0.0	0.1	0.0	0.0	0.0	0.0	0.0	0.0	0.0
Parties	7.5	0.0	10.6	0.8	3.6	1.3	7.4	3.2	7.2	0.1
AR	0.0	1.5	0.0	0.1	0.0	4.5	0.0	5.6	0.0	7.3
President	0.0	0.0	0.0	0.0	0.0	0.6	0.0	0.6	0.0	3.4
Revolution	0.0	0.0	3.4	0.4	4.8	2.1	13.3	5.1	6.3	1.7
Nationalization	2.1	0.0	5.8	3.8	15.3	8.5	20.3	3.4	8.2	1.2
Privatization	0.0	2.3	0.0	0.5	0.0	1.5	0.0	0.0	0.0	2.4
Unions	0.0	0.0	0.0	0.6	0.0	5.0	0.0	3.40	0.0	0.3
Prof. associations	0.0	1.4	0.0	1.0	0.0	0.5	0.0	0.0	0.0	0.4
Capitalist class	0.0	1.4	0.0	.5	0.0	0.5	0.0	0.0	0.0	0.0
Strikes	3.2	0.5	10.3	1.5	12.9	3.7	11.2	3.0	11.1	3.3
Other	1.3	0.0	0.2	0.3	1.0	1.2	1.0	6.0	4.8	0.8
DNK/NR	11.0	8.2	18.1	10.3	17.8	15.9	16.3	3.8	21.5	21.9

Sources: Bacalhau (1978), Bruneau and Macleod (1986), and Bacalhau (1994).
Includes Vasco Goncalves, Mario Soares, PS/CDS and PS/PSD coalition governments.

TABLE 11
WHAT ARE SOLUTIONS TO THESE PROBLEMS?

	1984	1993
Government		60.7
A new government	9.7	
Legislature		5.0
President		4.1
A more powerful president	9.2	
Political parties		1.6
Capitalist class		5.1
Nationalisation	3.2	
Accession to the EEC		12.2
Workers		1.6
Prohibition of strikes	14.1	
Privatization	12.9	
No privatisation	1.2	
Government aid for nationalisation	9.4	
Increased production	3.9	
Increased investments	1.8	
Others	3.2	
DNK/NR	32.7	10.6

Sources: Bacalhau (1978), Bruneau and Macleod (1986), and Bacalhau (1994).

TABLE 12
WHAT ARE SOLUTIONS TO THESE PROBLEMS? (BY OCCUPATION)

	Self-employed	Salaried	Unemployed	Retired	Students	Housewives
Government	60.7	60.9	60.7	60.0	60.0	61.0
Legislature	5.6	5.5	3.3	4.7	5.6	4.2
President	1.6	2.8	6.6	3.6	1.6	4.2
Parties	0.8	2.5	0.0	0.8	1.6	1.9
Cap. class	4.8	3.9	6.6	7.6	6.4	4.7
EU	16.2	14.4	16.4	6.1	16.8	8.0
Workers	0.8	1.6	1.6	1.4	2.4	2.8
DNK/NR	9.5	8.5	4.9	15.8	5.6	13.6

Source: Bacalhau (1978), Bruneau and Macleod (1986), and Bacalhau (1994).

The above indicates that there are great variations of opinion regarding the main social problems are, their causes and the actors that respondents feel are most likely to solve social problems, according to their political preferences.

TABLE 13
WHAT ARE SOLUTIONS TO THESE PROBLEMS? (BY PARTY AFFILIATION)

	PCP	PS	PSD	CDS	None
Government	67.0	68.6	57.4	64.5	53.3
Legislature	7.2	4.7	4.2	4.5	7.8
Parties	2.8	0.7	2.4	0.7	1.9
EU	5.8	10.8	13.3	14.8	12.3
Cap. class	5.4	5.0	7.7	5.1	4.1
Workers	0.3	1.2	1.8	0.0	0.8
Presidency	6.8	4.2	0.8	5.2	3.1
Others	0.0	0.4	2.0	0.6	0.8
DNK/NR	4.6	4.5	10.3	4.6	15.5

Source: Bacalhau (1978), Bruneau and Macleod (1986), and Bacalhau (1994).

THE UNEMPLOYED

Table 14 shows how those surveyed respond to six statements about the political parties and how those who are unemployed hold different views from all other groups. More specifically, they are consistently less impressed with the positive aspects of political parties. It is possible to argue that this scepticism stems from the inability of the parties to resolve the country's problems and lack of employment in particular. The table uses a scale in which 5 indicates a high level of agreement and 1 complete disagreement.

Table 15 shows how the unemployed give the lowest scores to an Index of Democracy, which the authors constructed on the basis of questions, compared with all the other groups.

We developed an index of Democracy based on the sum of three different questions. The unemployed have the lowest level of any of the six employment status groups. These data are displayed in Table 16.

As shown in Table 15, the unemployed indicated in 1993 that they intended predominantly to vote for the PS and PSD, but also report that they intended to vote for the PCP more than any other group.

CONCLUSION

The data from the three surveys, undertaken during the 15 years in which Portuguese democracy was gradually consolidated and major economic and social changes took place, provide some indications of the political impact of unemployment. The surveys show that unemployment is clearly politically important. The population perceives unemployment as

TABLE 14
EVALUATIONS OF POLITICAL PARTIES BY EMPLOYMENT STATUS

	Employment Status					
	Self-Employed	Employed	Unemployed	Retired	Students	Domicile
Parties are only good for dividing people	3.3	3.2	3.4	3.4	3.2	3.6
Parties defend the interests of certain groups	4.0	4.0	4.0	4.0	4.1	4.0
Parties are all the same	3.9	3.5	3.6	3.6	3.6	3.8
It is thanks to parties that people can participate in politics	4.1	4.2	3.7	4.1	4.9	4.0
Without parties there cannot be democracy in Portugal	4.0	4.3	3.8	4.1	4.1	4.1
Parties are good for nothing	2.0	1.9	2.1	2.1	1.9	2.0
N	310	680	73	481	144	279

Source: Bacalhau (1978), Bruneau and Macleod (1986), and Bacalhau (1994).

TABLE 15
EVALUATIONS OF PORTUGUESE DEMOCRACY BY EMPLOYMENT STATUS

Employment status	INDEX				Mean
	++	+	–	– –	
Self-employed	29.0	50.7	17.2	3.2	3.057
Salaried	33.2	48.7	16.4	1.8	3.135
Unemployed	24.5	52.3	20.2	3.0	2.983
Retired	35.5	46.5	16.7	1.3	3.162
Students	41.0	44.9	6.8	7.2	3.195
Housewives	30.2	47.4	18.8	3.6	3.042

Sources: Bacalhau (1978), Bruneau and Macleod (1986), and Bacalhau (1994).

TABLE 16
PARTY AFFILIATION BY OCCUPATION

	Self-employed	Salaried	Unemployed	Retired	Student	Housewife
CDS	4.7	1.2	3.0	4.4	5.3	2.7
PSD	34.5	22.7	19.8	37.5	31.2	34.7
PS	31.6	44.1	38.5	31.5	25.1	39.3
PCP	0.8	4.9	13.4	3.9	2.1	3.4
Other	0.9	1.6	0.7	0.5	2.6	0.4
No vote	2.2	0.8	1.4	1.2	2.9	2.1
None	4.3	5.2	1.0	4.9	8.5	2.4
DNK	20.9	19.5	22.1	16.2	22.3	15.0
Base	310	680	73	481	144	279

Sources: Bacalhau (1978), Bruneau and Macleod (1986), and Bacalhau (1994).

a key social problem, particularly the unemployed themselves. Data on party affiliation and the causes of the country's problems shows that the definition of a crisis is political. It is also clear that the unemployed have different political orientations and voting preferences compared with the rest of the population. For perhaps obvious reasons, they are less positive about political institutions and show the highest preference of any of the groups for the PCP. What is most remarkable is the evolution of popular perceptions of what constitutes a 'crisis' and the growing importance of unemployment in this definition. Originally, the focus of the surveys was not unemployment but rather political institutions and legitimacy, and it was only as a result of the request to contribute to this volume that the data concerning unemployment was analyzed.

In conclusion, a great majority perceives that there is a 'crisis' in Portuguese society and that unemployment is a major component of that crisis. There are major variations according to political orientation regarding the causes of the crisis and its resolution. Finally, those who are unemployed differ substantially from all other groups on key political issues. These results not only make sense but also clearly demonstrate the links between unemployment and political attitudes and beliefs.

NOTES

1. The data from the first survey is reported in Mario Bacalhau, *Os Portugueses e a Politica Quatro Anos Depois do 25 de Abril* (Lisbon: Meseta, 1978); some of the data from the second is found in Thomas Bruneau and Alex Macleod, *Politics in Contemporary Portugal: Parties and the Consolidation of Democracy* (Boulder: Lynne Rienner, 1986); and from the third is found in Mario Bacalhau, *Atitudes, Opinioes e Comportamentos Politicos dos Portugueses: 1973-1993* (Lisbon: Heptagono, 1994). This last book also includes data from the two previous surveys as well as a survey conducted by Dr Bacalhau in 1973. Some of the data from the last survey dealing specifically with political parties is found in Thomas Bruneau, ed., *Political Parties and Democracy in Portugal: Organizations, Elections, and Public Opinion* (Boulder: Westview, 1997.)
2. Vincenzina Santoro, 'The Portuguese Economy Today: The View From Wall Street', *Camoes Center Quarterly* Summer/Fall 1997, p.6.
3. Data and description on all of this can be found in Antonio Reis, (ed.), *Portugal: 20 Anos de Democracia* (Lisbon: Circulo de Leitores, 1994).
4. Santoro states that net funding from all EU facilities grew from 0.5 per cent of GDP in 1986 to an estimated 4.2 per cent in 1996.
5. See Maria Joao Rodrigues, *O Sistema de Emprego em Portugal: Crise e Mutacoes* (Lisboa: Publicacoes D. Quixote, 1966) and idem, *Competitividade e Recursos Humanos*, 1994.

REFERENCES

Bacalhau, Mario (1978):*Os Portugueses e a Politica Quatro Anos Depois do 25 de Abril*, Lisbon: Meseta.

Bacalhau, Mario (1994): *Atitudes, Opinioes e Comportamentos Politicos dos Portugueses: 1973-1993*, Lisbon: Heptagono.

Bruneau, Thomas (ed.) (1997): *Political Parties and Democracy in Portugal: Organizations, Elections, and Public Opinion*, Boulder: Westview.

Bruneau, Thomas and Alex Macleod (1986): *Politics in Contemporary Portugal: Parties and the Consolidation of Democracy*, Boulder: Lynne Rienner.

Reis, Antonio (ed.) (1994): *Portugal: 20 Anos de Democracia*, Lisbon: Circulo de Leitores.

Rodrigues, Maria Joao (1966): *O Sistema de Emprego em Portugal: Crise e Mutacoes*, Lisboa: Publicacoes D. Quixote.

Rodrigues, Maria Joao (1994): *Competitividade e Recursos Humanos*, Lisboa: Publicacoes D. Quixote.

Santoro, Vincenzina (1997):'The Portuguese Economy Today: The View From Wall Street', *Camoes Center Quarterly* Summer/Fall, p.6.

Does Labour Under-Utilization Affect Political Attitudes? Southern Europe in Comparative Perspective

UGO M. AMORETTI

The under-utilization of the labour force is one of the most dramatic problems the European Union (EU) has to face. Since the first oil shock in the early 1970s, Europe has been plagued by a persistent scarcity of jobs which does not look as if it is going to diminish. As Figure 1 shows, the percentage of Europeans unsuccessfully looking for a job has increased over time and is currently more than twice the percentage of unemployed Americans or Japanese. Joblessness reaches dramatically high peaks in the 'South' of southern Europe, where one fourth to one third of the labour force cannot find work.[1] Although proposing different solutions, almost all political parties consider unemployment to be one of the most pressing problems of the day. Likewise, unemployment is one of the main concerns of ordinary citizens, who constantly rank it as the most important issue affecting society (Eurobarometer various issues).

Given this context, it is not surprising that unemployment has attracted the attention of so many social scientists. The large body of literature focusing on this issue can be divided into two broad components: the works dealing with unemployment as a dependent variable, and therefore analyzing the *causes* of unemployment (Hibbs 1977; Lange and Garret 1985; Layard *et al.* 1994; Crepaz 1995; Siebert 1997; Ljungqvist and Sargent 1998); and the works considering unemployment as an independent variable, and thus dealing with its *consequences* (Kiewiet 1983; Lewis-Back 1988; Powell and Whitten 1993; Alesina and Rosenthal 1995). The former examine the effects of

Draft versions of this article have been presented at the Department of Political and Social Science of the University of Genoa and at the Center of International Studies of Princeton University. I am grateful to all those who attended these presentations for their valuable comments. Igal Hendel and Fernando Pérez de Gracia provided me with helpful statistical insights. Special thanks go to Nancy Bermeo and Kruskaia Sierra-Escalante.

FIGURE 1

UNEMPLOYMENT RATES IN THE EU, USA, AND JAPAN 1970–96

Source: Organisation for Economic Co-operation and Development (1986, 1996, and 1998).

politics (chiefly parties and institutions) on the economic performance of a given country, while the latter analyze the impact of the main economic variables – such as the unemployment rate – on political matters, especially voters' behaviour and electoral outcomes.

This literature has provided a better understanding of unemployment and the complex relations existing between economics and politics. Yet, no comparable literature exists for underemployment. The reasons for the inattention to underemployment have deep roots. On the one hand, unemployment statistics and the division of the working age population into *economically active* and *inactive*, on which western countries have been relying upon since the Depression of the 1930s do not lend themselves to examining any form of labour under-utilization other than unemployment.[2] On the other hand, under-utilized members of the labour force have traditionally been – at least until the 1970s – only a small portion of western countries' population, thus having limited appeal to social scientists.

In the pages that follow I try to fill part of the gap outlined above by assessing the magnitude of underemployment as compared to unemployment and analyzing whether both phenomena affect political attitudes in southern Europe.

In the first section I define the two concepts. Then, I sketch some hypotheses about how labour under-utilization may affect political attitudes. In the third section, I estimate the magnitude of unemployment and underemployment, placing the southern European countries in a broader European perspective. The fourth section analyzes how, if at all, the under-utilized members of the labour force differ from the adequately employed in terms of political interest, trust, and ideology. Finally, a concluding section discusses the results and points out the implications for further research.

THE UNDER-UTILIZATION OF LABOUR FORCE: DEFINITIONS

According to the international standard definition of *unemployment*, working-age people can be categorized as unemployed if they are without a job but available to work and actively seeking employment in the considered span of time (Hussmanns 1994: 94). Although this standard definition is not unquestioned, it highlights the main constitutive elements of unemployment: joblessness, availability for work, and willingness to accept employment.

Underemployment is a broad concept embedding several types of labour force under-utilization. According to the International Labour

Organization, underemployment exists when employed people who are not working full-time would be able and willing to work more, or when the income or productivity of employed people would be increased if they worked under improved conditions of production or were transferred to another occupation which takes into account their occupational skills (International Labour Organisation 1964: 22).

As the above definition stresses, underemployment is a multidimensional concept that embodies two broad components (International Labour Organisation 1976: 33-4; Clogg 1979: 3; Nayak 1990: 9; Hussmanns, Mehran and Verma 1990: 121; Hussmanns 1994: 99-104): *visible* underemployment, characterized by an insufficient volume of available work, and *invisible* underemployment, identified by under-utilization of skills, low income, or low productivity.[3] Thus, underemployment actually refers to four very different characteristics of labour under-utilization: the *time* spent working, the *income* derived from it, the *productivity* of the worker and, finally, the *skill* or human capital utilization on the workplace.

Whereas measuring unemployment is a relatively straightforward process, generally based on responses to surveys questioning the interviewee's current job status and willingness to work, underemployment is much harder to measure. With the exception of the time component, which lends itself to a relatively easy quantitative measurement, the other three 'invisible' dimensions of underemployment are qualitative features of work and therefore much more difficult to detect (Clogg 1979: 3).

Even though underemployment has been usually perceived as having particular relevance in developing countries, notably in connection with agriculture (Hopkins 1985; Nayak 1990), it has recently acquired new importance among the industrialized countries because of changes in labour markets (Hussmanns, Mehran and Verma 1990: 122).[4]

HYPOTHESES

Drawing from the existing literature on unemployment and political participation, in this section I propose some hypotheses about the political effects of labour under-utilization. As pointed out by Anderson (2000), many studies have analyzed the effects of economic distress on mental health and psychological well-being, finding that the unemployed are more likely to show low levels of self-confidence, be depressed and be engaged in a variety of deleterious behaviours. Although these studies do not directly examine how unemployment affects political attitudes, they implicitly suggest that the unemployed are likely to be less involved in political activities.

The way unemployment may influence political attitudes, however, is not straightforward. As stated by Schlozman and Verba in the now classic study *Injury to Insult: Unemployment, Class, and Political Response* (1979), unemployment may affect the political attitudes and behaviours of those who experience it by both decreasing and increasing political participation. Joblessness can be an incentive for the unemployed to be more active, especially since their joblessness affords them more free time. Yet, the unemployed could decrease their involvement in politics precisely for the same reason: given their status, they could withdraw from social life, lose self-esteem, and spend all their available time looking for employment or an alternative source of income (Schlozman and Verba 1979: 235-7). Moreover, since political attitudes and behaviours are influenced not only by unemployment but also by other factors (e.g. age, gender, or social status), joblessness may counteract or reinforce the effects produced by the latter, enhancing or lowering an already high or scarce disposition to take part in political life (Schlozman and Verba 1979: 236-7).

Examining political participation in the United States, Schlozman and Verba found that jobless citizens were less likely to take part in political life than employed ones, regardless of whether the measure of participation was political interest, voting, or other political activities. However, these differences were significantly reduced once they controlled for the socio-economic status (SES) of the interviewees, to the point that the lesser of political involvement of the unemployed appeared to be more the consequence of their social background than the result of being out of work (Schlozman and Verba 1979: 349). Brady *et al.* (1998) have recently sustained this conclusion, showing that mid-1990s political participation in the United States is still strongly structured on the basis of the SES and that stratification in political activity is roughly as pronounced as it was in the mid-1970s.

In the European context, but without controlling for the SES, Anderson (2000) has pointed out that, on the whole, in the mid-1990s the unemployed participate less in political life, are less satisfied with the way democracy works in their countries, and are less interested in politics than their employed counterparts. However, unemployment does not seem to lead to political extremism. When compared with the employed, the unemployed place themselves further to the left but are not significantly more likely to be located at the extremes of the political spectrum.

On the basis of the findings of the above studies, in this article I extend the analysis of labour under-utilization by examining – in a broad European perspective – the political effects of both unemployment and underemployment in contemporary southern Europe. Since the underemployed share with the unemployed the experience of being under-utilized, I expect them to be politically less involved and more radical than the fully employed. However, given that the underemployed are at the margin of the labour market but not completely excluded from it, I also expect them to be politically more involved and moderate than the unemployed. Thus, my first hypothesis is that the underemployed should be less interested in politics than the fully employed but more positive than those totally out of work. Secondly, I hypothesize that the underemployed will be less positive about the national government than the employed, but more than those without a job. Finally, the third hypothesis is related to political ideology and predicts that the underemployed will be more extremist than the employed but less extremist than the unemployed.

Summarizing, I expect the negative consequences of labour under-utilization to be stronger for those who are less utilized, thus assuming that under-utilization can be considered an ordinal variable rather than a nominal one.

LABOUR UNDER-UTILIZATION IN SOUTHERN EUROPE: DATA, MEASURES AND SOCIAL FEATURES

In order to test these hypotheses, I use a Eurobarometer data set from 1995 (Eurobarometer 44.1) based on national surveys of mass publics in the fifteen EU member states. Samples include about 1,000 interviewees per country, with the exceptions of Luxembourg (about 500 people), United Kingdom (about 1,300 people), and unified Germany (about 2,000 people).[5] Whereas the whole data set involves almost 15,000 respondents, my working sample is composed of 9,081 interviewees because I consider only those economically active (i.e. employed or unemployed interviewees between 15 and 64 years old, excluding homemakers, students and the retired). The unemployed are identified through a question assessing their occupational status and, at 1,032, amount to 11.4 per cent of the working sample.

TABLE 1
SOCIAL CHARACTERISTICS OF THE UNEMPLOYED, THE UNDEREMPLOYED, AND THE ADEQUATELY EMPLOYED IN THE EUROPEAN UNION

	Unemployed			Underemployed			Adequately Employed		
	% of Total	% of Unem.	N	% of Total	% of Under	N	% of Total	% of Empl.	N
By Occupation									
High Level									
Professionals	1.0	0.2	2	12.1	2.6	24	86.9	2.4	172
Business Proprietors	1.1	0.3	3	13.6	3.9	36	85.2	3.2	225
Employed Professionals	6.1	1.4	14	11.3	2.8	26	82.7	2.7	191
General and Top Managers	5.2	1.1	11	9.0	2.1	19	85.8	2.5	181
Medium-High Level									
Middle Managers	4.6	5.1	53	11.5	14.3	132	83.8	13.5	960
Desk Workers	8.4	11.1	115	11.9	17.6	163	79.8	15.4	1097
Supervisors	8.9	1.6	17	6.8	1.4	13	84.3	2.3	161
Medium-Low Level									
Self-Employed	2.8	1.9	20	13.6	10.7	99	83.6	8.5	607
Sales and Transportation Personnel	7.4	3.1	32	10.6	5.0	46	81.9	5.0	354
Employed not at the Desk (service sector)	9.9	11.5	119	10.9	14.2	131	79.1	13.3	949
Low Level									
Farmers and Fishermen	2.6	0.8	8	12.2	4.1	38	85.2	3.7	265
Skilled Manual Workers	15.2	24.5	253	7.5	13.5	125	77.3	18.1	1288
Other Manual Workers	21.5	19.9	205	7.7	7.9	73	70.8	9.5	674
Never Had a Paid Job	100.0	16.1	166	—	—	—	—	—	—
NA	100.0	1.4	14	—	—	—	—	—	—
All Respondents	11.4	100.0	1032	10.2	100.0	925	78.4	100.0	7124
By Gender									
Women	13.9	52.1	538	9.4	39.4	364	76.8	41.9	2982
Men	9.5	47.9	494	10.8	60.6	561	79.7	58.1	4142
All Respondents	11.4	100.0	1032	10.2	100.0	925	78.4	100.0	7124

	Unemployed			Underemployed			Adequately Employed		
	% of Total	% of Unem.	N	% of Total	% of Under	N	% of Total	% of Empl.	N
By Age									
15-24	21.2	25.1	259	8.0	10.6	98	70.8	12.1	865
25-39	10.0	37.2	384	11.7	48.3	447	78.3	42.1	2999
40-54	8.7	26.1	269	10.3	34.6	320	81.0	35.2	2510
55-64	12.9	11.6	120	6.5	6.5	60	80.6	10.5	750
All Respondents	11.4	100.0	1032	10.2	100.0	925	78.4	100.0	7124
By Years of Education									
Less than 5	10.8	2.4	25	—	—	—	89.2	2.9	207
Between 6 and 8	14.6	13.8	142	—	—	—	85.4	11.6	829
Between 9 and 13	12.5	60.0	619	2.0	10.6	98	85.6	59.7	4253
Between 14 and 19	8.2	18.8	194	20.2	51.5	476	71.5	23.6	1682
Greater than 20	9.4	5.0	52	63.1	37.9	351	27.5	2.1	153
All Respondents	11.4	100.0	1032	10.2	100.0	925	78.4	100.0	7124

Source: Eurobarometer (1996).

TABLE 2
SOCIAL CHARACTERISTICS OF THE UNEMPLOYED, THE UNDEREMPLOYED, AND THE ADEQUATELY EMPLOYED IN SOUTHERN EUROPE

	Unemployed			Underemployed			Adequately Employed		
	% of Total	% of Unem.	N	% of Total	% of Under	N	% of Total	% of Empl.	N
By Occupation									
High Level									
Professionals	—	—	—	16.7	3.8	9	83.3	2.9	45
Business Proprietors	—	—	—	12.9	3.4	8	87.1	3.5	54
Employed Professionals	—	—	—	11.8	1.7	4	88.2	1.9	30
General and Top Managers	—	—	—	4.5	0.4	1	95.5	1.4	21
Medium-High Level									
Middle Managers	3.8	2.9	7	11.5	8.8	21	84.7	10.0	155
Desk Workers	6.6	7.6	18	13.6	15.5	37	79.9	14.1	218
Supervisors	7.7	0.4	1	7.7	0.4	1	84.6	0.7	11

	Unemployed			Underemployed			Adequately Employed		
	% of Total	% of Unem.	N	% of Total	% of Under	N	% of Total	% of Empl.	N
Medium-Low Level									
Self-Employed	2.7	4.2	10	15.4	23.5	56	81.9	19.3	298
Sales and Transportation Personnel	9.8	4.2	10	10.8	4.6	11	79.4	5.2	81
Employed not at the Desk (service sector)	10.3	8.0	19	9.8	7.6	18	79.9	9.5	147
Low Level									
Farmers and Fishermen	2.5	1.2	3	12.6	6.3	15	84.9	6.5	101
Skilled Manual Workers	16.3	22.7	54	11.1	15.5	37	72.6	15.6	241
Other Manual Workers	17.9	14.7	35	10.2	8.4	20	71.9	9.1	141
Never Had a Paid Job	100.0	33.6	80	—	—	—	—	—	—
NA	—	0.4	1	—	—	—	—	—	—
All Respondents	11.8	100.0	238	11.8	100.0	238	76.4	100.0	1543
By Gender									
Women	16.1	53.4	127	11.0	36.6	87	72.9	37.3	575
Men	9.0	46.6	111	12.3	63.4	151	78.7	62.7	968
All Respondents	11.8	100.0	238	11.8	100.0	238	76.4	100.0	1543
By Age									
15-24	25.7	34.0	81	11.7	15.5	37	62.5	12.8	197
25-39	12.1	43.7	104	15.0	54.2	129	72.9	40.6	626
40-54	5.7	14.7	35	9.5	24.4	58	84.8	33.7	520
55-64	7.8	7.6	18	6.0	5.9	14	86.2	13.0	200
All Respondents	11.8	100.0	238	11.8	100.0	238	76.4	100.0	1543
By Years of Education									
Less than 5	10.4	9.2	22	—	—	—	89.6	12.3	190
Between 6 and 8	10.3	21.8	52	—	—	—	89.7	29.4	454
Between 9 and 13	13.8	45.8	109	7.8	26.1	62	78.4	40.2	620
Between 14 and 19	11.7	20.6	49	25.8	45.4	108	62.5	17.0	262
Greater than 20	6.6	2.5	6	74.7	28.6	68	18.7	1.1	17
All Respondents	11.8	100.0	238	11.8	100.0	238	76.4	100.0	1543

Source: Eurobarometer (1996).

TABLE 3
SOCIAL CHARACTERISTICS OF THE UNEMPLOYED, THE UNDEREMPLOYED, AND THE ADEQUATELY EMPLOYED IN CENTRAL AND NORTHERN EUROPE

	Unemployed			Underemployed			Adequately Employed		
	% of Total	% of Unem.	N	% of Total	% of Under	N	% of Total	% of Empl.	N
By Occupation									
High Level									
Professionals	1.4	0.3	2	10.4	2.2	15	88.2	2.3	127
Business Proprietors	1.5	0.4	3	13.9	4.1	28	84.7	3.1	171
Employed Professionals	7.1	1.8	14	11.2	3.2	22	81.7	2.9	161
General and Top Managers	5.8	1.4	11	9.5	2.6	18	84.7	2.9	160
Medium-High Level									
Middle Managers	4.8	5.8	46	11.5	16.2	111	83.7	14.4	805
Desk Workers	8.8	12.2	97	11.4	18.3	126	79.8	15.7	879
Supervisors	9.0	2.0	16	6.7	1.7	12	84.3	2.7	150
Medium-Low Level									
Self-Employed	2.8	1.3	10	11.9	6.3	43	85.4	5.5	309
Sales and Transportation Personnel	6.7	2.8	22	10.6	5.1	35	82.7	4.9	273
Employed not at the Desk (service sector)	9.9	12.6	100	11.1	16.4	113	79.0	14.4	802
Low Level									
Farmers and Fishermen	2.6	0.6	5	12.0	3.3	23	85.4	2.9	164
Skilled Manual Workers	14.9	25.1	199	6.6	12.8	88	14.9	18.8	1047
Other Manual Workers	22.5	21.4	170	7.0	7.7	53	70.5	9.6	533
Never Had a Paid Job	100.0	10.8	86	—	—	—	—	—	—
NA	—	1.6	13	—	—	—	—	—	—
All Respondents	11.2	100.0	794	9.7	100.0	687	79.0	100.0	5581
By Gender									
Women	13.3	51.8	411	8.9	40.3	277	77.8	43.1	2407
Men	9.7	48.2	383	10.3	59.7	410	80.0	56.9	3174
All Respondents	11.2	100.0	794	9.7	100.0	687	79.0	100.0	5581

	Unemployed			Underemployed			Adequately Employed		
	% of Total	% of Unem.	N	% of Total	% of Under	N	% of Total	% of Empl.	N
By Age									
15-24	19.6	22.4	178	6.7	8.9	61	73.6	12.0	668
25-39	9.4	35.3	280	10.7	46.3	318	79.9	42.5	2373
40-54	9.4	29.5	234	10.5	38.1	262	80.0	35.7	1990
55-64	14.6	12.8	102	6.6	6.7	46	78.8	9.9	550
All Respondents	11.2	100.0	794	9.7	100.0	687	79.0	100.0	5581
By Years of Education									
Less than 5	15.0	0.4	3	—	—	—	85.0	0.3	17
Between 6 and 8	19.4	11.3	90	—	—	—	80.6	6.7	375
Between 9 and 13	12.2	64.2	510	0.9	5.2	36	86.9	65.1	3633
Between 14 and 19	7.5	18.3	145	19.0	53.6	368	73.5	25.4	1420
Greater than 20	9.9	5.8	46	60.9	41.2	283	29.2	2.4	136
All Respondents	11.2	100.0	794	9.7	100.0	687	79.0	100.0	5581

Source: Eurobarometer (1996).

The employed are classified on the basis of 13 different categories. To assess the extent to which respondents falling within each of these categories are underemployed, I apply the Labour Utilization Framework (LUF) initially proposed by Hauser (1974). According to this approach, a worker is defined as underemployed if his or her education is more than one standard deviation above the mean education in his or her current occupation.[6] As stated earlier, underemployment can be defined in different ways each involving a number of unresolved difficulties. In this article, I specifically focus on *one* of its kinds: the by-product of the mismatch between citizen skills and the jobs available. I suspect this mismatch to be particularly relevant in contemporary EU labour markets.

Educational levels greatly differ across Europe, from an average of more than 16 years in Denmark to an average of less than 9 years in Portugal. Therefore, the cut-off points used to identify the underemployed are determined by adding one standard deviation to the national average levels of education previously calculated for each country.[7]

On the basis of these cut-off points, 918 respondents – equal to 10.1 per cent of the sample – can be classified as over-qualified for their job and hence underemployed by mismatch. Tables 1, 2, and 3 sketch a synthetic portrait of the unemployed and the underemployed as compared to the adequately employed.

In both southern Europe and the EU as a whole, citizens with low and medium-low status occupations have been hardest hit by unemployment. Moreover, the majority of the unemployed are women, have between nine and 13 years of education, and belong to the 25-39 age cohort of the population. However, whereas in southern Europe unemployment is particularly widespread among the young, central and northern countries display a higher percentage of over-40 unemployed. This finding suggests that while in the south one of the main causes of joblessness is the initial barrier to entry into the labour market, in the rest of the EU unemployment is more a long-term issue. In fact, this view is corroborated by looking at the percentage of those who have never had a job, who are more than a third of southern unemployed compared to about a tenth of the unemployed of the other countries.

Contrary to unemployment, underemployment hits men more than women and, by definition, people with higher levels of schooling. Once more, Europeans between the ages of 25 and 39 represent the bulk of under-utilization, while its distribution among the occupational categories is more even, ranging from a relatively low 7.5 per cent among supervisors to a relatively high 14.0 per cent among shop owners and craftsmen.

Table 4 shows the distribution of unemployment and underemployment by country. Not surprisingly, unemployment is slightly higher in southern Europe (11.8 per cent) than in the other EU countries (11.2 per cent). More interestingly, this table shows that underemployment goes from a low 8.0 per cent in Ireland to a high 12.5 per cent in Portugal, with the southern European countries performing once again worse than the rest of the Union. While in southern Europe underemployment is 11.8 per cent, the remaining EU countries have two percentage points lower of mismatched workers (9.7 per cent). It is interesting to note that all the four southern European countries suffer from an underemployment level that is above the EU average. Further, whereas Portugal is the southern European country with the lowest rate of unemployment (9.0 per cent), it is instead the one plagued by the highest rate of underemployment (12.5 per cent). This suggests that, especially in Portugal, people who would otherwise be unemployed find a solution to the lack of proper jobs by taking positions for which they are over-qualified. It further suggests that unemployment and

TABLE 4
UNEMPLOYED AND UNDEREMPLOYED RESPONDENTS BY COUNTRY
(AS PERCENT OF NATIONAL LABOUR FORCE)

Country	Unemployed		Underemployed	
	Percent	N	Percent	N
South	*11.8*	*(238)*	*11.8*	*(238)*
Greece	10.6	(55)	11.9	(63)
Italy	11.5	(55)	11.1	(53)
Portugal	9.0	(47)	12.5	(65)
Spain	16.2	(81)	11.4	(57)
Centre-north	*11.2*	*(794)*	*9.7*	*(687)*
Austria	5.5	(34)	9.9	(62)
Belgium	14.8	(82)	8.1	(45)
Denmark	10.8	(68)	11.9	(75)
Finland	16.0	(90)	8.9	(50)
France	8.6	(53)	9.2	(57)
Germany	14.5	(188)	9.0	(117)
Ireland	12.5	(62)	8.0	(40)
Luxembourg	8.8	(36)	10.7	(43)
Netherlands	6.9	(36)	11.7	(61)
Sweden	8.1	(50)	11.0	(68)
United Kingdom	12.9	(95)	9.2	(69)
EU	*11.4*	*(1032)*	*10.2*	*(925)*

Source: Eurobarometer (1996).

underemployment are complementary phenomena and that both must be taken into account when analyzing labour markets.

The particular relevance of the complementary relationship between unemployment and underemployment in the south can be partially explained by the characteristics of the southern countries' welfare states. Historically, these countries' public expenditure for social protection, as a percentage of GDP, has been much lower than in central and northern Europe. Today, although it has steadily increased, this disparity remains (Eurostat 1997). Therefore, it is not surprising to find such a high rate of underemployment. Faced with the choice of being unemployed or accepting jobs below their skill level, southerners tend to choose the latter. Given the allocation of state monies, it is very costly to be unemployed.

Before proceeding, it is worth noting a few caveats related to the data and the method employed to assess underemployment. First, regarding the data, this working sample over-represents the smaller countries and therefore does not reflect the exact composition of the entire EU labour

TABLE 5

INTEREST IN POLITICS OF UNDEREMPLOYED, ADEQUATELY EMPLOYED, AND UNEMPLOYED RESPONDENTS BY COUNTRY

	Underemployed						Adequately Employed						Unemployed					
	Frequently		Occasionally		Never		Frequently		Occasionally		Never		Frequently		Occasionally		Never	
	%	N	%	N	%	N	%	N	%	N	%	N	%	N	%	N	%	N
South	*22.0*	*(52)*	*55.5*	*(131)*	*21.6*	*(51)*	*19.4*	(300)	*53.8*	(833)	*26.7*	(413)	*16.4*	(39)	*45.0*	(107)	38.2	(91)
Greece	24.6	(15)	49.2	(30)	26.2	(16)	29.5	(119)	49.5	(200)	21.0	(85)	20.0	(11)	47.3	(26)	32.7	(18)
Italy	34.0	(18)	54.7	(29)	11.3	(6)	27.8	(103)	58.2	(216)	13.7	(51)	21.8	(12)	50.9	(28)	25.5	(14)
Portugal	15.4	(10)	56.9	(37)	26.2	(17)	9.0	(37)	50.9	(209)	39.9	(164)	12.8	(6)	29.8	(14)	57.4	(27)
Spain	15.8	(9)	61.4	(35)	21.1	(12)	11.3	(41)	57.3	(208)	31.1	(113)	12.3	(10)	48.1	(39)	39.5	(32)
Centre-north	*25.5*	(174)	*60.0*	(409)	*13.6*	(93)	*16.2*	(904)	*61.3*	(3420)	*21.6*	(1206)	*16.5*	(131)	*52.5*	(417)	*30.1*	(239)
Austria	21.7	(13)	63.3	(38)	15.0	(9)	19.4	(101)	63.7	(332)	15.7	(82)	26.5	(9)	47.1	(16)	26.5	(9)
Belgium	13.3	(6)	57.8	(26)	28.9	(13)	11.3	(48)	59.9	(255)	28.2	(120)	9.8	(8)	54.9	(45)	34.1	(28)
Denmark	40.0	(30)	56.0	(42)	4.0	(3)	19.0	(92)	61.4	(298)	19.0	(92)	25.0	(17)	48.5	(33)	26.5	(18)
Finland	14.0	(7)	60.0	(30)	22.0	(11)	15.8	(67)	64.3	(272)	19.4	(82)	14.4	(13)	60.0	(54)	23.3	(21)
France	40.4	(23)	47.4	(27)	12.3	(7)	17.3	(88)	59.6	(303)	23.0	(117)	17.0	(9)	62.3	(33)	20.8	(11)
Germany	28.7	(33)	66.1	(76)	3.5	(4)	16.8	(167)	66.3	(659)	15.0	(149)	18.1	(34)	59.6	(112)	20.7	(39)
Ireland	20.0	(8)	62.5	(25)	17.5	(7)	16.2	(64)	48.5	(192)	34.1	(135)	14.5	(9)	27.4	(17)	58.1	(36)
Luxembourg	18.2	(8)	61.4	(27)	18.2	(8)	16.6	(55)	57.1	(189)	25.7	(85)	13.9	(5)	41.7	(15)	44.4	(16)
Netherlands	31.1	(19)	57.4	(35)	9.8	(6)	14.4	(61)	69.3	(294)	14.4	(61)	22.2	(8)	55.6	(20)	22.2	(8)
Sweden	25.0	(17)	57.4	(39)	17.6	(12)	15.1	(76)	66.6	(335)	17.9	(90)	12.0	(6)	62.0	(31)	24.0	(12)
United Kingdom	14.9	(10)	65.7	(44)	19.4	(13)	14.9	(85)	51.1	(291)	33.9	(193)	13.7	(13)	43.2	(41)	43.2	(41)
EU	*24.6*	*(226)*	*58.8*	*(540)*	*15.7*	*(144)*	*16.9*	*(1204)*	*59.6*	*(4253)*	*22.7*	*(1619)*	*16.5*	*(170)*	*50.8*	*(524)*	*32.0*	*(330)*

Source: Eurobarometer (1996).

force. Nonetheless, given that my main goal is to assess the political effects of labour under-utilization rather than merely estimate its magnitude, this does not constitute a significant problem. Second, this survey was not specifically designed to analyze labour under-utilization and thus provides only a very general estimate of the magnitude of underemployment by mismatch. Given the exploratory nature of my study, however, this survey offers a good starting point for a first analysis of the under-utilization of labour, which may be further examined with a more fitting data set once some of its basic features are investigated.[8]

Finally, regarding the method, the statistical procedure followed to establish if a worker is underemployed may generate upwardly biased figures. Because of the way they are calculated, the cut-off points measure the mismatch between the education of a single worker and the current average education of all other people having the same job as determined by the labour market and its imperfections, but do not necessarily estimate the magnitude of underemployment.[9]

FINDINGS

Interest in Politics

Interest in politics is measured by asking respondents how frequently they discuss political matters when getting together with friends. If the hypothesis I derived from previous studies of unemployment and labour marginalization is correct, interest in politics should be higher among the adequately employed, lower among the underemployed, and even lower among the unemployed.

Table 5 displays the distribution of unemployed, underemployed, and adequately employed respondents by country. The southern European unemployed, as expected, are not very interested in politics. A striking 38.2 per cent of them never discuss politics when getting together with friends. Surprisingly, the underemployed are the most interested in politics. Only 21.6 per cent of them fail to talk about political matters with friends, compared to a higher 26.7 per cent of the adequately employed.

This pattern is confirmed in the other EU countries as well. Almost a third of the central and northern European unemployed (30.1 per cent) never talk about politics, compared to only 13.6 per cent of the underemployed, and 21.6 per cent of the adequately employed. Although the propensity to discuss politics among friends is clearly lower in the southern countries, the trends that emerge when all the respondents are considered do not differ: the unemployed remain the group least interested in politics (32.0 per cent of them never discuss politics), while the underemployed are the most interested (only 15.7 per cent of them do not talk about politics with friends, compared to 22.7 per cent of the adequately employed).

In the south the only exception to this finding is Greece. There, the hypothesized relationship between employment status and interest in politics is apparently correct. In central and northern Europe, this is also the case of Finland, whereas in Austria, Belgium, and Sweden there is virtually no difference between the underemployed and the adequately employed. France, finally, is a unique case, given that the adequately employed are the least interested in politics, followed by the unemployed and the underemployed. Overall, my hypothesis is corroborated in only two countries (Greece and Finland) out of 15. While the unemployed – as expected – are clearly the least interested in politics throughout the EU (with the exception of France), the underemployed are the most interested, both in southern and central-northern Europe, and – although with different margins – in 11 of the 15 EU countries. Hence, contrary to what I anticipated, it seems that only the greater marginalization suffered by the unemployed affects interest in politics. Underemployment appears instead to boost it.

These data, however, do not clarify whether the different propensity to be engaged in political discussions displayed by each of the three groups is the outcome of the experience of under-utilization itself or, on the contrary, a spurious effect produced by the demographic and social characteristics of the unemployed and the underemployed. Political attitudes, in fact, may be influenced not only by respondents' status in the labour market but also by other socio-economic variables. The patterns here observed might be more the result of the socio-economic background of the interviewer rather than the consequence of their employment status. As previously noted, the unemployed, the underemployed, and the adequately employed do have a different socio-economic profile.

If under-utilization influences political involvement (either increasing or decreasing it), people belonging to the three different labour force categories should display varied degrees of interest in politics once controlling for other variables. Figures 2 and 3, however, show that once occupational and education levels are taken into account, the effects of both forms of under-utilization blurs. Whereas unemployment seems to reduce the interest in politics at the low and medium-low occupational

FIGURE 2
INTEREST IN POLITICS BY OCCUPATIONAL LEVEL AND EMPLOYMENT STATUS

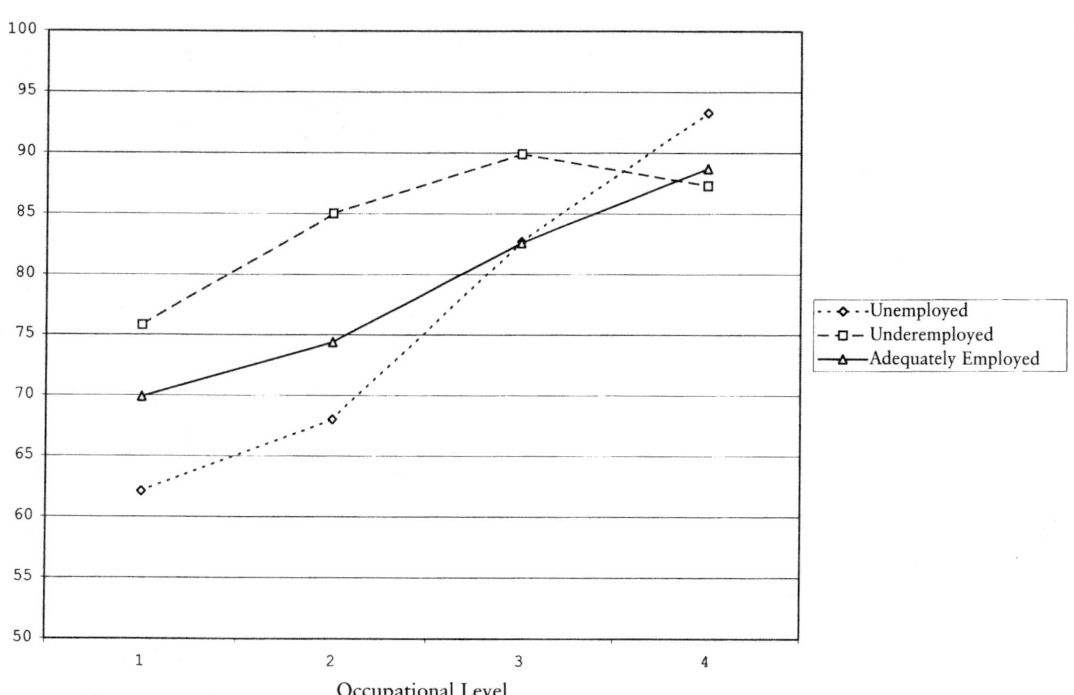

Source: Eurobarometer (1996). See Table 1 for occupational levels.

FIGURE 3
INTEREST IN POLITICS BY EDUCATIONAL LEVEL AND EMPLOYMENT STATUS

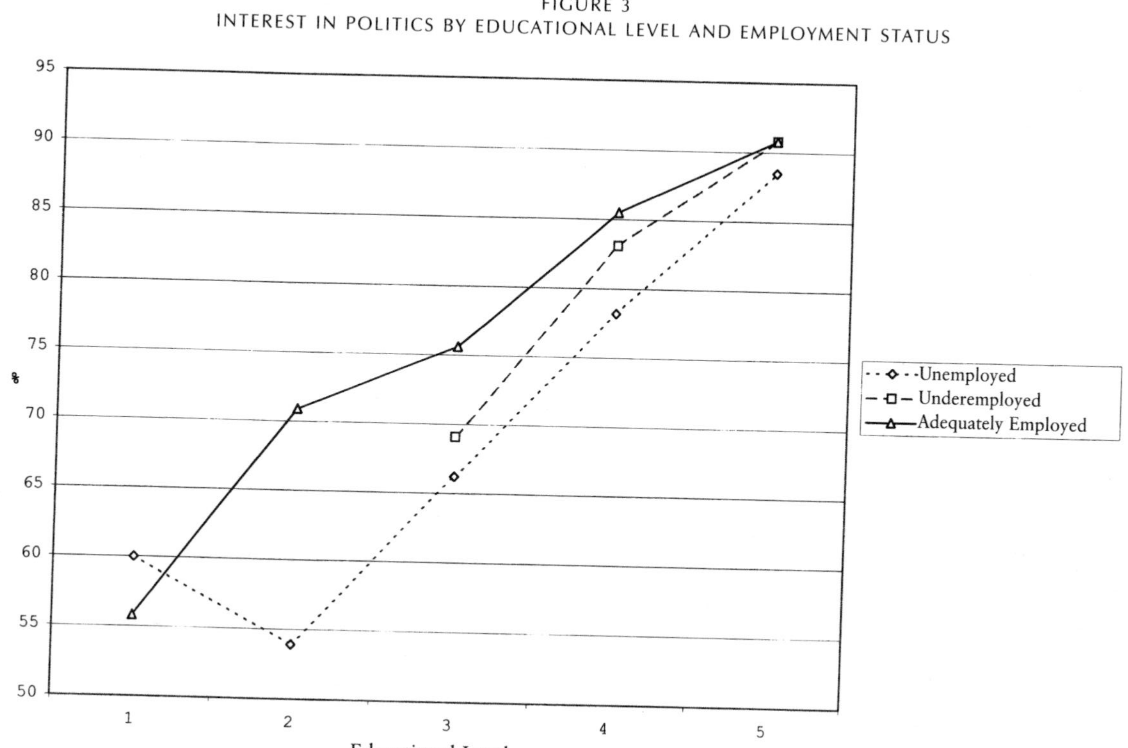

Source: Eurobarometer (1996). See Table 1 for educational levels.

levels, it has no influence on the medium-high category and appears to have a positive effect on those belonging to the high occupational level. On the other hand, the underemployed are generally the most interested in politics, but become the least involved when those with a high level job are considered. Therefore, unemployment and underemployment seem to have opposite effects on low and high occupational categories: whereas joblessness appears to reduce the interest in politics of the former and increase that of the latter, the consequences of underemployment are antithetical.

Figure 3 shows that the higher interest in politics displayed by the underemployed is probably an artefact of their greater education. At each educational level, the adequately employed – and not the underemployed – are in fact the more interested in politics, except among those with more than 20 years of education, for whom employment status is virtually irrelevant. These findings suggest that occupational and educational levels are more closely related to interest in politics than employment status.

However, to clarify whether holding a job – whether adequate or not – makes a difference in the propensity to talk about political questions with friends, I made use of logistical regression analysis. For each country, into an equation predicting political interest, I entered employment status along with other socio-economic variables that are supposed to be related to interest in politics: education, gender, age, occupational level, and household income.[10] Tables 6-A to 6-D show the results I obtained in the four southern European countries. Although exhibiting only a modest impact on the likelihood of being engaged in political discussions, education is statistically significant in Italy, Portugal, and Spain and, overall, in ten out of the 15 EU countries.[11] Likewise, age is statistically significant in nine countries. Employment status, instead, is insignificant across the EU, in the south as well as in the other countries. Clearly, the statistical analysis strengthens the argument that any difference among the unemployed, the underemployed, and the adequately employed in terms of political interest is due more to the selective recruitment of the unemployed and the underemployed from disadvantaged social groups than to their employment status.

Political Trust

Political trust is estimated by asking interviewees whether they think they can rely on their national government or not. Does working at a job below one's skill level lead one to be less satisfied with the way the political system works and thus less prone to trust the government? Does unemployment lead to even greater dissatisfaction? Table 7 shows that no clear pattern emerges across the EU on this issue. Whereas the unemployed are generally less trusting towards their national government, there is virtually no difference between the adequately employed and the underemployed. As was the case with interest in politics, cross-country differences exist; furthermore, in several countries, the employment status of the interviewees seems to have no significant effect on their level of trust.

Differences in political trust among the adequately employed, the underemployed, and the unemployed are not particularly meaningful in southern Europe. Predictably, the percentage of interviewees thinking it is possible to trust the national government is smaller among the unemployed (37.0 per cent). The adequately employed and the underemployed, nonetheless, are just slightly more trustful, and what is most striking is actually the low confidence towards the national government exhibited by all three categories. In none of the southern European occupational groups did a majority of interviewees believe it is possible to trust the national government.

Turning to central and northern Europe a different picture emerges. Whereas the unemployed are, as predicted, the most pessimistic group (43.3 per cent of them do not trust the national government), the adequately employed and the underemployed are definitely more optimistic. However, as was the case in southern Europe, the difference between these last two groups is quite small (1.4 per cent). Thus, the hypothesized relationship between employment status and political trust is not corroborated by the data, as is further indicated by the statistical analysis. None of its component variables of a model in which political trust is a function of employment status, education, gender, age, income and occupational level proved significant in more than three EU countries.[12]

Rather, the only significant difference seems to be that between southern and central-northern respondents, with the latter displaying an overall higher level of political confidence. The unemployed, the least positive segment of the central and northern labour force, trust their national government more than any southern European occupational group.

Finally, at the country-level, several exceptions to the patterns identified above can be noticed. In the southern countries, for instance, the underemployed are the least trusting group in Greece and Spain, and

TABLE 6-A
LOGISTICAL ANALYSIS OF INTEREST IN POLITICS, GREECE

Variable	B	S.E.	Wald	df	Sig	R	Exp(B)
Empl. Status			.3258	2	.8497	.0000	
Empl.Status (1)	–.1146	.2430	.2224	1	.6372	.0000	.8917
Empl.Status (2)	.1511	.2706	.3118	1	.5766	.0000	1.1631
Education	–.0214	.0402	.2838	1	.5942	.0000	.9788
Gender	–.1573	.1143	1.8931	1	.1689	.0000	.8545
Age	.0351	.0103	11.7331	1	.0006	.1327	1.0358
HH Income			1.9238	4	.7498	.0000	
HH Income (1)	–.1975	.2701	.5348	1	.4646	.0000	.8208
HH Income (2)	–.1038	.2276	.2080	1	.6483	.0000	.9014
HH Income (3)	.2625	.2049	1.6409	1	.2002	.0000	1.3002
HH Income (4)	.0773	.2216	.1216	1	.7273	.0000	1.0803
Occupation			6.3298	3	.0966	.0244	
Occupation (1)	–.5267	.2533	4.3233	1	.0376	–.0648	.5906
Occupation (2)	–.3438	.2070	2.7597	1	.0967	–.0371	.7091
Occupation (3)	.2403	.2506	.9193	1	.3377	.0000	1.2716
Constant	.4200	.7803	.2898	1	.5904		
–2 Log Likelihood	523.275						
Extent of Fit	506.625						

Source: Eurobarometer (1996).

TABLE 6-B
LOGISTICAL ANALYSIS OF INTEREST IN POLITICS, ITALY

Variable	B	S.E.	Wald	df	Sig	R	Exp(B)
Empl. Status			.6307	2	.7295	.0000	
Empl.Status (1)	.0855	.3035	.0793	1	.7783	.0000	1.0892
Empl.Status (2)	–.2742	.3727	.5414	1	.4618	.0000	.7602
Education	.1057	.0470	5.0644	1	.0244	.0874	1.1115
Gender	–.2970	.1486	3.9949	1	.0456	–.0705	.7431
Age	.0138	.0132	1.0844	1	.2977	.0000	1.0139
HH Income			6.4378	4	.1688	.0000	
HH Income (1)	–.3178	.3102	1.0492	1	.3057	.0000	.7278
HH Income (2)	.6320	.3839	2.7109	1	.0997	.0421	1.8814
HH Income (3)	–.5401	.2689	4.0338	1	.0446	–.0712	.5827
HH Income (4)	.1968	.3446	.3260	1	.5680	.0000	1.2175
Occupation			8.4669	3	.0373	.0784	
Occupation (1)	–.6171	.3113	3.9293	1	.0475	–.0693	.5395
Occupation (2)	.5550	.2946	3.5492	1	.0596	.0621	1.7419
Occupation (3)	.1428	.2938	.2362	1	.6270	.0000	1.1535
Constant	–.0042	.9848	.0000	1	.9966		
–2 Log Likelihood	362.069						
Extent of Fit	487.738						

Source: Eurobarometer (1996).

TABLE 6-C
LOGISTICAL ANALYSIS OF INTEREST IN POLITICS, PORTUGAL

Variable	B	S.E.	Wald	df	Sig	R	Exp(B)
Empl. Status			1.9030	2	.3862	.0000	
Empl.Status (1)	–.3002	.2398	1.5661	1	.2108	.0000	.7407
Empl.Status (2)	.1192	.2544	.2195	1	.6394	.0000	1.1266
Education	.1098	.0347	10.0111	1	.0016	.1071	1.1160
Gender	–.4875	.0995	24.0163	1	.0000	–.1776	.6142
Age	.0152	.0085	3.1528	1	.0758	.0406	1.0153
Occupation			8.1672	3	.0427	.0557	
Occupation (1)	–.5183	.1854	7.8192	1	.0052	–.0913	.5955
Occupation (2)	–.1864	.1765	1.1154	1	.2909	.0000	.8300
Occupation (3)	.2738	.2405	1.2966	1	.2548	.0000	1.3150
Constant	–1.0371	.6012	2.9757	1	.0845		
–2 Log Likelihood	626.887						
Extent of Fit	517.737						

Source: Eurobarometer (1996).
Note: Data on Households Income not available for Portugal.

TABLE 6-D
LOGISTICAL ANALYSIS OF INTEREST IN POLITICS, SPAIN

Variable	B	S.E.	Wald	df	Sig	R	Exp(B)
Empl. Status			1.1238	2	.5701	.0000	
Empl.Status (1)	–.2025	.2093	.9370	1	.3331	.0000	.8166
Empl.Status (2)	.1169	.2707	.1864	1	.6659	.0000	1.1240
Education	.0691	.0330	4.3803	1	.0364	.0619	1.0716
Gender	–.0930	.1026	.8219	1	.3646	.0000	.9112
Age	.0163	.0090	3.2352	1	.0721	.0446	1.0164
HH Income			5.9021	4	.2066	.0000	
HH Income (1)	–.4257	.2305	3.4103	1	.0648	–.0476	.6533
HH Income (2)	–.1583	.2122	.5565	1	.4557	.0000	.8536
HH Income (3)	.3648	.2314	2.4853	1	.1149	.0279	1.4402
HH Income (4)	.2343	.2036	1.3245	1	.2498	.0000	1.2640
Occupation			.6696	3	.8803	.0000	
Occupation (1)	.1413	.1939	.5316	1	.4659	.0000	1.1518
Occupation (2)	.0620	.1908	.1057	1	.7450	.0000	1.0640
Occupation (3)	–.0622	.1877	.1099	1	.7402	.0000	.9397
Constant	–.6883	.6571	1.0971	1	.2949		
–2 Log Likelihood	602.432						
Extent of Fit	501.051						

Source: Eurobarometer (1996).

TABLE 7
TRUST TOWARDS THE NATIONAL GOVERNMENT OF UNDEREMPLOYED, ADEQUATELY EMPLOYED, AND UNEMPLOYED RESPONDENTS BY COUNTRY

	Underemployed				Adequately Employed				Unemployed			
	Can		Cannot		Can		Cannot		Can		Cannot	
	%	N	%	N	%	N	%	N	%	N	%	N
South	*41.9*	*(99)*	*52.1*	*(123)*	*41.3*	*(639)*	*50.2*	*(778)*	*37.0*	*(88)*	*50.4*	*(120)*
Greece	42.6	(26)	45.9	(28)	52.7	(213)	44.3	(179)	52.7	(29)	45.5	(25)
Italy	35.8	(19)	56.6	(30)	28.6	(106)	56.1	(208)	16.4	(9)	56.4	(31)
Portugal	56.9	(37)	43.1	(28)	46.0	(189)	51.6	(212)	46.8	(22)	46.8	(22)
Spain	29.8	(17)	64.9	(37)	36.1	(131)	49.3	(179)	34.6	(28)	51.9	(42)
Centre-north	*53.7*	(336)	*37.1*	(253)	*52.3*	(2920)	*38.0*	(2119)	43.3	(344)	*44.0*	(349)
Austria	45.0	(27)	45.0	(27)	50.9	(265)	37.4	(195)	61.8	(21)	29.4	(10)
Belgium	37.8	(17)	53.3	(24)	32.9	(140)	54.9	(234)	35.4	(29)	47.6	(39)
Denmark	66.7	(50)	25.3	(19)	65.6	(318)	29.7	(144)	50.0	(34)	42.6	(29)
Finland	58.0	(29)	40.0	(20)	53.7	(227)	41.1	(174)	50.0	(45)	41.1	(37)
France	47.4	(27)	38.6	(22)	46.5	(236)	46.5	(236)	50.9	(27)	41.5	(22)
Germany	43.5	(50)	44.3	(51)	47.0	(467)	36.9	(367)	35.6	(67)	45.2	(85)
Ireland	45.0	(18)	37.5	(15)	51.8	(205)	33.8	(134)	50.0	(31)	35.5	(22)
Luxembourg	72.7	(32)	20.5	(9)	74.0	(245)	17.8	(8.2)	61.1	(22)	22.2	(8)
Netherlands	80.3	(49)	18.0	(11)	76.9	(326)	17.9	(76)	63.9	(23)	25.0	(9)
Sweden	58.8	(40)	30.9	(21)	49.7	(250)	41.0	(206)	38.0	(19)	58.0	(29)
United Kingdom	40.3	(27)	50.7	(34)	42.3	(241)	51.6	(294)	27.4	(26)	62.1	(59)
EU	*50.7*	*(465)*	*41.0*	*(376)*	*49.9*	*(3559)*	*40.6*	*(2897)*	*41.9*	*(432)*	*45.4*	*(469)*

Source: Eurobarometer (1996).

the most trusting in Italy and Portugal. What is astonishing, however, is the extremely low level of trust displayed by Italians: regardless of their position in the job market, about 56 per cent of the Italian labour force think it is not possible to trust their national government. It is not difficult to imagine that the exceptionally low confidence shown by Italians is probably due to the endemic corruption that has historically permeated Italian politics. Finally disclosed to the public in the first half of the 1990s – thanks to the new international scenario, the rise of new political actors, and the action of the judicial power – this widespread corruption (Rhodes 1997) has remarkably lowered Italians' trust towards politics, and ultimately led to the end of an entire party system and a complete realignment of electors (Di Virgilio 1994; Bartolini and D'Alimonte 1996; Ignazi and Katz 1996).

Summarizing, no clear trend emerges from examining labour force trust towards the national government. On the whole, the unemployed seem to be less trustful both in the south and in the centre-north, whereas among those who have a job, it is hardly possible to distinguish between the adequately employed and the underemployed. Yet, several cross-country differences exist across the EU and, once controlling for the effects of other socio-economic variables, no consistent pattern emerges. This finding reinforces the conclusion reached in the prior section: political attitudes are not the outcome of under-utilization itself but the result of the socio-economic features of the unemployed and the underemployed.

Political Ideology

The last hypothesis I test in this work deals with political ideology. Are under-utilized members of the labour force more likely to embrace extreme political stands because of their less than adequate position in the labour market? To answer this question, I examine unemployed, underemployed and adequately employed respondents' self-location along the political spectrum. First, I compute their mean self-placement in the ten point left-right scale. Then, I examine whether and to what extent they are inclined to opt for one of the two ends of the political spectrum, by calculating the percentage of respondents choosing the extreme categories (identified by the values 1, 2, 9, and 10) of the left-right continuum. Similar mean values, in fact, could hide very different distributions of respondents along the political spectrum.

On the whole, Table 8 shows that the position in the job market makes little difference in one's placement along the left-right continuum.

TABLE 8
MEAN LEFT-RIGHT PLACEMENT OF UNDEREMPLOYED, ADEQUATELY EMPLOYED, AND UNEMPLOYED RESPONDENTS BY COUNTRY

	Underemployed		Adequately Employed		Unemployed	
	Mean	Sd	Mean	Sd	Mean	Sd
South	*4.98*	*1.97*	*5.03*	*2.15*	*5.02*	*2.12*
Greece	4.85	1.94	5.40	2.01	5.43	1.63
Italy	4.61	2.04	4.84	2.37	5.27	2.55
Portugal	5.10	2.03	5.11	2.12	4.57	1.88
Spain	5.33	1.86	4.69	2.04	4.88	2.15
Centre-north	*5.08*	*1.96*	*5.27*	*1.45*	*4.98*	*1.88*
Austria	5.43	2.05	5.33	1.88	5.05	1.68
Belgium	5.35	1.63	5.27	1.89	5.19	1.71
Denmark	5.19	2.11	5.75	1.88	5.10	2.14
Finland	6.36	1.83	5.63	1.73	5.03	1.95
France	4.74	2.14	5.04	2.34	4.84	1.94
Germany	4.49	1.68	5.04	1.80	4.86	1.80
Ireland	5.26	2.03	5.52	1.66	4.93	2.06
Luxembourg	5.03	1.98	5.25	1.64	5.22	1.91
Netherlands	4.57	1.94	5.25	1.70	4.74	1.83
Sweden	5.13	2.02	5.10	1.96	5.17	2.03
United Kingdom	5.15	1.70	5.23	1.73	4.93	2.06
EU	*5.05*	*1.96*	*5.23*	*1.96*	*4.99*	*1.93*

Source: Eurobarometer (1996).

As the mean and standard deviation values show, both in the south and in the centre-north, respondents assume a normal distribution regardless of their job situation. Mean values range from a low 4.5 of the German underemployed to a high 6.4 of the Finnish underemployed, whereas standard deviation scores go from 1.5 of the adequately employed outside of the south to 2.6 of the Italian unemployed.

Looking at single countries provides additional evidence of the lack of any consistent relationship among the adequately employed, the underemployed, the unemployed and their mean placements along the left-right continuum. In southern Europe, the unemployed are the furthest left group in Portugal, the furthest right in Greece and Italy, and the central group in Spain. In central and northern Europe, instead, they are the group furthest left in Belgium, Denmark, Ireland, the United Kingdom, Austria, and Finland; the group furthest right in Sweden; and the central group in Germany, France, Luxembourg, and the Netherlands. Likewise, the positioning of the underemployed follows no clear pattern.

Having established that there is no meaningful connection between the under-utilization of the labour force and mean placement along the

TABLE 9
EXTREME LEFT-RIGHT PLACEMENT OF UNDEREMPLOYED, ADEQUATELY EMPLOYED, AND UNEMPLOYED RESPONDENTS BY COUNTRY

	Underemployed		Adequately Employed		Unemployed	
	Percent	N	Percent	N	Percent	N
South	*12.18*	*(29)*	*14.14*	*(219)*	*13.87*	*(33)*
Greece	14.55	(8)	10.64	(43)	5.45	(3)
Italy	14.55	(8)	19.95	(74)	25.45	(14)
Portugal	17.02	(8)	13.87	(57)	12.77	(6)
Spain	6.17	(5)	12.40	(45)	12.35	(10)
Centre-north	*10.85*	*(74)*	*8.78*	*(490)*	*10.08*	*(80)*
Austria	13.33	(8)	9.40	(49)	5.88	(2)
Belgium	4.44	(2)	10.09	(43)	7.31	(6)
Denmark	13.33	(10)	7.84	(38)	11.76	(8)
Finland	8.00	(4)	4.96	(21)	8.89	(8)
France	15.79	(9)	17.13	(87)	13.21	(7)
Germany	7.83	(9)	8.25	(82)	9.04	(17)
Ireland	12.50	(5)	6.57	(26)	14.52	(9)
Luxembourg	11.36	(5)	5.14	(17)	8.33	(3)
Netherlands	11.48	(7)	5.90	(25)	11.11	(4)
Sweden	14.71	(10)	11.53	(58)	12.00	(6)
United Kingdom	7.46	(5)	7.72	(44)	10.53	(10)
EU	*11.22*	*(103)*	*9.94*	*(709)*	*10.95*	*(113)*

Source: Eurobarometer (1996).

left-right continuum, I evaluate whether a less than adequate position in the labour market has any effect on the propensity to take an extreme political stand. To this end, Table 9 shows the percentage of the adequately employed, the underemployed, and the unemployed located at the two extreme ends of the political spectrum.

As we can observe, there is little difference among the three groups. In the whole sample, extremism involves less than 11.0 per cent of the respondents, without major variation among the three occupational categories. A comparison between southerners and other Europeans shows that whereas 14.1 per cent of the southern adequately employed choose an extreme location along the political spectrum, only 8.8 per cent of Europeans living in the other EU countries choose the same placement. Similarly, 13.9 per cent of the southern unemployed place themselves on the extreme ends of the spectrum, while in the centre-north only 10.1 per cent of the unemployed share the same view. Finally, 12.2 per cent of the underemployed in the south choose one of the poles of the political spectrum, compared to a lower 10.9 per cent of the other European underemployed.

A further indication of the lack of any consistent correlation between one's position in the labour market and political extremism comes from an examination of the percentages of respondents at the two extremes of the left-right continuum in each country. Whereas in Greece 14.6 per cent of the underemployed is extremist, compared to 10.6 per cent of the adequately employed and only 5.5 per cent of the unemployed, in Spain only 6.2 per cent of the underemployed assumes the same radical position, compared to 12.4 per cent of the adequately employed and the unemployed. The data on political extremism among the adequately employed, the underemployed, and the unemployed do not corroborate the hypothesis derived from the literature in any of the southern European countries. Nor is the hypothesis confirmed in the remaining countries of the EU. Rather, the most interesting finding is probably the existence of a north-south cleavage, on the basis of which respondents show different propensities to assume extreme stands (higher in the south, lower in the north) regardless of their job situation.

Several factors may explain this disparity. First, the southern and central-northern regions are not equally well off in economic terms. Greater financial stability can account for a reluctance to adopt extremist positions that may alter the status quo and factor uncertainty into the future. Second, welfare systems also differ. A scarce protection from the downturns of economy may make radicalism more appealing; there is little to lose for those who belong to the have-nots. Third, as already mentioned, educational levels are uneven throughout the EU. Southerners, who are on average less educated, may be more prone to answer to calls for radical solutions. Fourth, governmental effectiveness varies across the continent. Once again, southern Europe has historically experienced the downside of state action. Fifth, southerners' higher propensity to choose an extreme location may be affected by the legacies of southern European countries' authoritarian past, which may have produced a relative radicalization of the political market, both on its demand (citizens' preferences) and supply side (parties' platforms).

CONCLUSION

Unemployment and underemployment are widespread across the EU and roughly equivalent in size. Their political consequences, however, are apparently distinct. While unemployment seems to influence the political attitudes of those who experience it, underemployment – as I have defined it here – seems to have less obvious effects.

Regarding interest in politics and the possibility of trusting the national government, the unemployed turned out to be the group least involved in politics and least trusting among those examined. These findings confirm what prior studies on this subject had already highlighted: the attitudes of the unemployed tend to be different from the ones of people who have a job (Schlozman and Verba 1979; Anderson 2000). However, once controlling for SES variables, the limited involvement in political matters and the scepticism that characterize the unemployed turned out to be not the effect of joblessness itself but – as found by Schlozman and Verba (1979) in their study of unemployment in the United States – a consequence of the socio-economic characteristics of people out of work. Whatever the cause, however, what matters is that the reduced interest in politics shown by the unemployed is likely to affect their impact on the political system and, hence, the possibility that their voice is heard – and their needs met – by policy makers. The dramatic lack of jobs that characterises contemporary Europe as a whole is probably the best indicator of this policy implication.

On the other hand, the scarce confidence towards the national government shown by the unemployed confirms that people without a job are somewhat more alienated than the rest of the labour force. Again, my analysis points out that this is more the result of the socio-economic characteristics of the unemployed than the consequence of being without a job. As already shown by Schlozman and Verba (1979: 216-17), alienation is largely a consequence of the selective recruitment of unemployment, which hits especially people belonging to low social status groups whose propensity to participate is already inferior before the experience of being out of work. Thus, it is possible that the effects of unemployment in Europe do not differ from those displayed on the other side of the Atlantic: reduction of self-esteem, isolation, and withdrawal from the political and social arenas.

In contrast to the unemployed, the underemployed did not appear to be greatly affected by under-utilization. Both in south and centre-north Europe, as well as in 12 out of 15 countries, the underemployed were consistently more involved in politics than the adequately employed and the unemployed, whereas no meaningful difference between them and the adequately employed emerged when comparing their levels of political trust. Again, this turned out to be more the result of the peculiar characteristics of the underemployed, especially their higher levels of education, than the outcome of their position in the labour market. This suggests that in spite of having a job inferior to their qualifications, the underemployed are not hampered from exercising a greater impact on the political system.

Nonetheless, securing such an impact requires the underemployed to act together to some extent, which – in turn – requires them to be conscious of their common status in order to overcome the dilemmas of collective action (Olson 1965). Given that the attitudes of the underemployed do not differ from those of the adequately employed, the very existence of this awareness is questionable.[13]

In this context, it is not unreasonable to imagine a scenario in which European governments – unable to reverse the trend of rising unemployment begun in the 1970s – may pursue the goal of tackling the mismatch of labour demand and supply by stimulating various forms of underemployment. Given its negligible political salience, underemployment is politically free of cost and represents one of the easiest way out from the European unemployment labyrinth. This road, however, might eventually lead to a very undesirable social consequence. Since the inflexibility of the EU labour markets already favour – as pointed out by the European Commission (1997) – the existence of a vast area of precarious jobs, it is possible that in the future the interaction between these rigidities and the political opportunism of government officials may encourage the development of dual labour markets, made of a small portion of established employees enjoying a high degree of protection against being laid-off, and a large majority of others having little or no protection (European Commission 1997: 23; Siebert 1997).

One of the most important findings of this article was perhaps the cleavage between centre-northern and southern respondents, with the former displaying a much higher level of confidence in their domestic political institutions. The unemployed, the least trustful group among the other Europeans, were still more positive than even the south's most trusting category (the adequately employed), supporting the interpretation that political trust largely depends on factors other than the shortcomings of labour market.

This result is of great interest. On the one hand, it confirms the existence of a relationship between government effectiveness and legitimacy (Almond and Verba 1963). On the other, it highlights the comparatively worse setting in which southern Europeans political elites have to work nowadays. The long-standing government ineffectiveness suffered by southern Europe has eroded a great part of the *demos*' confidence in public officials, with the double effect of drastically reducing the trust of citizens and of making current efforts to improve governance even more difficult.

Political ideology, finally, did not appear to be significantly different among the unemployed, the underemployed, and the adequately employed. On the whole, the examination of political stands among southern Europeans (as well as among the other Europeans) showed that most citizens are concentrated around the central positions of the political spectrum. Moreover, about the same percentage of people with extreme views was found in each of the three categories, while some differences became visible across the fifteen countries of the Union. Therefore, an individual's position in the labour market seems to play a small role in determining ideology. Other factors must explain cross-country variations. These results corroborate the findings of Anderson (2000) and reassure us about the absence of any centrifugal drive that the vast under-utilization of labour, following the Weimar pattern, could induce.

Summarizing, while unemployment is associated with lower levels of political interest and trust, underemployment by mismatch is not correlated to any particular pattern of political attitudes. However, as already shown throughout this article, SES variables exercise greater influence on political attitudes than under-utilization does and can better help explain these findings. Yet, the explorative nature of this study calls for further research. In order to increase our understanding of the political consequences produced by labour under-utilization, future studies may wish to extend the analysis to the other forms of underemployment (by time, by income, and by productivity) that I did not consider here, or try to refine the analysis with better data (e.g. trying to introduce subjective measures of underemployment, running a longitudinal analysis to monitor respondents' attitudes over time, or assessing any eventual attitudinal difference induced by the length of under-utilization that has taken place). It may turn out that the political consequences of labour under-utilization are greater than they appear now.

NOTES

1. According to Eurostat (1998), Andalucía (Spain) suffers the highest rate of unemployment of Europe (32.0 per cent), followed by other southern Spanish (Extremadura, 29.5 per cent, Ceuta and Melilla, 26.4 per cent), and the southern Italian regions (Campania, 26.1 per cent, Calabria, 24.9 per cent, and Sicily, 24.0 per cent). However, these figures do not take into account the hidden economy, which is traditionally large in southern Europe (Eurostat 1982; Bermeo 1999).

2. According to this approach, the economically active group, also referred to as *labour force*, is made of people who either work for pay or profit or are actively seeking a job; whereas the economically inactive group is composed of people who do not work for pay or profit, do not look for employment and hence do not contribute to the formal gross domestic product (GDP). Since the 1930s, almost all labour market statistics have been collected and interpreted in light of this dichotomization, with the result that only a part of the labour markets' shortcomings and their political effects is usually captured (Sullivan 1979: 7-12).
3. A review of the literature reveals that sometimes the term underemployment is also referred to the persistency, in a given country, of substantial unemployment with no clear tendency to disappear (Drèze 1991). Here I do not consider this macro-level meaning and, instead, I focus on individuals' position in the job market. On the meaning of invisible underemployment as *disguised unemployment* see Robinson (1936).
4. Studies have especially analyzed cases related to particular sub-samples of the population of a given country, like young people and women (Ruiz-Quintanilla et al. 1996), inhabitants of urban areas (Sheets et al. 1987; Simpson 1992), ethnic minorities (Zhou 1993; Soltero 1996; Madamba 1998), or particular segments of the labour market, identifiable either in terms of occupation (Burris 1983) or education (Solmon et al. 1981; Kaufman 1982).
5. Within the sample of the United Kingdom, Northern Ireland is over-represented with about 300 interviewees; likewise, the former East Germany is over-represented within the German sample with about half of the interviewees.
6. Thus, three variables are needed to determine the mismatch for any worker: his or her occupation, his or her education (which serves as a proxy for skill level), and a mismatch cut-off for the occupation. Whereas occupation is here directly identified through a question asking for the job of each respondent, formal education can be assessed only indirectly. This Eurobarometer data set, in fact, includes information regarding *when* formal education was ended but not for *how long* it was attended. Hence, under the assumption that all interviewees began school at six years old, I have created a new variable 'Years of Education' by subtracting six years from the reported age they stopped attending formal education. Given the substantial homogeneity in the policies pursued by the European countries in this area, this is a reliable measure (Eurostat 1991: 38).
7. Given that men and women are unevenly distributed among the 14 occupational categories, I have also calculated two separate cut-offs (one for men and one for women) for each occupation. Differences, however, are negligible and thus I prefer to employ a unique cut-off point for each profession as determined by the mean education of all respondents falling inside that category.
8. For example, in a more accurate data set the number of occupational categories could be enlarged to obtain a higher degree of homogeneity within each of them; while the skills of interviewees could be reported more precisely, specifying not only the number of years spent at school, but also the degree achieved, possible periods of formation attended after having stopped formal education, or some measure of experience, which is an important factor of skill accumulation that can be achieved only in the workplace. This caveat, however, has also methodological implications. A major area of concern with the LUF approach, in fact, is usually identified in the use of completed years of education as a proxy for the skill level of each worker. As it has been noted, schooling as a proxy for the skills clearly does not take into account that the skill level of each person depends on a variety of inputs only in part identifiable with formal education (Sullivan 1978: 197-8; Clogg 1979: 11). Two people with the same number of completed years of education can actually have very different skills because of the different quality of education, on-the-job training, or skill accumulation through experience. Yet, a minimum level of formal education is often the first requirement to

qualify for certain jobs, and formal education may at least indicate a general level of culture that witnesses an ability of knowing how to learn. Therefore, although it is a less than optimal criterion to infer skills under-utilization, schooling does not take me too far from what I want to estimate.

9. This procedure, in fact, is silent about the waste of human capital that may be induced by the adverse conditions of the labour market, which may lead people towards under-qualified jobs. Even if I am unable to suggest a better measure, it is worth noting this point, especially with reference to the European labour markets where a non-skilled manual worker has an average education of ten years.
10. The model was set up following the work of Schlozman and Verba (1979: 244-54) and expecting those with a better education, a higher occupational level, a higher income, males, and middle-aged to display comparatively higher rates of interest in politics. I do not report the results of the analysis based on the OLS regression because they are not significantly different from those obtained with the logistical regression.
11. Data about central and northern EU countries not reported here.
12. Results based on logistical and OLS regression.
13. Moreover, since the way I estimated underemployment by mismatch tries to secure an objective assessment of underemployment, but fails to catch whether underemployed are subjectively aware of their condition, there is no direct way to assess whether the underemployed are conscious of their status or not.

REFERENCES

Alesina, A. and H. Rosenthal (1995): *Partisan Politics, Divided Government and the Economy*, Cambridge, MA: Cambridge University Press.

Almond, G and S. Verba (1963): *The Civic Culture. Political Attitudes and Democracy in Five Nations*, Princeton, NJ: Princeton University Press.

Anderson, C.J. (2000): 'Desperate Times Call for Desperate Measures? Unemployment and Citizen Behavior in Comparative Perspective', in N. Bermeo (ed.) *Unemployment in the New Europe*, Cambridge: Cambridge University Press (forthcoming).

Bartolini, S. and R. D'Alimonte (1996): 'Plurality Competition and Party Realignment in Italy: the 1994 Parliamentary Elections', *European Journal of Political Research* 29/1, pp.105-42.

Bermeo, N. (1999): 'What's Working in Southern Europe?', *South European Society & Politics*, This Issue.

Brady, H.E., K. Schlozman, S. Verba and L. Elms (1998): 'Who Bowls? Class, Race, and Changing Participatory Equality', paper presented at the 1998 Annual Meeting of the American Political Science Association, Boston, MA, 3-6 September 1998.

Burris, B.H. (1983): *No Room at the Top. Underemployment and Alienation in the Corporation*, New York, NY, Praeger Publishers.

Clogg, C.C. (1979): *Measuring Underemployment. Demographic Indicators for the United States*, New York, NY: Academic Press.

Crepaz, M. (1995): 'Consensus vs. Majoritarian Democracy: Political Institutions and their Impact on Macroeconomic Performance and Industrial Disputes', *Comparative Political Studies* 29/1, pp.4-26.

Di Virgilio, A. (1994): 'Dai partiti ai poli: la politica delle alleanze' [From Parties to Poles. The Politics of Alliances] *Rivista Italiana di Scienza Politica* 24/3, pp.493-549; reprinted in S. Bartolini and R. D'Alimonte (1995), *Maggioritario ma non troppo* [Majoritarian but not Too Much], Bologna: Il Mulino, pp.177-232.

Drèze, J.H. (1991): *Underemployment Equilibria*, Cambridge: Cambridge University Press.

Eurobarometer (1996): Eurobarometer 44.1, Brussels: Commission of the European Communities.

Eurobarometer (various issues): Standard Eurobarometer, Brussels: Commission of the European Communities.

European Commission (1997): *Employment in Europe*, Luxembourg: Office for Official Publication of the European Communities.

Eurostat (1982): *Multiple Job Holders. An Analysis of Second Jobs in the European Community*, Luxembourg: Office for Official Publication of the European Communities.

Eurostat (1991): *A Social Portrait of Europe*, Luxembourg: Office for Official Publication of the European Communities.

Eurostat (1997): *Eurostat Yearbook*, Luxembourg: Office for Official Publication of the European Communities.

Eurostat (1998): *Statistics in Focus*, Regions 3/98, Luxembourg: Eurostat Press Office.

Hauser, P.M. (1974): 'The Measurement of Labour Utilisation', *The Malayan Economic Review* 19/1, pp.1-15.

Hibbs, D.A. (1977): 'Political Parties and Macroeconomic Policies', *American Political Science Review* 71/4, pp.1467-87.

Hopkins, M. (1985): *Alternatives to Unemployment and Underemployment. The Case of Colombia*, Boulder, CO: Westview Press.

Hussmanns, R. (1994): 'International Standards on the Measurement of Economic Activity, Employment, Unemployment and Underemployment', in I. Chernyshev (ed.), *Labour Statistics for a Market Economy. Challenges and Solutions in the Transition Countries of Central and Eastern Europe and the Former Soviet Union*, Budapest, London, and New York, NY: Central European University Press, pp.77-105.

Hussmanns, R., F. Mehran and V. Verma (1990): *Surveys of Economically Active Population, Employment, Unemployment and Underemployment. An ILO Manual on Concepts and Methods*, Geneva: International Labour Office.

Ignazi, P. and R. Katz (eds) (1996): *The Year of the Tycoon: Italian Politics 1994*, Boulder, CO: Westview Press.

International Labour Organisation (1964): *Employment and Economic Growth*, Geneva: International Labour Office.

International Labour Organisation (1976): *International Recommendations on Labour Statistics*, Geneva: International Labour Office.

Kaufman, H.G. (1982): *Professionals in Search of Work: Coping with the Stress of Job Loss and Underemployment*, New York, NY: Wiley.

Kiewiet, D.R. (1983): *Macroeconomics and Micropolitics: The Electoral Effects of Economic Issues*, Chicago, IL: Chicago University Press.

Lange, P. and G. Garret (1985): 'The Politics of Growth: Strategic Interaction and Economic Performance in the Advanced Industrial Democracies, 1974-1980', *Journal of Politics* 47/3, pp.792-827.

Layard, R., S. Nickell and R. Jackman (1994): *The Unemployment Crisis*, Oxford: Oxford University Press.

Lewis-Beck, M.S. (1988): *Economics and Elections. The Major Western Democracies*, Ann Arbor, MI: University of Michigan Press.

Ljungqvist, L. and T.J. Sargent (1998): 'The European Unemployment Dilemma', *Journal of Political Economy* 106/3, pp.514-50.

Madamba, A.B. (1998): *Underemployment among Asians in the United States. Asians Indians, Filipino, and Vietnamese Workers*, New York, NY and London: Garland Publishing.

Nayak, P. (1990): *Disguised Unemployment and Underemployment in Indian Agriculture*, New Delhi: Radiant Publishers.

Olson, M. (1965): *The Logic of Collective Action. Public Goods and the Theory of Groups*, Cambridge, MA: Harvard University Press.

Organisation for Economic Co-Operation and Development (1986): *OECD Economic Outlook*, 40, Paris: OECD.

Organisation for Economic Co-Operation and Development (1996): *OECD Economic Outlook*, 60, Paris: OECD.

Organisation for Economic Co-Operation and Development (1998): *OECD Economic Outlook*, 63, Paris: OECD.

Powell, G.B. and G.D. Whitten (1993): 'A Cross-National Analysis of the Economic Voting: Taking Account of the Political Context', *American Journal of Political Science* 37/2, pp.391-414.

Rhodes, M. (1997): 'Financing Party Politics in Italy: A Case of Systemic Corruption', *West European Politics* 20/1, pp.54-80.

Robinson, J. (1936): 'Disguised Unemployment', *Economic Journal* 46/182, pp.225-37.

Ruiz-Quintanilla, S., S. Antonio, and R. Claes (1996): 'Determinants of Underemployment of Young Adults: A Multi-Country Study', *Industrial and Labor Relations Review* 49/3, pp.424-38.

Schlozman, K.L., and S. Verba (1979): *Injury to Insult. Unemployment, Class, and Political Response*, Cambridge, MA and London: Harvard University Press.

Sheets, R.G., S. Nord and J.J. Phelps (1987): *The Impact of Service Industries on Underemployment in Metropolitan Economies*, Lexington, MA: Lexington Books.

Siebert, H. (1997): 'Labor Market Rigidities: At the Root of Unemployment in Europe', *Journal of Economic Perspectives* 11/3, pp.37-54.

Simpson, W. (1992): *Urban Structure and the Labour Market. Worker Mobility, Commuting, and Underemployment in Cities*, Oxford: Clarendon Press.

Solmon, L.C., L. Kent, N.L. Ochsner and M.L. Hurwicz (1981): *Underemployed Ph.D.'s*, Lexington, MA: Lexington Books.

Soltero, J.M. (1996): *Inequality in the Workplace. Underemployment among Mexicans, African Americans, and Whites*, New York, NY and London: Garland Publishing.

Sullivan, T.A. (1978): *Marginal Workers, Marginal Jobs. The Underutilization of American Workers*, Austin, TX and London: University of Texas Press.

Zhou, M. (1993): 'Underemployment and Economic Disparities among Minority Groups', *Population Research and Policy Review* 12/2, pp.139-57.

Attitudes and Threat Perception: Unemployment and Immigration in Portugal

M. MARGARIDA MARQUES

In all the survey research conducted in Portugal since the 1980s, unemployment consistently appears as one of the top problems (see Bacalhau and Bruneau, this issue). In a nation-wide poll made in 1996, unemployment was the main concern for one in every three interviewees, ranking right after drugs (*Público*, 1 May 1996 : 2). Moreover, in spite of low average earnings, 85 per cent of those interviewed admitted they would give up wage increases in order to avoid job losses in their firms. Three quarters of the respondents even reported that they would accept a reduction in earnings (as the counterpart of less working hours) in order to prevent an increase in unemployment.

Another survey, conducted in 1994, showed that the majority of the Portuguese perceived the opportunity structure as inegalitarian, the main cleavage in society being that between the 'rich' and the 'poor' (Cabral 1995). In this context, employment emerged as a key scarce resource. The creation of employment ranked first among the major responsibilities of the State, though taking care of the unemployed was not among the main priorities (Cabral 1995: 14-17). Furthermore, mistrust toward the opportunity structure correlates strongly with low education levels as well as economic status, and 'materialistic' attitudes toward work (Rodrigues 1995: 52-5).

The concern with unemployment is curious given how very low Portuguese official unemployment looks in European terms. Official unemployment rates have been held generally to one digit, except at

---

Data gathering for this article was funded by Praxis XXI – CSH840/95 project. A special note of appreciation is owed to Rui Santos, my colleague at the Sociology department and at the Laboratory for applied social research, SociNova, for his helpful suggestions and comments, and to Nancy Bermeo and the anonymous reviewer whose contributions were fundamental to the making of this final version of the paper.

some exceptional moments, and the main concentration of joblessness has been in the area around Lisbon.

One of Portugal's few high unemployment episodes corresponds to the aftermath of de-colonization, and the sudden 'return' from the former African colonies of nearly half a million individuals (about 5 per cent of the Portuguese population).[1] Inevitably, an association between both phenomena emerged and gained widespread acceptance. Later on, in the early 1990s, a second wave of high unemployment occurred, just a few years after Portugal's adhesion to European Community. It was also the period when the first Schengen 'walls' were being built, and, in a counter-cyclical way, a fast increase in foreign population occurred in Portugal. That was the moment when immigration first arose as a political issue.[2] In a traditionally out-migration country, in-migration of such huge dimensions and in historical contexts of political agitation could not fail to have multiple effects.

In this context how does the fear of unemployment bear on attitudes toward foreigners in general, and particularly toward immigration, in Portugal? It is our intention in this article to show that there is a pervasive perception of threat associated with in-migration which may not directly correspond with individual and collective experiences of unemployment, nor be explained by deeply rooted or widespread xenophobic public attitudes.

Our evidence mainly comes from survey results published in newspapers, in Eurobarometer, and some scientific literature. Strictly speaking, the nature of available data does not allow the test of hypotheses; it rather supports arguments in order to build hypotheses. And this is in fact the aim of this paper: presenting and systematizing diverse evidence (published before 1998) in order to suggest interpretative paths. We shall support most of the arguments using data from Portugal, Spain, Italy, and Greece, therefore trying to disentangle the impact of cultural *versus* structural factors on attitudes. We shall however concentrate on the Portuguese case, whose sources we know the best, in order to explore further some of the aspects of the problem in focus.

The first part of the argument discusses employment and unemployment, showing how they are socially constructed and showing how public opinion is sensitive to which categories of people get or are entitled to get jobs (Maruani and Reynaud 1993). In a second section, we turn to analysing the evolution of work related values, by using survey data collected over a 20 year period, and using different methodologies.

Using data covering the four southern European countries (when available), we show that there are indeed important similarities among these societies, reflecting what might be a cultural pattern (as suggested by G. Hofstede). We ask if it impinges on attitudes toward foreign labour, and how these attitudes are expressed. In a third section, a brief overview of immigration evolution in these traditional out-migration societies of southern Europe provides the contextual perspective for understanding the results of the surveys made by Eurobarometer in order to monitor Europeans' perception of foreigners. In spite of difficulties in gathering together comparable statistical data on immigrants, it can be shown that there is no such thing as a common attitude toward foreign labour in southern Europe. Finally, we turn to national surveys conducted in Portugal, and show that foreign labour is not all lumped together into a single category. Instead, the image built on past experience of different categories of foreigners, together with perceived social distance, are important in moulding attitudes.[3]

THE SOCIAL CONSTRUCTION OF EMPLOYMENT AND UNEMPLOYMENT

Every comparison requires contextualization (Desrosières and Thévenot 1988), so before discussing the agents or causes of unemployment in Portugal, it is advisable to have an overview of the Portuguese labour force in the context of what is commonly called 'southern Europe', and of the European Union as a whole. Our overview begins with a discussion of the structure of employment and unemployment; and then offers a quick glance at the results of surveys on work related values.

Starting with the statistical data on the Portuguese labour force, it comes as no surprise that, on a series of simple indicators, Portugal is clearly part of the cluster of south European societies. Portugal experienced a late but rather abrupt withdrawal of youth from the labour force. It has a relatively low percentage of salaried workers (with Greece exhibiting exceptionally high rates of self-employment), a very low percentage of unemployment subsidy beneficiaries (with Spain being the outlier) and finally, low educational qualifications, even by south European standards. These trends are illustrated in Tables 1, 2, 3 and 4 below.

The comparison across southern Europe highlights the specificity of the Portuguese situation: the later and sudden withdrawal of the young from the labour force, and the still huge weight of low-skilled labour, related to the relatively late expansion of schooling, are indeed important examples of Portugal's uniqueness.

TABLE 1
YOUTH (AGED 15-24) PARTICIPATION RATE

	1977	1980	1985	1990	1996
Greece[b]	—	—	40.6	39.4	36.7[a]
Italy[b, c]	44.5	45.3	43.8	43.5	39.4
Spain	62.7	59.6	55.0	51.2	44.4
Portugal	68.2	69.3	64.3	60.4	44.3

Notes: [a]1995; [b]break in series in 1991 for Greece and 1992 for Italy; [c]age bracket [14-24].
Source: OECD (1997).

TABLE 2
WAGE EARNERS AND SALARIED WORKERS IN CIVILIAN EMPLOYMENT (%)

	1976	1980	1985	1990	1996
Greece[b]	47.6[a]	49.7	49.3	52.4	53.9[c]
Italy[b]	70.8	71.4	70.3	71.3	71.1
Spain	68.5	69.1	68.3	73.4	74.5
Portugal	64.8	67.6	67.7	70.6	71.3
	—	—	—	—	—
Germany	94.1	94.9	90.2	92.2	90.0

Notes: [a]1977; [b]break in series in 1991 for Greece and 1992 for Italy; [c]1995.
Source: OECD (1997).

TABLE 3
EMPLOYED POPULATION BY EDUCATION LEVELS IN 1997 (%)

	Low	Medium	High
Greece	51.0	31.3	17.7
Italy	53.4	35.9	10.7
Spain	59.7	17.0	23.3
Portugal	75.4	12.5	12.0
	—	—	—
Germany	18.2	57.7	24.1

Source: Eurostat cited in *Público* 8 October 1997.

The low percentage (in European terms) of wage earners is strongly related to the feebleness of the secondary sector in Portugal. Its quite recent growth is heavily dependent, among other things, on the institutional and legal changes that took place after the change in the political regime in 1974, which also naturally affected the institutional framework of unemployment, and therefore the nature of the ties of wage earners with economic activity.

In fact, only in 1985, i.e. one year before entering the European Community, and long after the unemployment rates started rising well above the 'frictional' levels (close to 20 per cent in the more industrialized districts like Setúbal), a decision was made to change the legal framework of unemployment insurance extending subsidy rights to those who had lost their jobs, calculated as a direct percentage of their former earnings (Decree-Law #20 of 17 January 1985).

Despite this new institutional framework, access to unemployment subsidies is still extremely limited. In this, Portugal is like the other southern European countries. Spain is the exception in using benefit incentives to cushion the shock of industrial restructuring (see also Maruani and Reynaud).

TABLE 4
PERCENTAGE OF UNEMPLOYED RECEIVING SUBSIDIES IN 1991

	Men	Women
EU	52	33
Greece	12	7
Italy	19	19
Spain	37	21
Portugal	18	16

Source: Eurostat cited in Maruani and Reynaud (1993: 38).

Despite these similarities with other southern European countries, Portugal is unique in other ways. Its unemployment benefit system is more gender blind than that of any country in the EU (excluding Italy). The size of the labour force as a percentage of the whole population is below the average for northern Europe but is far above the average for southern Europe (although Italy also steadily reaches and crosses the threshold of 40 per cent). This, in the European context, is the result of the comparatively large participation of women in the Portuguese labour force (Table 5) which cannot fail to impinge on gender relations. Since

TABLE 5
TOTAL LABOUR FORCE AS PERCENTAGE OF TOTAL POPULATION

	1976	1980	1985	1990	1996[b]
Greece	35.6[a]	35.8	39.2	39.6	40.6
Italy	39.1	40.5	41.6	43.2	41.1
Spain	37.6	36.1	36.4	39.5	41.1
Portugal	43.8	44.4	45.1	50.1	49.2
	—	—	—	—	—
Denmark	49.2	52.4	53.8	56.6	53.6
			Female labour force (aged 15-64)		
Greece	33.3[c]	33.0	41.8	43.6	45.9
Italy[d]	37.6[c]	39.6	41.0	45.9	42.7
Spain	33.8	32.2	33.4	41.2	46.2
Portugal[e]	53.4[c]	54.3	56.1	62.9	64.1
	—	—	—	—	—
Denmark	62.9	71.8[f]	74.5	78.5	74.1

Notes: [a]1977; [b]1995 for Greece and Germany, 1994 for Italy; [c]1974 for Portugal, 1977 for Greece and Italy; [d]14 to 64 years old; [e]Includes persons aged less than 15 years; [f]1981.
Source: OECD (1997).

gender relations are a structuring axis of the basic institutions in society, the high participation of women in the labour force has implications in small social units, namely the family, but also in the larger and macroscopic ones.

In other European countries women are frequently blamed for unemployment, based on the assumption that the vacancies opened by their withdrawal from the labour force would then be occupied by men. In Portugal, however, even when new legislation about part time work and early retirement was being discussed, the idea that the exclusion of women would be beneficial never really gained credence in public opinion. The results of systematic survey research prove the point (Franca *et al.* 1993).

This result is even clearer when one concentrates on the 1997 survey of a broad, national sample of firms: only 6 per cent of them said men ought to be given priority in hiring over women (Freire *et al.* 1998).

In a context where redistributed wealth necessarily mirrors produced wealth, which in this case means a tight budget (in comparison to north European levels of welfare), it comes as no surprise that, somewhere in the decision process of public administration bureaucracy, distortions may occur – be they systematic or random (see Mingione 1996).

TABLE 6
OPINIONS ON WHOM SHOULD BE GIVEN PRIORITY IN EMPLOYMENT

	EU	Italy	Spain	Portugal
Men have more right to jobs than women				
agree	33	42	30	33
disagree	55	44	60	58
People should retire earlier				
agree	47	52	52	58
disagree	38	31	32	28
The national (Italians, Spaniards, Portuguese, ...) workers should be given priority in hiring by employers, in relation to foreigners				
agree	62	72	76	86
disagree	27	15	14	7

Source: L. França (1993: 28)*.
Note: *This is the report of the results obtained in Portugal by the European Value Systems Study Group (EVSSG). The observation comprised only nine of the by then twelve countries of the EU (excluding Greece, Denmark and Luxembourg) (França 1993: 10–11); however, we shall call the total the EU results.

TABLE 7
THE IMPORTANCE OF RECRUITMENT CRITERIA

	Very/quite important	Little/not important	Doesn't know/ doesn't answer
Being a man (N=449)	5.8	90.5	3.8
Being young (N=450)	58.2	40.3	1.5
Being Portuguese, in face of foreigners (N=449)	40.7	56.1	3.1

Source: J. Freire *et al.* (1998: 179).

Women are, in fact, less prone to receive unemployment subsidies than men, as has been seen above; but one cannot realistically say that they are heavily discriminated against. However, Portuguese women do exhibit a much higher risk of unemployment and of remaining in long term situations of joblessness than men. In fact, they are also more prone to be caught in temporary jobs and other forms of precarious employment (including working from home and doing piecework).

New entrants in the labour market, namely young people, suffer from precarious employment as well. In fact, it is not the getting of a job that seems difficult; it is rather entering into a more or less stabilised position in the work force that proves to be the major obstacle faced by young people. Again, official figures point to relatively low rates of youth

TABLE 8
YOUTH (AGED 15-25) UNEMPLOYMENT

	1991	1995	1996
EU	16.3	21.5	21.6
Greece	22.9	27.9	—
Italy[a]	26.0	33.2	33.6
Spain	31.1	42.5	42.8
Portugal	8.8	16.6	16.2

Note: [a]July in 1996.
Source: EUROSTAT.

unemployment in Portugal (in spite of the sharp increase from 1991 to 1995) – contrasting with those of other south European 'partners', and even with the rest of the EU.

The predicament of young job seekers was characterised as a 'queuing situation'[4] and it is thus not surprising to see that, at a much higher level than women, 'older people' in the labour market are held as responsible for unemployment (Table 6). The Portuguese are much more supportive of early retirement than Europeans as a whole, though southern Europeans in general stand out as especially supportive. (Only south European countries surpass the 50 per cent mark in supporting early retirement.) The results of the 1997 survey (Table 7) confirm that nearly 60 per cent of the employees studied strongly supported giving preference to young people in hiring.

The systemic patterns in this evidence thus suggest that employment and unemployment have to be seen not just as economic institutions, but as social constructions as well (see Maruani and Reynaud 1993).

When foreigners are involved, therefore, it is to be expected that the reactions will also probably be socially constructed and non-random. In fact, one should keep in mind the heavy weight of unskilled or low skilled labour in Portugal, precisely the categories where mistrust toward the opportunity structure is highest (Cabral 1995: 27), and expect that reactions may reflect some sort of perception of increased competition with the arrival of foreign workers.

In fact attitudes are actually much more unfriendly toward foreign workers in the Portuguese labour force than toward women or older people, as shown in the results of the 1991 European survey already referred to (Table 6). The results of the 1997 nation-wide survey also show that more than 40 per cent of the workers of a sample of firms consider that Portuguese should be given preference over foreigners in hiring (Table 7).

Portugal, together with the two other south European countries considered in the EVSSG 1991 survey, reveals the highest scores of negative attitudes toward foreigners in the EU when the competition for jobs is involved. These negative attitudes persist even though the large majority of Portuguese are aware that people from minority groups are suffering some sort of discrimination in the job market (Eurobarometer: Second Survey of Racism and Xenophobia). The north Europeans, though their countries have much greater volumes of foreign population, have less negative attitudes. Thus while northern Europeans perceive only limited possible competition with foreigners in labour markets (as well as possibly expressing forms of solidarity towards immigrants which find only limited echo among southern Europeans), southern Europeans reveal an acute concern with the distribution of jobs seen as scarce resources.[5]

TABLE 9
ARE MINORITY GROUPS BEING DISCRIMINATED AGAINST IN THE JOB MARKET?

	Greece	Italy	Spain	Portugal	EU12
Tend to agree	90	79	89	86	71

Source: Eurobarometer 47.1, Special Edition on Racism and Xenophobia, 1997.

What explains this difference? Are southern European cultural factors at play? Or, is the difference explained by the fact that the relatively low skilled southern European labour force has a greater sense of vulnerability to competition from immigrants? These questions require further research.

WORK RELATED VALUES

In more general terms, one can see that work always scores high as an important domain in life in southern Europe. In the first Eurobarometer special edition on racism and xenophobia, a survey conducted in 1988, work ranked first in a list of twelve items described as human rights, in all the four countries considered. In the EU as a whole it ranked only third.

TABLE 10
HUMAN RIGHTS THAT SHOULD ALWAYS BE RESPECTED UNDER ALL CIRCUMSTANCES (RANK)

	Greece	Italy	Spain	Portugal	EU12
Education & training	3	2	1	2	1
Privacy	5	4	3	7	2
Work	1	1	1	1	3
Equality before the law	1	2	3	5	4
Information	4	5	5	3	7

Source: Eurobarometer Special Edition on Racism and Xenophobia, 1989.

The fact that in Portugal work ranks above education and privacy (which are the first and second most prized human rights in the EU as a whole) must be put in context. The results of 1991, 1994 and 1997 surveys (França et al. 1993; Rodrigues 1995; Cabral, Vala and Freire 1998) reveal a cultural pattern dominated by what might be termed 'materialistic' values (Inglehart). This dominant orientation, in turn, is associated with low economic and cultural status, and with high mistrust toward the opportunity structures. So, the high value put on work as a basic human right goes hand in hand with the notion of work as a scarce resource: these are two sides of the same coin.

The importance given to the domain of work has a considerable influence on the way people look at values such as professional pride, meritocracy and self-fulfilment. Conversely, it certainly affects the way people look at unemployment, and how they experience the concrete situation of joblessness. The patterns of influence manifest themselves from at least the late 1960s to the 1990s. In the late 1960s and early 1970s,[6] the transition period to a more fully integrated economy of southern Europe in the capitalist world system, the data collected by G. Hofstede suggests a common pattern of work related cultural traits. These include a heavy emphasis on *uncertainty avoidance* and compliance with the respect for social distances based on authority levels. On both the uncertainty and the authority measures, Italians ranked lower than other southern Europeans but still higher than most other Europeans.

Though 20 years is a long time, França (1993) still shows a pattern of value orientation which can be termed as typically south European. One result stands out which clearly singles out south European societies from all the others: it is the region where work comes immediately after the family, and clearly above friends in the priority scale of the surveyed population (Table 12).

TABLE 11
INDEX AND RANK IN 39 COUNTRIES

	'Power distance'	'Uncertainty avoidance'
First ranks	Philippines, Mexico, Venezuela	Greece, Portugal, Belgium
Greece	60 (16)	112 (1)
Italy	50 (22)	75 (16)
Spain	57 (19)	86 (8)
Portugal	63 (15)	(104) (2)
Last ranks	Denmark, Austria, Israel	Sweden, Denmark, Singapore
Mean of 39 countries	51	64

Source: G. Hofstede (1984: 77, 122)
Note: * from highest to lowest scores.

TABLE 12
VERY IMPORTANT?

	EU		Italy		Spain		Portugal	
	rank	%*	rank	%*	rank	%*	rank	%*
Family	1	96	1	99	1	99	1	97
Friends	2	90	3	92	3	91	3	83
Work	3	86	2	95	2	93	2	94
Leisure	4	83	4	82	4	82	4	75

Note: *Percentage answers 'very important'.
Source: L. França (1993: 16).

Uncertainty avoidance works against sharing what are perceived to be scarce resources, most of all when they pertain to a central realm of life such as work. In this context, the rise of unemployment, its structural modification (namely the rise of long term unemployment), and the sense of 'economic crisis' was bound to provoke fears and find anchor in perceived threats. In Portugal, despite the fact that the official unemployment rate is very low, because of the widespread mistrust of the opportunity system, survey research consistently reveals that the fear of unemployment is very intense – even more intense than in societies having higher unemployment rates. Women, as has been shown, are not envisioned as competitors and though late retirement is not so easily accepted, foreigners are, in fact, the 'preferred' scapegoat. The fear of unemployment can be projected on to foreigners with ease: this was the case in the 1980s, when racial clashes (between White Portuguese and Black African descent workers) occurred in the industrial suburbs of Lisbon where unemployment rates were extremely high. There are realistic fears (expressed by national associations' leaders, policy makers and trade union leaders) that the same situation may occur as soon as the intensive demand of labour for public works starts declining.

WHO ARE THE FOREIGNERS LIVING IN PORTUGAL AND HOW ARE THEY PERCEIVED?

Who is a foreigner? Not surprisingly, a country familiar with emigration, mass tourism, and now recent waves of immigration exhibits different behaviours towards different categories of foreigners.[7]

A study of the language used in Portuguese newspapers (Guibentif 1991) revealed migrants coming to Portugal for economic motives were not usually referred to as immigrants. Instead, and because of the large concentration among them of people coming from the former colonies in Africa, terms like Africans or Capeverdians (the first and at present the largest African community to settle in Portugal) were used in place of the term immigrant but with exactly the same meaning.

In a field observation, we were able to see just how misleading the term immigrant may be when used among White Portuguese. The fact of being traditionally an emigration society makes it easy for ordinary people to mix the meanings of the words 'immigrant' and 'emigrant'. On the other hand, people coming from the former colonies sometimes do not like to be called immigrants either.[8]

People coming from the former African colonies and their families form the bulk of the foreign population settled in Portugal. Though the community is surely much larger than official registration statistics indicate, the relative size of (Black) African immigration is greater in Portugal than in any other European country (Machado 1997; Cordeiro 1997; Justino et al. 1998). In Spain, Italy and Greece, OECD reports point to much more heterogeneous migrant inflows.[9]

So, even though in formal terms there seems to be a single trend of recent transformation of south European societies towards immigration, one should keep in mind this limited, albeit very important particularity.

The still very recent de-colonization of the African territories formerly under Portuguese administration (which occurred in the mid-1970s) and the increased influx of people arriving from Africa and Brazil (since the 1980s) were very powerful accelerators of transformation in Portuguese relations with the foreign-born. The 'other' coming from abroad was formerly portrayed as a tourist or a member of the wealthy societies where Portuguese labour migrated. This perception has now

TABLE 13
EVOLUTION OF THE LEGAL FOREIGN POPULATION ACCORDING TO THE CONTINENTS OF ORIGIN

	1986		1997	
Total number of foreigners	86,982	100	175,263	100
Europeans	24,040	27.6	49,747	28.4
Africans in general	37,829	43.5	81,717	46.6
Africans from former Portuguese colonies	36,799	42.3	77,600	44.3
Brazilians	7,470	8.6	19,990	11.4

Sources: Machado and SEF (1998).

changed and grown more complex.

Although there are no systematic enquiries on the topic from that period, the available data and literature suggest this was, in fact, the dominant image of foreigners, since the time that Portugal took initiatives to attract mass tourism, in the 1960s. The data above show the still important presence of other Europeans among the foreigners: but they are predominantly located in the sunbelt regions and the cities, and they are much less geographically concentrated than the people coming from Africa (Cordeiro 1997).

Today still, the average yearly volume of tourist arrivals in Portugal nearly matches the total population, more than 90 per cent coming from other European countries. Spain and Greece also depend heavily on European tourism (Boisseuvain 1994).

And it was also in the 1960s that emigration to other European countries (mainly France) was booming with almost one million departures in the 1960s alone. Although at a much slower pace, and under different forms (e.g. seasonal as well as permanent departures) emigration still continues regularly mobilizing important segments of the labour force in some regions (Alentejo, Beira Interior) towards Europe (e.g. Switzerland, Germany). But it is difficult to measure in the new institutional context of the EU, and we do not know how much of this goes to Europe and how much goes elsewhere (Peixoto 1983; Baganha and Peixoto 1996). The strongly-knit long distance relations that supported the chain migrations are now a guarantee of communication between differing social, economic and cultural contexts.

Portugal's experience with tourism and emigration may help explain why the concept of foreigner does not have the negative connotations it assumes in other societies, and why the term immigrant is so easily mistaken for emigrant. Yet, when one looks at the attitudes toward social

TABLE 14
TOURISM

Country	Total arrivals (millions)	Market share from Europe (%)
Greece	8,873,310	88.92
Italy	20,862,965	74.08
Spain	12,251,352	84.91
Portugal	8,019,919	92.56
Total Europe*	186,880,715	82.39

Note: *15 countries included
Source: World Tourism Organization cited in J. Boissevain (1994: 49).

TABLE 15
FEELINGS TOWARDS 'OTHERS'

	Greece			Spain			Italy			Portugal			EU12/15*		
	'93	'95	'97	'93	'95	'97	'93	'95	'97	'93	'95	'97	'93	'95	'97
NATIONALITY															
Disturbing	28	35	34	7	6	6	11	8	13	6	7	5	13	11	13
Not disturbing	70	64	64	91	93	93	86	90	83	93	93	94	83	86	83
RACE															
Disturbing	25	20	31	11	8	7	13	11	16	9	8	7	16	13	15
Not disturbing	74	79	67	87	91	91	84	86	81	90	91	92	81	84	81
RELIGION															
Disturbing	30	27	–	8	8	–	11	8	–	8	8	–	13	12	–
Not disturbing	69	72	–	88	91	–	84	90	–	90	91	–	82	85	–

Sources: Eurobarometer 39, 1993; Eurobarometer 42, 1995; Eurobarometer 48, 1998.
Note: * EU 15 in 1997, EU 12 in 1993 and 1995.

heterogeneity in the four southern European countries, all having undergone roughly the same experiences in the near past, there is no simple pattern.

According to Eurobarometer, the Portuguese and the Spanish societies appear to be much more tolerant than the rest of the EU – concerning issues related to nationality, race, or religion (Table 15). Greece appears as much less prone to accept heterogeneity than the rest of the EU, and Italy ranks as average. There is definitely not a clear south European pattern distinguishable in the data concerning the attitudes toward foreigners, as Table 15 makes clear.

TABLE 16
ATTITUDES TOWARDS NON-NATIONALS OF THE EC

	1991	1993	1995	1997
Greece:				
Too many	29	57	64	71
Lot, but not too many	47	34	33	27
Not many	12	4	2	1
Don't know	13	6	2	1
Spain:				
Too many	25	25	27	20
Lot, but not too many	41	44	45	47
Not many	21	20	25	23
Don't know	13	12	4	10
Italy:				
Too many	63	64	46	53
Lot, but not too many	29	29	43	35
Not many	5	5	8	9
Don't know	3	2	3	3
Portugal:				
Too many	18	25	30	28
Lot, but not too many	33	42	36	41
Not many	28	19	26	20
Don't know	21	14	8	11
EU 12/15:*				
Too many	50	52	43	45
Lot, but not too many	34	34	42	40
Not many	9	9	11	10
Don't know	7	6	4	6

Sources: Eurobarometer 35, 1991; Eurobarometer 39, 1993; Eurobarometer 42, 1995; Eurobarometer 48, 1998**
Notes: * EU 15 in 1997, EU 12 in 1991 and 1993; ** the exact formulation of the question, in 1997, didn't involve the reference to foreigners from outside EC.

Moreover, when one considers the perception of the volumes involved in the migration flows coming from outside the EU, the data corroborate the scenario of tolerance toward foreign workers in Portugal and Spain (Table 16): The same pattern of answers holds, although the values reflecting a negative assessment are much higher. Italy and Greece, however, score even higher than the EU average in the negative feelings towards foreigners.

The results of surveys of attitudes toward foreigners are clearly distinct from the single pattern observed for attitudes towards work. Therefore, if there is an influence of cultural factors on attitudes toward foreigners, it does not derive from a geographically based socio-cultural entity like southern Europe. Rather, these data suggest that one cannot make sense of this heterogeneity, without reference to specific categories of foreigners and to specific historical experiences between nationalities.

HUMAN RIGHTS AND FOREIGNERS' PARTICIPATION IN THE LABOUR MARKET

National surveys on value orientations toward immigration, race and ethnic relations may be of interest to further explore this orientation of research. Public opinion poll data on value orientation show that humanistic ideals prevail over 'materialistic' orientations, when broad migration issues are addressed.

TABLE 17
ON WHAT SHOULD IMMIGRANTS ISSUES BE DISCUSSED?

an economic basis	28.6%
a cultural and humanistic basis	46.0%
doesn't know/doesn't answer	25.4%

Source: Público, 2 August 1995, p.2.

Furthermore, two recent nation-wide polls revealed that the large majority (77 per cent) of Portuguese believe foreigners living in Portugal should have the same social rights as Portuguese (Cabral 1995: 18) and 29 per cent even believed that those coming from outside the EU should have their rights extended (Europinion #13 1997). Political rights (such as the right to vote in local elections) were also deemed acceptable by 83 per cent in another nation-wide poll (*Público*, August 2nd 1995). Concerning tangible social rights, however, and specifically, access to jobs, things appear to be quite different.

Especially interesting is one result obtained in a 1992 poll, concerning the perceptions of competition in the labour market from foreign workers.[10] As suggested before, the low rates of unemployment are no obstacle to the spread of feelings of insecurity crystallized in the presence of foreigners. Table 18 shows the relationship.

The fact that the percentage of respondents feeling threatened by foreigners rises nearly eight per cent in Lisbon where the majority of foreigners and particularly the bulk of Africans are settled, further supports this interpretation.

Consistent with these data, the results of an opinion poll taken two years later show that there is an even distribution between those who

TABLE 18
ARE IMMIGRANTS TAKING AWAY PORTUGUESE JOBS?

	Total	Lisbon
Yes	42.6	50.3
Maybe	13.8	11.0
No	43.6%	38.7%

Source: Público, 11 May 1992, p.3.

think Portugal should shut the doors to foreigners looking for jobs, and those who reject it (Villalobes 1994).

The large numbers involved in the rejection of foreigners allow us to think that it is indeed, a collective sense of insecurity which is being expressed. And furthermore, one can hypothesise that it affects different levels of the socio-economic hierarchy (see also Quillian 1995).

That professionals are affected by this insecurity is illustrated by a 'crisis' in the dental field that made the headlines some years ago when Brazilian dentists wanted to practice in Portugal and met with strong objections from the Portuguese medical dentists' association. The disagreement was apparently about the value of school credentials, but the Brazilians claimed it was a reaction of 'turf protection'. A joint decision involving professional organizations and State agencies of both countries seems to have put an end to the dispute (see *A Capital*, 23 July 1998).

In fact, only the migrant populations coming from Africa are heavily concentrated in manual work; this is not the case either for other Europeans nor for Brazilians, who, on average, possess qualifications superior to the average Portuguese. But this is not the single difference: whereas the former are concentrated almost exclusively around the capital; the settlement of Brazilians is dispersed throughout the country, and the other Europeans are concentrated in the sunbelt areas and around the big cities (for a thorough review of the demographic characterization of the foreign population in Portugal, see Cordeiro 1997).

So, instead of a reaction based on concrete experiences of tight and ferocious competition, what emerges from these data, (when keeping in mind the reduced unemployment experience of the Portuguese in general), is that a negative although diffuse perception of competition affecting the collectivity is being constructed and projected onto newly found scapegoats.

In sum, it seems that general human rights on the one hand, and concrete rights entailing the access of foreigners to perceived scarce goods, on the other hand, bring about quite different reactions from the Portuguese public. On human rights issues there is much more open-mindedness. On access to the national labour market there is much more reserve and even overt opposition.

But is there a clear cut, unique attitude toward foreigners? Are they perceived as a homogeneous collective 'other'? The available data show some interesting categorical cleavages. Relying once more on data from Eurobarometer Special Edition on Racism and Xenophobia from 1989, when Portuguese respondents were asked to name other nationalities, only other south Europeans, other Europeans in general, and Africans were mentioned in more than 10 per cent of the responses. When asked about other races, 61 per cent of the responses mentioned Blacks. Congruent with data on the very limited internal ethnic differentiation (when compared to neighbouring Spain, for instance) and on volume and national composition of foreigners in Portugal, this result reveals that ethnic and cultural diversity does exist in Portuguese society, but in comparison to other Europeans, Portuguese are in general much less familiar with social heterogeneity on racial, religious, national or ethnic grounds.

Concerning the feelings towards several categories of 'others', including foreigners, obtained in the 1995 opinion poll, one can clearly see that the latter are not the ones who attract the most negative feelings. Rather, three particular categories of nationals – Homosexuals, drug addicts and Gypsies – rank conspicuously higher in antipathy than any other ethnic category involved in the question.

With closer inspection of the categories involving foreigners or ethnic groups, one can acknowledge a distinction between those who are more and less familiar to, and more and less welcomed by the Portuguese. Arabs and Muslims, Asian Indians and Jews are not recognized as a separate social category by more than a third of the Portuguese public and are thus not a focus of this analysis.

Asian Indians are, in fact, numerous in Portugal (estimates point to more than 30,000), and some of them are Muslims – as are some of the Africans. They are however dispersed in a wide occupational bracket, and over-represented in business ownership and highly skilled professions (Ávila and Alves 1993; Malheiros 1996). Because most of them have Portuguese nationality it is not possible, through national statistics, to go much further in characterising their make up. Their non existence as a

TABLE 19
FEELINGS TOWARD SELECTED SOCIAL GROUPS

	Sympathy*	Antipathy*	Doesn't know/ Doesn't answer
Homosexuals	27.3	45.3	27.3
Drug addicts	34.4	43.6	22.0
Gypsies	45.9	36.4	17.7
Arabs and Muslims	37.3	27.3	35.4
Spaniards	56.7	24.9	18.4
Asian Indians	45.1	21.6	33.3
Blacks	61.1	21.1	17.7
Jews	46.7	20.1	33.2
Other Europeans	61.2	15.4	23.5
Brazilians	68.0	14.8	17.2

Source: Público, 2 August 1995, p.4.
Note: *The question allowed two categories for expressing the feelings: 'a lot' and 'a little'.

social category for one third of the respondents is quite intriguing and suggests that the way social ethnic categories are built in Portuguese public opinion deserves further attention.

Concerning the remaining four categories, one can see they all rate high in sympathy (above 50 per cent). Nonetheless, only Brazilians rate low in antipathy and in lack of familiarity (below 20 per cent in both). Europeans rate low in antipathy, but are beyond 20 per cent in lack of familiarity, whereas the inverse happens with Blacks and Spaniards. In sum, different categories of foreigners, corresponding to diverse historical experiences, and different *modes of economic incorporation* (A. Portes) in Portuguese society, generate differing public attitudes. As suggested by Bobo and Hutchings (1996) this is possibly not only the result of a simple majority-to-minorities relationship. It may also reflect the sedimentation process of minorities' perceptions of each other and of the majority itself.

How does the widespread feeling of work as a scarce resource impinge on the attitudes toward the access of foreigners to the national labour market? The data presented here support the idea that the perception of threat is related to the lack of confidence in the opportunity structure, which correlates with the low average qualifications of the Portuguese labour force. On the other hand, evidence about the sharp differences between the four southern European countries, and among Portuguese nationals toward different categories of foreigners, suggest that attitudes are structurally embedded. In conclusion, and following Bobo and Hutchings (1996) approach, we suggest two hypotheses[11] and the way to address them. First, that the perception of threat is a consequence of prevailing feelings of mistrust of opportunity structures in Portugal. Second, that the anchoring of perceived threat must be related to specific contexts of past historical experiences and to the constructed images of particular categories of foreigners. Future research should address not only the majority's perceptions of different minorities, but also the various minorities' perceptions of each other and of the majority itself. Concrete relations in the workplace and labour market must be included in our observations if we wish to go beyond the verbal expression of opinions. Only in this way is it possible to combine psychosocial and structural approaches and thus understand why some categories are more visible than others, while some of the minorities melt into the social fabric.

NOTES

1. 'Retornados', literally the 'people who returned', was the term coined after decolonization to refer to the people coming from the former colonies – some of whom were of Portuguese (mainland) descent.
2. See the articles written by José Leitão (a member of the political commission of the Socialist party, by then opposing the Liberal party in office, presently High Commissioner for Immigration and Ethnic Minorities) and Celeste Correia (then a member of the Capeverdian Association, now the Socialist Party MP in charge of immigration issues in the Parliament) in *Expresso*, 29 June 1991 (p.A8) and 28 September 1991 (p.A10).
3. Although focusing on the 'racial background' of groups in order to capture multiple interactions in a 'multiracial social context', L. Bobo and V. L. Hutchings (1996) suggest a general framework integrating psychosocial and structural factors which we also find suitable for the analysis we present here of the attitudes of Portuguese majority toward several minority groups – our purposes being however of a much more limited scope, and the reality under scrutiny much less ethnically differentiated.
4. Waiting for the older people to 'get out' of the labour market.
5. But see also the analysis made by L. Quillian (1995) of 1988 Eurobarometer results, showing that prejudice is a response to collectively perceived threat depending both on 'economic conditions' and 'the size of the racial or immigrant group'.
6. Observations made in two survey rounds (the first between 1967 and 1969, the second between 1971 and 1973), among employees of a high tech multinational corporation (Hofstede 1984: 40-45).
7. A recent survey by J. Vala should shed some more light on this topic.
8. Some of the older persons interviewed argued that they were Portuguese when they were born, and do not understand why they must now accept the official status of immigrant.
9. Data for the other south European countries available from SOPEMI annual reports, based on national statistics, doesn't allow an easily comprehensible systematization in a single table. See the analysis of technical problems in international comparisons in Tapinos and Delaunay (1998), and data specifications in SOPEMI statistical tables.
10. Analysis concerning reactions to foreigners' participation in the Portuguese labour market was also presented in Marques et al. (1998). Baganha (1996) presents an

exhaustive list of the polls made in Portugal since the 1980s, and until 1995, on all sorts of topics concerning foreigners and ethnic minorities.

11. See also Cabral (1995), Rodrigues (1995) and Portes and Rumbaut (1996).

REFERENCES

Ávila, P. and M. Alves (1993): 'Da Índia a Portugal: trajectórias sociais e estratégias colectivas dos comerciantes indianos' [From India to Portugal: social trajectories and collective strategies of Indian business owners], *Sociologia – Problemas e Práticas* 13, pp.115-33.

Baganha, M. and J. Peixoto (1996): 'O estudo das migrações nacionais' [The study of national migrations], in J.M.C. Ferreira et al. (org.): *Entre a economia e a sociologia*, Oeiras: Celta Ed., pp.233-9.

Baganha, M. (1996): *Immigrants Insertion in the Informal Economy. The Portuguese case*, Coimbra: mimeographed report.

Bobo, L. and V.L. Hutchings (1996): 'Perceptions of racial competition in a multiracial setting', *American Sociological Review* 61/6, pp.951-72.

Boissevain, J. (1994): 'Towards an Anthropology of the European Communities?', in V.A. Goddard, J.R. Llobera and C. Shore (eds), *The Anthropology of Europe*, Oxford: Berg, pp.41-56.

Cabral, M.V. (1995): 'Equidade social, "estado-providência" e sistema fiscal: atitudes e percepções da população portuguesa (1991-1994)' [Social equity, 'welfare state', and fiscal system: attitudes and perceptions of the Portuguese population (1991-1994)], *Sociologia – Problemas e Práticas* 17, pp.9-34.

Cabral, M.V., J. Vala and J. Freire (1998): *Atitudes sociais dos portugueses. Base de dados 1997. Orientações perante o trabalho* [Social attitudes of the Portuguese. 1997 data base. Work orientations], Lisbon: ICS-ISSP.

Cordeiro, A.R. (1997): *Immigrants in Portuguese Society. Some Sociographic Figures*, Lisbon: SociNova Working Papers 4, FCSH-UNL.

Desrosières, A. and L. Thévenot (1988): *Les catégories socio-professionnelles* [The socio-occupational categories], Paris: La Découverte.

European Commission (1989): Eurobarometer special edition on racism and xenophobia.

European Commission (1997): Eurobarometer 47.1, special edition on racism and xenophobia.

European Commission (1991, 1993, 1995, 1998): Eurobarometer 35, 39, 42, and 48.

Fernandes, J.M. (1992): 'Racista? Eu?' [Racist? Who, me?], *Público* 11 May, pp.2-3.

Fernandes, J.M. (1995): 'A face escondida do racismo' [The hidden face of racism], *Público* 2 August, pp.2-5.

França, L. et al. (1993): *Portugal. Valores europeus, identidade cultural* [Portugal. European values, cultural identity], Lisbon: IED.

Freire, J. *et al.* (1998): *Atitudes face ao emprego, trabalho e tempo livre* [Attitudes toward employment, work, and leisure], Lisbon: IESE and Observatório do Emprego e Formação Profissional, mimeographed report.

Guibentif; P. (1991): 'A opinião pública face aos estrangeiros' [Public opinion toward foreigners], in M. Céu Esteves (ed.), *Portugal, país de imigração*, Lisbon: IED, pp.63-74.

Hofstede, G. (1984): *Culture's Consequences. International Differences in Work-related Values*, London: Sage Publications.

Justino, D. *et al.* (1998): *Proceedings of the Metropolis International Workshop*, Lisbon 1998, FLAD, pp.273-304.

Machado, F.L. (1997): 'Contornos e especificidades da imigração em Portugal' [Contours and specificities of immigration in Portugal], *Sociologia, Problemas e Práticas* 24, pp.9-44.

Malheiros, J. (1996): *Imigrantes na região de Lisboa: os anos da mudança* [Immigrants in Lisbon: the years of change], Lisbon: Colibri.

Marques, M.M. *et al.* (1998): *Oeiras City Template.* http://www

Maruani, M. and E. Reynaud (1993): *Sociologie de l'emploi* [Sociology of employment], Paris: La Découverte.

Mingione, E. (1996): 'Urban Poverty in the Advanced Industrial World: Concepts, Analysis and Debates' in E. Mingione (ed.): *Urban Poverty and the Underclass. A Reader*, Cambridge: Blackwell Publishers, pp.3-40.

OECD (1997): *Labour Force Statistics 1976-1996.*

Oliveira, F.C. and A Cunha (1996): 'Solidários sim, militantes não' [Sharing solidarity yes, but not being militants], *Público* 1 May, pp.2-7.

Peixoto, J. (1983): 'Migrações e mobilidade: as novas formas de emigração portuguesa a partir de 1980' [Migrations and mobility: the new ways of Portuguese emigration from 1980 on], in M.B. Silva, M.I. Baganha, M.J. Maranhão and M.H. Pereira (eds), *Emigração e imigração em Portugal*, Actas do Colóquio Internacional sobre Emigração e Imigração em Portugal, Lisbon: Fragmentos, pp.278-307.

Portes, A and R. Rumbaut (1996): *Immigrant America: A Portrait*, Berkeley: University of California Press (2nd edition).

Quillian, L. (1995): 'Prejudice as a response to perceived group threat: population composition and anti-immigrant and racial prejudice in Europe', *American Sociological Review* 60/4, pp.586-611.

Rodrigues, M.L. (1995): 'Atitudes da população portuguesa perante o trabalho' [Attitudes of the Portuguese population towards work], *Organizações e Trabalho* 14, pp.33-63.

SOPEMI (1998): *Trends in International Migration. Annual Report*, OECD

Tapinos, G. and D. Delaunay (1998): *Peut-on parler d'une mondialisation des migrations internationales?* [Can one speak of a globalization of international migrations?], Paper presented at the OECD International conference on Globalization, migrations and development, Lisbon.

Villalobos, L. (1994): 'Venham, mas poucos' [Come, but not too many], *Semanário* 19 March, p.8.

Immigration and Unemployment in Greece: Perceptions and Realities

MARTIN BALDWIN-EDWARDS and
CONSTANTINA SAFILIOS-ROTHSCHILD

INTRODUCTION

Until the 1990s, modern Greece had never experienced significant levels of foreign immigration, although mass migrations of Greeks themselves have been significant. Greek identity or 'Greekness' can be considered 'an organic whole in which Greek Orthodoxy, the *ethnos* and the state are a unity' (Pollis 1992: 171); thus Greece considers itself ethnically homogeneous, although with a few minorities. Even mass tourism has been viewed as a necessary evil, tolerated for economic reasons. Within this context it can be understood that the recent influx of permanent, semi-permanent and temporary immigrants from a variety of countries has created negative feelings among many Greeks. Some are unhappy merely because so many other languages are spoken, which makes them feel that they are not in their own country. Other social changes such as higher (although still low) crime rates and rising unemployment, which might otherwise be attributed to modernization and economic developments, have become linked in the public view with immigration. In this paper, we attempt to chart the available evidence about the employment of (mainly illegal) immigrants, their likely relationship to the employment and unemployment of Greeks, and the perceptions of various actors within Greek society.

Trends in Employment and Unemployment

Over the 1980s, the formal Greek economy exhibited a modest increase in employment, alongside a large decline in agricultural employment (–27 per cent) and a smaller decline in manufacturing (–15 per cent). These declines were offset by increases in services – almost entirely through employment by the state. Over this period the female participation rate increased and the male rate declined, particularly for older men. The recorded unemployment rate increased from around 4 per cent in the early 1980s to over 10 per cent in the late 1990s, with typical southern European characteristics – high female unemployment, high youth unemployment and a very high incidence of long-term unemployment (Demekas and Kontolemis 1997: 84).

The problem with these data is that they do not adequately reflect, let alone explain, the Greek reality. Greece has a very large informal sector – conservatively estimated at 30-35 per cent of GDP (Lianos et al. 1996; Kanellopoulos 1992) along with an endemic tendency toward multiple job holding and unpaid family work. The precise overlap between recorded unemployment and actual unemployment can only be conjectured, although the extent of underemployment is probably significant. We should note a rural/urban distinction here as well as the gender difference. Table 1 shows these two parameters clearly.

TABLE 1
UNEMPLOYMENT RATES BY SEX AND AREA, 1997

	Urban %	Rural %
Male	8.3	4.9
Female	19.0	7.9

Source: **Labour Force Survey, 1998.**

Thus the high rate for urban women is at least partly explained by their frequent participation in the informal economy whilst declaring themselves unemployed. Male participation is more usually in the form of a second job, with one job in the formal economy, therefore men are less likely to declare themselves as unemployed. In the case of rural women, their higher rate is explained by the fact that they are underemployed as unpaid family workers, working one or two months during harvest; since many do not have other (non-farm) employment, they are classed as unemployed. Rural men without work tend to migrate to urban areas, hence the lower rural unemployment rate. Mass internal migration – usually to Athens – has been a consistent feature of twentieth century Greece and is the major cause of rural agricultural labour shortages.

Immigrants in the Labour Force

Greece has admitted few non-Greek immigrants as workers (a stock of around 30,000), although the number of legally present immigrants is much higher (approximately 80,000) (OECD 1998: 114-15). Throughout the 1990s these numbers have declined (Baldwin-Edwards 1998) whilst the estimated number of illegal immigrants has been escalating. Prior to the regularization procedure of 1998, these estimates were in the range 250-500,000 – between 6 and 12 per cent of the registered labour force (OECD 1998: 115). The recorded number of applications for the first stage of the regularization was 373,000 (Baldwin-Edwards and Fakiolas 1999), implying that the higher estimates are correct. Given that the vast majority of immigrants are of working age, and likely to be economically active, this shows their major role in the contemporary Greek economy. For comparison, we should note that the ratio of registered immigrants to labour force in the rest of Europe is typically within the range 3-8 per cent: only Germany, Austria and Switzerland are higher at 9, 10 and 18 per cent respectively (OECD 1998a). Even the comparable Italian problem with illegal immigrants takes its ratio up to a maximum of about 7 per cent. Thus Greece has an exceptional problem in the extent of its illegal immigrant population.

Since the vast majority of immigrants are illegal, we know very little about them – most notably their nationalities, gender and length of stay. In the recent programme for the legalization of illegal immigrants, 53 per cent of applicants were Albanian: this confirms the perception that the major nationality is Albanian. The regularization programme applications contradict earlier research, showing Egyptian, Bulgarian and Pakistani as the major nationalities after Albanian (see Baldwin-Edwards and Fakiolas 1999), although there are known to have been specific problems for some nationalities in the legalization programme. Previously, it was thought that the main groups were Polish, other Balkan, Filipino, Egyptian and Pakistani (Papantoniou et al. 1996: 56-7).

The unemployment rates of legally present foreign workers are consistently two to three times the levels of the indigenous populations in all European countries, whilst in the USA, Canada and Australia they exhibit almost identical levels (Leslie 1997: 57). Unpublished data from the NSSG (Papantoniou et al. 1996) show a rate of around 15 per cent unemployment, with migrants from certain regions at very high levels: Africa – 36 per cent; Oceania – 26 per cent; North America – 19 per cent; Middle East, South America, South Asia, eastern central Europe – 15 per cent. The lowest rates are for East Asia and the EU, which are at or below the Greek figure. These figures might suggest that the restrictive Greek immigration policy has been more effective than other European countries', in its implementation of some sort of strict *Gastarbeiter* policy. However, this is to ignore the massive illegal immigration and employment – with 15-20 illegal immigrants for every legal one.

The substantial economic literature on immigration and the labour market has appeared to reach no unequivocal conclusion about the impact of legal immigration on labour markets (Lianos et al. 1996; Borjas 1994; Friedberg and Hunt 1995). The less extensive literature on the impact of illegal immigration concludes generally that there are distributional consequences. These consequences are of two sorts. First, a systemic and admittedly theoretical one – that cheap immigrant labour permits the continuation of a traditional pattern of socio-economic development when the domestic labour supply is too costly for its productivity level. This may impede economic restructuring by channelling resources into the informal sector (Dell'Arigna and Neri 1987). The second consequence is a crucial empirical matter – of whether the immigrant labour is a substitute or complement for indigenous labour. If immigrants substitute for nationals, then wages will fall and the indigenous workforce may lose their jobs. If, on the other hand, immigrants are complementary then they enable the indigenous labour force to reach higher productivity levels in other sectors of employment (Jahn and Straubhaar 1999).

THE EMPIRICAL EVIDENCE

Almost all of the limited studies of immigrants in Greece have focused on Athens. We use here four surveys looking at immigrants in Athens and three in rural areas – the latter providing previously unpublished data.

Urban Areas

In urban areas, a 1993-94 study by Lazaridis and Romaniszyn (1998) found that Albanian men work primarily in the construction industry and women in domestic work and some tourist-related work such as cleaning.

Research undertaken in 1995-96 by Iosifides had a sample of 135 mainly illegal immigrants in the Athens area, with three nationalities covered – Albanian, Egyptian and Filipino. Labour market segmentation according to nationality and gender, with little relevance of education and training, are important conclusions (Iosifides 1998: 46) – although our reading suggests that gender is by far the more important variable.

Iosifides reaches two important conclusions regarding labour market competition with Greeks. First, that immigrant employment seems to be essential for the economic survival of many small businesses and actually enables employed Greeks in those firms to keep their jobs; secondly, that many jobs are created because of immigrants' availability at lower wages (p.38). Yet another important conclusion is that immigrants' employment is precarious and unstable (p.46): it may be that the level of earnings is not in itself a sufficient explanation for the disinterest of Greek workers in such employment. These findings tend to confirm the dual labour market hypothesis, initially advanced by Piore (1978).

Markova and Sarris's research (1997) of 100 Bulgarians in the Athens area appears to contradict other research findings – namely, their conclusion that immigrant employment is quite stable and that some 50 per cent of respondents are competing with Greeks for employment. These apparent contradictions are easily explicable, in our view. First, the sample taken was heavily biased (75 per cent) towards women, thus reflecting a specific submarket probably independent of nationality. Secondly, they report that there was almost perfect correspondence between the type of housekeeping work and the presence of native competition. 'Live-in' housekeeping work is taken almost exclusively by immigrants, whereas other housekeeping duties are still attractive to Greek women. Thus these two conclusions seem invalid as generalizations about the immigrant labour market in Athens.

Another study undertaken by Chtouris in March-April, 1998 in greater Athens with 300 illegal immigrants, concluded that the immigrants play a significant role in keeping small businesses competitive. About one fifth (21.4 per cent) of the immigrants are employed in small businesses and about one fifth (20.9 per cent) in construction and seasonal work and slightly less than one fifth (19.1 per cent) in personal or domestic services. The survey found that among those who answered regarding the size of their wages, 24.1 per cent earned less than 5,000 drachmas per day. It concludes that it is unclear how many jobs filled by immigrants would have been filled by Greeks, if tight controls on illegal labour were introduced: the very low wages motivate employers to hire immigrants and it is doubtful that Greeks would have accepted most of the jobs held by immigrants, even if the wages were slightly better. The survey also points out that the employment of immigrants in the service sector plays a very important role by facilitating the work of women with high skills, as well as for the care of old people (Shugart 1998).

Rural Areas

The detailed 1993 socio-economic study by Lianos and others (1995), examining legal and illegal immigrants in four provinces of northern Greece, showed that while illegal immigrants substitute for Greek unskilled workers, many of the jobs they held would not have been performed by Greek workers. Thus, illegal immigrants have substituted (net substitution) only about 5.8 per cent of jobs held by Greeks. This is particularly true in agriculture where 21.6 per cent of unskilled farm jobs seem now to have been replaced by immigrants, mainly illegal ones. On the other hand, the study found that illegal immigrant employment in agriculture has contributed potentially 0.4 per cent to Greek GDP and employment in construction has a potential net contribution to Greek GDP of about 1 per cent.

A study by Lazaridis and Romaniszyn (1998) of Albanians in Corfu found that they all worked in unskilled agricultural work (e.g. olive harvesting) and that they were usually paid half the wages of Greek workers.

In the TSER research programme examining the social exclusion of men and women smallholders, research was conducted in the rural areas of four prefectures of Greece: Karditsa, Chania (Crete), Evia, and Lesvos.[1] Two hundred and ninety-eight interviews were conducted over the period March-September 1998. Of these interviews, 205 were conducted with women farmers and 92 with men farmers, the large majority of whom were smallholders, that is with farms of less than 4.5 ha.

There is considerable social, economic and cultural differentiation between the four prefectures. Karditsa and Chania are the most traditional areas in which patriarchal values are still prevalent and powerful. Evia and Lesvos are more 'modern' areas, with Lesvos being the more progressive region. There is also considerable variation with regard to the numbers of immigrants available for agricultural work. Karditsa has the largest number of immigrants, predominantly Albanians and Lesvos, has the fewest immigrants. This is largely due to geographical reasons, Karditsa being the nearest area to Albania, Lesvos being the more remote area and also the one with a very heavy presence of the army, because it is a border area with Turkey. The number of immigrant workers available influences the wages they receive as well as the number of farmers who use them. Thus in the three villages of Lesvos studied, the majority of smallholders (65.3 per cent) who hired workers and of farmers with more than 4.5 ha, Greeks (80.0 per cent) hired Greek workers whom they usually paid 15,000 drachmas for pruning and

12,000 for unskilled agricultural work. Only about one third (34.7 per cent) of smallholders and one fifth (20.0 per cent) of farmers with more than 4.5 ha hired Albanians – mostly in combination with Greek men or women workers. Greek workers were hired for pruning and other skilled agricultural work and Albanians for heavy and unskilled agricultural work involved in the harvesting of olives. The wages of Albanians ranged between 8,000 and 10,000 drachmas but they also received meals – occasionally three meals a day.

In Karditsa, on the other hand, where there is the highest concentration of immigrants, again the majority of smallholders (69.7 per cent) who hired workers (about 46.4 per cent of all farmers studied hired workers), hired Greek men and women. In this area many women still work as waged agricultural workers, thus half of the Greek workers hired are women (or slightly more than one third of all hired workers). Although it appears that Albanians replace women agricultural workers in unskilled agricultural work, this may not be true. It is a fact that there is a differential in the level of wages: for the same unskilled agricultural work, such as hoeing and harvesting cotton or tobacco, women are paid 5-6,000 drachmas and Albanians are paid 3-4,000 drachmas. Albanians, however, are offered meals in addition – in some cases, three meals a day. Sometimes both Greek women and Albanians are hired as seasonal workers, the latter for heavy unskilled tasks.

Some of the interviewed women working as agricultural labourers voiced their feelings regarding the competition faced from Albanians and their fear that they are being displaced by them – since they claim that they can now find fewer work opportunities in agriculture. It must be noted, however, that because of the great number of Albanians available in rural Karditsa, they are competing with each other for work, thus depressing the level of their wages. These are about half the wages of Greek male workers, who are paid only 6-7,000 drachmas but are not offered meals. Similar wage differentials between Greek and Albanian male workers in agriculture have also been reported by other researchers in villages in Corfu, another area which because of its proximity to Albania has large numbers of illegal Albanian immigrants (Lazaridis and Romaniszyn 1998).

In Evia, where there is a small number of Albanians, again the majority of farmers (63.2 per cent) do not hire seasonal agricultural workers. Of those who hire seasonal workers, about an equal number hire Albanians and/or Greeks and only in one case, a Greek woman is hired as a seasonal worker. Also it is interesting to note that there is no difference between the agricultural wages paid to Albanians and Greek workers. One farmer commented: 'some think that they pay less when they pay the Albanians 5,000 drachmas; when, however, you calculate the cost of the meals you give them, it is the same cost for Albanians or Greeks.'

Finally, in Chania, Crete, where there is a considerable number of foreign agricultural workers, including Rumanian and Russian-Pontian in addition to Albanians, more than half of the farmers do not hire workers. Of those who hire seasonal agricultural workers, they predominantly (90 per cent) hire immigrants, mostly Albanian but also a mixture of Albanian and Rumanian or Albanian and Russian-Pontian workers. There is no evidence that they displace Greek workers since very few Cretans are willing to work as seasonal agricultural workers and the wages of Greek and foreign workers are about the same – 6-7,000 drachmas.

Interpreting the Data

The crucial differentiation regarding the employment patterns of illegal (and, to some extent, legal) immigrants is not so much nationality and educational level or training. Rather, the determinants appear to be the rural-urban setting and the immigrant's gender. Thus we find male immigrants predominantly in construction and unskilled heavy agricultural labour, whilst women are concentrated in housekeeping and childcare. The rural-urban differentiation has been adequately dealt with in the literature, whereas little attention has been paid to gender differentiation.

It seems that existing fears and claims made about the impact of illegal immigrants on the labour market are not based on sound evidence. First, the data from Athens – as well as from the study of rural areas – do not show that Greek workers are being displaced (with the possible exceptions of Greek female seasonal workers in agriculture in Karditsa and Greek 'live-out' housekeepers in Athens). Instead, it appears that in most cases the immigrants perform work that Greeks are not willing to undertake and are thus complementary to the native labour force.

Secondly, it is not true as a generalization that immigrants (and particularly Albanians, who are the majority) always work for very low wages. In the case of agriculture, in most instances if the meals offered to illegal immigrants are also counted, there is little difference between the wages of Greek and Albanian workers performing the same work.

There seem to be two important parameters determining earnings – the local supply-demand relationship and a temporal 'learning curve' of the immigrants. Thus wage levels depend primarily on the number of available immigrants in an area, the level of demand for unskilled labour and the extent to which Greeks are willing to perform the same work with reasonable wages. A secondary factor may be a 'learning curve' (e.g. Markova and Sarris 1997) whereby initially immigrants are ill-prepared and obstructed by linguistic difficulties. As time goes by, they gain experience in the labour market and ability in the Greek language and are then able to bargain and show preferences with respect to working conditions.

Thirdly, it is evident that Albanians and illegal immigrants in general are valuable – even essential – for small businesses' survival, particularly in agriculture. This is true also for individuals, particularly working women and the elderly. There is a corresponding positive effect on Greek GDP.

GREEK PERCEPTIONS OF IMMIGRANTS

The 1991 Immigration Law was passed explicitly as a restrictive response to the inflow of illegal Albanian migrants, and makes no attempt to deal with the role of immigrant labour or their position in Greek society (Glytsos 1995: 168-9). Thus the award of work permits is very limited (see above) and has led to massive illegal immigration and employment of foreigners; this situation led to the 1998 Legalization Programme, attempting to regularize the status of most illegal immigrant workers (see below). Karydis (1992, 1993) has argued forcefully that the 'dangerous Albanian' stereotype was invented initially by the police, taken up by the media and subsequently used by the state as the putative cause of increased criminality.

We might expect this negative construction of immigrants to be reflected in opinion polls. In the Atttica area, a 1995 survey of 500 households asked respondents to list the five most important effects of foreign workers in Greece: 73 per cent chose 'increase unemployment', 56 per cent 'increase crime' and 53 per cent 'decline in wages' amongst the five choices.[2] However, the same survey asked respondents to list the three most pressing problems in Greece: illegal immigrants were cited by only 7.5 per cent, ranked tenth out of twelve choices. Unemployment was ranked third at 45.5 per cent.

A 1993 poll taken in Kavala found 90 per cent of respondents agreeing that immigrants take jobs from Greeks, and 84 per cent that they constitute a public danger.[3] Another 1995 survey of 1,000 young people (15-29) in the Salonica region showed 93 per cent agreeing that foreigners increase unemployment, 88 per cent that they contribute to increased crime; on the other hand, 81 per cent agreed that immigrants do jobs which Greeks avoid.[4] Yet another survey of 1,000 people in the same year in Thessaloniki shows that employment status has no bearing on the views of the respondents, with employed, unemployed, students and 'others' ranking unemployment as the main effect of immigration (90-95 per cent), followed by increased crime (85-90 per cent).[5] Although there was much acceptance that they do the jobs avoided by Greeks (80-86 per cent) there was little recognition that they help the economy (14-21 per cent). It must be noted that all these polls were taken in northern Greece which borders emigration countries such as Bulgaria and Albania and such negative feelings may spring from the threateningly high numbers of immigrants in these areas.

The research of Lianos et al. in northern Greece showed 66 per cent of respondents perceiving that illegal immigrants have very much intensified unemployment among unskilled workers. This much lower figure can probably be explained by the fact that their survey was carried out amongst political and economic elites. Participants were chosen for their socio-economic status and superior knowledge of immigrant employment; these characteristics might be expected to lead to a greater appreciation of immigrants' contribution to the Greek economy.

In the research undertaken by Safilios-Rothschild described above, a distinction seemed to emerge between common beliefs and personal experiences. Those Greeks who had come into direct contact with, and actually employed, Albanians tended to find them hard-working and reported that they had no complaints.

Formal Responses to the Draft Decree for Legalization[6]

The Committee for the Regularization of Illegal Immigrants – set up in 1997 to prepare the two Presidential decree laws for the legalization of illegal immigrants – invited and received statements from ministries, prefectures, trades unions, employers' associations and others. (For trades unions and associations the statements are resolutions taken in extraordinary meetings.) These statements encompass a wide range of views, which appear to reflect different interests (of governmental agencies and private sector actors), and also different perceptions, apparently linked with regional variations. We advance some explanations later in this paper.

(a) Ministries. An unequivocally positive position appeared from the Agriculture Ministry, supporting legalization and acceptance of immigrants. The Ministry noted an acute shortage of agricultural labour, primarily through rural-urban migration of young people and the declining working capacity of ageing farmworkers. The higher wage costs created by shortage of manpower have made Greek products uncompetitive in European and world markets; the employment of immigrants has brought economic relief by stabilizing wages and matching increased seasonal labour demand. Mention is also made of certain sectors (sheep, pigs, cows and poultry) where harsh working conditions have resulted in no Greeks being prepared to work and the vast majority of employees are illegal immigrants.

The Ministry of Foreign Affairs opposed the legalization, on the grounds that it would give rights to the immigrants and might lead to more immigration. Both Foreign Affairs and Defence feared the possible creation of ethnic or religious groups. The Ministry of National Economy noted that it has no information about the role of immigrants in the labour market.

(b) Prefectures. Twenty-nine out of 52 prefectures submitted reports. Almost all supported the employment of immigrants in agriculture, although some with very restrictive conditions – such as 3-month permits. The Athens prefecture noted its major role in issuing foreigners' permits across the metropolitan area of Attica, and recommended initial 1-year permits renewable after examination of the labour market to avoid creating Greek unemployment. Two border prefectures – Drama, bordering Bulgaria and Thesprotia, bordering Albania – asked for both legal and illegal immigrants to be deported, admitting only ethnic Greeks. Two regions – Karditsa and Evritania – commented on the threat to law and order and to Greek society from illegal immigrants, requesting controlled seasonal agricultural workers and deportation of all illegal immigrants. The Peloponnesus prefectures admitted the need for agricultural workers, but with very restrictive conditions. The islands – most particularly the prefectures on Crete – insisted on confining workers to agriculture and for seasonal work only.

(c) Trades Unions. The General Confederation of Labour, in line with its history of positive action (Papantoniou et al. 1996: 149-50), set out extensive rights and protection of illegal immigrant workers, with the ultimate objective of acquiring their trade union membership. The

agricultural unions commented that immigrants have saved Greek agriculture from disaster, and that bureaucratic procedures should be abandoned in order to encourage their employment and avoid increased food prices. One suggestion was that employment of less than 6 months should be excluded from the registration procedures, although farmers should submit personal data of employed immigrants to the authorities. The only opposition to immigrants is shown by the Musicians' Union, which opposed regularization unless approved specifically in each case by the Union.

(d) Employers' Associations. All set out a very positive assessment of the role of immigrants in the Greek economy, with some reservations about not displacing Greeks. Three out of the five respondents reported that serious labour shortages pertain in their industry. The Federation of Industries in northern Greece noted that a few years ago many jobs were not filled in the agricultural sector – especially harvesting and animal husbandry. The Association of Greek Fish Farmers comments that 2,000 people are employed and that they are dependent on illegal Albanian workers for competitive exports. Deportation of these illegal workers would destroy their firms because of the disinterest of Greeks in the hard work of fish farming. The Flower Producers in Trizinia note similarly that flower production could not continue without immigrant labour, and that Indians have been employed for many years and now specialize in such jobs.

SOME TENTATIVE CONCLUSIONS

In terms of Greek perceptions, we posit here four variables as having considerable explanatory power. Most important seems to be the immigrant/population ratio – largely depending on proximity to 'sending countries'. Also important are the variables of the urban-rural and male-female disjunctures. Finally, although of lesser importance, we note the public-private disjuncture.

The opinion poll data are too poor to know whether there is any gendered dimension, although it seems that Greeks are more fearful of single young men than of married men with families or single women. The rural-urban dichotomy is only to be expected. First, the inhabitants of cities are universally more tolerant of immigrants; secondly, many of the rural areas are border regions which have had mass influxes of illegal immigrants and much petty crime. There the high immigrant/native ratio reinforces the rural effect – leading to high negative perceptions. Even in the city of Thessaloniki, which might be expected to show urban tolerance, we note a much higher affirmation in opinion polls that 'immigrants cause unemployment' (typically about 90 per cent) than in Athens (70 per cent or lower). The submitted opinions of prefectures cited above fit this pattern very clearly. Athens was supportive of immigration, although concerned to protect Greek jobs; some border regions wished to stop all immigration of other than ethnic Greeks, whilst other rural areas recognized the need for immigrant labour but abhorred its illegality.

One consensual point is the perceived need for the Greek state to regulate immigrant labour and prevent illegal migration. A public-private dichotomy is evidenced in the public reality of their illegality, which is inconsistent with the immigrants' important – even crucial – function in the economy. The role of the media in reporting issues of crime and immigration is a major factor in shaping public opinion; thus we can also find the dichotomy in the sense that, in contrast with very high response rates in opinion polls to the alleged criminal behaviour of (Albanian) illegal immigrants, those who have had actual experience of Albanians seem to have few or no complaints. This aspect of Greek perception has not been adequately studied, however, and requires further investigation.

The role of the trades unions is interesting, in that if they perceive immigrant labour as threatening their members' interests, they might be expected to take a stand against it. Throughout the 1990s the major unions have been nothing but supportive of immigrants' rights, and most particularly of the right to legal status. This position is similar to that of unions in Italy and Spain (Watts 1999), but is not illogical. In line with the perceptions of the employers' associations and of some ministries and prefectures, they seem to accept that immigrants are for the most part either filling vacant posts or actually creating employment where it would not otherwise exist. If there is a danger to their members' interests, it lies in illegal immigrant labour weakening the bargaining power of unions. Thus the rational course is to promote the legalization of all immigrants and attempt to recruit them into relevant unions. At the same time, one must recognize that there is a discourse going on in organizations: thus the official positions are unlikely to exist at all levels. Two sorts of dissenting claim have been reported: that 'the seemingly bottomless pool of cheap labour provided by migrants was pushing Greeks out of jobs' (Shugart 1998) and that immigrants are responsible for the downward spiral of wages in the construction industry (Lazaridis and Romaniszyn 1998).

What of the legalization programme currently underway? In principle, the Greek state wishes to avoid replacing Greek workers with immigrants. Award of a Green Card requires examination of labour market conditions, but given the limited indicators available (along with the knowledge that even the USA failed to achieve the same objective) it is possible that legalized immigrants will be competing with Greeks in the future. The latest available data suggest that so few have been awarded Green Cards, and most of those for a period of only one year, that the dual labour market will be preserved. Thus it can safely be predicted that the linkage between illegal immigration and unemployment of Greeks is unlikely to increase in the near future.

In fact, illegal status is most likely a defining condition of employment, and probably most regularized immigrants will rapidly revert to it through their unemployability in the formal economy. This has been the experience of Italy, in its several regularization programmes (Reyneri, 1999). To a great extent, the underground economy is a market response to over-regulated and uncompetitive labour markets in an increasingly global economy; immigrant participation in it is extensive and market-driven. Only wholesale reform of the Greek labour market – which looks impossible – is likely to change that (Jahn and Straubhaar 1999).

For the future, we can discern several contradictory trends. First, that as contacts between Greeks and immigrants increase, the public-private dichotomy may diminish – leading to greater acceptance of immigration as a beneficial phenomenon both economically and socially. Second, that the localized extent of immigration and the very illegality of it, are serious problems for the population; thus some public policy measures are necessary in both respects. (It is difficult to imagine that state capacity can rise to this level, however, with the current weak regulation of the labour market.) Third, that as economic reform, privatization and deregulation proceed in Greece, the loss of over-protected state employment will force large numbers of low- and medium-skilled Greeks onto the labour market. Future competition for jobs in the private sector may lead to direct competition with immigrant labour, especially with skilled immigrants who are not using their skills at present. Thus the unknowable balance of these competing forces will be crucial in determining harmonious or conflictual immigrant relations.

NOTES

1. The unpublished data presented here were collected by Constantina Safilios-Rothschild within the context of a Targeted Socio-Economic Research Contract SOE2-CT97-3044 with DG XII of the Commission of the European Communities with the title: 'The Social Exclusion of Women Smallholders'.
2. Conducted by the Athens Labour Centre (KAPA); elaborated in OECD (1997).
3. Conducted by OPINION on behalf of the Lambrakis Foundation, Jan-Feb 1993 in Kavala. Cited in Papantoniou et al. (1996).
4. Elaborated in OECD (1997).
5. Elaborated in OECD (1997).
6. These summaries are taken from the synopses presented in Fakiolas (1998).

REFERENCES

Baldwin-Edwards, M. (1998): 'The Greek Regularization: a comparative analysis with the Spanish, Portuguese and Italian experiences', University of Reading, Centre for Euro-Mediterranean Studies Working Paper, April 1998 [on Web at http://www.rdg.ac.uk/EIS/].

Baldwin-Edwards, M. and R. Fakiolas (1999): 'Greece: the Contours of a Fragmented Policy Response', *South European Society & Politics* 3/3.

Borjas, G.J. (1994): 'The Economics of Immigration', *Journal of Economic Literature* 32/4, pp.1667-1717.

Dell'Arigna, C. and F. Neri (1987): 'Illegal Immigrants and the Informal Economy in Italy', *Labour* 1/2, pp.107-26.

Demekas, D. and Z. Kontolemis (1997): 'Labour Market Performance and Institutions in Greece', *South European Society & Politics* 2/2, pp.78-109.

Fakiolas, R. (1998): 'Μετανάστευση' [Immigration], in X. Petrinioti and G. Koukoules (eds), *Επετηρίδα Εργασίας 1997* [Greek Labour Yearbook 1997], Athens: Panteion University Press, pp.19-34.

Friedberg, R.M. and J. Hunt (1995): 'The Impact of Immigrants on Host Country Wages, Employment and Growth', *Journal of Economic Perspectives*, 9/2, pp.23-44.

Glytsos, N. (1995): 'Problems and Policies Regarding the Socio-economic Integration of Returnees and Foreign Workers in Greece', *International Migration*, XXXIII/2, pp.155-76.

Iosifides, T. (1997): 'Immigrants in the Athens Labour Market', in R. King and R. Black (eds), *Southern Europe and the New Immigrations*, Brighton: Sussex Academic Press, pp.26-50.

Jahn, A. and T. Straubhaar (1998): 'A Survey of the Economics of Illegal Migration', *South European Society and Politics*, 3/3.

Kanellopoulos, C. (1992): 'The Underground Economy in Greece: What Official Data Show', Discussion Paper no.4, May 1992, Centre for Planning and Economic Research (KEPE), Athens.

Karydis, V. (1992): 'The fear of crime in Athens and the construction of the "dangerous albanian" stereotype', *Χρονικά* 5, pp 97-103.

Karydis, V. (1993): 'Migrants as a political enterprise: the Greek-albanian case', *Χρονικά* 8, pp.93-6.

Lazaridis, G. and K. Romaniszyn (1998): 'Albanian and Polish Undocumented Workers in Greece: A Comparative Analysis', *Journal of European Social Policy* 8/1, pp.5-22.

Lianos, T.P., A.H. Sarris and L.T. Katseli (1996): 'Illegal Immigration and Local Labour Markets:The Case of Northern Greece', *International Migration*, XXXIX/3, pp.449-84.

Markova, E. and A. Sarris (1997): 'The Performance of Bulgarian Illegal Immigrants in the Greek Labour Market', *South European Society & Politics* 2/2, pp.57-77.

OECD (1997): '1996 SOPEMI Report on Greece', prepared by Nikos Petropoulos, mimeo – 32 pp + 32 tables.

OECD (1998): *Trends in International Migration: SOPEMI Annual Report*, Paris: OECD.

OECD (1998a): *Employment Outlook*, Paris: OECD.

Papantoniou, A., M. Papantoniou-Frangouli and A. Kalavanou (1996): 'Migrants' Insertion in the Informal Economy: Deviant Behaviour and the Impact on Receiving Societies', Greek Report of TSER project, Athens, December 1996, mimeo – 160 pp + 20 tables.

Piore, M. (1979): *Birds of Passage. Migrant Labor and Industrial Societies*, Cambridge: Cambridge University Press.

Pollis, A. (1992): 'Greek National Identity: Religious Minorities, Rights, and European Norms', *Journal of Modern Greek Studies* 10, pp.171-95.

Reyneri, E. (1998): 'The Mass Legalization of Immigrants in Italy: Permanent or Temporary Emergence from the Underground Economy?', *South European Society & Politics* 3/3.

Shugart, D. (1998): 'Small Businesses Might Not Survive Without Immigrants', *Kathimerini* 15/May [English Edition].

Watts, J. (1998): 'Italian and Spanish Labour Leaders' Unconventional Immigration Policy Preferences', *South European Society & Politics* 3/3.

Unemployment and the Political Economy of the Portuguese Labour Market

MANUEL VILLAVERDE CABRAL

The direct political and electoral impact of unemployment in Portugal tends to be significantly absorbed by the social structures of the country's labour market. This is why there has been little organized collective resistance to unemployment emanating from the Portuguese labour movement since the 1974 revolution.

In combination with other important socio-economic features of the Portuguese labour market that will also be discussed, the comparatively low weight of wage earnings in family incomes in most parts of Portugal seems to account for the equally low overall impact of unemployment on Portuguese politics. Furthermore, in recent years, the parts of the country most struck by unemployment were also those where a local left-wing political culture already prevailed. It is this and not unemployment *per se* which accounts for the unusually radical attitudes of the Portuguese unemployed.

As a result of these mediating factors, when unemployment did have some political and electoral impact, in the 1980s and the 1990s, it was constructed as simply part of a generally negative 'economic climate' prevailing in the country, rather than as a singular and direct mobilizing factor against the government of the day.

WAGES AND FAMILY INCOMES

The first point one needs to make about the political economy of the Portuguese labour market is, therefore, the structurally low weight of wages in overall family incomes in Portuguese society. While the importance of remittances from abroad has declined in recent years, income from sources *other* than labour (both wage labour and self-employment), as a share of overall family income, has increased consistently since the early 1980s.

It is not possible to deal here in any detail with the expansion of the Portuguese welfare state as a consequence of the democratization of the Portuguese political system (Esping-Andersen 1988). However, special mention must be made of social security transfers, namely pensions massively allocated to the elderly even when they had not made any financial contribution to the system during their working life. These non-wage related sources of income are especially important in Portugal's less developed regions. Such transfers account presently for some 20 per cent of family incomes and up to one third of regional income in areas like the Alentejo in the rural south and Trás-os-Montes in the north-east.

TABLE 1
SOURCES OF FAMILY INCOME (%)

Year	Wage-labour	Self-employment	Social security	Other*
1981	50	19	11	20
1990	47	14	14	25
1996	46	12	18	24

*Remittances; ownership; non-monetary sources of income
Source: Instituto Nacional de Estatística [National Institute of Statistics].

Another important feature of Portugal's political economy worth mentioning in this context is the country's low ratio of labour revenue to GDP. In fact, Portugal seems to share this particular feature with the other southern European countries. In the late 1980s the figures were, according to the comparative study carried out at the Portuguese Ministry of Employment (Almeida and Ribeiro 1997), 53 per cent in Portugal, 50 per cent in Spain, 49 per cent in Italy and 47 per cent in Greece. If correct, these figures suggest the need for comparative research into the specificity of southern European political economy. For now, one can only draw attention to the potential effects of relatively low labour revenue on the social impact of unemployment.

REGIONAL DISPARITIES IN WAGE LABOUR

The second distinguishing feature characterizing the structure of Portugal's labour market is the uneven regional distribution of rates of wage labour and, consequently, the regional unevenness of the weight of wages in family incomes. Such disparities are further reinforced by differential age structures, since the regions where traditional economic activities still prevail, such as farming, tend also to be those where the population is older and the economic impact of remittances from abroad is greater.

The latest regional breakdown of the share of wage-earners in the labour force is the 1991 Census, but we are entitled to believe that significant changes may have occurred since then. Indeed, the Employment Survey carried out quarterly estimated the share of wage-earners in the working population for 1995 at only 70 per cent.

TABLE 2
WAGE-EARNERS AS % OF THE WORKFORCE (1991 BY REGIONS)

Status	Portugal	North	Centre	Lisbon	Alentejo	Algarve
Wage-earners	77	76	69	81	71	71
Employers	6	7	6	6	5	7
Self-employed						
Family-helpers	15	15	22	12	18	21

Source: Instituto Nacional de Estatística [National Institute of Statistics].

According to Table 2, the regional distribution of wage-earners in the workforce varies significantly from over 80 per cent in the so-called 'Region of Lisbon and the Tagus Valley' to under 70 per cent in the central region (Coimbra). Actually, in all regions but Lisbon the share is below the national average. Since the 'statistical region' of Lisbon is substantially larger than the actual Metropolitan Area, if we had access to the breakdown for the exclusively urban areas of Lisbon and Setúbal, the relative weight of wage-earners in the labour force would be even greater, particularly when compared with the rural areas of all the regions north of the Tagus.

Conversely, only in the Lisbon area is the weight of self-employment in the working population lower than the national average. More importantly, we know from an older survey of the late 1970s that only in the districts of Lisbon and Setúbal was the weight of wages in family incomes above 50 per cent (Cordovil and Santandré 1980). Due to the ageing structure of most regions and the ensuing impact of social security payments, as well as remittances and other non-wage sources of family income, we have reason to believe that these structural differences between the Lisbon-Setúbal conurbation and the rest of the country may, if anything, have increased in recent years.

In fact, the latest regional breakdown for the sources of family income (1995-96) has just been made public, confirming the low weight of wages in most of the country. As expected, for a new historical low, the national average weight of wages was just under 46 per cent. Only in the Lisbon region did wages account for half of family income.

TABLE 3
SHARE OF WAGES IN REGIONAL FAMILY INCOME (1995-96)

Region	Value (%)
North	48
Centre	39
Lisbon	50
Alentejo	41
Algarve	40
Portugal	46

Source: Instituto Nacional de Estatística [INE National Institute of Statistics].

The only significant new evidence is that the pattern in the northern region comes closer now to the Lisbon pattern though there is reason to believe that this may be due to massive under-reporting of other sources of income in the north, namely income from self-employment. At any rate, it is striking that in highly populated and economically active regions such as central Portugal and the Algarve, the reported weight of wages in family incomes is no more than 40 per cent. The same reason mentioned above for the northern region may also apply here.

To sum up the regional pattern of labour markets and income sources, it seems clear that in most of Portugal, wages make only a limited contribution to the regional economy and therefore to family standards of living. Conversely, the social impact of unemployment, if and when it increases, tends to be very unevenly distributed throughout the country and often concentrated in the area of Lisbon and Setúbal as well as a few other towns struck by specific economic conjunctures.

These profound regional differences are not new in Portuguese society. Indeed, it is fair to say that the militant section of the Portuguese industrial working class has remained, since its political rise in the twentieth century, geographically isolated as well as socially separated from all prospective allies such as the urban lower middle classes and the peasantry. Its only 'class ally' has been historically the rural proletariat of Alentejo whose members are now very much reduced (Cabral 1979).

THE DECLINE OF WAGE-LABOUR AND THE RISE OF SELF-EMPLOYMENT

In the past half-decade, soon after the beginning of the process of European monetary convergence following the Maastricht Treaty in 1992, the Portuguese labour market has experienced a slight but steady reduction of wage-labour alongside a rise in self-employment.

Following the first ever wave of modern unemployment in Portugal in the early-middle 1980s[1] (when the officially unemployed were more than 10 per cent of the working population), Portugal has known, in recent years, a decline of wage labour due to increasing de-industrialization coupled with the privatization of banks, industries and utilities nationalized in 1975. This trend has been especially obvious in those parts of the country where manual and non-manual salaried workers tended to be dominant.

Though the figures are erratic and difficult to interpret, there seems to be a steady trend of decline in wage labour beginning in the early 1990s. The latest figures indicate that in 1995 the number of wage-earners in the workforce had decreased over 6 per cent as compared to 1992, while the number of self-employed continued to increase their share in the working population up to over 20 per cent in the same period.

Quite frequently, these new self-employed workers are former wage-earners who took advantage of redundancy payments to start a small business. Half of the 200,000 people who lost their salaried jobs since 1993 became in fact 'their own bosses'. If one bears in mind that while the number of self-employed keeps growing, the share of income derived from self-employment has dropped relatively since the early 1980s, it is thus far from obvious that the change has been for the better as far as overall family incomes are concerned. However, part of the alleged success of these new self-employed may be due to the kind of income under-reporting that the Portuguese fiscal system allows. Wage-earners cannot under-report so easily.

There is, indeed, a new 'myth' in Portuguese society about the success of some of these self-made businessmen for whom, as the saying goes, 'unemployment was a blessing in disguise'. Coupled with the current liberal ideology stressing the virtue of creating one's own job, there is here a new cultural ingredient undermining the resistance that wage-earners might otherwise have to mass redundancies. This 'myth' adds to the relative political isolation of the unemployed and is enhanced by a number of governmental programmes encouraging the unemployed and first-job seekers to engage in self-employment.

TABLE 4
CONTINENT (%)

	Number (10^3) 1995		Annual change (%) 1994/93		1995/94	
	Employment	Wage-earners	Employment	Wage-earners	Employment	Wage-earners
Total	4225.3	3040.4	–0.1	–2.0	–0.6	–1.0
Agriculture	465.1	54.2	2.3	–8.6	–2.4	–7.8
Fisheries	12.4	9.6	–15.1	–16.5	–12.1	0.0
Mining	16.8	15.0	–10.7	–16.7	–4.0	–3.2
Manufacturing industry	972.0	834.6	–0.2	–1.2	–3.6	–3.8
Food	105.0	88.7	1.1	–1.1	–4.9	–4.9
Textiles	330.9	289.8	2.4	2.1	–7.0	–6.5
Wood & Paper	114.7	92.1	–7.6	–8.0	1.2	–0.9
Chemicals	116.5	106.5	–4.5	–3.0	–2.1	–3.7
Metal works	107.4	87.7	0.9	–2.0	–2.6	–2.4
Machinery	97.2	87.9	15.3	15.0	–1.8	–0.1
Motor industry	40.6	38.2	–12.7	–13.4	3.3	2.1
Furniture	59.7	43.7	–8.8	–15.2	–2.3	–3.5
Electricity, Gas & Water	34.6	32.5			–5.7	–3.3
Building & Public works	340.3	242.3	–2.8	–4.2	2.9	1.1
Services	2384.1	1852.2	–0.3	–1.9	0.7	0.3
Commerce & Tourism	819.2	464.4	–1.0	–4.3	0.2	–1.5
Transportation & Communications	133.5	111.4	–1.1	–2.7	–8.4	–10.8
Banking & Insurance	137.4	128.1	–4.2	–4.4	1.9	1.2
Information, Research & Development	183.0	120.6	7.6	1.3	10.3	8.7
Public Administration	307.9	305.0	–1.7	–1.4	3.0	2.8
Education	303.4	292.5	2.8	2.3	1.1	1.2
Health	191.0	180.3	1.8	1.0	–1.7	–1.5
Others	259.1	201.5	–2.7	–5.1	–0.4	4.1

Source: INE (IEmployment Survey).

Equally important from a sociological viewpoint, is the fact that the decline of wage labour has been most felt in manufacturing industry, the only significant exception being the motor industry (due to the Ford-Volkswagen motor-works, near Setúbal, which is now Portugal's major exporter). Unfortunately we have no detailed regional breakdown of this process of de-industrialization, though it is clear that it struck the south harder than the north (see Table 6 below), with no compensation in the Lisbon region through increased employment in the service sector.

BACK TO FARMING?

Another point that proves critical to understanding how structural factors mediate the effects of unemployment is a surprising new feature of the Portuguese labour market. Though data from the Employment Survey is as yet only available through the media, a striking new trend has been noticed: employment in agriculture, after decades of steady reduction, has started to rise regularly since 1993. By the end of 1996, employment in agriculture had risen to 12.5 per cent of the working population from an historical low of 11 per cent in 1992 (Público 21 Sept 1996). It is hard not to see here an *effet pervers* of the policies of privatization and downsizing of firms and utilities.

At any rate, this is undoubtedly an amazing feature from the viewpoint of the modernization of Portuguese economy. Given the age structure of these new farmers (they tend to be men over 50) and the small size of their farms, mostly located north of the Tagus, such a phenomenon illustrates two crucial features of the Portuguese labour market.

First, it is well known to scholars familiar with the social geography of Portuguese farming that these regions correspond to the realm of the traditional peasantry (Freitas *et al.* 1976). This re-deployment of peasant strategies is a clear indication of the depth of current under-employment in the Portuguese economy, to the extent that it is fair to speak of real unemployment hidden not only from statistics but indeed from the eyes of society. On the other hand, it also shows that the traditional flexibility of local labour markets is still very much alive in Portugal and can be used by the rural population in 'bad times', namely when there are no alternative salaried jobs for some or most of the members of the peasant family.

Rural sociologists and anthropologists will also easily recognize the 'moral economy' that leads these men, when they lose their jobs at the age of 50 or more, to go back to the plots they had officially abandoned but had never ceased farming, with the help of their families, rather than to face a community where the unemployed tend to be morally equated with the lazy and the useless. Of course, this will not make their farms more profitable than before, but it keeps them from the dole queue and conceals their situation from the public eye. Governments of the day can only thank them for both. According to the data available, in about three years the number of small farmers in Portugal has increased by 50,000, accounting for a large proportion of the so-called new jobs created during that period.

THE MULTI-JOB TRADITION AND THE INFORMAL ECONOMY

These recent developments lead to another feature of the Portuguese labour market brought to light over a decade ago during the recession of the early-middle 1980s. Mainly in rural areas, but also in newly urbanized ones where the links with the countryside have not been entirely severed, there is a long tradition of multi-jobs carried out within the family either as a group or serially by individual family members. This is a kind of labour division within the family geared towards the maximization of its collective income that reminds one of the traditional peasant economy. As a result, both the productivity and the income per hours worked by all the members of the family are of course much lower than in a full-fledged salaried economy.

The technical term coined to describe this multi-job tradition is 'pluriactivity' and, according to the 1979 agricultural census, more than 80 per cent of rural families were engaged simultaneously in farming and some other paid jobs, either near their residential areas due to the 'diffuse industrialization' of the countryside, or away from home thanks to modern daily or weekly commuting (Lima 1986; Almeida 1986). To some extent, these job arrangements within the family unit are a kind of functional equivalent of emigration and have a similar impact on the structure of the national labour market. They absorb outright unemployment at the same time that they contribute to prevent open reactions against it.

This is also the kind of social model that continuously fuels the so-called underground economy in ways that have been described in the early 1980s (Cabral 1983). At present, though economic activity is high, the new pressures upon wage-labour seem to have led again to a revival of underground strategies though we do not have reliable data to assess this in detail. At any rate, the spread of informal economic strategies, while distorting the formal labour market, shows how traditional strategies are adapted to the opportunities opened by the modern economy. The spread of informal economic strategies also contributes to the survival of the 'welfare society' in the face of a feeble welfare state (Santos 1990; Rhodes 1996).

It is this set of social practices that accounts for Portugal's comparatively high rate of occupation coupled with low economic productivity. It is as if the labour market were still 'socially embedded', to use Karl Polanyi's expression. Such an embeddedness makes room not only for male adults but also for women (though women, more often than not, are in jobs that focus on traditional female tasks and are confined to the domestic realm, such as the 'putting out system' or work on the family farm). Despite the increase in schooling, this set of social practices also makes room for young people and even for children, not infrequently as unpaid family helpers (still 2 per cent of the national workforce in 1991 and maybe more nowadays).

All these features give the Portuguese labour market, especially outside the area of Lisbon and Setúbal, a high degree of plasticity. These features also give the market an opacity that prevents unemployment from being felt in the way it is supposedly felt in societies where the population relies more exclusively on income from wage labour and the labour market is not embedded in family and community networks.

In the Lisbon area, instead, the rise of unemployment is currently kept under control mainly due to huge investment in public works and construction, which in turn add new forms of flexibility and opacity to the labour market. In effect, the construction boom relies massively on the employment of immigrant workers who have been coming from Portugal's former African colonies since the mid to late Seventies, precisely when Portuguese emigration was brought to a halt by the 'oil crisis'.

In the past two years, about 55,000 jobs were created in this sector, particularly for the International EXPO '98 and a few other big projects. Most of these jobs are manned by immigrant workers, while about 30,000 jobs disappeared in the services and the manufacturing industry during that period in the Lisbon metropolitan area.

As occurred before in other European countries, this trend adds another distorting factor to the Portuguese labour market whose implications have just started to be studied (Baganha 1997; 1998). At any rate, it is doubtful that, if and when the construction boom ceases, immigrant workers will return to their homelands as the official view suggests, but it is useless to speculate now about the potential impact of unemployment among immigrant labour. In fact, due to their precarious legal status, if and when they become redundant, immigrant workers have no incentive at all to report to the official 'job centres'; such under-reporting tends in turn to conceal the real figures for national unemployment.

REAL AND CONCEALED UNEMPLOYMENT

A word needs to be said now about true rates of unemployment in Portugal. It is not possible to enter into the subtleties of statistical criteria that keep changing in the European Union in order to conceal real unemployment from public awareness. Let us concentrate on the official figures. Comparatively low as they appear, neither the figures for *strictu sensu*[2] nor even for *latu sensu*[3] unemployment account for under-employment, namely for people who work less than 15 hours a week and whose numbers have risen from 13 per cent of the workforce in 1987 to 22 per cent in 1995.

TABLE 5
UNEMPLOYMENT

Year	Unemplyment (stictu sensu) Numbers (10^3)	%	Unemplyment (latu sensu) Numbers (10^3)	%
1974	111.7	2.9	156.7	4.0
1975	137.9	3.5	173.1	4.4
1976	189.1	4.7	253.1	6.2
1977	215.5	5.3	295.0	7.2
1978	204.8	5.1	318.0	7.7
1979	164.6	4.0	324.4	7.7
1980	152.4	3.7	317.1	7.4
1981	165.3	3.9	345.2	7.9
1982	146.0	3.5	306.6	7.1
1983	365.7	7.8	487.6	10.1
1984	393.9	8.4	495.7	10.4
1985	405.4	8.7	497.3	10.4
1986	393.6	8.4	478.7	10.0
1987	329.2	7.0	402.3	8.4
1988	272.9	5.7	338.9	7.0
1989	243.5	5.0	294.7	6.0
1990	231.1	4.7	273.6	5.5
1991	207.5	4.1	244.2	4.8
1992	194.1	4.1	262.5	5.5
1993	257.5	5.5	331.3	6.9
1994	323.8	6.8	403.8	8.3

Source: INE (Employment Survey).

According to official reports, visible under-employment grew 30 per cent from 1993 rising to 65,000 people in 1995. According to the same reports, another 130,000 people were also available for work if given the chance. These individuals are mainly women at home and young people who have registered at the government 'employment centres' but do not qualify as unemployed. The sum total of these prospective workers would raise the share of concealed unemployment in the labour force by another three or four percentage points. Recently the daily newspaper *Diário de Notícias* put the estimated figure for overall real unemployment at 14 per cent, though it is true that the numbers of those officially registered at the 'employment centers' have been steadily declining for the past year and a half.

Furthermore, a large number of young people have been kept off the dole thanks to a whole set of 'vocational training courses' financed by the European Union and to a series of temporary schemes subsidizing self-employment. Altogether, these palliatives kept 63,000 people off the dole in 1991 and over 100,000 off the dole in 1994. According to the latest media reports (October 1997), nearly 150,000 were in this position in 1996.

In our recent survey (1997) about social attitudes among young people from 15 to 29 years old, we found only 6 per cent unemployed overall but up to 7.5 per cent unemployed among working class youngsters. We also found that over two-thirds of Portuguese young people had joined the workforce before they were 18 years old while one third of all young workers had been unemployed at least once in their lives, especially in the Lisbon area where those who were or had been unemployed rose to 46 per cent (Cabral and Pais 1998).

To conclude this section, it must be underlined that the Portuguese labour market, while accommodating high rates of employment and 'pluriactivity', also conceals pervasive under-employment. Such a model is if anything strengthened by the fact that there is very little financial support for the unemployed. Indeed, though unemployment rose steadily from 1992 to 1996, the number of people receiving financial aid kept declining due to the increasingly strict criteria imposed on the unemployed for receipt of benefits. In average terms, they got the equivalent of the minimum wage (about US$350 per month) which is less than half the national average earnings, which in turn are the lowest in the European Union. There is therefore little incentive in Portugal to indulge in voluntary unemployment. Indeed, redundancy payments and unemployment benefits together rose only from 0.2 to 0.4 per cent of family incomes during the period of highest unemployment in recent times.

SOCIAL ATTITUDES TOWARDS UNEMPLOYMENT

As a result of all these features of the Portuguese labour market, social attitudes towards unemployment are very mixed in Portugal and, if anything, popular feelings tend to blame the unemployed for their misfortune. There is indeed enough survey data to confirm that most people in Portugal still share an ethic which Maria de Lurdes Rodrigues has aptly described in terms of work as social duty as opposed to work as individual achievement (Rodrigues 1995).

Furthermore, the majority of respondents to our surveys repeatedly support the notion that job creation is the government's main task, but on the other hand they are clearly not prepared to give any special aid to the unemployed. In other words, most Portuguese believe that the government should provide a job for everyone but, at the same time, they also think that everybody is morally bound to accept any occupation available irrespective of his or her vocation. Accordingly, most working people attach less value to schooling and improving their 'human capital' than to working and making an individual effort to earn a livelihood (Cabral 1997b). Under such a traditional moral economy, it is not surprising that there has been little tradition, in Portuguese society, of solidarity – other than that provided by family networks – and of organized struggle against unemployment.

If anything, in recent years, the increasing flexibility of labour contracts, the rise in part-time jobs and the threats to pensions and to the welfare state have led to a heretofore virtually unknown fear of losing one's job. Moreover, as mentioned earlier, unemployment does not strike evenly across the country nor across occupational and age groups.

As can be gathered from the variations of employment over time, shown in both Tables 6 and 7, the region of Lisbon and Setúbal has paid the highest price in job losses, in particular in manufacturing industry. Table 7 in particular shows again the decline of wage earners, especially male workers who decreased by 8 per cent from 1992 to 1995. It is therefore the historical core of the Portuguese militant working class that has been most severely hit by the current socio-economic trends.

Among young people under 25, official unemployment was more than twice the national average (16 per cent versus 7 per cent) when it reached its peak in 1995. In the Lisbon area and Alentejo, youth

TABLE 6
EMPLOYMENT BY REGIONS AND SECTORS

	Numbers (10^3) 1995				Variation 95/94 (%)			
	Total	Primary	Secondary	Tertiary	Total	Primary	Secondary	Tertiary
North	1589.4	180.3	665.3	743.5	–0.1	–6.0	–1.7	3.0
Centre	825.0	200.3	255.2	369.5	0.8	–0.3	0.5	1.5
Lisbon	1462.6	47.2	373.2	1042.7	–2.1	–4.3	–4.2	–1.1
Alentejo	205.0	34.2	46.3	124.5	0.3	4.0	–7.0	2.3
Algarve	143.1	15.3	23.8	104.0	–1.1	–0.3	0.8	–1.7
Continent	4225.1	477.3	1363.7	2384.1	–0.6	–2.6	–2.1	0.7
Azores	86.9	17.7	19.6	49.6	–2.0	4.3	–11.2	–0.2

Source: INE (IE/OEFP).

unemployment was more than three times the national average. There is no way of telling how much unemployment affects the attitudes of young unemployed people, but although their numbers seem to have decreased since 1995, we found in our 1997 survey that youngsters who are or have been unemployed tend to take a more radical stand against the establishment than their age peers who are employed or in school. Indeed, young unemployed people support the Communist party twice as much as young people at work and four times as much as students (Cabral and Pais 1998).

Using a different approach and entirely different data, Christopher Anderson reached a similar view of the Portuguese unemployed in his comparative analysis of political attitudes among the unemployed in the European Union (Anderson 1997). Indeed, while his general conclusion is that

> European unemployed are somewhat less involved in political affairs than the employed (...) there are also some noteworthy cross-national differences. The most prominent are Italy and Portugal... Unemployed voters in Portugal are also noteworthy because they were more extreme in their political views than employed ones and also furthest to the left of the employed. Moreover, they were significantly more interested in politics than the employed and just as likely to vote.

Actually, while C.J. Anderson takes the view that dissatisfaction with democracy may be a consequence of marginalization from the political life of a given country, we believe that such dissatisfaction can also be a

TABLE 7
EMPLOYMENT BY STATUS

	Numbers (10^3) 1995			Variation (%) 1991/90			Variation (%) 1993/92			Variation (%) 1994/93			Variation (%) 1995/94		
	HM	H	M	HM	H	M	HM	H	M	HM	H	M	HM	H	M
Employers	273.8	204.5	69.4	12.0	11.4	14.2	2.0	0.5	6.7	1.9	2.4	0.4	–2.0	–2.1	–1.7
Self-employed	825.6	451.7	374.0	5.5	3.7	7.5	–0.2	–1.4	1.2	4.8	5.5	4.0	2.7	5.5	–5.0
Wage-earners	3040.1	1639.0	1401.1	1.4	0.1	3.3	–2.8	–3.3	–2.2	–2.0	–2.6	–1.1	–1.0	–2.1	0.4
Family helpers	81.2	33.7	47.6	8.5	–2.6	15.6	3.1	3.2	3.0	14.9	15.1	14.7	–11.7	–9.7	–13.0
Members of co-operatives	4.4	2.2	2.0	–18.6	–24.0	22.2	–10.7	–27.3	42.9	128.0	93.8	160.0	–22.8	–29.0	–23.1
Total	4225.2	2331.1	1894.1	3.0	1.4	5.1	–2.0	–2.6	–1.1	–0.1	–0.5	0.4	–0.6	–0.9	–0.3

feature of the national civic culture. At any rate, in all four southern European countries, both the employed and the unemployed, irrespective of rates of unemployment, are much less satisfied with democracy than in the other EU member countries. Of all southern Europeans, the Portuguese were in fact the most satisfied with the political regime (at a rate of 50 per cent), but the gap in 'democracy satisfaction' between the employed and the unemployed was the second largest in Europe, the latter being predictably much less satisfied. The Portuguese unemployed were indeed those who placed themselves further to the left of the political spectrum and virtually the only ones in Europe who were more interested in politics than the employed.

THE POLITICAL AND ELECTORAL IMPACT OF UNEMPLOYMENT

The unique properties of the Portuguese unemployed result from the fact that unemployment has tended to occur mainly in the urban and rural areas where a left-wing political tradition already prevailed. Whether or not those who crafted the monetary and economic policies of the 1980s (before accession to the European Community in 1985) and the 1990s (after the Maastricht agreement in 1992) were aware of the impact of such policies on the class composition of the Lisbon 'red belt' and the Alentejo, the fact remains that policy change in Brussels did not alter substantially local political beliefs. If anything, it may have strengthened old feelings against the incumbent authorities. Conversely, traditionally conservative regions and social strata seem to have been spared most of the hardship and consequently had no strong motives to change their ideological allegiances.

From a political and electoral viewpoint, it seems fair to say, therefore, that unemployment has operated in Portugal, in the past decade and a half, as a contextual part of the general economic climate prevailing in the country, rather than as a direct mobilizing factor. In turn, the economic mood is of course a complex mix of numerous factors that individuals and social groups evaluate according to their own social position and criteria. To add to the complexity, some of those factors are not exempt from political manipulation by the governments of the day, such as pensions and wages in the public sector.

By and large, the trade unions have been rather ineffectual in dealing with either of the two 'waves' of high unemployment that the country has known since 1974. In fact, they suffered dramatically from the changes in the labour market (de-industrialization, de-localization, decontractualization, down-sizing, immigrant labour increase, etc.). According to the latest report, trade unions seem to have lost one third of their members since the middle 1980s (Cerdeira 1997). In the face of unemployment, the unions confined themselves with little success to token marches against factory closures.

With the exception of the Communist Party, which in this field acts mainly through the unions it controls, the other Portuguese political parties have virtually no tradition of direct involvement in social issues or movements. Even for the Socialist party, unemployment therefore seldom became a mobilizing issue. In fact, public awareness of the growth of unemployment occurred more often than not due to the responses of the media to sporadic events, to statements from political outsiders or to statements from the Catholic Church, which has come to adopt a rather strong position on social matters such as poverty and racism.

In the recent past, however, unemployment has been a relevant issue on the political agenda two times. Each time has predictably coincided with statistical unemployment peaks. The first occurred in 1983-85 when (among a whole set of factors) unemployment and wage-arrears[4] clearly contributed to deep disenchantment with the '*bloco central*' government, the grand-coalition between the Socialist and the Social-Democratic parties then engaged in securing accession to the European Community.

'Hunger marches' promoted by the Communists, strong pronouncements from the Bishop of Setúbal and systematic press campaigns mounted by the followers of President Eanes, who was about to launch a new political party (the *Partido Renovador Democrático*), all account undoubtedly for the political mood which led to the electoral collapse of the Socialist Party in the 1985 general election as well as the temporary success of the newly created populist party led by Eanes.

The second episode occurred ten years later, when unemployment was reaching a new peak. The protracted economic recession initiated in 1991-92 was definitely part and parcel of the demise of Prime Minister Cavaco Silva and of the electoral defeat of his party, the PSD, in the 1995 general election. It is difficult, however, to single out the weight of unemployment from the other economic factors and, above all, from the specific political ingredients of the time, namely the accusations of arrogance and sleaze increasingly addressed to the 'orange majority' (a reference to the colours of the PSD). It is likely, nonetheless, that the rise of unemployment in the 1990s contributed to reverse dramatically Cavaco Silva's success among working class voters in previous elections (1987 and 1991).

The revolt against ten years of '*cavaquismo*' (1985-95), as the period came to be called, was above all a cross-party attack from left and right against the 'the dictatorship of the majority', as President Mário Soares once called it. The wave of discontent spread then from the urban areas to the rest of the country, after the spontaneous rebellion of commuters from the communist boroughs south of the Tagus against the rise of the Lisbon bridge toll in the Summer of 1994 (Cabral 1997a).

To conclude, especially in the 1980s but also in the 1990s, unemployment accounted significantly for the negative economic climate of both periods, but it was only one ingredient among others explaining the incumbent's electoral rejection. As pointed out, the specific political effects of unemployment and its weight in political change are difficult to establish because, in Portugal, unemployment affects the population's living standards very differently according to regions, economic sectors and occupational status. Finally, unemployment struck mainly those urban and industrial social groups in which a left-wing civic culture had long prevailed. These social groups were therefore already prone to vote against both the Socialists and the Social-Democrats, which have alternated or allied in office for most of the time since the consolidation of Portuguese democracy and would have been blamed for unemployment in the first place.

NOTES

1. Indeed, it must be noted that until the early 1980s, Portugal had known virtually no unemployment since the early 1960s. Due to massive emigration, the former relationship between supply and demand in the labour market, which used to be clearly unfavourable to wage-earners, was drastically reversed. Moreover, before the Sixties the modern notion of unemployment – massive numbers of workers thrown into sudden lack of economic resources – hardly fit the Portuguese experience, which was best described, as regards the condition of poor job-seekers both in the countryside and urban areas, as 'lack of work' (*falta de trabalho*) to use a common expression of those years that has almost vanished from today's vocabulary.
2. *strictu sensu*: Unemployed individuals who took active steps to find a job during the week previous to the survey.
3. *latu sensu*: Unemployed individuals available for work but who did not took active steps to find a job during the week previous to the survey.
4. Wage arrears – in Portuguese, *salários em atraso* – were indeed a striking feature of the 1980s which illustrates the reluctance of Portuguese society to deal with overt unemployment. Employers, instead of closing their factories or laying off the workforce, just stopped paying any wages, while the workers went on labouring and called for State intervention.

REFERENCES

Almeida, J.F. (1986): *Classes sociais nos campos: camponeses parciais numa região do Noroeste*, Lisboa: Instituto de Ciências Sociais/Presença.

Almeida, M.H. and Ribeiro, M.E. (1997): *Os níveis de rendimentos dos Portugueses e o quadro geral da respectiva formação, distribuição e aplicação no contexto comunitário*, Lisboa: Ministério da Qualificação e do Emprego.

Anderson, C.J. (1997): *Desperate times call for desperate measures? Unemployment and voter behavior in comparative perspective*, paper presented at the conference on Unemployment effects: The Southern European Experience in Comparative Perspective, Princeton University.

Baganha, M.I. (ed.) (1997): *Immigration in Southern Portugal*, Oeiras: Celta.

Baganha, M.I. (1998): 'Immigrant involvement in the informal economy: the Portuguese case', *Journal of Ethnic and Migration Studies* 24/2, pp.367-85.

Barreto, A. (ed.) (forthcoming): *A Situação Social em Portugal, 1960-1997*, Lisboa: Instituto de Ciências Sociais.

Cabral, M.V. (1979): *Portugal na alvorada do século XIX: forças sociais, poder político e crescimento económico de 1890 a 1914*, Lisboa: A Regra do Jogo.

Cabral, M.V. (1983): 'A economia subterrânea vem ao de cima: estratégias rurais perante a industrialização e a urbanização', *Análise Social* 19/ 76, pp.199-234.

Cabral, M.V. (1997a): *Crónicas realistas. Política e sociedade em Portugal nos anos Noventa*, Oeiras: Celta.

Cabral, M.V. (1997b): *Cidadania política e equidade social em Portugal*, Oeiras: Celta.

Cabral, M.V. and Pais, J.M. (eds) (1998): *Jovens portugueses de hoje*, Oeiras:Celta

Cerdeira, M.L. (1997): 'A sindicalização portuguesa de 1974 a 1995', *Economia e* Trabalho, Lisboa: Ministério da Qualificação e do Emprego 1/1, pp.46-53.

Esping-Andersen, G. (1993): 'Orçamentos e democracia: o Estado-Providência em Espanha e Portugal', *Análise Social* 28/122, pp.589-606.

Freitas, E.; J.F. Almeida and M.V. Cabral (1976): *Modalidades de penetração do capitalismo na agricultura: estruturas agrárias em Portugal continental, 1950-1970*, Lisboa: Presença.

Lima, A.V. (1986): 'A agricultura a tempo parcial em Portugal – uma primeira aproximação à sua quantificação', *Análise Social* 22/91, pp.371-9.

Rhodes, M. (ed.) (1996): 'Southern European Welfare States', special issue of *South European Society and Politics* 1/3.

Rodrigues, M.L. (1995): 'Atitudes da população portuguesa perante o trabalho', *Organizações e Trabalho* 14, pp.33-63.

Santos, B.S. (1990): *O Estado e a sociedade em Portugal, 1974-1988*, Porto: Afrontamento.

Relying on Stop-gap Measures: Coping with Unemployment in Greece

NEOVI M. KARAKATSANIS

Traditionally, unemployment has not been seen as a major problem in Greece. As in Portugal where the concept had little meaning prior to 1974 (see Bacalhau and Bruneau, this volume), in Greece unemployment was virtually non-existent during the 1960s and 1970s and averaged only 2.4 per cent from 1975 to 1981 – a period in which many other OECD countries saw the emergence of significant unemployment problems. Several important factors served to keep unemployment low. First, a massive exodus of approximately one million Greeks from 1955 to 1970 – over 10 per cent of the total population – to Western Europe, Australia, and North America helped eliminate competition for marginal jobs and keep unemployment down (Tsoukalas 1987: 194). Acting as an added shield against unemployment was a bloated public sector, so large that today it employs nearly forty per cent of Greek salaried workers (OECD 1996: 59). A long tradition of self-employment, occupying approximately half of the labour force, was another contributing factor to historically low unemployment levels, as were very ungenerous unemployment benefits which limited the availability of unemployment insurance to a maximum of 12 months and offered some of the lowest benefits by international standards, thereby creating a disincentive for people to remain unemployed (OECD 1996: 81; Schömann 1995: 10; Symeonidou 1996: 73). In short, due to a multiplicity of reasons, unemployment has virtually been a non-issue for decades.

More recently, however, the situation has changed. Climbing to unprecedented post-war levels by Greek standards, official unemployment reached over 10 per cent in 1995 and unofficial estimates put it even higher at 12 per cent. This was brought about by many factors. The severe international economic crises and recession of the late

---

I would like to thank Nancy Bermeo for proposing this article and the anonymous reader whose suggestions were very thoughtful and useful.

1970s and early 1980s, in conjunction with intense competition from other low-wage economies in light-manufactured goods, led to a large loss of Greece's market share. Additionally, the second oil shock hit at a time when Greek wages were bloated, real investment was in decline, the gross domestic product was nearly stagnant, inflation was on the rise, and deindustrialization was beginning to hit. This, coupled with substantial immigration as Greeks returned from recession-hit north and central Europe, greatly exacerbated the unemployment problem, almost tripling the unemployment rate over the course of the 1980s (National Statistical Service of Greece, various years).

In the 1990s, unemployment increased even more as did Greece's labour supply – this time by the entry of legal and illegal immigrants from former Communist bloc countries. Furthermore, the effects of continuing socio-economic modernization had negative repercussions on unemployment. Increased urbanization as well as the inevitable agricultural decline which modernization entails led to a further rise in unemployment as people – especially youth – abandoned the countryside and a life of farming for Greece's major cities where jobs are scarce and where the new arrivals lack necessary skills for gainful employment. In addition, as governments struggled to meet strict EMU criteria through significant restructuring to make the economy more efficient and competitive, unemployment was further exacerbated. Thus, the prospects for employment are far from encouraging, especially for youth and women who today face extremely high levels of unemployment for extended periods of time.

As Table 1 illustrates, Greek unemployment is characterized by a significant dualism: certain social groups are over-protected against unemployment while others are under-protected and relegated to being long-term or permanently unemployed. As with the other southern European countries, the burden of unemployment in Greece falls mostly on the shoulders of the youth and women. Male heads of household, by contrast, are rarely unemployed. Heads of household enjoy virtually full employment (with only about 2 per cent being out of work), while first-time job seekers – especially youth – have very high rates of unemployment (over 29 per cent) with women also suffering disproportionately (15 per cent) (OECD 1996: 63). This dualistic tendency is particularly troublesome if one considers the fact that these high-risk groups (women and youth) are also likely to experience unemployment for longer periods of time (Kostaki and Ioakeimoglou 1997). In fact, the proportion of the unemployed who have been out of

TABLE 1
GREEK UNEMPLOYMENT RATES (BY GENDER AND AGE)
1983-1995

Age	1983	1987	1992	1995
		Women		
15-19	33.8	39.9	44.2	49.2
20-24	28.0	31.3	34.4	37.8
25-29	16.4	16.1	17.9	22.5
30-44	8.0	7.5	10.6	10.4
45-64	3.8	3.0	5.1	5.8
65+	0.6	0.5	0.7	1.9
Total	11.7	11.3	14.2	15.3
		Men		
15-19	16.9	15.0	19.0	22.5
20-24	17.2	18.6	18.2	19.8
25-29	8.8	8.1	9.5	11.7
30-44	4.2	3.4	3.3	4.8
45-64	3.5	2.7	2.8	3.7
65+	0.3	0.4	0.9	0.5
Total	5.8	5.1	5.4	6.7

Source: Symeonidou (1998): 187.

work for more than 12 months in Greece increased from 32.3 per cent in 1983 to 50.5 per cent in 1994 (Symeonidou 1996: 73).

It is interesting to note that this dualism is largely the result of traditional cultural norms and practices. Specifically, the Greek economy and social system favour job stability for *male heads of household*, whom society expects to be the main (but not necessarily the only) provider for the family. An indication of the importance of family status is the set of criteria used in the 1980s to make public sector hiring decisions. According to a mid-1980s law, number of children, level of family income and other indicators of family status were to be more important in making hiring decisions than professional qualifications and other work experience (OECD 1991: 88)! Furthermore, government regulations make dismissal of core workers in the formal economy (both in the private and public sectors) very difficult and costly. Job stability is so heavily emphasized in Greece that, when compared to other OECD countries, Greece has the lowest rates of inflow to and outflow from the ranks of the unemployed as well as one of the lowest shares of dismissed workers in total unemployment (OECD 1996: 63). High statutory severance payments that increase proportionally over time also bias the degree of protection toward older employees by making it highly unlikely that they will be dismissed. Thus, thanks to such government regulations and cultural practices that promote job stability, core workers – especially male heads of households – enjoy virtual life-long employment in Greece. They do so, however, at the expense of non-privileged 'outsiders' – mostly women and youth – who remain unemployed for extended periods, usually years at a time.

In addition to visible unemployment, invisible unemployment is also a serious problem in Greece. Traditional cultural values and attitudes placing the proper role for women within the home, where they provide the family with unpaid domestic assistance, have kept many women from joining the formal labour force as well as from registering as unemployed. Likewise, similar values also encourage youth to remain at home, reliant on family support for extended periods of time. Unlike in the United States, for example, where it is typical of university students to hold part- or full-time jobs while in school, irrespective of their family's socio-economic status, few Greek students work while enrolled in university. In fact, many young people are kept out of the labour market, out of the competition for scarce jobs, and kept from formal unemployment by the excessively long periods of time they are enrolled as students – usually well in excess of five years. In addition to prolonged university enrolment, young men are also kept out of the labour market by their extensive period of compulsory military service. As a result, invisible unemployment is also quite high in Greece.

By the time visible unemployment surpassed the 10 per cent mark in 1995, however, it had become increasingly evident that the economy was in the midst of crisis, that youth and women were particularly high-risk groups and that the unemployment problem would likely deepen in future years. As Haris Symeonidou (1996: 74) writes, '[d]eindustrialization, mass redundancies, the closing of numerous "ailing" firms and the stagnation of investments [were] all indications that unemployment [would] rise and the existing situation [would] worsen.' Thus, in the face of economic deterioration and with their 'marching orders' from the European Union, Greek political elites, political analysts and students of public policy turned increased attention to the causes and consequences of unemployment, as well as to possible structural reforms and active labour market policies that could generate future employment.

Strikingly absent from this debate, however, were the voices of the vast majority of the Greek population. In fact, unlike in Portugal and

Spain, where 'unemployment was a major concern of the population' (Bacalhau and Bruneau, this volume), the effects of unemployment and underemployment in Greece appear to have been a far greater concern for analysts and the government than for the public at large. In fact, at no point in recent Greek political history has unemployment surfaced as a major political issue on which political parties explicitly battled. Even at the height of recent unemployment – when it has reached levels unprecedented for generations accustomed to virtually full (male) employment – neither the socialist PASOK government nor the opposition felt compelled to treat it as the most critical public policy issue, as unemployment has been in virtually every other OECD country. In fact, the government of the day remained in power and continues to pursue economic and structural reforms as it strives to achieve its main public policy goal – economic and monetary union – a goal destined to increase the level of unemployment in Greece (at least over the short-term). Moreover, the Greek public has shown relatively little angst about high and rising levels of unemployment in Greece compared to other Europeans. A recent Eurobarometer survey of young Europeans found that only 9.6 per cent of Greek respondents (the lowest percentage of all 17 countries in which the survey was conducted) answered that they would 'accept any job whatever the conditions' if unemployed. In contrast, 19.2 per cent of Italian youth, 19.5 per cent of Spanish youth, and 13 per cent of Portuguese youth answered that they would accept any job if unemployed. In the same survey, 24.1 per cent of Greek youth (the highest average amongst the 17 participating countries) answered that they would 'accept a job only if it was stable, well paid and if it was appropriate to my level of qualification' if unemployed. This compared to 11.3, 7.2 and 4.2 per cent in Italy, Portugal and Spain, respectively (Eurobarometer 1997: 67). Indicative of these attitudes is the response of a 23 year old Greek woman when asked whether unemployment is a critical problem in Greece: 'The media tell us it's a problem and that we should be concerned, but none of us really seem to be. It doesn't affect us. Most of us who are unemployed are waiting either for the "perfect" job or for someone else to find that job for us.'[1] This attitude is typical of many Greeks – even those in high-risk categories – who, while concerned about securing the 'perfect' job for themselves and other members of their family, do not seem to be genuinely alarmed by the unemployment 'problem' in general.

This article will seek to explain why this has been the case. It will argue that, as in Spain, where networks of social policies help government cope with the crisis, or as in Portugal, where a strong 'welfare society' (de Santos 1991; Hespanha 1993) has sprung up to fill the gaps in social welfare provision, in Greece too the traditional and informal coping strategies of both families and government have been instrumental in providing a cushion for the unemployed, making unemployment less of an issue for the average Greek. Specifically, I will argue that the *quid pro quo* relations inherent in both Greek political clientelism as well as in personal familism have protected most Greeks against the negative consequences of unemployment by informally institutionalizing several stop-gap measures.

THE FAMILY AS STOP-GAP MEASURE

One of the most important coping strategies in Greece – characteristic of southern European traditional culture in general – is the strong support network offered by the extended family to its unemployed members. Several reasons – all of them predominantly cultural in nature – can be given for this. First, there still exist the remnants of traditional peasant culture where access to inheritance is linked to the obligation – rather than the choice – to care for fellow kin. This is closely related to socially ascribed roles for women – mothers, daughters, and daughters-in-law – who are expected to carry out the necessary care-giver roles prescribed by society and who construct their identities on the basis of family responsibility – serving as the backbone of 'family welfare' (García and Karakatsanis, forthcoming; Chletsos 1993; Pantelidou-Malouta 1988). Facilitating this crucial welfare function is the family's reliance on a collective domestic income, pooled from a variety of sources and work relations, which facilitates the family provision of welfare. In this regard, the Greek family serves three important and complementary roles. It serves as a unit of employment, providing jobs in family-owned businesses or farms when others cannot be found. It provides an informal placement service, helping job-seekers find employment through personal and other family connections. And, finally, it is a provider of income assistance to unemployed family members and others in need.

As an employer, it is not uncommon for the Greek family to own a small family-operated business which provides work to several family members at any given time. Reflecting this phenomenon is the fact that the number of people in the average economic unit in Greece is two (compared to the European average of six). These small businesses, engaged in retail sales, tourism, and craft industries, provide some family members with unofficial or informal work and others with formal employment. Unofficial work is primarily performed by women and youth, is usually outside the realm of traditional wage labour, and is considered as unpaid 'assistance' to the family's head of household who is the owner of the 'shop.' Such 'assistance' also predominates in agricultural work on family farms, where women and youth 'assist' in the fields, remain largely unregistered in employment statistics and go unpaid for their labour (Stratigaki and Vaiou 1994; Zafeiri-Kampitsi 1993). As a result of such traditional practices, family-owned businesses and farms soak up Greece's excess labour supply, helping to keep official unemployment low.

In addition to providing family members with jobs in family-owned businesses, the extended family also provides an informal placement service, helping unemployed family members and friends locate prospective employers through personal acquaintances and connections. This phenomenon is so widespread, in fact, that there is virtually an economy of influence in Greece – that is, of the personal influence and connections, the *meson*, that often serves as the most reliable route to gainful, usually public sector, employment. In fact, such connections are so important that, according to a recent survey of Greek workers, less than 10 per cent of those surveyed indicated that the government-run job placement office, Manpower Employment Organization (OAED), had actually helped place them (OECD 1996: 83). Instead, most Greek workers acknowledge their reliance on informal networks of personal assistance to routinely find work. As a result, the job a person holds often has more to do with whom one knows rather than with the merit, experience or skills of the job-seeker. Thus, Greek families not only lower the number of job seekers by providing work for unemployed family members (both formally and informally) in family-owned businesses, but they also provide informal assistance, helping find work for job-seekers through personal connections and friendships.

As in the other countries of southern Europe, however, perhaps the most important way the family protects society against the ills of unemployment is by pooling family resources to support unemployed family members. Unlike the traditional northern European breadwinner model, in which the head of household traditionally works outside the home and provides the family with its means of sustenance, the Greek family has traditionally relied on a 'family wage' (García and Karakatsanis, forthcoming) that is pooled from a variety of work relations and sources. The strategy behind this arrangement involves pooling the income of the highly-protected head of household with the incomes of other family members, some of whom may be employed full- or part-time in the formal economy as well as others engaged in contract or informal work in the underground economy. Thus, in addition to the wages of the male head of household, Greek women contribute to the family wage with income derived from their employment in the formal economy as well as from their informal employment (baby-sitting, cleaning, catering and other domestic work) and/or paid irregular work (secretarial work done from home, casual jobs in services, retail, tourism, and industrial home working). Second, youth also contribute to a lesser degree through their work in door to door sales, express delivery, distribution of advertising materials, and summer jobs. Third, income from government subsidies (especially to farmers), old age and disability pensions as well as interest and other types of income accrued from property ownership, rentals, and savings may also be added to the family wage. Fourth, multiple-job holdings – 'pluriactivity' – by the same family member are often common in contributing towards the family wage. This is especially true in farming where, in addition to agricultural income, farmers often supplement their pay with other forms of wage employment (especially on a part-time basis), both through the use of limited time contracts as well as from work in the large underground economy (especially tourism). Finally, the family wage also benefits disproportionately from the unpaid 'assistance' of family members, especially women and youth, who work informally as unpaid family help (Hadjimichalis and Vaiou 1990: 94-95).

Since income from any single source of pay is relatively low in Greece, pooling income from various sources tends to reduce the dependence of households on any single source of pay, lowers the threshold of the minimum necessary and acceptable wage, allows families a relatively high standard of living and provides surplus income to be used in assisting unemployed family members and others in need. In sum, as in other southern European countries, income pooling has allowed the Greek family to fill privately a large gap in government social welfare provision. The family provides social assistance to the unemployed while relieving the state of the need to expend increased resources on unemployment and other social benefits.

Facilitating the generation of the family wage and this system of family welfare is a high degree of cross-generational family cohabitation, resulting in a high frequency of social contacts between family members whom society teaches to assist each other at times of need rather than rely on the state (for a similar phenomenon in Spain and Italy, see Guerraro and Naldini 1996). In this cultural milieu, where pre-marital cohabitation and single-person living arrangements are neither widespread nor positively sanctioned by society, unemployment benefits for first-time job seekers are non-existent and are largely viewed as unnecessary both by society and government alike. Instead, generous income assistance is provided by the extended family and most first-time job seekers are happy to rely on such financial support for relatively long periods of time rather than accept undesirable jobs that they do not consider up to their high standards. According to one EC survey, in fact, some two-thirds of Greek youth indicated that they wished to find employment in the highly-prized public sector – that is, in a job which would guarantee them permanent, well-paid employment with exceptional benefits (OECD 1990: 24). As a result, Greek youth are patient and perfectly content to remain in their parents' homes, waiting for such appointments and choosing financial dependence on their family until a relatively advanced age. With such attitudes being the norm rather than the exception, it is not surprising that the vast majority of young people live at home until marriage, regardless of whether they are employed, unemployed, or students. Thus, Greek youth prefer unemployment and dependence on family to independence and fairly low-pay private sector jobs.

Moreover, parents tend to reinforce the dependent relationship of children by providing generously and expecting little in return. Looking after one's children and assisting them financially – well into marriage, in fact – is virtually demanded by a society which stigmatizes parents who opt out of such arrangements, criticizing them for having forsaken their parental responsibilities. Yet another form of parental assistance in Greece has been the dowry system, which continues to be practised informally. Traditionally, the dowry system was one aspect of arranged marriages, in which the bride's family was obligated to provide its future son-in-law with a negotiated amount of cash, property, livestock and other goods in exchange for his willingness to marry their daughter. The size or amount of the dowry varied, depending on the bride's socio-economic status, and came from years of family savings, the earnings of the girl herself, the sale of family property, immigrant remittances sent from abroad, or even from borrowing. In traditional Greek families, social expectations also tended to obligate the eldest son – especially if the father was deceased – to remain unmarried and to provide a dowry to his sisters (Kourvetaris and Dobratz 1987: 157). Only once his sisters were 'situated,' could he himself settle down to marry. While no hard evidence exists on this phenomenon today (since official dowries were abolished in 1983) and while dowry-less marriages are becoming more commonplace in Greece, the practice of dowry-giving continues for many families, even though it has become informal and difficult to measure. Concerned that their children should be 'settled' (Symeonidou 1996: 81) when married, Greek parents continue to provide homes, household furniture, appliances, linen, blankets, land and/or rental properties to them at the time of their marriage. Thus, rent-free living goes a long way towards offsetting the consequences of low pay, underemployment and unemployment for many young couples. This is yet another way in which the Greek family continues to serve a crucial – albeit informal – welfare function.

Finally, it is important to emphasize that economic need is not the primary explanation for such strongly family-oriented, or 'familistic', tendencies. The economic argument is, in may ways, secondary to the cultural motivation. Such practices are as common among well-to-do families as they are in less-privileged ones. Greek society teaches members of families that one's primary 'duty' is to the collectivity rather than to the self and stigmatizes individuals who choose to opt out of the reciprocal, *quid pro quo* relations inherent in familistic practices. Thus, a strong cultural component is involved, whereby society places value on familism and corresponding low importance on notions of individualism and independence. As a result of this cultural peculiarity, neither widespread discontent nor demands to alter such practices have yet been widely voiced.

THE STATE AS STOP-GAP MEASURE

Thanks in large part to the important, albeit informal, role played by the family in providing social assistance to the unemployed, as well as to the relatively low levels of unemployment historically, the Greek state has given very little direct financial remuneration to the unemployed. Table 2 illustrates, in fact, that in contrast to the high priority given to other aspects of social expenditures, formal labour market policies make up less than 10 per cent of total state social expenditures – or about half the EU average for such programmes. Offsetting the lack of formal transfers to the unemployed, the Greek state has dealt with unemployment through a variety of mechanisms, all of which have sought to lower the size of the labour force while reducing the unemployment rate (especially for primary heads of household). In so doing, it has expanded disability and other pensions (to reduce the labour supply), relied on extensive public sector recruitment (to lower unemployment) and facilitated the institutionalization of labour market rigidities (to protect the employment of primary heads of household).

TABLE 2
DISTRIBUTION OF SOCIAL EXPENDITURES (1993)
(AS A PERCENTAGE OF TOTAL GOVERNMENT EXPENDITURES)

	Greece	EU
Old Age	50	29
Survivors	9	7
Disability	11	8
Unemployment	5	9
Health	20	23
Active Labour Market Policies	2	4
Other	2	19

Source: OECD (1997): 65.

The first way in which the Greek state has attempted to deal with unemployment – albeit informally – has been through its heavy reliance on, and abuse of, disability and other pensions to lower the size of the country's active labour force. Specifically, pensions and other types of income support – income support that has traditionally contributed to the family wage and, indirectly, to family welfare in general – have been blatantly distributed by political parties during election years in exchange for electoral support. Particularly during election years in the 1980s, expenditures on pensions and other income-supporting transfer payments made up the vast bulk of substantial increases in government spending. Table 2 illustrates that in 1993, pensions accounted for 70 per cent of all social benefits, in contrast to an EU average of only 44 per cent (see, also, Petmezidou-Tsoulouvi 1992: 131). It is interesting to note that governments were willing to go to great lengths to achieve such high budgetary allocations to the pension funds – all in an effort to shore up electoral support. To this end, successive governments not only abused the loose eligibility requirements and early retirement provisions, but also relied upon disability pensions when the more stringent eligibility criteria for old age pensions could not be met (OECD 1996: 82). It should come as little surprise, then, that the total number of pensioners in Greece far exceeds the population aged over 65. While such activities were consciously carried out for the express purpose of securing voters' electoral support, they were also instrumental in keeping down the size of the labour force and unemployment.

In addition to increased recourse to pensions, the second way in which the government informally coped with and ultimately disguised unemployment was through its extensive patronage-based recruitment to the Greek public sector, which over the past two decades has ballooned to astronomic levels, acting as the main source of employment creation in the country. As with the granting of pensions, successive Greek governments sought to bolster their electoral support by adding thousands of employees to the public payroll during election years. According to one observer,

> The parties' traditional reliance on the purchase of support by state patronage was increased by the appearance of genuine competition between them, and by the new power of voters. It was largely for this reason that state expenditure on welfare and jobs in the public sector – both of which had risen gradually in the twenty-five years up to 1974 – increased steeply in the following fifteen years (Close 1993: 228).

As political elites distributed favours through public sector employment, the state's apparatus was consciously and systematically penetrated by party members. To accommodate party faithfuls and to provide them with much-coveted public sector employment, the number of existing positions and departments were increased and new ones created. To manufacture as many positions as possible, the state encouraged early retirement (with very generous pensions), freeing up public sector positions for new-hires. As the state's policies made public sector employment a reality for more individuals, it was able to limit unemployment. Data point to the widespread use of such practices: from 1981 to 1990, general government employment grew at three times the rate of private-sector employment, increasing at a rate of approximately 30 per cent throughout the 1980s. Today the larger public sector employs an astounding 30 to 40 per cent of the Greek workforce – about double the OECD average (OECD 1991: 81; 1996: 59, 81). It is important to note, however, that while acting as a shield against unemployment, the astronomical growth of the public sector has been a tremendous drain on state revenues and has been responsible for huge budgetary shortfalls. Furthermore, the growth in the number of public service positions has led to overstaffing and underemployment, allowing public servants the time and opportunity to earn additional income in Greece's large informal economy (Kanellopoulos 1992: 28-9).

The third way in which the Greek state has informally coped with unemployment is through the institutionalization of a highly rigid labour market – restricting dismissals by private and public employers, preventing unilateral reductions in working hours by management and awarding extremely generous severance payments to dismissed workers. Specifically, Greek law prohibits the reduction in a firm's workforce by over 2 per cent per month and requires prior authorization by the Ministry of Labour – authorization that is difficult to acquire and routinely denied. Such restrictions primarily benefit privileged 'core' workers who enjoy full-time employment, relatively stable contracts, high wages, generous social security and other fringe benefits and virtually complete protection from dismissal. In contrast, 'outsiders' – particularly youth and women – are virtually unprotected and relegated to long-term or even permanent unemployment. Employers refrain from hiring new 'permanent' employees during periods of economic growth when they perceive the cost of dismissing those employees during periods of economic down-turn as prohibitively high. Finally, social pressures and cultural norms have tended to reinforce such practices since Greek society approves of the dependence of youth and women on their families, fathers, and husbands. In short, this informal stop-gap measure of the state is itself a culturally-supported practice that ultimately reinforces the reciprocal relations inherent in familism.

Finally, it was to protect the employment of core workers that government subsidies were allocated in the mid-1980s to the so-called 'problematic' industries – some 40 industries employing over 25,000 workers. The state's willingness to pursue policies that were, in economic terms, wasteful and counterproductive should be seen in light of the fact that the Greek economy and social system favour job stability for core workers. To preserve such jobs and to keep social peace, the Greek state decided to absorb these companies' one billion dollar indebtedness rather than allow those industries to close, forcing thousands out of work. Even though, as then Under-secretary for Industry, Vasso Papandreou, declared, it might have been more cost-effective to shut the ailing industries down and simply keep on paying workers their wages, the government decided to create a holding company to oversee and continue running these firms (Spraos 1991: 183; Hadjiyannis 1990: 171-2; and *Το Βήμα* 1986). Thus, keeping unviable industries in operation at an extremely high budgetary cost can best be understood when viewed through the lenses of a culturally-supported practice – one that traditionally protects the employment of core-employees (primarily heads of household) and reinforces the Greek familistic practices that have traditionally provided for the unemployed in Greece.

FUTURE TRENDS

Due to the informal stop-gap measures of both the family and state, the unemployment problem in Greece has not been, until very recently, a major concern of the public. For example, Eurobarometer surveys conducted in the 1980s and 1990s (when unemployment was on the rise) indicate that, compared to other Europeans, Greeks tended to be more optimistic about economic conditions, including unemployment. In 1981, when asked whether the number of unemployed in their country was likely to increase, decrease or remain the same in the coming year, only 14.7 per cent of Greeks responded that unemployment was likely to increase (compared to a European average of 62.3 per cent) while 46.8 per cent of Greek respondents answered that it was likely to decrease (compared to a European average of 13.9 per cent) (Eurobarometer 1981). A 1983 Eurobarometer also indicated relative optimism concerning the issue of unemployment. When asked whether, in their view, unemployment was likely to disappear or remain unsolved if the economy were to pick up, 54.8 per cent of Greeks answered that it was likely to disappear (over double the European average of 24.3 per cent), while only 24.5 per cent answered that the unemployment problem would remain unsolved (compared to a European average of 67.2 per cent) (Eurobarometer 1983). Even as unemployment rates began to reach alarming levels between 1989 and 1994, Greeks still appeared to assign less significance to the problem than did their European counterparts: in 1989 (when unemployment reached 7.8 per cent), fewer Greek respondents (38.9 per cent of those surveyed) ranked unemployment as the most important issue facing the country, compared to 46.2 per cent of Portuguese, 51 per cent of Italians, and 60.9 per cent of Spanish respondents. By 1994 (when unemployment had peaked at 10 per cent in Greece), the number of Greeks ranking it as one of the top three issues facing the country remained virtually unchanged (68.4 per cent) as compared to 1989 (70.5 per cent). In contrast, Italians, Spaniards and Portuguese assigned unemployment a higher and increasing significance. While, as we have seen, the percentage of Greeks assigning a high importance to unemployment decreased slightly (by 2.1 per cent) from

1989 to 1994, the percentage of Italians, Spaniards, and Portuguese increased by 8.9, 9.2 and 12.3 per cent respectively (Eurobarometer 1989, 1994).

These attitudes of the Greek public are likely to change in the not-too-distant future, however, as the effects of unemployment are likely to be felt by more Greeks in a more intensified manner than ever before. Just as unemployment reaches critical levels in Greece, the traditional stop-gap measures of both the family and the state are failing, and gradually disappearing. Due to cultural, demographic, and structural transformations currently underway, the unemployed in Greece will no longer be able to rely on the informal coping mechanisms that have compensated for shortages of public social welfare provision for so long.

Already, structural transformations – transformations heretofore experienced by other OECD countries – pose a real challenge to the state's ability to deal informally with unemployment in Greece. As the Greek economy was forced to enter a phase of economic discipline in the 1990s, industrial restructuring became an important cornerstone of government policy. As a result, Greek firms are increasingly being forced to rely on their own efforts and efficiency gains rather than on generous government subsidies, fiscal exemptions, currency devaluations, subsidized low-interest loans and other types of assistance that have traditionally come to their 'rescue' (OECD 1992: 34, 82). This trend has been particularly difficult as a large number of small family-owned firms are pushed to consolidate and to adapt to a new generation of products and more efficient production techniques. As a result of such restructuring, manufacturing industry already shed some 21 per cent of its employees between 1981 and 1995 (OECD 1996: 56). Moreover, unprofitable state-controlled enterprises have also begun to come under scrutiny as governments have realized that the funds to keep them afloat are no longer available. As a result, such firms are increasingly relying upon lay-offs or are being sold or liquidated altogether. In contrast, profit-generating firms are being floated on the stock market and privatized (either in part or in full). Reflecting such closures and privatizations, total employment in public enterprises declined by approximately 11,000 in 1991 (2 per cent of total public employment) and more significant future reductions seem certain as the public sector will continue to undergo long-promised structural reforms in the immediate future. In addition, the government is also showing increased willingness to resort to privatization in order to raise revenues – the success of the partial privatization of OTE, the public telecommunications company, has contributed proceeds accounting for 3 per cent of GDP in 1998, more than the total proceeds of privatization from the previous seven years combined (Pangalos 1999). Moreover, the government has also taken an increasingly hard-line stance on the ailing and debt-ridden state-controlled airline, Olympic Airways, threatening closure unless cost-cutting and restructuring proceeds. In sum, restructuring efforts continue to have widespread consequences on the labour force: many workers have already lost their jobs and an increasing number – including 'core' members in the formal economy – are in danger of becoming redundant in the not-too-distant future. Further job losses are therefore destined to occur.

Reflecting this trend in structural transformations, the size of the public sector has also begun to shrink. In addition to working towards the privatization of a number of profitable public enterprises and government-owned banks, massive lay-offs in 1990 of central government personnel with fixed term contracts reflected the government's new-found preoccupation with reducing general government expenditures and acquiring efficiency gains from a slimmer, healthier public sector. As a result, a 10 per cent reduction in public sector employment has been announced by the central government, as has its intention to replace only one of every two retirees in future years. To make this a tangible possibility, many of the loopholes used by ministers to hire public servants in the various ministries and other government offices on fixed-term contracts (for whom recruitment criteria are less stringent) have been narrowed. Thus, as the effects of these and other measures – designed to keep public sector recruitment relatively low – are put into practice, unemployment is likely to rise. Undoubtedly, the problem will be most acute when core workers themselves begin to be affected by such structural change.

Steps are also being taken to do away with many of the labour market rigidities that have become institutionalized in Greece. Increasingly, the government has come to believe that in order to make firms more efficient and competitive, employers must be given greater latitude in making hiring and firing decisions at the firm level. The underlying belief is that greater flexibility of the labour market, while leading to increased levels of short-term unemployment, should over the long-run lead to higher rates of job creation and increased productivity. As a result, many labour market rigidities have already begun to be dismantled as additional recourse to part-time and fixed-term contracts have moved the labour market towards greater liberalization and flexibility. Thus, even though peripheral workers with little to no employment protection are likely to be affected by labour market reforms, it is the core male workers who have traditionally enjoyed the benefits that such rigidities offer who are likely to lose their privileged employment status over the longer term. This will be a transformation of the most significant kind and will undoubtedly have adverse consequences on both the family wage (to which the male head of household contributes disproportionately) and, through it, the entire system of family welfare.

Finally, reform of the Greek pension system is also likely to increase the labour supply and, through it, the level of unemployment in Greece. Reacting to budgetary limitations as well as to European Union demands that pension reforms be instituted in order to stem the system's deteriorating financial position and combat its abuse (Venieris 1996: 266-7; OECD 1997: 65), the state has been pushed to undertake important pension reform. Specifically, reforms enacted from 1990 to 1992 raised the degree of disability required to receive a full or partial disability pension, specified the specific medical criteria for each level of disability, and tightened verification procedures. Future pensions are to become increasingly less generous than those allocated to the current generation of employees. In addition, a drastic reduction in the number of new disability pensions have already been effected – 26 per cent of all pensions in 1989 to 15 per cent in 1995 (OECD 1996: 82; OECD 1997: 85). Regardless of these and other reforms, however, some argue that pensions still remain too generous to make the system viable. Reform came 'too late' and was 'insufficient' to restore system viability (OECD 1997: 85). Thus, despite the positive impact of reform, pension expenditures are still set to increase due to demographic factors such as the ageing of the population and urbanization.[2] As a partial response to earlier pension reform that was only partly successful, 1996 legislation indexed minimum pensions to the consumer price index, rather than to average earnings,[3] introduced Greece's first-ever means testing of certain pensions, unified pension rights and obligations for all public and private sector employees, and increased the retirement age of women to 65. Clearly, these reforms – and likely future ones to be effected after the next general election – reduce the government's ability to combat unemployment by 'pensioning off' people out of the labour market. An increase in the labour pool is thus virtually inevitable, as those who in the past would have been eligible for pensions must now seek active employment. Barring any dramatic transformation of Greece's economy over the short- to medium-term – and a concomitant increase in the demand for workers – this change too almost certainly spells higher unemployment.

Unfavourable demographic trends are also likely to put upward pressures on unemployment. First, the agricultural sector – which still represents over 20 per cent of employment in Greece – is in the process of steady decline – a decline likely to be accelerated by Common Agricultural Policy reforms as some sectors face substantial price cuts in the near future. Moreover, Greece and some of the other southern European countries will also likely experience a large continuing loss of jobs in agriculture as widening of the European Union dictates that, over the longer-term, subsidies and other financial supports be shifted away from southern Europe towards the newer, 'poorer' countries of east-central Europe. In short, as an ever-increasing number of people (especially youth) abandon agriculture for other forms of employment and as agriculture becomes less profitable with the reduction and elimination of subsidies, structural unemployment is likely to rise.

Illegal immigrants are also contributing to the unemployment problem in Greece despite the fact that, to the present, most of the half-million illegal immigrants have not competed for work with Greek citizens. Except for jobs in construction, most illegal immigrants are employed as unskilled workers, performing household tasks and agricultural work that most Greeks refuse to do. Nonetheless, this is currently changing and is likely to continue to change in future years as the state, in an effort to bring illegal immigrants into the formal economy where taxes can be collected and to place them on more of an equal footing with other members of the workforce, has decided to introduce work permits for illegal immigrants, legalizing their stay in Greece. As illegal immigrants turn from underground and intermittent employment to formal full- or part-time work and become part of the domestic labour force, formal unemployment is likely to experience increased upward pressures as these workers begin to compete with Greeks for 'real' jobs.

In addition to structural transformations and demographic changes, a third trend that is likely to increase unemployment is the transformation of the Greek family. Declining marriage rates, later ages at which young people marry, rising divorce rates (even though still quite low) and attitudinal shifts concerning sexual relations before marriage are bringing about a cultural revolution in Greece. Women – the backbone of family 'welfare' – are beginning to challenge their traditional roles and dependent positions within the family as increasing numbers of them attain higher levels of education and enter the formal labour market in search of employment (Hadjimichalis and Vaiou 1990: 101-2). Their participation rate has increased over the past 15 years – from about 40 per cent in 1981 to almost 45 per cent in 1995 – but still remains below the OECD average of about 60 per cent. Moreover, the higher the level of women's educational attainment, the higher their participation rate. While less than 60 per cent of women with only a high school education participate in the labour force in Greece, 85 to 90 per cent of women with a college education do. At this higher level of educational attainment, women approximate the equivalent male participation rate of 95 per cent (Ioakeimoglou, Kaminioti, Kostaki and Skopelitou 1998: 96-7; see also, Symeonidou 1998). Since younger women are generally better-educated and since increasing education is positively related to labour force participation, women's participation in the work force is likely to increase substantially in the future, bringing inevitable consequences to the family and its traditional welfare role.

Moreover, women are not the only societal group whose participation rate is likely to increase due to the cultural transformation currently underway. The attitudes of young people are also being altered as more of them begin to seek greater levels of independence from their families, choosing to live on their own or with non-family members. In future years, these young people, who have made a conscious decision to sever dependence on the family, are likely to turn to the state rather than to the extended family network for financial assistance when out of work.

Even though modernizing social trends have come slowly, divorce rates remain low, and cohabitation and single-person living arrangements are still relatively rare in Greece, studies indicate that Greeks are increasingly acquiring 'modern' attitudes. In this, Greeks are not alone: liberalizing attitudes have taken root throughout all of southern Europe. Moreover, attitudinal modernization is likely to accelerate from one generation to the next (Martin 1996: 28), as greater emphasis is placed on personal fulfilment and happiness (Kotzamanis 1997: 101-2). As more and more Greeks adopt modern attitudes, as greater numbers of women leave the home to enter the formal labour market, and as increased numbers of young people move out of their parents' homes to live on their own or with roommates, not only is the size of the labour force likely to be altered – with real consequences for unemployment – but the number of women available to engage in domestic care-giver functions as well as the horizontal extension of kinship networks to encompass traditionally large families is likely to decline. These cultural and social transformations will thus have an undeniable and perhaps irreversible effect on the family provision of welfare (Guerrero and Naldini 1996: 62). As Haris Symeonidou (1996: 84) rightly asserts, the 'family cannot be regarded as a welfare state substitute in the long term.'

CONCLUSION

In conclusion, unemployment has reached a critical juncture in Greece, now at an all time high of over 10 per cent. Not surprisingly, the unemployment issue which, until recently, has not been a very salient issue for the average Greek is now becoming as critical for Greeks as for other Europeans. According to a 1998 Eurobarometer, 65 per cent of Greeks agreed with the statement that 'in the twenty-first century, unemployment will be at least as common as today.' This percentage was very much in line with the European average of 64 per cent. Moreover, Greeks tended to be somewhat more pessimistic about the overall economic situation than their European counterparts: 39 per cent of Greek respondents disagreed with the statement that 'in the twenty-first century, the overall economic situation in (our country) will improve' (compared to a European average of 34 per cent) (Eurobarometer 1998, B.67).

Unfortunately, both increased levels of unemployment as well as the new-found pessimism of the Greek electorate have come at a time when the state as well as the family have reached critical milestones of their own. The state has realized that it can no longer afford the informal stop-gap measures which, in the past, were able to help keep the size of the labour force in check, the rate of unemployment low, and the employment of the primary head of household protected. Yannis Stournaras, chairperson of the Council of Economic Advisors at the Ministry of National Economy and Finance, recently argued that the government will press on with proposed reforms – reforms likely to increase unemployment – regardless of the political costs: 'The ultimate goal of the government is to bring the country to economic and monetary union (EMU) by January 1, 2001. ... This government has proven that it does not care about the political cost,' he argued (Pangalos 1999). The family, for its part, is showing the first signs of disintegration as women are marrying at later ages (or choosing to stay unmarried), divorce rates are beginning to rise, mothers are seeking employment outside the home, and young people are taking the first steps towards single-person living (Kotzamanis 1997). Thus, the informal stop-gap measures of both the state and the family which provided a cushion for the unemployed in past years will soon cease to exist. As a result, just as the state is least able to afford it, it will have to establish viable and extensive labour market policies to deal with excessive unemployment. To put it simply, modernization brings its own peculiar challenges and difficulties. As Greek society modernizes, it brings in its wake modern problems – ones which a modernizing Greek state will be increasingly called upon to address.

NOTES

1. Personal interview conducted in Athens, Greece on 17 August 1998.
2. The pensions of urban dwellers are higher than those of their rural counterparts.
3. From about 1981 to today, the income of the average Greek pensioner – including all sources of pension-related income – has remained well above the average earnings of Greek workers, remaining at about 130 per cent of average earnings for most of the 1980s (OECD 1997: 78-9).

REFERENCES

Chletsos, M. (1993): 'Η Κρίση της Κοινωνικής Ασφάλισης και οι Γυναίκες στην Ελλάδα,' ['The Crisis of Social Security and Women in Greece'], in T. Doulkeri (ed.), *Η Κοινωνική Ασφάλιση στην Ελλάδα*, [Social Security in Greece], Αθήνα: Εκδόσεις Παπαζήση, pp. 173-186.

Close, D. H. (1993): 'The Legacy,' in D. H. Close (ed.), *The Greek Civil War, 1943-1950: Studies of Polarization*, London: Routledge.

Euro-barometer (1981): "Euro-barometer 16: Noise and Other Social Problems," Brussels: Directorate General.

Euro-barometer (1983): "Euro-barometer 19: Gender Roles in the European Community," Brussels: Directorate General.

Euro-barometer (1989): "Euro-barometer 31A: European Elections, 1989: Post-Election Survey," Brussels: Directorate General.

Euro-barometer (1994): "Euro-barometer 41.1: Post European Election," Brussels: Directorate General.

Eurobarometer (1997): "Eurobarometer 47.2: Young Europeans," Brussels: Directorate General XXII, Education, Training and Youth, p. 67.

Eurobarometer (1998): "Eurobarometer 49: Report," Brussels: Public Opinion Analysis Unit, European Union, p. B.67.

García, S. and N. M. Karakatsanis, (forthcoming): 'Social Policy, Democracy and Citizenship in Southern Europe,' in R. Gunther, P. N. Diamandouros and G. Pasquino, (eds.), *Changing Functions of the State in the New Southern Europe*, Baltimore: The Johns Hopkins University Press.

Guerrero, T. J. and M. Naldini (1996): 'Is the South so Different?: Italian and Spanish Families in Comparative Perspective,' *South European Society & Politics* 1/3 (Winter), pp. 42-66.

Hadjimichalis, C. and D. Vaiou (1990): 'Flexible Labour Markets and Regional Development in Northern Greece,' *International Journal of Urban and Regional Research* 14/1 (March), pp. 1-24.

Hadjiyannis, S. (1990), 'Democratization and the Greek State,' in R. H. Chilcote, S. Hadjiyannis, F. A. López III, D. Nataf and E. Sammis (eds.), *Transitions from*

Dictatorship to Democracy: Comparative Studies of Spain, Portugal, and Greece, New York, NY: Taylor & Francis New York Incorporated.

Hespanha, P. (1993): *Vers une Société-Providence Simultanément Pré- et Post-Moderne*, Coimbra: Centro de Estudos Sociais.

Ioakeimoglou, E., O. Kaminioti, A. Kostaki, and T. Skopelitou, (1998): 'Εκπαίδευση, Φύλο και Τρόπος Ένταξης στην Αγορά Εργασίας της Ελλάδας,' ['Education, Gender, and Means of Placement in the Greek Labour Force'], in L. Maratou-Alipranti and A. Chatzegianni (eds.), *Ανεργία, Εργασία, Εκπαίδευση-Κατάρτιση στην Ελλάδα και στην Γαλλία*, [Unemployment, Work, Education-Preparation in Greece and France], Αθήνα: Εθνικό Κέντρο Κοινωνικών Ερευνών, pp. 91-108.

Kanellopoulos, C. (1992), 'The Underground Economy in Greece: What Official Data Show,' Discussion Paper #4, Athens: Centre of Planning and Economic Research.

Kourvetaris, Y. A. and B. A. Dobratz (1987), *A Profile of Modern Greece in Search of Identity*, New York: Oxford University Press.

Kostaki, A. and E. Ioakeimoglou (1997): 'Διερεύνηση της Επίδρασης των Δημογραφικών Παραγόντων στη Μακροχρόνια Ανεργία,' ['Study of the Influence of the Demographic Components in Long-Term Unemployment], *Επιθεώρηση Κοινωνικών Ερευνών*, [The Greek Review of Social Research] 94/3, pp. 185-200.

Kotzamanis, V. (1997): 'Γαμηλιότητα και Διάλυση των Εγγάμων Συμβιώσεων στην Ελλάδα. Μια Πρώτη Δημογραφική Προσέγγιση,' ['Marriage and the Dissolution of Marriage in Greece: An Initial Demographic Approach'], *Επιθεώρηση Κοινωνικών Ερευνών*, [The Greek Review of Social Research] 94/3, pp. 61-152.

Martin, C. (1996): 'Social Welfare and the Family in Southern Europe,' *South European Society & Politics* 1/3 (Winter), pp. 23-41.

OECD (1990): *OECD Economic Surveys: Greece, 1989-1990*, Paris: OECD.

OECD (1991): *OECD Economic Surveys: Greece, 1990-1991*, Paris: OECD.

OECD (1992): *OECD Economic Surveys: Greece, 1991-1992*, Paris: OECD.

OECD (1996): *OECD Economic Surveys: Greece, 1995-1996*, Paris: OECD.

OECD (1997): *OECD Economic Surveys: Greece, 1996-1997*, Paris: OECD.

Pangalos, Philip (1999): "Government's Economic Guru Insists Convergence Targets Will Soon Be Met: Yannis Stournaras Tells the *Athens News* that Reforms will Proceed Regardless of Political Cost," *Athens News-Electronic Edition*, Athens, p. http://athensnews.dolnet.gr/SpecialEditions/Business99/1iig12.htm.

Pantelidou-Malouta, M. (1988): 'Γυναικείο Ζήτημα και Κράτος Πρόνοιας,' ['Women's Issues and the Social Welfare State'], in T. Maloutas and D. Oikonomou (eds.), *Προβλήματα Ανάπτυξης του Κράτους Πρόνοιας στην Ελλάδα. Χωρικές και Τομεακές Προσεγγίσεις*, [Problems of Welfare State Development in Greece: Special and Sector Approaches], Αθήνα: Εξάντας, pp. 183-220.

Petmezidou-Tsoulouvi, M. (1992): *Κοινωνικές Ανισότητες και Κοινωνική Πολιτική*, [Social Inequalities and Social Policies], Αθήνα: Εξάντας.

Rompolis S. and M. Chletsos (1995): *Η Κοινωνική Πολιτική Μετά την Κρίση του Κράτους-Πρόνοιας*, [Social Policy After the Crisis of the Social Welfare State], Θεσσαλονίκη: Παρατηρητής.

de Santos, B. (1991): *State, Wage Relations and Social Welfare in the Semiperiphery: The Case of Portugal*, Coimbra: Centro de Estudos Sociais.

Schömann, K. (1995): 'Active Labour Market Policy in the European Union,' Discussion Paper, Berlin: Wissenschaftszentrum Berlin für Sozialforschung.

Spraos, J. (1991): 'Government and the Economy: The First Term of PASOK 1982-84,' in S. Vryonis, Jr. (ed.), *Greece on the Road to Democracy: From the Junta to PASOK 1974-1986*, New Rochelle, NY: Aristide D. Caratzas Publisher.

Stratigaki, M. and D. Vaiou (1994): 'Women's Work and Informal Activities in Europe,' *Environment and Planning* A/26, pp. 1221-1234.

Symeonidou, H. (1996): 'Social Protection in Contemporary Greece,' *South European Society & Politics* 1/3 (Winter), pp. 67-86.

Symeonidou, H. (1998): 'Απασχόληση και Ανεργία των Γυναικών στην Ελλάδα. Αξιολόγηση Σχετικών Πολιτικών,' ['Employment and Unemployment of Women in Greece: Assessing the Worth of Certain Policies'], in L. Maratou-Alipranti and A. Chatzegianni (eds.), *Ανεργία, Εργασία, Εκπαίδευση-Κατάρτιση στην Ελλάδα και στην Γαλλία*, [Unemployment, Work, Education-Preparation in Greece and France], Αθήνα: Εθνικό Κέντρο Κοινωνικών Ερευνών, pp. 181-201.

Tsoukalas, K. (1987): Κράτος, Κοινωνία, Εργασία στην Μεταπολεμική Ελλάδα, [State, Society and Employment in Post-War Greece], Αθήνα: Θεμέλιο.

Το Βήμα [The Step], Athens: Greece, 10 August 1986.

Venieris, D. N. (1996): 'Dimensions of Social Policy in Greece,' *South European Society & Politics* 1/3 (Winter), pp. 260-269.

Zafeiri-Kampitsei A. (1993): 'Η Ασφάλιση των Γυναικήν Εμπόρων—Προβλήματα Προοπτικές,,' ['Insuring Female Merchants—Perspective Problems'], in T. Doulkeri (ed.), *Η Κοινωνική Ασφάλιση στην Ελλάδα*, [Social Security in Greece], Αθήνα: Εκδόσεις Παπαζήση, pp. 197-203.

What's Working in Southern Europe?

NANCY G. BERMEO

In February, 1999 a large and boisterous group of unemployed workers organized a demonstration in the southern Italian city of Naples. Though their physical appearance was not particularly notable, their location and demands were extraordinary. The rally took place outside a small African consulate where the unemployed were petitioning to become citizens of Gabon. Their leader explained that non-EU nationals were inscribed on special affirmative action lists that facilitated their acquisition of jobs. 'The state gives rights and prerogatives to those from far away but forgets about the citizens of the south. We are neither racists nor xenophobes. We just want to have equal opportunities.'[1]

This incident is, in many ways, emblematic of how southern Europeans are reacting to unemployment in the late 1990s. Their target was the state and not the private sector. Their demands used rights discourse and were built around an explicit comparison. Their tactics were quite literally spectacular, designed to attract the mass media and their effects on actual policy-making were probably nil. The incident is most emblematic in illustrating how the unemployed are straining to craft new identities and new means of extracting more responsiveness from their states.

Why do the most salient political consequences of high unemployment most often take this form and not others? Why is it, for example, that the unemployed are not the foundation of large, extremist parties? Why are they not more permanently visible and more effective as a petitioning group? Does unemployment have political consequences that we have ignored or, do the unemployed behave more or less like their employed peers?

Unemployment is certainly a salient political issue 'looming ever larger' in the polls and in the media (Offe and Heinz 1992: 2). The fact that it is either rising or extremely high in most European states suggests that it will remain salient for some time. Yet, as these essays demonstrate, rising unemployment has not been associated with rising extremism or destabilization in Europe's south. This trend challenges the findings of a number of scholars who have studied a broader sample of European countries and concluded that higher rates of unemployment facilitate the growth of the extreme right (Betz 1994; Kitschelt 1995; Jackman and Volpert 1996).

The fact that such a seemingly negative stimulus would not provoke a more negative response is puzzling. In the wealthier European countries we might attribute this response to the strength of welfare state provisions. In Britain we might conclude that an electoral system that discourages new parties is key. In other countries, the political moderation of the unemployed might be attributed to a lack of class consciousness (Verba and Scholzman 1977). None of these arguments holds in southern Europe. Indeed, the southern European puzzle proves particularly perplexing.

Historically, the opposition to liberalized labour markets has been stronger in the south than anywhere on the continent. From the forces promoting autarchy and corporatism on the historic right, to the relatively strong anti-market parties on the left, virtually every country in the region has had a strong historical tradition of resistance to free labour markets. Even the major dictatorships in the region provided strong protection for jobs. Rising unemployment is clearly an effect of liberalizing the European labour market, so why does the reversal of such long-standing protections not provoke a greater response?

Institutionally, the states of southern Europe seem least well equipped to compensate the unemployed with state assistance. Democratization brought the expansion of rudimentary welfare states across the region, but the safety nets of the south are of recent manufacture and broad weave. With relatively weak welfare states, we might expect the unemployed of the south to lead the continent in their level of dissension, but this seems not to be the case.

Attitudinally, the citizens of the south have the lowest political trust levels in all of Western Europe. As our essays ably demonstrate, individual citizens scapegoat immigrants in ways that are not too dissimilar from their counterparts elsewhere in Europe. What prevents political entrepreneurs from capitalizing on distrust, capturing the frustrations borne of unemployment and forging parties and movements like Le Pen's?

We can easily imagine a number of grim scenarios deriving from rising unemployment in Europe's south, yet none have come to pass. What's working in southern Europe to militate against these negative outcomes? This is the central question motivating this essay. I address the question by examining four explanations derived from the essays in this volume and the broader literatures on political mobilization and participation. They concern: the nature of state compensatory schemes, the nature of left coalitions in the south, the nature of work itself, and the nature of the family. Though southern Europe embraces (at a minimum) Portugal, Spain, Greece and Italy, I concentrate almost exclusively on the first three countries for the sake of continuity with the preceding essays.

STATE COMPENSATION FOR THE UNEMPLOYED

Southern European welfare states are smaller, in the aggregate, than welfare states in the rest of Western Europe but this tells us little about either the scope of compensatory schemes or their effects. Are the states of the south mitigating the negative effects of high unemployment through selective spending on the unemployed?

As a number of the preceding essays illustrate, compensatory policies for the unemployed have been key components of trade union-government bargaining in every country of the southern tier. Trade unions have been successful in lobbying for expanded compensatory policies in every country, though the benefits offered vary considerably across states, across time, and even across regions within certain states. The complexity of benefit allocation formulas prevents a detailed discussion of each country's system, but, at a general level, they fall far below the European average. As Cabral makes clear, Portugal's benefits are extremely modest, composing 0.4 per cent of family income in recent times (Cabral: 14, this volume). Greece seems to have an even more modest benefit program while Spain has the most generous. The first column in Table 1 shows the variation in unemployment benefits in each of the countries in southern Europe.

Survey research has confirmed the notion that compensatory payments to the unemployed play some role in mitigating political disaffection and extremism. Research in Spain, for example, illustrates that at the peak of unemployment (under the Socialists) the jobless not only shunned extremism, but proved just as likely as the employed to vote for the ruling Socialist party. The ruling party's ability to attract the votes of the unemployed was attributed in part to its compensatory programmes (Maravall and Fraile 2000).

It would be ironic if compensatory schemes did not serve some compensatory, ameliorative function but it would be unwise to conclude that compensatory schemes were a sufficient explanation for the puzzle

TABLE 1
BENEFIT PACKAGES ACCORDED THE UNEMPLOYED: SOUTHERN EUROPE IN COMPARATIVE PERSPECTIVE

	Single Person	Single Parent with 1 Child	Couples with 2 Children
Southern Europe:	*44*	*51*	*46*
Greece	30	32	28
Italy	34	41	43
Portugal	58	54	52
Spain	53	75	59
EUR12 Rate	51	62	61
Other Europe:	*55*	*70*	*69*
Belgium	60	64	59
Denmark	57	73	68
France	74	84	79
Germany	52	75	76
Ireland	24	47	57
Luxembourg	81	84	84
Netherlands	70	89	74
UK	23	45	57
EUR12 Rate	51	62	61

Source: adapted from Helen Fawcett and Theodoros N. Papadopoulos (1997: 15).
Note: Figures include housing costs and represent rate at which total assistance packages replace average male earnings before unemployment.

posed above. Three problems immediately come to mind. To begin with, access to unemployment benefits varies greatly. Large percentages of the unemployed do not qualify for state compensation schemes at all and many citizens lose their benefits over time. The behaviour of the many individuals in both these categories requires another explanation. Second, the citizens in states with meagre compensation programmes are not more disaffected or extremist than those in states with more generous programmes. On the contrary, as Karakatsanis and Amoretti explain, the unemployed in Greece are not especially mobilized nor especially alienated despite the fact that benefits to the unemployed are the lowest in the EU (Symeonidou 1996: 73). Finally, the states in which movement entrepreneurs have been most successful in forging an association between unemployment, xenophobia and alienation are states in which compensatory schemes are much more developed than those we see in the south. The case of France, where the packages offered to the unemployed are superior to anything offered in southern Europe illustrates the point. Table 1 illustrates the contrasts between France and the rest of the south and between the south and the rest of Europe.

LINKS TO LEFT COALITIONS

Compensatory payments provide a partial explanation for why the unemployed in Europe are not channelling their energies into extremist activities but much of the puzzle is left unsolved. Is it possible that the unemployed are linked to the democratic order through what Rand Smith, and others, call the 'left coalition'? That is, do the parties of the left and the labour unions linked to these parties provide an effective organizational alternative to semi-loyal or disloyal groups?

This hypothesis is intuitively appealing. As Amoretti's article illustrates, the unemployed in southern Europe are disproportionately working class and therefore drawn from the core constituencies of the Socialist and Communist left. Strong ties to previously existing organizations would make the unemployed less available for mobilization by movement entrepreneurs of any sort. Since left coalitions have historically been both vociferous proponents of full employment and active advocates for compensatory payments to the jobless, unemployed people from outside the working class might be drawn to traditional left coalitions as well. Are the connections between the unemployed and left coalitions strong enough to weather the recruitment drives of new, anti-system groups?

This question requires a sustained research project of its own but several of the essays collected here give us important leads. Most show some affinity between the unemployed and the traditional left political parties. Cabral, Bruneau and Bacalhau highlight the connections between Portugal's unemployed and the Portuguese Communist Party. Burgess and Encarnación observe the same association in Spain, and Smith makes the association in both Spain and France.

Yet, there are several reasons to be cautious about giving these associations too much explanatory weight. To begin with, we have little information on their strength and can thus only speculate on their durability in the face of competing claims. Social democracy in Greece, Portugal and Spain 'has been much less well entrenched as a social force' than in the rest of Europe (Rhodes 1996: 9). Given that party identification is declining in most states (Ignazi 1996; Schmitt and Holmberg 1995), that 'switching party allegiances is less and less a traumatic experience' (Ignazi 1996: 550), and that party preferences are notoriously fluid in both southern Europe and France (Morlino 1996; Bartolino and D'Alimonte 1996) our speculations might lead us to predict weakness and availability rather than their opposite.

Amoretti's research gives us additional reasons to be cautious. He shows that the ideological self-placement of the unemployed is not very different from the employed and therefore implies that a sizeable proportion of the unemployed are not connected to left wing parties at all. The Portuguese unemployed are disproportionally on the left (as is confirmed by Cabral, Bacalhau and Bruneau) but the ideological differences between the unemployed and the rest of the active population in Spain, Greece and Italy is negligible.

Amoretti also illustrates that most of the southern unemployed are disinterested in politics altogether. Though a portion of the unemployed are clearly politically engaged (even more engaged than the employed in Italy and Portugal) the little evidence we have on party affinity suggests, at best, that the left coalition hypothesis is only partially true.

The explanatory power of this hypothesis grows more questionable if we consider the connections between the unemployed and the other component of the left coalition. The linkage between labour unions and the unemployed has long been problematic. Though trade unions in most southern European countries have special programmes for the jobless and have sometimes even established unions *of* the unemployed, union leaders almost always give priority to their *working* rank and file. The incentives to do so are usually overwhelming. Wage earners elect union leaders and help fund union activities.[2] Those who lose their jobs generally lose their capacity and willingness to play either of these roles. Those who have never had a job, have never had a personal link to a union at all. Given the high percentage of first-time job seekers in the ranks of the unemployed, this is a sizeable component of the jobless population.

The essays collected here illustrate that relations between unions and the unemployed are intensely problematic in Europe's south. Burgess, Encarnación, Cabral, Sepheriades and Smith all highlight how unsuccessful southern European unions have been in their fight to block plant closures and privatizations. Though unions have organizational incentives to fight against any government measures that increase unemployment and therefore lead to 'lower entry and higher exit rates' (Visser 1996) their capacity to do so has been extremely limited. At least one well respected scholar argues that unions will not fight to protect jobs at all unless they become convinced that the union itself is threatened (Golden 1997).

Glatzer, Burgess and Encarnación show how unions in Portugal and Spain successfully extracted concessions from the state to compensate for job losses, but each explains how success has varied over time.

Sepheriades sees an even bleaker picture in Greece, arguing that 'concession bargaining' has been unsuccessful altogether. Currently, we do not know how (or even if) this limited success affects the links between the unemployed and left coalitions. We do know that rising unemployment has had a devastating impact on union density throughout the south. We also know that Sepheriades' call for greater solidarity between unions and the unemployed in Greece is echoed in Portugal, Spain and Italy as well (Stolleroff 2000; Richards and Polavieja; and Olney 1996). The disjuncture between unions and the unemployed may be remedied in the future but it is wide enough now to detract significantly from the weight we can accord the left coalition hypothesis.

Compensatory policies and ties to left coalitions seem at best, only partial explanations for the puzzle of working class behaviour in the south. More powerful explanations derive from the nature of work in the southern economies and the structure and role of the southern family.

THE NATURE OF WORK IN THE SOUTH

The title of this essay is a *double-entendre* meant to underscore the fact that working takes different forms in different economies. The term unemployment is linked to a particular and restricted concept of 'working.' As J. Garraty explains, '...only those who work for wages or a salary, who are at liberty to quit their jobs, yet who also may be deprived of them by someone else, can become unemployed' (Garraty 1978: 5). The concept of unemployment is so intimately bound up with a particular form of labour that the term was rarely used before the 1890s. The concept of *official* unemployment (the phenomenon which we most often measure and discuss) is connected to an even more restricted definition of working: that recognized and regulated by the state.

Official unemployment is thus a condition associated with the official wage economy, but a citizen's experience of unemployment will be mediated by the range of other interrelated economies available as alternative means of support. The wage economies in Portugal, Spain, Italy and Greece are supplemented by sizeable non-wage and informal economies and both of these supplemental economies help to mitigate unemployment's most negative effects. Cabral, Sepheriades and Karakatsanis illustrate this convincingly in their essays on Portugal and Greece but the connections can be made across the south and merits more discussion.

By 'informal economy' I mean 'market activity in legal goods and services that is not registered with the state, not taxed, ...and not subject to any other state imposed regulation on business' (Warren 1994: 92). The term embraces a wide range of activities, including labour in clandestine factories, artisan production, and paid but unregistered work on farms or in homes and hotels. Though synonymous with the underground or black economy, and therefore often associated with some sort of social underworld, the informal economy is not the realm of 'destitute people on the margins of society' but rather, an alternative 'process of income generation' intimately bound up with the formal economy (Castells and Portes 1989: 12).

All the countries in southern Europe have extensive informal economies (Gough 1996: 15). Italy has one of the largest informal sectors in the industrial world, producing at least 25 per cent of the country's GDP (Warren 1994; *The Economist* 1997). The importance of the Greek and Portuguese informal economies is discussed by Sepheriades, Karakatsanis and Cabral. Spain's informal sector is not discussed above but is particularly noteworthy given the high rate of official unemployment there.

Spain's informal sector provides an important source of income for the officially unemployed. Estimates of what percentage of Spain's labour force is working 'off-the-books' vary according to region, sector of activity and mode of measurement, but there can be little doubt that the informal economy absorbs 'a significant segment of the population' (Benton 1990) probably constituting between 21 and 25 per cent of total employment (Union Sindical de Madrid 1994; Muro et al. 1988). Scholars estimate that the informal sector employs as much as 40 per cent of the workforce in the hotel industry (de Miguel 1988) and nearly 30 per cent in other services in the 1980s. Estimates of the percentage of informal workers in the textile and clothing industries varied from 25 per cent to as high as 50 per cent (Miguelez Lobo and Rebello Izquierdo 1990a). Table 2 gives an overview of the informal sector in various branches of the Spanish economy.

Because so much of Spanish economic activity is geographically concentrated, much of the sectoral variation described above is reflected in regional differences. In general, the informal economy is largest in regions with the highest level official unemployment, the largest agricultural sectors, the heaviest dependence on tourism or a large presence of manufacturing and consumer goods industries. Regions that share two or more of these qualities are likely to have the largest informal

TABLE 2
SIZE OF THE INFORMAL SECTOR BY NATURE OF ACTIVITY: SPAIN
(PERCENTAGE OF TOTAL EMPLOYMENT)

Activity		Activity	
Domestic Services	60.4	Commerce	24.9
Tailoring	42.9	Textile Industry	23.4
Shoe Industry	37.8	Education and Research	20.4
Personal Services	34.5	Construction	18.7
Leather Industry	32.0	Food Industry	17.6
Agriculture, Hunting, and Fishing	30.9	Publishing and Art Industry	16.9
Hotels	26.1	Car Repairing	16.2

Source: Unión Sindical de Madrid (1994: 42).

economies. Murcia, Castile la Mancha and Andalucia exemplify the point (Miguelez Lobo 1988a: 3; Miguelez-Recio 1988).

The informal economy in Portugal is much like the Spanish with informal activity concentrated in traditional industries, services and tourism. It produces an estimated 22 per cent of GDP. Estimates of the size of the informal workforce in textiles and footwear run as high as 33 per cent nation-wide (de Sousa Santos 1994; de Sousa 1985 as in Miguelez Lobo and Rebello Izquierdo 1990b: 16) and as high as 45 per cent in the northern industrial district of Braga. Estimates of the proportion of workers in the informal economy in selected economic activities include 20 per cent of the workforce in manufacturing, 17-25 per cent of the workforce in services, and 50 per cent of the workforce in construction (Miguelez-Lobo and Rebello Izquierdo 1990b).

In Portugal, as in the rest of southern Europe, the informal sector is a complement to activities in the formal economy. As a result, informalization is most important in regions with a high concentration of tourism and agriculture. Between one-third and two-thirds of the labour force in the districts of Bragança, Vila Real and Viseu are working off-the-books in either full-time or part-time jobs. In the district of Faro, where tourism and food-processing provide seasonal work, the percentage of the labour force engaged in informal work may be as high as 50 per cent. The seasonal nature of the demand for labour in Portugal has given rise to the widespread practice of 'creating de facto flexibility' where there are 'legal rigidities' (European Commission 1997c: 185-6).

No one knows how many of the officially unemployed are working in the informal sector in Portugal, but a broad range of scholars agree that 'clandestine work' plays an important 'compensatory role, offsetting the negative effects of economic policies' and giving both workers and employers improved 'capacity to adapt to market variations' (Miguelez-Lobo and Rebello Izquierdo 1990b: 18). The fact that official wage labour is, as Cabral notes, a small percentage of family income is no doubt due to the supplementary weight of informal income (Cabral: 2, this volume).

The Greek informal sector is thought to be the largest in southern Europe, producing close to one-third of the official GDP (Soldatos 1995: 305; European Commission 1997b: 126). It is centred in the same sorts of activities as elsewhere in the south and reaches its peak in the construction industry where an estimated 70 per cent of all jobs are unregistered (European Commission 1997b: 126). Many of these construction jobs go to illegal immigrants but most of the less physically demanding positions in the informal sector are held by native born Greeks from working class and middle class backgrounds (Baldwin-Edwards and Safilios-Rothschild; European Commission 1997b: 126).

Reliable figures on the sectoral and regional distribution of the informal economy in Greece are not available but scholars agree on a few general points. In the Islands, most informal activity derives from tourism. In the centres of Athens and Thessaloniki, the informal sector is concentrated in services and commerce. On the outskirts of these cities, clandestine manufacturing is dominant with clothing, toys, decorations and leather goods produced by homeworkers.

The informal sector is of great importance to the unemployed and underemployed in Greece, especially during the tourist season when, according to at least one expert, 'anyone who is prepared to accept a low wage and irregular conditions can find a job' (Mingione 1990: 36).

As extensive as the informal sector is, it is important to note that not all of the officially unemployed find work there. Informal work is, as Sepheriades says, an important form of 'unemployment relief' but we do not know how many of the unemployed have access to it. We do know that 'officially recorded job loss in one sector' has historically been 'translated into more underground employment in the same sector' (Benton 1990: 37). We can also be certain that the masses of workers losing jobs in the formal sector and the younger workers who never got a position in the formal sector in the first place represent 'a willing labour force for the unregulated economy' (Benton 1990: 33) throughout the south. Younger people who have never gained a position in the formal labour market may be the subgroup of the unemployed most likely to find informal work (Mingione and Magatti 1995: 77). Since they do not qualify for unemployment subsidies in the first place, the number of citizens who are drawing unemployment benefits while working full time in the informal sector is probably much smaller than critics of unemployment subsidies maintain (Miguelez-Lobo and Rebello Izquierdo 1990a; Mingione and Magatti 1995).

The unemployed who have access to the agricultural sector of the southern countries have access to an additional and important coping mechanism that lies at the intersection of the informal, the formal and the non-wage economy. Part-time farming is growing increasingly important in Portugal, as Cabral explains, but the pattern can be observed throughout the south. The nature of agricultural work varies. Sometimes it involves seasonal work at harvest and planting times done by women who are officially unemployed or inactive. Other times it involves older unemployed male workers who lose their jobs in the formal sector and return to working small inherited properties of their own. A third and very common variant involves individuals who work part-time on their own small family farm and part-time in informal manufacturing (Miguelez Lobo and Rebello Izquierdo 1990b: 13). In most cases, farm work produces an important part of family income either in kind or in cash (Miguelez Lobo and Rebello Izquierdo 1990a). The fact that a large section of the working (and would-be-working) class in Greece owns land is thought to have decreased 'tensions' as well (Mingione 1988: 16). Throughout southern Europe 'family work', especially in agriculture, 'seems to be acting counter-cyclically' 'as a cushion against wage-employment losses' (European Commission 1997c: 182).

THE FAMILY AS FALLBACK

The subject of family income brings us to the subject of the southern family and to the key role it plays in mitigating unemployment's most negative effects. There are, of course, variations in family structure across the southern countries and between regions within the same country. There is also, however, a broad consensus in the sociological literature that the southern family has qualities that distinguish it from families elsewhere in western Europe. Three of these qualities are directly relevant to the plight of the unemployed.

First, and fundamentally, southern European families have closer internal ties than families in the rest of Europe. Community studies and survey research indicate that southern European families interact more frequently and have a substantially greater sense of mutual obligation between generations than families in the rest of western Europe (World Values Survey 1990-93; Guerrero and Naldini 1996; Wall 1995: 454). The differences are not universal, of course, but they are consistent enough that scholars write of the southern family and its roles in geographically specific terms. Leibfried writes of the 'primary solidarities and mutual obligations' that lie at the foundation of what he calls the Latin Rim regime[3] (Leibfried 1993). Roussel writes of the 'southern European family model' and contrasts it with two other models that fit the rest of Europe (Roussel 1995). Guerrero and Naldini write likewise of a southern family model characterized by 'a higher sense of duty to parents and family' and a 'high intensity and wide extent of family and kinship networks' (Guerrero and Naldini 1996: 60-1).

The sense of mutual obligation intrinsic to the southern family has a welfare function that works to the benefit of the unemployed in Portugal, Spain and Greece. In Greece, as Karakatsanis argues, the supportive role of the family serves as a counterweight to the state's very weak welfare provision. The Greek family plays what Symeonidou and others deem ' a crucial role in social protection' (Symeonidou 1996: 67). In Portugal, families seem to play a similar role. Scholars write of a 'welfare society' that supplements the official and poorly developed welfare state. In Portugal (as in the rest of southern Europe) 'the family fills the gaps' providing social protection 'based on personal connections, affective links' and 'networks of exchange and sociability' (Martin 1996: 34-5; Hespanha 1995; Arriscado Nunes 1995; de Sousa Santos 1992). A survey of the long-term unemployed in Portugal revealed that only 12 per cent saw state benefits as their main means of support. Over 50 per cent said they were supported by their families instead (Mendes and Castro Rego 1992 as in Pereirinha 1996: 210). In Spain as well, families cope with unemployment 'through intrafamiliar redistribution.' It is the Spanish family (in tandem with the burgeoning Spanish welfare state) which ensures that 'extreme poverty and social exclusion are very limited' despite record levels of unemployment (Laparra and Aguilar 1996: 108).

The arenas in which 'intrafamiliar redistribution' takes place are typically the family business (or farm) and the family residence. These are the second and third characteristics of the southern European family that assist the unemployed. Small, family owned businesses in the service sector are a key component of southern economies and are on the rise. Given the sense of familial obligation discussed above, they are a natural locale for the absorption of the unemployed either as official or unofficial workers. Table 3 suggests how the dynamic works and how it contrasts

TABLE 3
PERCENTAGE OF YOUNG PEOPLE EMPLOYED BY FAMILY: SOUTHERN EUROPE vs. EU12

Country	Percentage
Greece	69
Italy	65
Portugal	58
Spain	61
Southern Europe	63
EU12	39

Source: Adapted from Gough (1996: 14).

with patterns of behaviour in the rest of the EU.

The third characteristic of the southern family that assists the unemployed derives from residential patterns. Southern families are more likely than other families to live either near one another or with one another. Households embracing three generations are a long-standing component of the southern European family model (Guerrero and Naldini 1996: 60-1). The data presented in Table 4 show how residential patterns differ among regions and how the context in which the unemployed live varies as a result.

Southern residential patterns help to mitigate the negative consequences of high unemployment in a variety of ways. First, and most obviously, they shield the unemployed from the fluctuations of the housing market. The effects of this shielding process are dramatic: despite dramatically higher rates of unemployment, Madrid's rate of homelessness is ten times less than the rate in New York and five times less than the rate of Paris (Laparra and Aguilar 1996).

Southern European residential patterns assist the unemployed in a second way by enabling them to live off (and contribute to) pooled income. Many of the unemployed live in a single household with three sources of income: one earned by a male adult with full-time official employment; a second earned by a second adult with part-time employment or a job in the informal sector; and finally, a third source of income in the form of an old age or disability pension contributed by an older member of the family (Wall 1995: 454; Laparra and Aguilar 1996: 89).

The role of pensions is particularly important in the south. Over 34 per cent of all households receive old age pensions in the south, while only 23 per cent do so in the north (Pereirinha 1996: 201). In Spain, nine out of ten Spaniards of retirement age live with their children or their

TABLE 4
THE FAMILIAL RESIDENCE PATTERNS OF THE UNEMPLOYED: SOUTHERN EUROPE AND REST OF EUROPE COMPARED

	Households with Unemployed[1]	Households with 1 Adult		Households with 2 Adults		Households with 3 or more Adults + Children
		Single Person[2]	Single Parent	With No Children	With Children	
Greece	7.80	7.95	1.54	11.0	13.14	9.36
Italy	9.40	5.32	1.28	7.65	12.46	9.94
Portugal	4.00	2.43	2.40	10.48	17.74	16.17
Spain	17.70	2.71	1.18	7.51	16.64	17.74
France	10.20	15.14	4.26	18.16	18.29	7.90
EUR8	8.06	20.47	5.38	17.08	17.31	7.89
EUR12	8.62	15.18	4.12	14.44	16.53	9.68

Notes:
[1] As % of total number of households.
[2] Aged 15 to 64 years. Households with persons aged 65 or more years are excluded from the presentation.
Source: Adapted from Helen Fawcett and Theodoros N. Papadopoulos (1997: 4).

children's families (Almeda and Sarasa 1996: 158). Southern pension provisions are relatively generous, if judged in terms of replacement criteria. The southern welfare states are known as 'pensioner welfare states' (Symeonidou 1996: 74) because a disproportionate amount of public spending goes toward pension payments (Leibfried 1993) and because the southern states have some of the highest replacement rates for retirement benefits in Europe. People who meet the maximum contribution criteria receive retirement benefits equal to 107 per cent of average earnings in Greece, 97 per cent in Spain, and 94 per cent in Portugal (Stathopoulus 1996: 146) .[4] Pensions, especially those for state employees, are the basis of the 'dualist' welfare system that characterizes the south: one in which citizens in certain sectors of the economy or state benefit from 'generous' and even 'very generous protection' while citizens in other occupations or in the informal sector get few state provisions at all (Martin 1996: 33). For the unemployed of the south, familial links to citizens in the first category have greater utility than elsewhere. Even without the presence of a pensioner, the 'existence of several sources of income' helps to produce a more 'comfortable' standard of living than living alone (Miguelez Lobo and Rebello Izquierdo 1990b: 5).

The most important benefits the unemployed gain from the southern family may not be material but social. The continued pattern of multigenerational residence reinforces 'the social capital of even the most disadvantaged families' (Almeda and Sarasa 1996: 167). Unemployment may mean economic marginalization but it does not mean social marginalization as long as the extended family integrates the unemployed in the larger community. Continuities of behaviour and belief are not so surprising when so many other continuities counterbalance the effect of individual joblessness. Daily contacts with people who are working and who have networks and resources that may mean a job in the future make the difference between hope and hopelessness.

The coping mechanisms outlined above serve positive functions but are highly problematic in themselves. Working in the informal sector is a mixed blessing. Informal work is surely better than destitution but it affords neither the physical nor the social protections offered in the official economy. Union representation is impossible, working conditions are sometimes Dickensian, wages are almost consistently lower than in the official economy and workers who labour off-the-books have no legal recourse when they are not paid at all (Ybarra 1989; Portes, Castells and Benton 1989).

The problems intrinsic to the informal economy are not confined to those who work there. The informal sector costs the state and state welfare programmes a great deal. The loss of enterprise and personal income taxes is obvious, but more pernicious, perhaps, is the loss of contributions to pension funds. By 2015, nearly one out of five southern Europeans will be over 65. Many more will have been forced into early retirement (European Commission 1997). How will the pensions for these citizens be generated if nearly one-quarter of the labour force works outside of the existing social security system today? Who will replace the current cohort of core, middle aged breadwinners if a large percentage of today's younger Europeans are forced to labour only in the underground economy?

The fact that the family is the fallback for the unemployed is not all good either. The family's welfare function puts an extraordinary burden on women as caretakers and thus contributes to pernicious gender inequality. The reliance on families as welfare institutions forces citizens who have no family networks to rely on their own devices and also hampers the growth of the welfare state (de Sousa Santos 1992). Laparra and Aguilar justifiably call the reliance on the southern family 'integrated precariousness' (Laparra and Aguilar 1996: 92) but the fact that the unemployed are integrated and not marginalized helps to explain why the behavioural continuities are as they are.

Tony Judt has recently written eloquently of the *exclus* in France and the more industrialized regions in Europe. They are people who have lost access not simply to full-time work in the official economy but to *'the social liaisons that accompany'* a position inside *'conventional channels of employment or security'* (Judt 1997: 100). Southern Europe is certainly not without its own *exclus*, but the excluded are not as numerous as pure economics would dictate. Familial networks provide a channel of security and a set of continuous social liaisons that many of the unemployed elsewhere simply do not have.

Perhaps it is the nature of these liaisons that explains why the unemployed of the south behave so much like the other members of their traditional communities when it comes to politics. They are still *part* of their communities and thus part of whatever traditional political cultures their communities embrace.

They are also part of the multiple economies their communities rely on for survival. The people of the south have a long tradition of using multiple economies to cope with the vicissitudes of capitalism on Europe's periphery. These coping mechanisms are as rational now as ever before. The great irony of the south's late economic development is that its very unevenness has turned out to be an asset. Late development has meant the continued survival of institutions that predate advanced capitalism. These institutions provide the southern unemployed with options that their counterparts in the more advanced regions of the continent lack.

The *exclus* who stand centre stage in Judt's essay are those from the oldest industrial heartlands of Europe. They are workers whose families were caught up in capitalist industrial production generations ago. They are workers with no connection to farming; no strong tradition of self-employment; and no easy access to the informal sector. Most importantly, they are workers whose 'community has collapsed' (Judt 1997: 96) taking long-standing political cultures with them.

In France, Judt tells us, these collapsed communities have turned to the National Front. In these towns the unemployed behave as we would expect, channelling their anger and frustrations into extremism – 'into one long scream of resentment' (Judt 1997: 96). Will the unemployed of the south eventually turn in this direction as well? Le Pen's popularity is certainly sobering and not irrelevant to the south. He has mobilized hordes of non-voters and transformed them into constituents with exceptional voter loyalty (Guyomarch 1993). He attracted between 18 and 30 per cent of the votes of the unemployed in the 1995 Presidential election and in so doing outdistanced all other candidates on the left and right by a wide margin.[5] Making substantial gains in the working class constituencies as a whole, Le Pen attracted twice as many working class votes as the Communist candidate and outdistanced the Socialist candidate by approximately six percentage points (Shields 1995: 28-9). Whatever strength ties to the left-coalition had in the past, they are being challenged in France at least. Indeed, Le Pen relies 'largely, if not exclusively, on voters who during an earlier era would have voted for social democratic or communist parties' (Berman 1997: 108).

There are, happily, important distinctions between France and its southern neighbours. In the classical south, high levels of dissatisfaction seem still to be associated with a disengagement from politics (Villaverde Cabral 1995: 200; Morlino and Tarchi 1996). Though party identification with most of the political spectrum is generally low, researchers have discovered in some regions, at least, 'a tight electoral seal surrounding the left' (D'Allimonte and Bartolini 1997: 125). There is movement between parties on the left but not across the spectrum altogether. The prospects of Communists defecting to far-right parties is unimaginable as of now in Portugal (Cunha 1997: 30; Bacalhau and Bruneau, this volume) and probably equally unlikely in Spain or Greece. In all three countries, the relatively recent experience with right-wing dictatorship has made voters of all sorts wary of the ultra-right (Costa Pinto 1998; Karakatsanis 1996; Aguilar 1995).[6]

Whether these differences will continue in the future is impossible to predict – as is the emergence of an individual leader like Le Pen – but we can take stock of factors that might help or hinder the expansion of right-wing extremism. The continued viability of the coping mechanisms outlined above will be key, as will the nature of the more explicitly political institutions discussed in the preceding essays. I consider both sets of factors in my conclusion.

CONCLUSION

The future of the informal economy in southern Europe is uncertain. On the one hand, states are under increasing pressure to curtail informal activity as a means of raising tax income. (The current Greek government has reportedly made progress toward this goal and other states are attempting reforms as well.) On the other hand, the fact that states are undertaking fiscal reforms may give 'informal entrepreneurs' new incentives to hide their incomes. Informalization 'is an integral part of a more generalized restructuring' process (Benton 1990: 39) throughout the south and one of the main reasons that the 'self-employed' constitute a growing part of the southern European labour force (Rhodes 1996: 6). Southern states are hurt by the informal sector because of tax losses but they may continue to tolerate informalization because the costs of eradicating it will be high, it provides a safety-valve that contributes to 'social peace,' (Miguelez-Lobo and Rebello Izquierdo 1990b: 21) and it is deeply embedded in the social fabric of southern society (ECETF 1994: 70). If the formal deregulation of the labour market is as difficult as Glatzer's research suggests, the de facto de-regulation provided by the informal sector may continue to have appeal.

Whether the southern family will continue to serve its current welfare function is more questionable (Esping-Andersen 1999). At least two researchers have found that the southern family model 'adapts well to lasting employment shortages and to the scarce availability of social services' (Guerrero and Naldini 1996: 62-3) but adaptation may prove more and more difficult over time. Women are carrying the heaviest burdens in the familial welfare system and may eventually be unable or unwilling to perform the role of 'compulsory altruists' (Symeonidou 1996: 80). Declines in fertility will decrease the number of women caregivers even without any changes in mentality (Guerrero and Naldini 1996). Demographic and cultural changes lead Karakatsanis to predict an eventual decline in both the number of women available to perform the domestic care-giver role and the number of young people willing to play an active role in extended kinship networks.

The spread of individualistic values may make it impossible for the family to fill the gaps left by the welfare state in the future (Symeonidou 1996: 84). The spread of families themselves may make the model nonviable if individuals have to move farther from their original kin (and residence) to find work. Government efforts to stimulate labour mobility will disturb existing residential patterns and thus jeopardize a key coping mechanism. Spain's legislative initiatives to force recipients of unemployment benefits to accept jobs anywhere in the country (Glatzer, this volume) will do precisely this.

If familial housing patterns change, the informal sector may eventually become less accessible too. Research on Britain reveals that individuals usually need the resources of a household to enter the informal sector in the first place. Acquiring informal work usually requires a home to do homework, basic funds for materials, or money for transportation. Most of all, it requires social contacts (Pahl 1987: 46).

Immigration may change the dynamic for the worse as well. Research has found that the National Front thrives in those areas where high rates of unemployment combine with high rates of immigration and crime (Lewis-Beck and Mitchell 1993). Immigration is increasing rapidly throughout the south. Indeed the southern countries are now net importers of population (Garcia and Karakatsanis 1999). Since a number of researchers have found that popular anxiety about immigration varies with the relative size of immigrant communities, this is a destabilizing trend (Kitschelt 1996: 276; Fuchs, Gerhards and Roller 1993). The essays by Marques, and Baldwin-Edwards and Safilios-Rothschild show how certain immigrant groups are already being constructed as threatening to southern jobs and society and both forecast that the process of scapegoating will continue. As the number of (mostly illegal) immigrants rises, it is likely to spread, and to be directly linked to unemployment (Stathopoulus 1996: 152).

Whether changes in the nature of the southern family and in the size and composition of immigrant communities will facilitate the growth of extremism among the unemployed in southern Europe will depend a great deal on how already established political institutions react to the unemployed and their needs. Herbert Kitschelt is wise to remind us that the future of Europe's extreme right depends, not simply on socio-economic developments, nor on the strategic behaviour of extreme-right elites, but on 'the political opportunity structures' created by 'their competitors' (Kitschelt 1995: 278). The essays collected here have much to say about two institutions that compete with the extreme-right: socialist parties and trade unions. Despite the many differences between the cases discussed, a common theme emerges that has a direct bearing on opportunity structures. Simply put, it is that unemployment is threatening the social solidarities of the past. The breakdown of long-standing social solidarities expands the opportunities for the crafting of problematic replacements.

Rand Smith states the theme most explicitly in his essay, concluding that the 'major casualty of Europe's unemployment crisis may be the dissolution of the fraternal party-labour relationship that has sustained European social democracy for the past century' (Smith: 28). This is certainly an ominous forecast but it resonates with themes in the other essays as well. Virtually all of the Socialist parties discussed herein have drifted from their moorings in their respective labour movements. Faced with what Smith describes as the 'trade-off between capitalist efficiency and social solidarity', they have each opted for the former. Their embrace of capitalist efficiency was (and is) decidedly uneasy: the policy vacillations mapped out by Miguel Glatzer are ample proof of this. Yet, all the volume's essays that focus on trade unions emphasize how little power labour had to reverse decisions on plant closures, to stop privatizations or to marshal state funds for permanent job creation. With the possible exception of Spain, no socialist party has stood by 'the unemployed' as a key constituency for a sustained period of time. The dissolution of previous bonds and commitments opens opportunities for competing parties to both represent and redefine the interests of the jobless.

The opportunities to represent and redefine the interests of the jobless are opened further by the current divisions *within* the working class. The party-labour divide explored by Smith is only one of the multiple fissures threatening the solidarities of the past. Other essays show how divisions within the working class are weakening what might have been solidaristic class associations: Burgess and Encarnación show how organized labour failed to find a means of successfully representing the divergent interests of Spain's highly segmented labour force. Sepheriades shows how Greek trade unions have failed to forge solidarities between public and private sector workers, and between workers in the formal and informal economies. Marques, Baldwin-Edwards and Safilou-Rothschild illustrate that trade unions in both Portugal and Greece have tried, but largely failed, to promote more multi-cultural mentalities and alliances among their base constituencies. Across southern Europe, categories of workers who might have joined together as solidaristic class allies are divided instead by ethnic, national and racial identities.

Fears and dilemmas produced by unemployment either exacerbated or stimulated each of the divided solidarities reviewed above. The institutions that were (and are) most immediately hurt by the breakdown of solidarities are trade unions. Cabral, Smith, Sepheriades and Burgess each plot the trajectory of institutional decline. In Portugal, trade union membership has dropped by one-third since the mid-1980s. In France, membership dropped from 30 to 14 per cent in 15 years. In Greece, between 1982 and 1995, density dropped ten percentage points- to 27 per cent. In Spain, trade union membership dropped 50 per cent in three years, recuperated and then began to decline again in 1994.

With trade unions shrinking, much of the organizational space once occupied by class associations lies vacant. Movement entrepreneurs now have the opportunity to fill these spaces with associations built around other identities. Solidarities built around national or ethnic identities are predictable alternatives. They may be especially appealing for citizens who find themselves both out of work and out of place in newly heterogeneous neighbourhoods and states. To date, these citizens have not been mobilized in the south. As Amoretti and others have shown, their disinterest in politics is their distinguishing and dominant trait. Their disinterest surely hurts the quality of European democracy, but their active engagement in xenophobic movements will hurt the content of democracy as well. The southern European left would be wise to craft associational alternatives for the unemployed before the extreme right offers its own.

So far, the unemployed struggle with a negative identity: they are defined quite literally by what they are not (i.e. working). The National Front and similar parties have the double appeal offering the jobless both a positive identity (based on nationality) and a convincing argument about who is accountable for their fate. In years past, when trade union discourse 'was not losing its appeal' (Sepheriades) and when 'the voice of labour' had a broader audience (Encarnación), the unemployed had a ready answer to questions about accountability. It derived from a critique of capitalism and focused responsibility on capitalists and their allies.

Today this critique has lost ground. As Richard Sennett reminds us, even labour parties rarely hold employers (or capitalism) accountable for unemployment today (Sennett 1999: 18-19). The xenophobic right has entered the void with an alternative story-line: people are unemployed not because of the greed of others but because of the presence of others. The problem is not capitalism but globalization. The responsible parties are the immigrants who cross national boundaries and the politicians who seek to alter what those boundaries mean. National Front slogans such as '2 Million Unemployed = 2 Million Immigrants' have broad appeal in France. They may yet find a market in the south.

NOTES

1. *La Stampa* 16 February 1999 p. 10. The spokesperson was Vincenzo Guidotti who leads a Neapolitan organization of the unemployed called the Light Blue Union.
2. Burgess explains that Spain's factory council system encourages 'union leaders to be attentive to the interests of workers beyond their dues – paying membership' but the focus is still on those who are working in the firm.
3. Leibfried includes France in the Latin Rim category. Judging from the differences illustrated in Tables 1 and 4, I would not do so.
4. The exception here might be Portugal. Though Portugal's system, like the others, was funded by employment-based contributions, salaries and wages have been so low there that payments are still relatively modest (Pereirinha 1996).

5. The first figure comes from a BNV poll. The second from an IFOP poll. A MORI poll reported a figure of 24 per cent. Shields explains that the National Front might not be attracting masses of voters from the old core Communist constituency but is attracting new and formerly unmobilized voters who would probably have voted communist in the past (Shields 1995: 29).
6. Likewise Kitschelt attributes the relative weakness of extreme right parties in Germany and Italy to the legacies of a fascist past (Kitschelt 1996: 275-7).

REFERENCES

Aguilar, P. (1995): *La Memoria Histórica de la Guerra Civil Española (1936-1939): Un Proceso de Aprendizaje Político*, Madrid: Centro de Estudios Avanzados en Ciencias Sociales.

Almeda, E. and S. Sarasa (1996): 'Spain: Growth to Diversity', in V. George and P.T. Gooby (eds), *European Welfare Policy*, London: Macmillian Press.

Arriscado Nunes, J. (1995): 'As Solidariedades Primarias e os Limites da Sociedade-Providencia', *Revista Critica de Ciencias Sociais* 42, pp.5-25.

Benton, L.A. (1990): *Invisible Factories: The Informal Economy and Industrial*

Development in Spain, Albany: State University of New York Press.

Berman, S. (1997): 'The Life of the Party', *Comparative Politics* 29/1, pp.101-22.

Betz, H. (1994): *Radical Right-Wing Populism in Western Europe*, New York: St. Martin's Press.

Castells, M. and A. Portes (1989): 'World Underneath: The Origins, Dynamics, and Effects of the Informal Economy', in M. Castells, A. Portes and L.A. Benton (eds), *The Informal Economy: Studies in Advanced and Less Developed Countries*, Baltimore, MD: Johns Hopkins University Press.

Costa Pinto, A. (1998): 'Dealing with the Legacy of Authoritarianism: Political Purges and Radical Right Movements in Portugal's Transition to Democracy', in S.V. Larsen (ed.), *Modern Europe After Fascism*, New York: Columbia University Press.

Cunha, C. (1997): 'The Portuguese Communist Party in Portugal', in T. Bruneau (ed.), *Political Parties and Democracy in Portugal*, New York: Westview Press.

D'Alimonte, R. and S. Bartolini (1997): 'Electoral Transition and Party System Change in Italy', *West European Politics* 20/1, pp.110-34.

De Miguel A. (1988) *España oculta: la Economia Sumergida*, Madrid: Espasa Calpe.

Esping-Andersen, G. (1999) *Social Foundations of Postindustrial Economics*, Oxford: Oxford University Press.

European Commission (1994): *Growth, Competitiveness, Employment. The Challenges and Ways Forward into the 21st Century. White Paper*, Luxembourg: Office for Official Publications of the European Communities.

European Commission Demographic Report (1997): *Employment and Social Affairs*, Social Protection and Social Action, Luxembourg: Official Publications Office.

ECETF (1995): Mingione, Enzo and Mauro Magatti *The Informal Sector: Follow-up to the White Paper*, Luxembourg: European Communities.

European Commission (1997a): *Employment in Europe*, Luxembourg: Office for Official Publications of the European Communities.

European Commission (1997b): *Labour Market Studies. Greece*, Luxembourg: Office for Official Publications of the European Communities.

European Commission (1997c): *Labour Market Studies. Portugal*, Luxembourg: Office for Official Publications of the European Communities.

European Commission (1997d): *Labour Market Studies. Spain*, Luxembourg: Office for Official Publications of the European Communities.

Eurostat (1991): *Social Portrait of Europe*, Brussels-Luxembourg: Office for Official Publications of the European Communities.

Eurostat (1996): *Income Statistics for the Agricultural Household Sector*, Luxembourg: Office for Official Publications of the European Communities.

Eurostat (1997): *Eurostat Yearbook*, Brussels-Luxembourg: Office for Official Publications of the European Communities.

Fawcett, H. and T. Papadopoulos (1997) 'Social Exclusion, Social Citizenship and Decommodification: An Evaluation of the Adequacy of Support for the Unemployed in the European Union', *West European Politics*, 20/1. pp.1-30.

Garcia, S. and N. Karakatsanis (1999): 'Social Policy, Citizenship and Democracy in Southern Europe', in R. Gunther, P.N. Diamandorous and G. Pasquino (eds), *Changing Functions of the State in the New Southern Europe*, Baltimore: Johns Hopkins Press, forthcoming.

Garraty, J.A. (1978): *Unemployment in History: Economic Thought and Public Policy*, New York, NY: Harper and Row.

Golden, M. (1997): *Heroic Defeats: The Politics of Job Loss*, Cambridge: Cambridge University Press.

Gough, I. (1996): 'Social Assistance in Southern Europe', *Southern European Society and Politics* 1/1, pp.1-23.

Guerrero, T.J. and M. Naldini (1996) 'Is the South so Different? Italian and Spanish Families in Comparative Perspective', *Southern European Society and Politics* 1/3, pp.42-66.

Guibentif, P. (1996): 'The Transformation of the Portuguese Social Security System', *Southern European Society and Politics* 1/3, pp.219-39.

Guyomarch, A. (1989): 'The 1993 Parliamentary Elections in France', *Parliamentary Affairs* 46/4, pp.605-26.

Harding, P. and R. Jenkins (1989): *The Myth of the Hidden Economy*, Milton Keynes: Open University Press.

Hespanha, P. (1995): 'Vers une Société Providence Simultanément pré et Post-Moderne. L'état des Solidarités Intergérationnelles au Portugal', in C. Attias-Donfut (ed.), *Les Solidarités Entre Générations. Vieillesse, Familles, Etat*, Paris: Nathan, pp.209-21.

Ignazi, P. (1996): 'The Crisis of Parties and the Rise of New Political Parties' *Party Politics* 2/4, pp.549-66.

Jackman, R.W. and K. Volpert (1996): 'Conditions Favouring Parties of the Extreme Right in Western Europe' *British Journal of Political Science* 26/4, pp.501 21.

Judt, T. (1997): 'The Social Question Redivivus', *Foreign Affairs* 76/5, pp.95-117.

Karakatsanis, N. (1996): *Unnegotiated Transition, Successful Outcome: The Process of Democratic Consolidation in Greece*, unpublished dissertation manuscript, Cleveland: Ohio State University.

Kitschelt, H. (1995): *The Radical Right in Western Europe*, Ann Arbor: University of Michigan.

La Stampa (16 February 1999): 'The Unemployed: We Want to Become African' p.10.

Laparra, M. and M. Aguilar (1996): 'Social Exclusion and Minimum Income Programmes in Spain', *Southern European Society and Politics* 1/3, pp.87-114.

Leibfried, S. (1993): 'Towards a European Welfare State? On Integrating Poverty Regimes into the European Community', in C. Jones (ed.), *New Perspectives on the Welfare State in Europe*, London and New York: Routledge, pp.133-56.

Lewis-Beck, M.S. and G.E. Mitchell (1993): 'French Electoral Theory: The National Front Test', *Electoral Studies* 12/2, pp.112-27.

Maravall, J.M. and M. Fraile (1999): 'The Politics of Unemployment: The Spanish Experience in Comparative Perspective', in N. Bermeo (ed.) *Unemployment in the New Europe*, Cambridge University Press, forthcoming.

Martin, C. (1996): 'Social Welfare and the Family in Southern Europe', *Southern European Society and Politics* 1/3, pp.23-41.

Miguelez Lobo, F. and O. Rebello Izquierdo (1990a): 'Irregular Work in Spain', in

European Commission (1990), *Underground Economy and Irregular Forms of Employment (Travail au Noir)*, Luxembourg, Office for Official Publications of the European Communities.

Miguelez Lobo, F. and O. Rebello Izquierdo (1990b): 'Irregular Work in Portugal', in European Commission (1990), *Underground Economy and Irregular Forms of Employment (Travail au Noir)*, Luxembourg, Office for Official publications of the European Communities.

Mingione, E. (1990): 'The Case of Greece', in European Commission, *Underground Economy and Irregular Forms of Employment in Europe*, Luxembourg: Commission of the European Communities.

Mingione, E. and M. Magatti (1995): 'The Informal Economy: Follow-up to the White Paper', in *Social Europe Supplement* 3/95, United Kingdom: European Commission, Directorate-General for Employment, Industrial Relations and Social Affairs.

Muro, J. et al. (1988): *Analisis de las Condiciones de Vida y Trabajo en España*, Madrid: Ministerio de Economia y Hacienda.

OECD (1986) *Employment Outlook*, Paris, OECD.

OECD (1997): *Labour Force Statistics*, Paris: OECD.

Offe, Claus and Rolf G. Heinze (1992): *Beyond Employment: Time, Work and*

the Informal Economy, London: Polity Press.

Olney, S.L. (1996): *Unions in a Changing World: Problems and Prospects in Selected Industrialized Countries*, Geneva: ILO.

Pahl, R.E. (1987): 'Does Jobless Mean Workless? Unemployment and Informal Work' in L. Ferman, S. Henry and M. Hoyman (eds), *The Informal Economy: The Annals of the American Academy of Political and Social Science*, pp.36-46, 493.

Pereirinha, J.A. (1996): 'Welfare States and Anti-Poverty Regimes: The Case of Portugal', *Southern European Society and Politics* 1/3, pp.198-218.

Polavieja, J.G. and A. Richards (1999): 'Trade Unions, Unemployment and Working Class Fragmentation in Spain', in N. Bermeo (ed.), *Unemployment in the New Europe*, Cambridge University Press, forthcoming.

Portes, A., M. Castells and L.A. Benton (1989): 'Conclusion: The Policy Implications of Informality', in A. Portes, M. Castells and L.A. Benton (eds), *The Informal Economy: Studies in Advanced and Less Developed Countries*, Baltimore: The Johns Hopkins University Press.

Rhodes, M. (1996): 'Southern European Welfare States: Identity, Problems and Prospects for Reform', *Southern European Society and Politics* 1/3, pp.1-22.

Roussel, L. (1995): 'Vers une Europe des Familles?', *Futuribles* 2000, pp.47-62.

Royall, F. (1998): 'Le Mouvement des Chômeurs en France de L'hiver 1997-1998', *Modern and Contemporary France* 6/3, pp.351-65.

Schmit, H. and S. Holmberg (1995): 'Political Parties in Decline', in H.D. Klingerman and D. Fuchs (eds), *Citizens and the State*, New York, NY: Oxford University Press.

Sennett, R. (1999): 'Work and its Narratives: An Address to the British Sociological Association', 9 April 1999 (unpublished manuscript).

Shields, J.G. (1995): 'Le Pen and the Progression of the Far-Right Vote in France' *French Politics and Society* 13/2, pp.21-39.

Soldatos, G.T. (1995): 'The Structural Consequences of the Underground Economy. The Case of Greece', *Jahrbücher für Nationalökonomie und Statistik* 214/3, pp.301-23.

Sousa Lobo, M.I. (1985): 'Estrutura Social e Productiva e Propenção a Subterraneidade no Portugal de Hoje', *Analise Social 21* pp.87-89.

Sousa Santos, B. de (1994): *Pela Mão de Álice. O Social e o Político na Post-modernidade*, Porto: Afrontamento.

Stathopoulos, P. (1996): 'Greece: What Future the Welfare State?', in V. George and P.T. Gooby (eds), *European Welfare Policy*, London: Macmillian Press, pp.136-55.

Stoleroff, A. (1999): 'Unemployment and Trade Union Strength in Portugal', in N. Bermeo (ed.), *Unemployment in the New Europe,* Cambridge University Press, forthcoming.

Symeonidou, H.(1996): 'Social Protection in Contemporary Greece' *Southern European Society and Politics* 1/3, pp.67-86.

The Economist (1997): 'Survey: Italy' 8 November, pp.3-26.

Union Sindical de Madrid-Region de CC. OO. (1994): *El Trabajo Sumergido en la Comunidad de Madrid*, Madrid: Ediciones GPS.

Verba, S. and K.L. Schlozman (1977): 'Unemployment, Class Consciouness and Radical Politics: What Didn't Happen in the Thirties', *The Journal of Politics* 39, pp.291-323.

Villaverde Cabral, M. (1995): 'Grupos de Simpatía Partidária em Portugal: Perfil Sociográfico e Atitudes Sociais' *Análise Social* 30/130, pp.175-205.

Wall, K. (1995): 'Apontamentos Sobre a Familia na Politica Social Portuguesa', *Analise Social* 30/131-2, pp.431-58.

Warren, M.R. (1994) 'Exploitation or Cooperation? The Political Basis of Regional Variation in the Italian Economy' *Politics and Society,* 22/1, pp.89-115.

World Values Survey (1990-93): Surveys coordinated and documented by Ronald Inglehart, Ann Arbor: University of Michigan, ICPSR No.6160.

Ybarra, J.A. (1989): 'Informalization in the Valencian Economy: A Model for Underdevelopment', in A. Portes, M. Castells and L.A. Benton (eds), *The Informal Economy: Studies in Advanced and Less Developed Countries*, Baltimore: The Johns Hopkins University Press.

ABSTRACTS

Unemployment and Union Strategies in Spain

KATRINA BURGESS

This article examines the strategies adopted by Spain's two major unions, the General Workers' Union (UGT) and the Workers' Commissions (CCOO), in response to the crisis of unemployment that has plagued Spain since the late 1970s. I argue that the UGT and the CCOO have passed through three phases during this period: (i) divided unionism and social pacts contributing to a dramatic rise in temporary employment; (ii) unity of action and resistance to further flexibilization of the labour market; and (iii) joint negotiations ending the long-standing taboo against granting concessions on job security for permanent workers. After analyzing each of these periods, I conclude that the unions' strategic choices can be explained by the institutional context in which they were operating, their search for solutions to the insider-outsider dilemma, and political learning.

A Casualty of Unemployment: The Breakdown of Social Concertation in Spain

OMAR G. ENCARNACIÓN

This essay examines the consequences of high unemployment on governance and policy-making in Spain. It contends that a casualty of the unemployment crisis is the end of consensus on macroeconomic policy born with the transition to democracy in 1977 and sustained through 1986. This development is illustrated in an analysis of the breakdown of the process of social concertation defined as the collective pursuit of economic goals among the government, employers and trade unions. The unemployment crisis undercut the government's emphasis on cross-class consensus, raised the costs for labour's participation in public policy and eroded proclivities for co-operation among employers.

Unemployment, Informalization, and Trade-Union Decline in Greece: Questioning Analytical and Prescriptive Orthodoxies

SERAPHIM SEFERIADES

The first part of this paper briefly examines the merits of neo-classical arguments regarding the causes of the recent upsurge in Greek unemployment. By examining features of the Greek labour market (especially the large and eminently 'flexible' informal sector) it suggests that the experience of Greece casts doubt on the view that labour-market flexibility can serve as a cure to unemployment. The second, and major part, examines trade union decline. Unlike the situation in most European countries, rising unemployment has not affected the mobilizing capacity of the Greek labour movement. More than a century after its emergence, however, this movement has yet to overcome its historically embedded low trade-union density. This does not prevent the outbreak of militant strikes, but hampers their effectiveness. In recent years union leaders have attempted to address this problem by trying to curb the movement's traditional penchant for confrontational action, in favour of a co-operative model of industrial relations. In the background of a weak and retrenching welfare state, however, this has led to concession bargaining which, instead of improving, has further worsened the problem of declining union credibility and density.

Rigidity and Flexibility: Patterns of Labour Market Policy Change in Portugal and Spain, 1981–96

MIGUEL GLATZER

Liberalization of labour market policy is a notoriously difficult political enterprise. This article presents a modified scheme that codes and aggregates labour market policy change. The model is applied to the cases of Spain and Portugal, where, for different reasons, liberalization of labour market policy has been high on the policy agenda since the early 1980s. Despite the presence of majority governments for much of this period, the results indicate that liberalization of labour market policy frequently fails and is often delayed. Furthermore, successful liberalization often occurs in policy packages where liberalization in one area of labour market policy is traded for greater rigidity in another.

Unemployment and the Left Coalition in France and Spain
W. RAND SMITH

This article compares how recent Socialist governments in France and Spain addressed the policy dilemmas and political dynamics of unemployment. Despite contrasting initial approaches to unemployment, the governments of François Mitterrand and Felipe González eventually adopted economic approaches emphasizing business profitability and investment over the reduction of unemployment, while at the same time enacting measures to cushion the shock for unemployed and displaced workers. This policy proved controversial, as the unemployment issue undermined the cohesion of the Left political coalition on three levels: within the Socialist parties themselves, between the Socialists and other Left parties, and between the Socialist parties and their allies in the labour movement. The pattern of those divisions differed between France and Spain, however, creating contrasting political dynamics. In France, the chief conflicts occurred within the Socialist Party (PS) and between the PS and its ally, the French Communist Party, whereas in Spain the principal disputes were between the government and organized labour. The article examines the origins and implications of these conflicts within the Left coalitions.

Political Crises and Unemployment: Popular Perception in Post-revolution Portugal
THOMAS BRUNEAU and MARIO BACALHAU

This essay utilizes data from three nation-wide public opinion surveys in Portugal conducted between 1978 and 1993 to analyze the relationship between unemployment and political behaviour. It shows that the unemployed hold different political attitudes from those in other employment categories. The essay also analyzes the concept of 'crisis' and demonstrates the centrality of unemployment for the perception of a crisis in Portuguese society. The centrality of government in both creating and resolving the crisis is also discussed.

Does Labour Under-Utilization Affect Political Attitudes? Southern Europe in Comparative Perspective

UGO M. AMORETTI

Social scientists have often analyzed unemployment but have largely overlooked underemployment. This essay examines how both forms of labour under-utilization affect political attitudes. It begins with a discussion of the magnitude of underemployment within Southern Europe and then compares its political consequences to those of unemployment. The analysis, based on Eurobarometer data, shows that unemployment and underemployment are roughly equivalent in size. However, even if the unemployed and the underemployed appear at first to be partially affected by their under-utilization, the statistical analysis points out that – once socio-economic status is controlled for – the impact of both forms of under-utilization is negligible.

Attitudes and Threat Perception: Unemployment and Immigration in Portugal

M. MARGARIDA MARQUES

Unemployment consistently appears in Portuguese opinion polls as one of the nation's most serious problems. Yet, official rates of unemployment are comparatively low in European terms. Relying on statistical data on the composition of the labour force on the one hand, and on survey results on attitudes toward work, foreigners, and the opportunity structure, on the other hand, we show that there is a pervasive collective feeling of threat associated with employment seen as a scarce resource, which is being crystallized on immigrant labour. We hypothesise that it is a feeling structurally embedded in low labour force qualifications, dominant mistrust toward the opportunity structures, and perceived social distances between different social categories.

Immigration and Unemployment in Greece: Perceptions and Realities

MARTIN BALDWIN-EDWARDS and CONSTANTINA SAFILIOS-ROTHSCHILD

The massive extent of illegal immigration to Greece in the 1990s has coincided with increases in unemployment and crime, as well as conflicting with traditional Greek ethnic homogeneity. Available evidence suggests that immigrant labour is almost wholly complementary to the native labour force – even to the extent of enabling the survival of entire industries – and therefore is not a cause of higher Greek unemployment levels. The employment and Greek perception of illegal immigrants vary substantially across the country: a framework of analysis is presented, which suggests four variables as being important. These are the local immigrant/population ratio, and the dichotomies based on gender, rural-urban and public-private distinctions. One important consensual point emerges – opposition to the presence of illegal immigrants. Responses and solutions differ, however, in line with our analytic framework.

Unemployment and the Political Economy of the Portuguese Labour Market

MANUEL VILLAVERDE CABRAL

In this paper the author deals with the specific structures of the Portuguese labour market in order to account for the impact of unemployment on electoral behaviour. The low weight of wages in family incomes, the regional disparities in wage labour and the multi-job tradition in Portuguese society are examined to explain social attitudes towards unemployment. These features are shown to constrain the resistance that the working classes might have otherwise opposed to unemployment. In conclusion, the author argues that unemployment had a limited impact on the electorate's behaviour as part and parcel of the recessive 'economic climate' prevailing at the time of the 1985 and 1995 general elections.

Relying on Stop-Gap Measures: Coping with Unemployment in Greece

NEOVI M. KARAKATSANIS

This article seeks to explain why, despite unprecedented post-war levels of unemployment and extremely ungenerous unemployment benefits, unemployment has not been a major issue of concern for the average Greek voter. It argues that the quid pro quo relations inherent in both Greek political clientelism as well as in personal familism have protected most Greeks – even those in the highest-risk categories – against the negative consequences of unemployment by informally institutionalizing a number of stop-gap measures. But, just as unemployment has reached critical levels, these traditional stop-gap measures are beginning to disappear. The unemployed in Greece will no longer be able to rely on the informal coping mechanisms which have compensated for shortages of public social welfare for so long. As a result, the effects of unemployment are likely to be felt by more Greeks in a more intensified manner in the future.

What's Working in Southern Europe?
NANCY BERMEO

This concluding essay explains why unemployed southern Europeans have not become involved in extremist or xenophobic political movements despite relatively weak welfare states and rising levels of immigration. Drawing on material from the collection's essays and from the general social science literature on Southern Europe, the article concludes that expanding state welfare provisions have explanatory power in the Spanish case but that the two factors that are 'working' most to mitigate the negative political consequences of unemployment are the informal economy and the southern family. How long these coping mechanisms will be effective will depend on the actions of political parties and class associations discussed in the preceding chapters.

BIOGRAPHICAL NOTES

Ugo M. Amoretti received his PhD in Political Science from the University of Florence in 1998 and is a Visiting Research Fellow at the Center of International Studies of Princeton University. His research interests include political economy, voting behaviour, federalism, ethnic conflicts, and labour markets. He is currently directing a research project on federalism and territorial conflict funded by the Friederich Ebert Foundation.

Mario Bacalhau is an instructor and researcher at the Universidade Lusofona in Lisbon, Portugal. From 1972 until the present he has periodically conducted nation-wide public opinion surveys in Portugal, and published books and articles analyzing the results of these surveys for Portugal's political development.

Nancy Bermeo teaches at Princeton University and writes on political economy and regime change. She is the author of a book on Portuguese democratization entitled *Revolutions Within the Revolution* and the editor of *Liberalization and Democratization*, *Civil Society Before Democracy* and *Unemployment in the New Europe*. These last two books are the fruit of projects sponsored by the Southern European Research Group, which she directs.

Thomas Bruneau is an instructor at the Naval Postgraduate School in Monterey, California. Between 1973 and 1995 he was particularly active in researching and writing on Portugal's political transition. He has collaborated with Dr. Bacalhau in publishing four books on Portuguese politics.

Katrina Burgess is an Assistant Professor of political science in the Maxwell School of Citizenship and Public Affairs at Syracuse University. A specialist in Latin American politics, she has a PhD in politics from Princeton University, where she completed a dissertation on party-union relations in Mexico, Spain, and Venezuela. She has administered projects on US-Mexican relations at institutes in Washington and Los Angeles, and co-edited *The California-Mexico Connection*, published by Stanford University Press in 1993.

Manuel Villaverde Cabral was born in 1940. He holds a doctorate in History from the University of Paris and is currently a senior researcher at the Institute of Social Sciences, University of Lisbon. He was a research fellow at St Antony's College, Oxford, and hold the chair of Portuguese History at King's College London. He has published extensively on Portuguese history and society, and has recently written a book on *Political citizenship and social fairness in Portugal* (Lisbon, 1997).

Omar G. Encarnación is Assistant Professor of Political Studies at Bard College. He received his PhD in politics from Princeton University. His essays on the political and economic dynamics of regime change in Iberian Europe and Latin America have appeared in *Comparative Politics*, *Comparative Political Studies*, and *West European Politics*. In 1994 he was a Fulbright Fellow in Spain and a scholar-in-residence at the Center for Advanced Study in the Social Sciences of the Juan March Institute in Madrid. He is currently completing a book manuscript on the causes and consequences of divergent labour responses to the politics of democratization.

Miguel Glatzer is a Research Fellow at the Watson Institute for International Affairs, Brown University. He is completing a book-length study of employment policy and late welfare state development in Portugal and Spain. Forthcoming articles analyze the changing role of the non-profit sector in the administration of the Portuguese welfare state as well as the impact of European Monetary Union on Portuguese and Spanish social and labour market policy and industrial relations. With Dietrich Rueschemeyer, he is co-ordinating a research project that compares the impact of globalization on social policy in both advanced industrialized societies and middle income countries.

Neovi M. Karakatsanis is Assistant Professor of Political Science at Indiana University South Bend. Her primary research interests focus on southern European public policy and on the processes of democratic consolidation in southern Europe. Her most recent publication, 'Do Attitudes Matter? The Military and Democratic Consolidation in Greece,' appeared in *Armed Forces & Society* (1997).

M. Margarida Marques is a Professor at the Department of Sociology at the Faculty of Social Sciences of the New University of Lisbon, and a researcher at the Laboratory for applied social research, SOCINOVA, in the same institution. Her present research interests include labour force mobility, and ethnic minorities' social and political participation.

Constantina Safilios-Rothschild is a Research Professor at the National Centre for Social Research in Athens, Greece and is co-ordinating a research programme on 'Causes and Mechanisms of Social Exclusion of Women Smallholders' carried out in five European countries. She has a Masters and a PhD in Sociology from Ohio State University and she was for many years a Professor of Sociology at Wayne State University, the University of California at Santa Barbara and the Pennsylvania State University, the Agricultural University in Wageningen in the Netherlands and a Senior Research Associate at the Policy Center of the Population Council in New York City. She has done sociological research in Detroit, Honduras, the Coast Guard Academy, Kenya, Burkina Faso, Uganda and Bangladesh and she has led many development missions in Africa and Asia for the World Bank, the United Nations and the European Community.

Seraphim Seferiades is Fellow and Tutor at Churchill College, Cambridge. He has been a Hannah Seeger Davis Post-Doctoral Fellow at Princeton University, Athens and a Jean Monnet Fellow at the European University Institute. He has taught at the University of Athens and Panteion University, Athens. His research focuses on social and political movements, and the examination of the Greek labour movement in a comparative perspective.

W. Rand Smith is Associate Dean of the Faculty and Professor of Politics at Lake Forest College. He has published *Crisis in the French Labor Movement: A Grassroots Perspective* (1987), *The Left's Dirty Job: The Politics of Industrial Restructuring in France and Spain* (1998), and articles on French and Spanish political economy in such journals as *Politics & Society*, *Comparative Politics*, *British Journal of Industrial Relations*, and *West European Politics*.

INDEX

Crisis and Transition in Italian Politics

Martin Rhodes and Martin Bull, *European University Institute, Florence* (Eds)

> *'... one of the best books on the recent Italian political crisis published in English.'*
>
> ***Regional & Federal Studies***

> *'indispensible to students of Italian Politics.'*
>
> ***Contemporary Politics***

256 pages 31 tables, 8 figs 1997
0 7146 4816 7 cloth
0 7146 4366 1 paper
A special issue of the journal West European Politics

FRANK CASS PUBLISHERS
Newbury House, 900 Eastern Avenue, Ilford, Essex, IG2 7HH
Tel: +44 (0)20 8599 8866 Fax: +44 (0)20 8599 0984 E-mail: info@frankcass.com
NORTH AMERICA
5804 NE Hassalo Street, Portland, OR 97213 3644, USA
Tel: 800 944 6190 Fax: 503 280 8832 E-mail: cass@isbs.com
Website: www.frankcass.com